I AM DAMO SUZUKI

I AM DAMO SUZUKI

DAMO SUZUKI
AND PAUL WOODS

OMNIBUS PRESS
London / New York / Paris / Sydney / Copenhagen / Berlin / Madrid / Tokyo

Cover by Fresh Lemon
Picture research by the authors

ISBN: 978.1.78305.971.3
Order No: OP56474

Special Edition:
ISBN: 978.1.78760.213.7
Order No: OP58102

Exclusive Distributors
Music Sales Limited,
14/15 Berners Street,
London, W1T 3LJ.

Designed and Typeset by Evolution Design & Digital Ltd (UK)
Printed in the UK.

A catalogue record for this book is available from the British Library.

Visit Omnibus Press at www.omnibuspress.com

CONTENTS

INTRODUCTION BY DAMO SUZUKI

As I've said here everybody has their own story, finding their own mission.

I met many people – friends and not friends, with love or without love. It's not a matter of character: I appreciate everybody who came and played a part in my life. I'd like to say proudly, "Thank you!"

If you brought love, you protected me and built a warm nest.

If you brought me conflict, you made me stronger and gave me motivation.

Even if you invited me to another room, you led me to many situations I was able to solve.

I'm so happy to meet people.

There are many kinds of people who appear in this book.

I should say thanks to everybody I met on my path.

Share your good vibes with the one next to you.

INTRODUCTION BY PAUL WOODS

Damo Suzuki had no reason to agree to the writing of this book.

After all, there was already a definitive, authorised Can biography underway – and to some, that segment of the 1970s when the 'krautrock' underground approached mainstream acceptance is the historical slot that he fits into. To say that this irks Can's 'seasonal worker' vocalist may be akin to noting how the modern German music scene wouldn't appreciate being lumped in with *oompah* and *Schlager*.

For several decades now, Damo has been a peripatetic musical catalyst, independently touring the world to perform with a bewildering variety of musicians and bands. Leaving the greater part of the concerts open to randomness and chance, it's a distant cultural echo of how Holger Czukay picked him off of a Munich street to sing for 'That German Band' in the spring of 1970.

Yet I'm not sure if the founder of Damo Suzuki's Network always sees it that way. He's aiming for something almost metaphysical, if not overtly spiritual: "randomly creating time and space in the moment".

So it was in a similar spirit of experiment and of adventure that Damo signed up for this book. He opted out of participating in the fine official Can book (not at this writer's instigation, though I appreciate his loyalty) to produce something else entirely.

"This book will be about my philosophy, thoughts and dreams," he informed me. The fact that it would also follow those lesser-trodden tracks of his life became ever more intriguing – creating a kind of travelogue with random musical accompaniment.

By the time it was commissioned, however, Damo's world had shrunk to the size of his park-view Cologne apartment. By accident not design, the theme of facing up to serious illness became a major strand of our narrative – beginning with its genetic routes in family tragedy; its personal eruption in the 1980s; its cruel resurgence in recent years, which he has fought with incredible resilience.

It's perhaps a major irony of this work, then, that it's been delayed not as much by Damo's battle against ill health – though this surely played its part – as by its writer's more mundane crisis. Our subject just wanted to get on with things: when he was able, when he was not undergoing treatment or under sedation, he was always ready to talk. I, on the other hand, was daunted by finding myself outside the independent publishing industry where I'd worked for many years. It'd take many months before I was able to transfer my skills and regain a place in the world.

That Damo put up with this situation (albeit not always comfortably) is one measure of the man. But then, as his many friends and 'Sound Carriers' (collaborators in the never-ending, ever-expanding Network) point out, we're not dealing with any kind of 'rock star' here – but rather with an extraordinary human being, lacking the grotesque ego that seems to be a requirement of the music industry.

In the light of his struggle, my own gradually diminished to nothing. I was usefully shamed by how quickly he was striving to get back to his Never-Ending Tour, by his refusal to accept a life-threatening condition as any kind of lifelong impediment. Damo hopes that this memoir will inspire anyone who's facing adversity – particularly the kind of physiological threat he's had to face. I can only second that unequivocally.

For all the difficulties inherent in this book, I'll still argue its deferred deadline (as tolerated by our long-suffering publisher, Omnibus Press) added further dimensions. At every stop-gap there were more family members, partners present and past, musical collaborators (including the late, great Jaki Liebezeit) and bio-documentary makers stepping forward to speak about their relationship with Damo Suzuki. That this was driven by a sense of amazement, sometimes amusement, but always affection, is, I believe, reflected in the pages herein.

"Music, to me, is not so interesting," says Damo, insisting his lifelong wanderlust is fuelled by endless curiosity about people rather than an ambition to refine his musical technique. So it is here; in our chronicle of his lifelong travels you'll find recollections of people and impressions of places, with occasional references back to particular gigs or tracks.

It's fortunate, perhaps, that he inspires such affection among musicians, who bring their art-form to our narrative. All will speak of Damo's singular personality; his sometimes inscrutable philosophy; his belief in the overriding force he calls Energy.

Energy seems to bear something in common with the power source we tap into from the grid; the electricity that powers amplifiers and PA systems. But to Damo it's a far more universal power, transcending the scientific and becoming an existential force – perhaps even a moral or religious (or even dietary) power. Readers are invited, as this writer had to, to interpret what Energy may mean in the life of Damo Suzuki – or indeed, whether we find a parallel in our own lives.

Whatever our conclusions, long may it continue to energise.

Paul Woods, summer 2018

FOOTNOTE:
"I asked some person to translate my essay," says Damo. "He told me it's ungrammatical: 'Your English is not really perfect but it's you and it has some kind of charm, so it's okay.'"

In this spirit, Damo's own words throughout this book are edited both to read easily and to retain the mode of his speech. In the occasional extracts from his DamoSuzuki.com blog, in the second half of our narrative, the text is left unedited except where apparent mistakes have occurred.

PROLOGUE BY DAMO SUZUKI

I travel from place to place, creating the time and space of the moment. Damo Suzuki's Network consists of ever-changing Sound Carriers – local musicians.

This kind of network started after what I saw on TV breaking news at JFK Airport, early in the morning of March 19, 2003. It was five or six o'clock and I'd just flown from San Francisco via Las Vegas. I was quite tired; sleep seemed like just a word for something that didn't really exist. I saw then on the TV screen that the US was bombing Iraq. I was sad, disappointed and angry at the same time, as millions of people all over the world had taken to the street to protest against the bombing before it happened.

Since 9/11 this world has been changing in many ways, but mostly for the worse. One of my Sound Carrier friends often quotes a sentence I wrote at the time: "USA has been talking too much 'freedom', if you have enough sex you don't talk about sex, if you have enough money you don't talk about money."

So I started thinking of what I could do to take a stand against violence. For violence is everywhere, not only on the battlefield – it is at home, in society, at school, at the office…

I thought that maybe I could make something that would oppose it, because violence occurs when people have not communicated and their feelings have been ignored. I thought there and then: *'I am going to make a kind of music that can communicate directly with the people.'*

And I find that, with music, this is possible. I decided on music as a weapon against violence. Damo Suzuki's Network had actually been on the road since 1997, but in 2003 I began to to perform with local Sound Carriers – over seven thousand local musicians from more than forty countries since then. In the main, I don't know the Sound Carriers before the performance; we've just met for the first time, without any rehearsal, just a soundcheck before we go on the stage.

It's instant composing. Music is communication – the absolute opposite of violence. Just like the Sound Carriers on stage, the people in the audience start from the point of zero and come together with us in transmission.

What I like to offer with music is the creation of positive energy, not merely stopping at the music itself. I don't force anyone to believe in my words, but, with the energy that we create on the stage, each person in the audience may go away with an open mind, to find him/herself and to go his/her way. (We're already manipulated and pushed around enough by the system anyway.) Just to be as free as God created a human being. Free to walk and to breathe, free to eventually find one's own path… free to decide: Who am I? Where do I go?

I don't have a booking agency or manager. I arrange shows, book flights and travel mainly alone. I'm a one-man company because I like to keep myself free, I arrange everything on my own. I'm a DIY person, but I'm also living a normal middle-class life in the sense that I'm not rich.

I just don't like to belong anywhere any more. I have to be free from any form or structure, free to live like Damo Suzuki, no stamps, no microchips, belonging only to the time and space of the moment. I'd rather open up these spaces in my life.

People who come to my concerts may do so because I was once a seasonal worker in That German Band, for sure. But that's why I like to keep on the road: eventually, people come just for my 'living' work, not for days past, so many millions of years before.

I'd like to keep doing this until my days are over. This is my Never-Ending Tour.

CHAPTER ONE

A CHILD OF THE RISING SUN

When the sun no longer rose so high in the East, it was a pivotal time for the former Chrysanthemum Empire. Children born to a post-imperial Japan in those post-war years would grow up as members of a hybrid culture, which increasingly assimilated the ways of its Western conquerors.

The triumphalist empire that celebrated its emperor as a god and marched over its East Asian neighbours was no more. While the subtle scents of incense still wafted on the breeze, a tradition which conflated the symbols of Shinto and Buddhism with militarism gave way to a more pacific (in all senses) way of life: a work ethic combining family duty with national pride; the corporate salaryman; technological innovation which would, over time, utilise the new obsession with electrical gadgetry in order to sell it back to its birthplace, the West.

This is the period of transition that Kenji Suzuki was born into, in Ōiso on January 16, 1950. The southern part of that prefecture, the Syonan area that neighbours Tokyo, lies beside the Pacific Ocean, and was at that time a holiday resort for Japan's politicians or wealthy elite. Kenji's recall of the era evokes the cultural ripples of the time; his memories of his own early life are slightly more nebulous.

"It's not a huge town," he acknowledges from distant memory. Endlessly curious eyes that have viewed much of the world retain his childhood environment as a series of images.

"It was in a much more traditional Japanese style," testifies Kenji, "because the main cities were destroyed by bombardment. I was born in a tiny village where there were old-style Japanese houses."

But it was the modernist styles of reconstruction that would become prevalent in post-war Japan. "Many Japanese cities are like that, much more so than thirty or fifty years before. It's the last time I can remember when each place had its own identity. Now, here in Europe, or maybe the USA or Australia, everything looks the same. You can find on every corner stupid American hamburger shops and American cafés. So if you arrive at any station you find the same city, the same constructions."

Besides his motherland's architectural identity, however, runs an avenue of recall that leads to somewhere much more personal.

"I think that the earliest memories of many people are maybe from five or six years old," says the man also known as Damo. "Before that you cannot remember. I can remember, at five years old, when my father died. As a small kid I didn't know the meaning of dying. That day, so many people were appearing at my home, dressed in dark clothes, speechless, that I was wondering, 'Why are all these people here?' That is my oldest memory."

But abiding memories of his dad are few. A smiling paternal face, a diminutive foreshadowing of the man that his small son might become. For a verbal portrait of Daiji Suzuki, we have to turn to his daughter Hiroko, Kenji's elder sister.

HIROKO SUZUKI

He was a handsome guy; when he was on holiday he'd wear a silk hat and cane like a dandy at that time. He invited me to Ginza often, also to the line dance show at Nichigeki Music Hall. While my mother was a serious person, at a banquet on a festival day he danced naked; he seems to have been a very funny guy and friendly to everybody.

Once he even brought me to his office in Sakuragichō, Yokohama. After World War II, sometimes he worked as an interpreter for the US military as he was able to speak English. While my mother was busy running her home farm, he was lonesome; he cooked takoyaki and spoke with me awhile.

A benign presence lost to his children in his thirties, the hard-working architect at Japan Rail was fleetingly glimpsed in the Suzuki family home.

14

It was the aspirational dawn of Japanese reconstruction, and Suzuki-San left young Kenji only a visual recollection of a man he never really knew.

By the time the boy had reached eight years old, the bereaved family relocated to Atsugi in the centre of the Kanagawa prefecture, a forty-five-minute train journey on the Odakyu line from Shinjuku, the centre of Tokyo. "At that time it had a population of maybe forty thousand people," he looks back. "Nowadays it is getting to maybe six times the population and I cannot find anything similar at all. So it is not really my home, there is nothing I can remember there. Nothing is the same."

Their resolute and industrious mother was the saviour of the family, although she would require help in raising her only surviving daughter and three sons. "My mother was a physically small woman," acknowledges the second son who shares his late parents' stature. "My father had died quite young; she was in her mid-thirties and now had to take care of her other three kids and me.

"She was working hard. My older brother, Isamu, and my sister, Hiroko, who were in junior high school, lived in another place in Ōiso with my uncle. (My mother had five sisters and five brothers.)

"My younger brother, Hiro, and I were living together with my mother. I also had one sister who was three years older than me, but she'd died. There is a story that she died in a traffic accident; at that moment she had me in her arms, she covered me, and that is why I didn't die too. But I'm not sure if this is true or not, because I didn't ask my mother about it.

"Hiro and I moved with my mother to Atsugi, where she opened an ice block shop – not ice cream but ice blocks, because almost no family had a refrigerator, unlike today. So they had to buy ice to put in a refrigerator which was not electric. The shop had a freezing compartment and could store four or five blocks of ice. The size of an ice block was 1050 (height) × 560 (width) × 260 (depth) mms; its weight was 135 kg.

"When she got an order from a customer she slid out the ice block from its compartment, cutting it to the size the customer wanted with a chainsaw. Also she offered a carry-home service, covering the ice with coarse cloth to protect it from melting during transportation by bicycle. At the beginning she did all this work alone; later she found a young worker to help. In the winter she changed her store to a fruit shop, mainly oranges and apples. Also at this time she had many canaries, which she would make money from if her canary won at a competition."

HIROFUMI SUZUKI

My mother was working hard from morning to evening. We were not a rich family, but we never felt we were poor. My mother was working with a smile on her face, never showed the hard life. Also we helped her, I think.

As a youngest brother, Kenji treat me good many times, but sometimes I was hit by him on my head from his frustration. Then I thought, 'I don't need a brother!' Now we're grown up, I'm happy that I'm not an only child, happy to have a brother.

"We lived on two floors," continues Kenji, recalling his mother's industrious pragmatism. "The first floor (the ground floor in Europe) had a freezing compartment; beside that was a space with kitchen, small living room and bath. We slept on the second floor, where there was also one room specially for canaries.

"When I woke up for a pee it was horrible. I had to go downstairs, through the ice block shop in darkness, to arrive at the toilet. It was even worse in that the toilet was not modern like today; you could see endless space from the pot and sometimes a cold wind blew. But this process was a kind of adventure when the nights were long.

"When we moved to apartment houses in a new area, my mother opened a grocery store with help from her younger brother. She sold pickles, dry and boiled meats, frozen goods, dried fish, fresh vegetables and fruits, tofu and alcohol (beer, whisky, sake, syoutyu, wine), like a small supermarket. One good thing of this period is that we children could eat expensive food that needed to be consumed fresh before it went bad. The less positive aspect is that we couldn't choose what we liked to eat.

"The first floor was the shop, warehouse and bathroom. My small dog was in the warehouse. On the second floor there was a small living room, dining room and kitchen, and another room I used as my learning corner. At night it became a sleeping space for me and my younger brother; some time later, when my older brother moved to Atsugi, he and my mother slept in the small dining room; when my sister came she also slept there. We also had quite a good-sized balcony on the second floor, mainly used to dry washed clothes."

It provided a lifelong lesson in the stoic practicalities of survival. The term 'hard work' is often used as a rationale by those who draw profit from the labours of others; as experienced by the Suzuki children, however, hard work was an exercise in existential necessity.

"My mother was doing many things," testifies Kenji, "as she was really strong. When all her kids had grown up, finished school or university, and were able to live without support from her, she learned *chigiri-e*. A few years later she became a teacher of this discipline, in which visual images are created by tearing coloured paper. My mother always loved to read books and had acquired a lot of knowledge. She researched whatever she became curious about; she couldn't stand not knowing about it. She had studied at high school, which was unusual for females at that time, and had even played tennis."

Most remarkably perhaps, Kimie Suzuki, a woman dedicated to family, work and duty, was not opposed to the shoots of non-conformism that would sprout from the personality of her middle son. "My mother didn't speak that much," confirms Kenji, "but I learned a lot from her. It was a hard time for her when she lost my father, she had to take care of four children, but all of us were well educated – except for me, as I wanted to quit school. I think she was quite sad when I left Japan, but she allowed me to go and gave me my freedom. I was lucky to have such a mother.

"As I left Japan, my mother said to me, 'Wherever you go, you have to eat good things; you have to promise!' She also told me: 'Eat fresh salad with many colours, each colour is light.'"

The quiet matriarch would finally leave this existence several decades hence, in the year 2013. The reverence her children hold for her is still observable. "It was quite a shock, although I knew that she would be dying soon as she was ninety-three years old. For almost the last ten years before, she had suffered from a form of Alzheimer's. Sometimes I'd meet her for maybe half an hour before she could truly remember who I was. It was quite a sad time for us as her children, because she was losing many of her memories."

In the early years of this decade, Kenji 'Damo' Suzuki returned briefly to the country and the culture that bore him. His odyssey of personal remembrance began at the very roots, at the house in Ōiso where he was born – a high-ceilinged domicile to his childhood imagination, now revealed as a modest abode seemingly too small to house a whole family.

"We had a small garden and behind it was a nice pond where I would hunt frogs," he reminisces. "It's just beside the national road that runs from Tokyo to Osaka. Behind this road was the beach, which I could get to in only a few minutes and where I spent a lot of time in the summer."

In his retracing of a lifetime's steps, the adult Damo picked up only the faintest scent of Japan's formerly dominant spiritual traditions. As a young Japanese kid, he'd never felt truly at one with Shinto and its symbolic icons of the Nipponese islands.

"Actually, I don't know if they believed or whether it was the same as in Britain," he demurs, "where people seem to believe in the Church of England but it's just a tradition. Later on in Atsugi there was a Shinto temple with a garden; they had TV and maybe twenty or thirty people came there to watch it."

It was television, rather than the mythical shades of the past, that pointed to a future for modern Japanese culture. Although most families had yet to purchase a TV set of their own, by the time he was ten years old Kenji was receiving his first diluted taste of Western pop culture. "But we had only two public broadcasting and one private station at the time, so it was totally different from now, and not many radio stations either. You couldn't hear that much popular music – maybe some dance tunes and easy listening on the radio.

"It was the beginning of the sixties. I was quite influenced at the time by pop music, but traditional Japanese music was just strange to me. Listening to early Japanese music is quite a niche today, but I could not go back to three hundred or four hundred years before. But then traditionally-based Japanese popular music, *kayōkyoku*, was almost like a *canzone* or *chanson*, nothing to do with the local blues-oriented music of the Anglo-Saxons."

Kayōkyoku assimilated Western musical styles into a Japanese idiom, starting with the *lied* of classical music and moving into a hipper post-war groove with the Nipponisation of swing and easy listening rhythms.

"The texture of kayōkyoku's lyrics was quite strange to foreigners," reflects the adult Kenji. "You needed to be Japanese to understand what it was communicating about the trees or flowers; each plant had a cultural meaning. If you are thinking about only one stone on the beach, there is a different meaning that can be ascribed to each of the stones." From the *kiku* (chrysanthemum) that symbolises survival and rebirth to the lotus flower whose ornamental likeness is used as holders for the incense sticks derived from it, floral imagery was a legacy of Shinto.

"Then I heard 'Sukiyaki' by a composer named Hachidai Nakamura, with lyrics by Rokusuke Ei. They made a kind of light pop music that I'd never heard before in Japan. I guess they are really the pioneers of Japanese pop – but if I say 'pop music' now, it is something to do with the mainstream. Then there were different cultural expectations."

'Sukiyaki', as sung by twenty-something Japanese crooner Kyu Sakamoto, was a jauntily catchy lyric of loneliness, augmented by tuneful whistling and a rhythm that wouldn't sound out of place at the more pop-oriented end of Nashville country music. It was a cultural crossover that became a rare foreign language hit in the US.

"Kayōkyoku and *enka* – which was also traditional Japanese music – were something I couldn't get into, but with the 'Sukiyaki' song – it's called '*Ue o Muite Arukō*' in Japanese ['I look up when I walk' – nothing to do with the Japanese dish which US distributors felt might strike a chord with the home market] – I had this fresh feeling which, in Japanese popular culture, didn't exist until then. Pop music in Japan at that time was Japanese singers covering music from abroad, but singing in Japanese. US culture was quite strong then, because, as with Germany and Italy, if you had lost a war then the culture of the country that won would be imported."

Today, Damo remains convinced that the post-war culture of 'winner takes all' persists. But for his younger self, as with many others, the predominance of Western pop culture was a double-edged sword. "Many people got into pop culture via US culture. I was living quite near to US military bases, so I was probably influenced much more than people who were living in other parts of Japan.

"I can remember one TV series that I was quite fond of at the beginning of the sixties, called *Route 66*. Two guys were travelling down Route 66, from Chicago to Santa Monica, 3939.67 kms by Chevrolet Corvette. They had adventures and love affairs in each different location for 116 episodes, it was like a road movie on TV. This programme may have motivated me to travel. To live every day with skill."

A middle-American riff on the beatnik auto-bohemianism of Jack Kerouac and his fictionalised friends in *On The Road*, *Route 66* followed the weekly adventures of a corporate dropout and his underemployed sidekick crisscrossing the USA. Its framework supported a compendium of themes ranging from the social problems of the era (1960–64) to the old Hollywood of silent comedy and monster movies. Most tellingly for the times, it took its name from a song that was an ode to the freedom of America's Interstates and highways; originally a jazz-inflected hit for the (Nat) King Cole Trio, 'Route 66' entered the R&B/rock'n'roll canon via Chuck Berry's electric version – sold back to the USA by a bunch of white English R&B copyists called The Rolling Stones.

"It got me into international music for the first time," confirms the adult Kenji. "In my early teens I didn't have much interest in buying anything that was coming from the radio, so this became my first source of musical culture."

But before Western music came a nascent wanderlust, in part inspired by the Chino-panted hipsters who traversed Route 66. "I was not very good in school, but I was interested in geography and I was good at it. I spent quite a lot of time just gazing at a World Atlas and dreaming about going somewhere. I was more interested in dreaming, in my own visions."

More localised inspiration came from a new Japanese visual culture that took the raw *bang-pow!* of American comic books and turned it into something distinctively, peculiarly Eastern. "I was also painting from when I was maybe eight years old," recalls Kenji, although his was not the standard dabbling in watercolours. "I began by painting comics, and at that time I was quite into Osamu Tezuka – this guy is a pioneer of Japanese comics."

Now praised as the godfather of manga, the late, lamented and very prolific Tezuka is famous in the USA and Europe for *Astro Boy* – spawning the first Japanese TV cartoon series to become a hit in the West, which also gives him some claim to be the godfather of anime. Stanley Kubrick's *2001: A Space Odyssey* might have contained a less scientifically clinical, more wide-eyed sense of visual fantasy if Tezuka had afforded the time to leave his home studio for a year and work as the film's art director.

"I like Tezuka's artwork a lot," emphasises Kenji, "and even now I have his complete works, up to 200 comic books by him. He was a hard worker and, as far as I know, painted more than 250,000 pages of comics altogether. He genuinely gave hopes and dreams to young boys like me. When I was maybe seven, eight years old he was my hero. He was for me the greatest person I could imagine."

Already pioneering his pop-culture field during World War II, Tezuka was studying to be a medical doctor before he switched over to comic art full time. In the tradition of a literary visionary like H. G. Wells, both his fantasy mangas like *Lost World* and his later anime cartoon adaptations reflect his optimistic view of science.

"I'm not so interested in his anime," demurs Damo, "it's much more interesting to turn from one page to another page. If you see film or anime it's quite automatic – you don't have to think so much. The book is supported by your brain. If you see already-finished stuff with your eyes, the brain doesn't work so much. If you read a book, every word can be imagined. If I read manga comics, they give much more impact." It's a personally existential attitude towards the imagination that persists in his own art form to the present day, but first came to fruition as a schoolboy.

"I made a hand-painted magazine for only a few of my schoolmates, every three days or so. I painted another comic for each person. Not printed, but hand-painted one by one! Because I was having quite a lot of fun and I wanted to paint, my first ambition was to be a comic artist. It was ten pages each time for three different persons. Each book was totally different. I did this for a couple of months and they paid me money – but not much, 10 or 20 yen or something. Maybe it was a bit less sophisticated because I was only a kid. I didn't know anything about love or mafia-type things – maybe I painted schoolboy stuff that was going on at the time."

After a short while, however, the young schoolboy decided neither his talent nor his ideas were equal to his inspiration. In the manner of so many early ambitions, he let it drop.

His dreams would never die, though. In many ways he would remain a lifelong romantic. In the earliest part of his adolescence, at least a year before he reached his teens, he focused his romanticism upon a love object no older than himself. "I wrote a love letter to my schoolgirl friend but I was too shy to speak with her," he smiles affectionately at the bashful little dreamer he once was, "and maybe she was waiting for me to speak with her. She knew that I loved her, but I was not able to express it."

It wouldn't be that long before his attraction to the opposite sex bore fruit. Before that, however, young Kenji began his life's on-off love affair with music. It started with the gift of a musical instrument from Hiroko, his sister.

"Every birthday she would buy me a clarinet, a saxophone, an organ," he remembers with evident affection, "and at the same time she was a member of a classical music society. She was getting one or two classical LPs every month, so that was the musical education I had. It was Western classical music, but only the popular composers – Mozart, Beethoven, Johann Strauss, mainstream classics."

It bred a lifelong habit. Whether or not his life was currently entwined with rock music, in its varying shapes or mutant forms, classical music provided a structure that both man and boy could take refuge in. Then there were the less formalised aspects of Western music, like the jazz that briefly held sway among students before the age of rock music (as opposed to rock'n'roll) dawned.

"I bought 'Take Five' by Dave Brubeck so I could play saxophone to it," says the man we now call Damo of the early sixties instrumental hit. "Not like on the record, but it allowed me to think, *'If I can listen to something then I can play its melody.'* But I wasn't really being creative, I was just covering the track."

The lilting sax melody inspired by Middle Eastern airs made it the best-selling jazz record of all time. Given a subsequent lifetime's experience of improvised music, one might think Damo Suzuki had a natural feel for the genre. But one might be wrong.

"I don't really know what jazz is," he demurs. "The really strange thing is that people can recognise jazz by the percussion and so on, but even jazz musicians cannot explain it. One night I was discussing with some young people, 'What is jazz?' and one of them said, 'Jazz is sex' – which is okay, sometimes jazz is sexy.

"But there are so many words that apply to other music too: 'improvisation' is not only jazz, there is a form of folk music from Russia that is always improvised. Once I played with a string quartet, well-educated classical musicians, but we improvised too – so I don't know, what is jazz?"

It's perhaps fitting that the maverick lone voice behind the peak recordings of Can and, more contemporarily, the live onstage compositions of the Damo Suzuki Network should question any musical labels. But his initial musical training came conventionally packaged.

"For three years I played clarinet in the junior high school brass band," he recounts, "rehearsing three or four days a week after school lessons. We were rehearsing mainly march music. There were many sports clubs and events in the school – baseball club, soccer club – and if they were playing against another school team then we would go to play music to support them. Once again, I wasn't really being creative but I probably composed my first pieces at this time."

But there was a new musical revolution sending out sound waves from the West. A world away from the discipline of a woodwind section, it started (and mostly ended) with the brutally simple, electrically amplified line-up of lead guitar/rhythm guitar/bass guitar/drums.

"When I was maybe twelve or thirteen, in 1963, 'electronic music' didn't mean what it does now," explains Damo, "it meant an instrumental surf-rock band like The Ventures." Picking up on the vocal-free 1950s guitar styles of Duane Eddy and Link Wray, and their early sixties UK counterparts The Shadows, surf rock ventured into realms far outside the beach-boy harmonies of Jan & Dean, extending to the experimental guitar sounds of Hendrix influence Dick Dale.

"This was quite a popular style in Japan at the time," Damo recalls of his American-influenced youth, "so very young kids were copying The Ventures or The Astronauts," the latter proving more popular in Japan than in their homeland. "It started the *eleki* [electric guitar] boom when many kids formed bands to copy their guitar heroes. In the middle of the boom, there were many bans on schoolboys playing eleki as the PTA and teachers were protesting against this movement. They stamped on boys who had ambitions to make this music, branding them as failures."

Looking back on the eleki boom, it's remarkable that performers like Yūzō Kayama, a clean-cut Hank Marvin figure augmenting his instrumental twang with songs that sounded like a Nipponese Bobby Vee, should be seen as encouraging juvenile delinquency. But this new music was the product of an alien culture, seemingly at odds with centuries of codified Japanese tradition.

Despite this cultural conservatism, the older Kenji remembers, with just a hint of nostalgia, how "it was a really good time when I was fourteen or fifteen years old. After I came to junior high school, I went around with one girl who was half American and half Japanese. I was almost entirely listening to soul music, so maybe I was connecting that with this girl. We met quite often. At that time I was not much interested in my studies at school, as my girlfriend had much more importance in my life."

23

The diminutive teenager, his straight black hair growing gradually longer, would grab the attention of girls on both sides of the East/West divide. His adolescent instincts aside, the same period saw the flowering of a natural curiosity about life outside of the prescribed norm – the first stirrings of a cultural outsider.

"In Japan, every high school at that time had a uniform," he remembers of the prevailing conformism. "Sometimes I pretended to go to high school, but in a train station or elsewhere I'd take off my uniform to change into normal clothes. I was much more interested in going to a big city like Yokohama and hanging around, listening to live Japanese bands covering American and British bands. So I didn't have time for studying at all, I had another interest.

"Then, when I was fifteen or sixteen years old, there was the *wasei* pop boom, with major groups like The Tigers, The Tempters and hundreds of other bands who covered American or British styles but sung Japanese lyrics over Japanese-style melodies." Itself a response to the 'British invasion' of the USA, which reinterpreted black American R&B by provincial English white kids, wasei was the beginning of what we now know as J-pop – adding the odd Eastern inflexion to the less threatening side of the rock music revolution.

"It was based in part on Japanese traditional music but it wasn't to my taste," confirms Damo, "though they had quite a lot of success. I was much more interested in listening to original music from abroad."

Once again, Damo claims this pop-cultural colonisation was imposed via military defeat: "That is why so much American music came, American movies, American TV – this is part of propaganda. That people have to listen to this music is kind of a punishment because we lost the Second World War.

"But of course it gains popularity and people think, *'Oh this is good music, I like this!'* They want emotional compensation for losing a war. It just happened like this, but through these sources I learned to listen to British music. Also I listened to soul musicians like James Brown, because I found the groove really good. I also liked The Righteous Brothers, who were quite different. It got to other kids too but I didn't listen to a special category of music – I was quite curious about many directions."

In rock and pop music, the listener should always be sceptical of any performer claiming 'authenticity' – though, for young Japanese kids of the mid-sixties, the British beat-boom bands of the time must have sounded like the real thing. Forming a band must have seemed like the quickest way to enter an electrifying new world; initially though, the young Kenji tried a different route to this bright new modernity.

"When I was in the second year of high school, at age sixteen," he recalls, "I went to actor training school for a few weekends when school was out. I wanted to be an actor for only a short time. Their first lessons were in fluent Japanese speaking, which was boring for me, so I quit at an early stage."

This brief flirtation had less to do with thespian ambitions than an intoxication by female glamour. "At that time I liked two actresses especially: Junko Ikeuchi, aged early thirties, a beautiful woman perfectly dressed in a kimono, and Mariko Kaga, in her early twenties, who I found a pretty sexy beast. She was the Japanese Brigitte Bardot – very cute and popular with young men. I also met my cousin, Jyunko, at the training school, as she was trying to be an actress.

"It was a good choice not to be an actor. I didn't have the talent, it was just a kind of kid's dream." But neither would he follow the more obvious path of forming a band.

"I was much more interested in managing one, so I arranged some concerts when I was fifteen or sixteen years old. Shortly before that I started listening to British music, because by the mid-sixties The Beatles had played concerts in Japan."

Prior to the Liverpudlian moptops' arrival there was already a 'B-pop' scene of sorts in Japan – this was the bland smiliness of Peter & Gordon ('A World Without Love') and The Honeycombs, whose stomping, Dave Clark Five-style, female drummer provided the backbeat of their manufactured pop hit, 'Have I The Right?'. But Kenji Suzuki was going for a bigger, bolder beat.

"During that period I established a music lovers' club called the Scouser Club, to support British bands," he reminisces. The term 'scouser' denoted the Fab Four's hometown of Liverpool; but as Kenji quickly realised, the British invasion emanated from all compass points of an island nation of similar size to Japan: from The Animals in the north-west to the Stones in the south-east.

"We were mainly young boys from Atsugi and Numazu in the neighbouring prefecture of Shizuoka," he says, glancing back down the corridor of years. "At that time, although British bands seldom came to Japan, I used to go to concerts to hear what Western countries' young people were listening to. I wasn't a Beatles fan but I had all of their LPs, and then I went on to The Rolling Stones, whose albums I had too – but after a while I got fed up with them too, and went on to The Kinks."

The Kinks, centring round north London brothers Ray and Dave Davies, are where British rock really begins. Their raw riffing debut singles, 'You Really Got Me' and 'All Day And All Of The Night', are oft credited as the template for heavy metal; the wry disaffection of Ray's mid-sixties lyrics have, according to Damo, "a kind of punk texture"; in seeming contradiction of all this, The Kinks embraced a very English music-hall nostalgia, whereby the village green preservation society yearned to return to the past.

"I got really into The Kinks in about '66," he remembers with enthusiasm. "I started an unofficial Kinks Fan Club, which was a continuation of the Scouser Club and it really wasn't huge, only a few people of the same mind to avoid The Beatles and the Stones. I think this was before The Kinks LPs were released in Japan. We met regularly once a month or so, to listen to records on stereo equipment.

"At that time I used to go to Yamaha music shops at Dgenzaka, Shibuya, in Tokyo to buy imported vinyl LPs that were quite expensive. The minimum cost was 2,500 yen – compare this with a university graduate's first salary, which was around 35,000 yen at that time. I had to wait for maybe two or three months because it came by ship. I got all of the LPs by The Kinks before people in Japan could get them from King Records [the distributor of Pye Records, The Kinks' British label], and also many interesting products by unknown bands."

By this stage, the teenage Kenji was living to hear the latest music. "After a while I got American underground music like The Music Machine, ? & The Mysterians – garage-punk. I heard much of The Seeds, which was not released in Japan. I ordered two LPs, I guess – Sky Saxon's vocals were very special to me." Their US hit 'Pushin' Too Hard' featured the line 'all I want is to just be free / live my life the way I wanna be.' "Besides which I heard the Tamla Motown and Atlantic label styles of soul music.

"Magazines like *Cashbox*, *Billboard*, *NME* and *Melody Maker* were my literature," the inky music trade press, which sold hundreds of thousands of copies between them in that pre-internet age. "I wasn't a rich kid, but I made money to buy LPs as a caddy (I lived near to a golf course) or helping at a record shop near Hon-Atsugi railway station. Once, at a class reunion many years later (in 2004), my old schoolfriend told me I had enough money to invite a few friends to spend one or two days in Hakone; I paid for everything for them. I can't remember how much money I must have made, but once I bought a complete band kit – electric guitar, bass guitar, drum kit, amplifier, microphone."

The stage may have been set for Kenji to become a Japanese music impresario, if his wanderlust hadn't awakened. As it was, he was happy to neglect his school studies to keep funding his interests, rising at dawn to deliver newspapers on his bike and ride through a graveyard, feeling just a little spooked.

"I was thinking about travelling abroad when I was sixteen," he confirms, "because I was so much into Western music. I was also quite interested in other cultures, and I was reading magazines like *Heibon Punch* – which was established in 1964, a weekly Japanese men's magazine with A4-size naked women in the centre. I was very interested in getting information on what was going on in the men's world, which seemed cool." Indeed.

In those pre-feminist days, one test of a young man's sophistication was how closely he might aspire to the consumer lifestyle ethic of Hefner's *Playboy*, which included naked centrefold girls among the trappings of the good life. While the rising generation would espouse free love and sexual freedom, it never really got away from the idea of sex as a sensual reward for the young and hip.

But in any case, the impulse to leave behind the restrictions of his homeland – whether geographical or cultural – was now compelling. "Since I was a kid I'd had an interest in travelling in Japan," he reflects, "but I only went to a few places and didn't go very far. Up until the time my father died he was always quite busy, so there wasn't much possibility of travelling with him. I went to Southern Japan, Kyushu, and also the eastern part of Japan like Kyoto, Osaka. That's all, because it wasn't a time when people had enough money to travel – it was maybe fifteen years after the world war. Economically, Japan wasn't such a strong country at that time, maybe twenty-second or twenty-third in the world. Also at that time, transport wasn't as easy as today.

"But later my brother, Hirofumi, who is three years younger than me, was collecting butterflies as specimens and got me interested in it. So we went for a few days to Kirigamine in the Nagano prefecture with our sister, who by then was working in a bank."

The butterfly, in its manically fluttering beauty, is a symbol of love and devotion in Japan – at least when two of the creatures are placed together. Kenji Suzuki was attuned both to the life of the senses and that of the emotions, and this would remain true throughout his travels in Western Europe.

But at home his personality was not always so readily accepted. He looks back on an incident when he was eleven years old: "I liked a girl who was one year above me and I used to watch her. Then a kid of the same age called me to come behind a cinema. Fortunately, I was able to escape, as he was brandishing his knife."

It was the instinctive reaction of a young thug to sexual jealousy, but possibly also to someone he regarded as somehow different from himself. On his Western travels, such incidents would be mercifully few; the hippie era and its short-lived psychedelic revolution placed a premium on eccentric individualism, while Kenji (who would be reborn on his travels as 'Damo') had the unforeseen advantage of cultural novelty.

In Japan, however, his outsider status could cause resentment. He recalls a school trip to the south-west when aged sixteen: "It was not that much fun as there were so many schoolmates and ten teachers. I slept in the same room with ten or twenty boys; some of them didn't like me for some reason and beat me in the stomach so that the teacher could not see the next morning. Some put their pillows over me while many boys were beating me at the same time. I had good friends too, but it seems I had a similar amount of enemies. I don't know why they did this to me when I didn't harm them."

In school, his bad grades were mitigated by his sociable behaviour. "I was not a bad boy who made trouble. Only once my mother was called to come to the school, when I was sixteen. The teacher said to her: 'Your son avoided paying the book budget for our library.'"

His hard-working mother's aspirations had secured him a place at a private school in Odawara, in the eastern part of the Kanagawa prefecture. The boy would travel to Odawara – famous for its ancient castle – every day on the Odakyu line from Hon-Atsugi in thirty minutes.

Kenji's time there would come to an abrupt end, but still some mutual respect persisted between pupil and pedagogues: "After a while the teacher told her, 'Actually your son is right, he was saying in class, "We pay enough money to come to this private high school, we don't have to pay the budget for the library. You cannot manage with the payment we pay every month?"'

"But my most joyful moment was when school finished. My sister Hiroko remembers how she heard from my mother that I rebelled against school rules from a sense of injustice. The teacher said, 'If you're talking like that, don't come to school!' I took him at his word and stayed at home. As a philosophy of life, it might be better to leave this one blank."

In his final days at Odawara, Kenji had an experience which, in a strange way, pointed toward the open possibilities of the future. "I had a friend whose father owned a restaurant in front of Odawara station," he recalls, "which was doing well. Quite often I went there with some other friends, eating and drinking. During the examination period, I was walking down the street with my clique. Then I saw something flying over Odawara-Jyou castle; it went up, then moved to the right – left – down – up. It moved like an anime movie. It was not technically possible to make that kind of vehicle at that time; it's still not possible now. It was oblong, cobalt coloured and had no window. It was not made by any inhabitant of earth.

"'You guys, did you see?' No reply. I was sure I saw a UFO, even though I was under stress from examinations."

It was like a harbinger of the coming epoch, when all visions, however hallucinatory, would be valued, or even of the decades that followed – when the hidden truth would be forever 'out there', hanging in the ether.

Kenji's turning point had arrived. "Slowly, my eyes were opening as I became more interested in going somewhere else. Then, when I was seventeen, I quit high school; it was 1967. Why should I stay and study to enter university when I don't share the belief in bettering my social position? My whole life through, I had been never been satisfied to live like anyone else. It's my life. To quote a lyric I particularly like by The Kinks, 'I'm not like everybody else.'"

With the influence of Western popular culture becoming so tangible, many of Kenji's contemporaries spoke of travelling to the West. But out of all of them, he would be the only one to follow through on his plan.

Today, he looks back on his youthful gamble without regret; in fact he regards it as an ideal for living: "I recommend that young people stay a few years in other countries, it means more than going to school, especially if you have no motivation to study. Why waste your precious youth just hanging around? Better to go out and enjoy new fresh air, you'll learn many things by yourself."

Although his polite but persistent mannerisms and his calm reasoning remain resolutely Eastern, in 1967 Kenji Suzuki yearned to break out of his native Japan. "I went against the traditions we were taught to believe in at school," he affirms. "I'm not interested in the traditional way of things because there is no truth inside of it.

"If you wish to find the truth, you must break with tradition: 'Because my father was a Buddhist, and also my grandfather and grandmother...' but I'm not a Buddhist. Because I went on to travel alone, I would learn many things. I later realised a kind of truth: if you eat food and it has a good taste, then you will eat only good food. I think this statement has a kind of parallel to spirituality."

The almost infinite varieties of international cuisine would be a part of the young traveller's education. But for now, until he could set sail from home, he continued to hang out on the periphery of Tokyo's hidden subculture.

In 1968, the year Kenji Suzuki left Japan, a Japanese film entitled *Diary Of A Shinjuku Thief* would play the international art cinema circuit. Directed by Nagisa Oshima (later known for the controversial *Ai No Corrida*), it's a comedy of manners that conflates sex with the thrill of theft and begins in a bookshop in the Shinjuku neighbourhood. Shinjuku was where the young hipsters hung – the nearest Nipponese equivalent to America's beatniks or, latterly, the hippies.

"It is the part of Tokyo where so-called *Shinjuku kojiki* ('homeless people in Shinjuku' – in other words hippies) were meeting at that time. I was not really into it, but I liked it because it was not connected with traditional life and the normal ways. There was a kind of freedom – which is why I spent some time there, and also why I would later find myself in communes in Europe.

"But it was only a few people, so you cannot say 'hippie movement' like in Europe or America. I don't know how many there were but they had some kind of underground theatre and artistic movement, maybe from mid-'66 or '67. Because we had lost the world war and US culture had come to Japan, even our anti-establishment ideas had to come from somewhere else."

The Shinjuku kojiki were the nearest thing to a deviant subculture within an ethos of strict conformity. In a land of stringently applied laws few would risk the Western flirtations with hallucinogens or narcotics, but the sight of Japanese boys and girls in shades and smoking cigarettes would, at that time, have carried a similar cultural charge to the Beats.

As for Kenji, his own individualism was more light-hearted: "When my sister married, I'd visit her in Koganei-city in my new, self-designed boots. She thought a pop star had come, as I looked so cool!" But the decision he'd made was serious. Everything in his life would now be geared toward leaving his motherland.

"It was probably hard on my mother," he concedes, "but I wanted to go my own way. If I'd stayed longer in school to take examinations for university, it wouldn't have been any good because I had no interest in it. If the stronger interest lies in the other direction then that's the way you go."

But there was no overnight departure. First, he had to secure work with his uncle's company, which built water conditioning systems. "My uncle Isao was one of my mother's brothers," he explains. "After my father passed he came to visit us often. He was as supportive as a father to me and one of the people I respected most. He had three daughters, and I guess in a way he wanted to have a son. He played with me and Hirofumi, he made us laugh and be happy, even if only for a moment. I owe much to him."

As for the job itself, "It was really hard physical work, usually outside. I rode there on my bicycle – which was almost fifteen kilometres there and fifteen kilometres back home – even on rainy or stormy days. But I did it because I wanted to get my money together and get out of Japan."

It would not be the last time that Kenji Suzuki committed himself to hard labour out of necessity or, from a traditionally Japanese perspective, family honour. Seven months of knuckling down would raise enough for his planned sojourn, although he was only permitted by the government to leave with the bare minimum of currency at that time – 20,000 yen plus US$500.

The money was only likely to fund his travels for a matter of weeks, rather than months. "So I was trying to find personal sponsors. I wrote many letters to newspapers in Europe. The Swedish popular daily newspaper *Expressen* ran my letter: '*Young Japanese boy is looking for a family who support me – has interest to know your habit and culture.*'

The response was twenty-one letters from Sweden, as well as one from Belgium. Kenji's decision was made for him. "If it had come from another country then I'd have gone there. Because I didn't come from a rich family, I didn't have much money to travel. If any one place was welcoming me with a warm bed and food then I went to this place. It just happened to be Sweden.

"When I came out I didn't have any plan. I didn't have any plan for anything in my life. If you came out of Japan there were not so many aeroplanes, not so many transport possibilities. So I took a ship because it was the cheapest I could get at that price."

In the late 1960s, Sweden would gain a reputation as Scandinavia's capital of sexual liberation; the young Japanese boy was, as yet, unaware of such stereotyping. But still, he knew he was setting off into another world.

"At that time, leaving Japan was like leaving forever," the much older Damo recalls, "because if you leave on a ship people are throwing tapes, and the port is growing smaller and smaller, my mother and family and my brothers and my friends are getting smaller and smaller. It makes it much more sentimental.

"I had only a one-way ticket; I didn't have very much money. With these financial stakes, I have to survive in Europe. It is really a kind of life-changing event – I might not be able to come back to my home."

CHAPTER TWO

A JAPANESE BUSKER IN EUROPE

"On January 17, 1968, at the port of Yokohama, came a very important turning point of my life," says the man who, as a teenager, was still known as Kenji Suzuki. "My travels would take me to Sweden, via Siberia in midwinter." It was the day after his eighteenth birthday. A *bon voyage* that led towards a peripatetic not-quite-adulthood.

Waving a fond *adieu* were his mother, little brother Hiro and his 'clan' from high school, who'd hung out at Odawara station and, sometimes, at Shinjuku with him. The parting felt permanent and a little ominous. Around nine in the morning the sky was still pitch-dark, with snow and rain mixed in the air. The older man, by now so much more widely read than his younger self, might recognise the Western literary tradition of sympathetic atmosphere in his memories of that night.

It was, he recalls, "a very melancholy moment: the harbour brass band played that famous Scottish melody 'Auld Lang Syne', a farewell song. As it was ringing through the harbour, both the passengers and the people who were sending them off threw tapes."

The Russian liner's horn blew deep, displacing air under the dark grey winter sky. Heavy rain showers followed in the very next moment. "It was the start of my adventure and my farewell to the loved ones who stayed behind," he recollects.

As the ship sailed out of port and the figures on the harbour receded into miniature, Kenji felt an increasing sense that he might never return. "Travel at that time meant that you may or may not come back," muses the seasoned traveller of today. "There was no easy travelling; aeroplanes were rare and very expensive, only for rich people." The sentiment accompanying his departure was a deliciously sad feeling of estrangement from the past.

It was exile on a budget. The cheapest route to arrive in Europe from Japan at that time was all inclusive at around 70,000 yen. Travelling through Cold War-era Russia also entailed transfer costs and the price of every meal for each day he stayed there.

But still, the sense of adventure was palpable. "Strangely, I didn't even worry that I knew only a few words in English," says the older Kenji of his linguistic isolation. "It took some time to get out of my sentimental state, and I don't remember if I shared a cabin with someone. I took the cheapest cabin but maybe I was alone, as only crazy people or escaped criminals would have the idea of travelling in the middle of Russian wintertime."

Or perhaps someone wide-eyed and curious enough not to worry about a guardedly paranoid society. But then the Russian people themselves seemed open and approachable. In particular, the young Japanese with a healthy interest in *gaijin* girls felt drawn to the women.

"They looked pretty, beautiful even," he recalls, "and I decided I'd like to talk with them. Outside, the stormy winter weather ruled; the waves of the sea were not only misty, they seemed to be angry. Regularly at lunchtime or dinnertime, many passengers stayed in their cabin and didn't show themselves in the restaurant. Maybe they were dizzy from seasickness. I was in the restaurant every time; I wasn't worried that maybe in the next second the ship would be sinking."

Eating Russian food for the first time was an interesting experience for a lifelong *gourmand*; seeing the ladies at close quarters was even more interesting. "Everything I saw was something new that I'd never experienced before. It was my entrance to a new world."

And he was no longer alone. A disparate group of mainly young Japanese passengers were following their own sea-bound routes to Europe: "A guy in quite trendy clothes with long hair wanted to go to Paris to study fashion – he already looked the part. Another guy wanted to go to see the Winter Olympic Games in Grenoble, France. Two girls wanted to go to Romania and study, and so on. Everybody had their own story and their own goal."

After two and a half days riding the winter waves of the Japanese ocean, Kenji watched the Russian port of Nakhodka growing bigger from his cabin. By now acclimatised to the weather, without the benefit of shades the reflecting snow could still hurt his eyes. "But outside it was terribly cold, minus 30°C," he recalls with a visceral shudder. "I'd never really experienced this coldness; at this temperature your piss became an ice pole if your heart was brave enough for you to open your jeans."

It was a bracing start to his journey: by train to Khabarovsk; from Khabarovsk to Moscow by air. "When the train terminated at Khabarovsk they thought I was a girl, because I had long hair," says Kenji, "and directed me to the ladies' wagon. But after a while, two ladies complained about me: 'This is a boy!' So I had to go to the other wagon."

It was a common enough complaint in those days: 'Are you a boy or a girl?' To Soviet citizens it must have been all the more perplexing.

His sojourn in Moscow lasted a few days. "It was a big city in darkness," the grown-up Kenji recalls, "they didn't have much street light and where they did it was dull. All the people were in the same colours, grey or deep green, with a really deep winter coat, their heads naturally covered with that famous *ushanka*. Even in those cold winter days many people were on the street, forming queues in front of shops."[*]

His love of female company and unthreatening manner hooked him up with two Hungarian women, staying at the same hotel. While they must have been relatively youthful, to him they were senior and sophisticated enough to be regarded as 'ladies'.

"Their Indian friend invited me and some young Japanese passengers to their huge hotel room for drinks," he reminisces. "I felt I was falling in love with one of the two ladies, although we separated after a while, as she was not feeling well enough to travel abroad."

"I think I bought her flowers to say farewell," he recalls of his romantic aspirations, while staying discreetly coy. "I remember her name still, but this may not be the right place to record it. I remember it all quite well: she was so elegantly dressed and very beautiful."

---

[*] Later that same year, expatriate American singer-songwriter Scott Walker would make his own journey through Russia by rail; the unwanted attention of men who appeared to be KGB would divert his sympathy for communism toward a more humanistic existentialism. The young Damo, while a yea-saying nascent hippie, had no such faith in a creed that imposed 'equality' via grey conformism.

From Moscow it was a trip on the night sleeper to Helsinki, Finland: "my entry to the free world," as he describes arriving at his first European destination, without the compatriots who'd accompanied him thus far. "The world outside the window was shining, the trees were never-ending, the winter landscape unchanging," he thinks himself back into the moment. "Time was almost stopping, though my body was carried forward into infinity." Still, it was just another stop along the way to his Scandinavian destination.

At Stockholm harbour, the Swedish correspondent scheduled to support Kenji's stay for the next few months sent his female cousin along to pick him up. "My host lived a long drive from the city in a very quiet town; I stayed there for only one night. I found that he was a homosexual teacher, so I didn't want to stay there for longer than I had to." For the young Eastern traveller, some aspects of even a small European country could be too cosmopolitan.

Early the next day he made his first ever European hitchhike, to the small town of Gräsmark. "In the middle of the Swedish winter hitchhiking is not really a good idea," Kenji shivers at the memory, "in fact it's dangerous, but there wasn't much money so there were no other possibilities."

He was able to navigate his road trip with his thumb. Instead of Route 66, he was picked up by a series of car drivers on E18 – the road from Stockholm to Oslo, capital of Norway. "I got to Karlstad. The difficulty was from Karlstad to Gräsmark in poor traffic situations, cars carrying me for only short distances, waiting a long time in freezing cold weather. I passed through much woodland before finally arriving at Gräsmark. The cold still gave me a shock because I'd come from central Japan.

"It was quite different for me," Kenji recalls of the culture shift, "because Japan had a high population at that time and many houses were quite tiny. The streets were quite narrow. In Sweden it was very different because only seven or eight million people were living there. I was much surprised by the living standards: in Sweden they were at quite a high level and every place was totally clean."

Gräsmark was a compact microcosm of a small society. At the time it had a population of only fifty people: one petrol station, one church and one supermarket. "Actually it was much smaller than a supermarket," corrects Kenji, "but they had almost every kind of everything. In German it's called a Tante-Emma-Laden ('Aunt Emma's shop') – it's a much more private atmosphere, kind of a meeting place for village people talking about this and that.

"Now, they have a population of 250, a bigger supermarket, some guesthouses, a few international visitors and summer houses for big city people," he expands. But over the course of decades, the development itself doesn't seem so overly expansive. "Several years ago I went there again – after forty years or something, and it's still a beautiful place but it's totally different. This was the first place where I lived for a long time in Europe."

SIMON TORSSELL LERIN
Experimental musician (guitar) in a duo with Bettina Hvidevold Hystad (electronics)

We were in Japan and we met Damo in Osaka (2010), after a show. I had listened to Can records but I didn't know so much about Damo Suzuki's Network – we went to see one of the Network shows in Osaka, then after the show we got to meet him. He found out I was from Sweden, so he started to speak a little Swedish with me. Then he told me that before he was in Can, in the sixties, he stayed in Sweden for a few months. I'm from western Sweden, close to the Norwegian border, and it turns out that he stayed like thirty minutes away from where I grew up, in a small village of about two hundred people. We've got this connection so that was how our relationship started.

He told us about this place Gräsmark in the woods, in the west part of Sweden where he lived, quite close to where I'm from in Sunnemo. This place was so small and he hadn't met a Swedish person before who knew about it. So it was this strange coincidence that we meet in Japan and we find out that I'm almost from the same place where he stayed.

He talked about nature and snow and things like that. I think it was new to him. Since this place is quite remote in Sweden, there is no big city close to it. Especially in the sixties, the people who lived there didn't travel so much really. For him coming especially as the first Japanese person, I think he really stood out. He comes from outside of Tokyo somewhere, so to be a little bit isolated like that was something new to him.

In the wintertime it's usually around minus 10, but in January it can be minus 20. But in summertime it's very nice, it can be around 25 degrees. It's a very calm place: small lakes and small fountains and lots of forest. Now there are a lot of people farming; back then they worked more in the forests as well. The people are quite friendly – depending on where you are in this area, but usually they are interested in new people. So I think Damo quite liked it that everyone became curious when he came.

We didn't think so much about it for about two years, but then we started talking about it again just for fun: "I wonder if anybody still remembers him in this place Gräsmark? Do they know about Can or that he became a musician afterwards?" So we started relating to them the way that Damo had done, because he had sent an ad to the Swedish paper when he was still in Japan, when he was a seventeen-year-old: he wrote that he was interested in coming to Sweden and wondered if anyone could take him as a guest for one month, because he wanted to learn about Swedish traditions.

We decided to use the same approach; so we also got in touch with the local newspaper and we placed a small article where we asked: 'Does anybody remember Damo Suzuki who stayed in Gräsmark forty years ago? Does anybody have any memories of this?'

The same evening that this came out in the paper, a woman got in touch, a local hairdresser called Birgitta – because she didn't known about the 'Damo' name, she still called him Kenji. She called me and said: "Kenji was in the paper today – did you know he wanted to marry me?" [laughs]

So that was really quite interesting and it brings us to the start of our project* – we had contact also with Damo, so we sent him some photos she

---

* *Simon Torssell Lerin/Bettina Hvidevold Hystad with Damo Suzuki* – limited edition of 500 – white 12" heavyweight LP with 60-page book in box (released December 2013). Damo: "In the year 2010, I became sixty years old. To celebrate sixty is something special for Japanese as it is 5 × 12 zodiac. At least once in my life, I wished to know more about my native country, so I presented myself for my sixtieth birth year: I spent around three months travelling through the country I was born and grew up in before I left for Sweden. During this trip I met Simon and Bettina in Osaka at one of my Network performances.

"After a while, Simon contacted me, he and Bettina were both art students, they found the interest to do an art project that zooms into Damo Suzuki's life before he joined That German Band.

"In 2012, I went back to Gräsmark for the first time in forty years. There I met Gittan [her friends' pet name for Birgitta], her sister and a few other people knowing me from the end of the sixties when I lived there. Sadly I couldn't meet Helga, my Swedish mother, she died few years ago. All my memories came back like it all happened yesterday. Suddenly my body was covered by the time and space of that period of my life.

"Simon and Bettina's book project – their life connecting with my time and space when I was young – is not just research of my life. Simon and Bettina left their footprints on my life softly."

had from that time. That led to Damo being very interested and he asked me if I could help him come back and meet her again after forty years.

There are two parts to the book: the first part was always written from mine and Bettina's perspective, how we found things out on our journey together with him. The first part was about this Birgitta, the Swedish part of the story of the sixties before he joined Can. Then the second part of the book was about how we went with him on his Japan tour with the Network, we went to almost all of the concerts, and we photographed and videotaped the shows and met the Sound Carriers, and wrote about our experience of the concerts.

So the first part was where we went to all these archive things, we went to the Royal Library in Stockholm and found this old ad that Damo put in the paper in the sixties. We included that, it was quite interesting; we found some other articles about Damo when he was living in Gräsmark. The local paper wrote about him only because he was the first Japanese person in this village, so we found some quite funny newspaper articles from the sixties about him. Damo told us which paper it was in and we knew the times so we just had to search, but we had to do quite a lot of searching.

Helga Anderson was the matriarch who became the first European surrogate mother to the boy that became Damo. "The family Anderson treated me well," he recalls, "as if I was one of their sons. Every day they gave me 10 Swedish krone, even allowing me to stay in a separate house just next door to that small supermarket."

It was Mrs Anderson who introduced Damo to the local community. "I suddenly gained a reputation in the surrounding villages as a cute Japanese boy," he remembers with some satisfaction. "Schoolgirls, who had nothing to do after school other than cross-country skiing through the woods, visited me occasionally with their friends. So I wouldn't say it was a bad time." A lifelong love of femininity and the female form had already found expression back in his youth.*

---

* Damo: "I made a deeper, more lasting contact with one particular girl. This, and all the other stories about my life in a small village, would appear in the book forty years later by Swedish artist Simon Torssell Lerin and his Norwegian collaborator, Bettina Hvidevold Hystad, on my time in Sweden at the end of the sixties and my romance with a Swedish girl, Gittan. During this period, I learned not only how to communicate with young Swedish girls but also tried Norwegian skiing for the first time."

In a hamlet full of fair-complexioned Scandinavians, a long-haired Nipponese had obvious novelty appeal. "I'm quite small and some girls treated me like a puppet!" he remembers with amusement. "I don't like to say this now, but I think I was kind of cute. Also I had a guitar and saxophone, I could play some music and some young girls liked musicians."

Music was just an enjoyable pastime rather than an intended career, but it came together at random when Damo met back up with Syuji, the Japanese boy who'd been heading to the Grenoble Winter Olympics. Once the games were over, Syuji hooked up to stay with him for a few months.

"We became a duo, performing folk songs and other things on the local radio, as I'd brought a guitar, saxophone and clarinet with me." 'Folk', in this instance, seems to have been a hybrid of Eastern and Western musical styles and also languages – with odd English and Swedish words or phrases augmenting their native tongue.

"Syuji told me about the French culture, so I wanted to travel out of Sweden for maybe one or two weeks," he recounts. "I went to Switzerland to buy cigarettes – it was cheaper to buy them there, as Sweden was quite expensive and I'd been smoking since I was seventeen – and decided I would soon travel on to another country, Denmark or Germany."

It was the origin of Damo Suzuki's status as an honorary European – pre-dating his many years as a naturalised Deutschlander. "When the winter was over, we decided to move on to other places, get jobs and expand our activities. We reached Karlstad and met a kendo teacher, Takayama, who had been teaching the Japanese sport with a wooden sword for two years and allowed us to stay at his apartment until we found a place of our own."

The duo found a room in the cellar of a recently widowed woman. She proffered a letting contract which didn't allow bringing girls home. As Damo confirms, "This was easy to break for seventeen- and eighteen-year-old boys. I found an American girlfriend and Syuji a Swedish girl. We were both in love but the landlady was really angry. She took my saxophone and clarinet, and kicked us out of the room."

It was the end of the line for the jobless, incurably romantic duo. "I went to Töcksfors, near the Norwegian border, to work in a hotel as a dishwasher," recalls Damo, "as recommended by Okubo, another Japanese guy we met. Syuji went to Stockholm to seek work.

"One day, mine and Syuji's girlfriends visited me while I was working in the hotel; they didn't stay and talk for long before going home. My girlfriend didn't like to see me washing dishes, she only wanted to see me playing guitar and singing. It left them both speechless and it wasn't long before they disappeared."

For all his love of young women, Damo took the blow with grace. After all, he didn't really consider himself a *musician*.

He moved on again, this time to Gothenburg, the second biggest city in Sweden, where he worked again as a dishwasher and stayed with a bunch of young Japanese guys, with names like Ibaragi, Yamauchi, Watanabe and Kon. If Damo had been a novelty in Gräsmark, in urban Sweden he was one of a number of young men fleeing the stifling conformity and obligations of Japanese culture.

"Ibaragi was an amateur photographer," Damo recalls. "Yamauchi came from a rich family and had good manners, we found it easy to mimic him; both were students. I had trouble with Watanabe: I don't know what the reason was, but we fought in the middle of the kitchen at our work. Kon was a former military guy who played guitar and was a fan of Tom Jones. Then I moved to share a room with a kendo teacher."

At Christmas 1968, there was a hospitality centre in the middle of Gothenburg for foreign workers not able to share Christmastime with their own families, serving drinks and small snacks for no charge. Damo had now been in Sweden for almost a year, and it was here that he met the latest in a rapid-fire line of girlfriends.

"The kendo teacher lived in an old blockhouse on the fourth floor," he recalls of their social milieu. "Next door were a few young North American boys who had escaped the Vietnam draft; every day they had a party, full of marijuana smells and the loud music of The Doors and Hendrix."

The hippie culture had permeated all the way from Haight-Ashbury to northern Europe. While straight society may have feared its supposed radicalism, to most late teens and twenty-somethings it was just a throwing off of everyday norms in favour of an agreeable psychedelicism. As the R&B beat sound exploded outwards, so did many people's minds (if only temporarily). It was a cultural liberation that Damo found a perfect organic fit.

41

"This time I had young Swedish girls visiting me every day," he recalls of the pleasurable lifestyle he fell naturally into. Being an incurable romantic, he also fell in love with one of them. "We moved to Copenhagen, Denmark, to work and live together there without telling her mother. I was working in a restaurant as usual, but my girlfriend was getting homesick so we had to go back to Gothenburg. This time I don't know how we carried all the things we had with us, but we hitchhiked or took a train. It was still wintertime."

Back in Gothenburg, the tryst was surely over. "She became quite an angry person because she'd fallen pregnant," he recalls with a tinge of regret. "We stayed at her mother's apartment, but the time came when I had to move.

"In early spring I left Gothenburg to become a busker, travelling from town to town. First I travelled through the middle and southern parts of Sweden: Arvika, Borås, Enköping, Eskilstuna, Halmstad, Helsingborg, Jönköping, Kalmar, Karlskoga, Köping, Linköping, Malmö, Norrköping, Nyköping, Säffle, Trollhättan, Uddevalla, Uppsala, Västerås, Åmål, Örebro, every day it was a different city."

FROM 'CAN'S DAMO SUZUKI ON BUSKING ACROSS EUROPE IN THE LATE 60S', AS TOLD TO MIKE SHEFFIELD, *HOPES & FEARS*, OCTOBER 2015

I first began busking when I left my girlfriend in Gothenburg. I didn't work anywhere, I didn't even want to belong anywhere. I've always liked to have a greater sense of freedom in my life. And so I busked for one year, alone. I began in Sweden and then travelled to Denmark, Germany, and, finally, France.

I didn't make good money busking, but I would busk when I didn't have enough to eat or travel to the next spot. I would busk about once every three days. It's not a good business, you don't make very much money, but it was not necessary for me to have that much money to sustain my lifestyle. In the wintertime, I would find other ways to make money, like working at a restaurant or on a farm.

My busking was largely about improvisation. I had composed some pieces, but I couldn't play guitar well at all. I would do some improvisation with only two or three chords. I had to do something to survive.

As he'd later term it, it was 'the sound of the stone age' – a primitivism he cultivates to this day, becoming ever more sophisticated as it ascends from the primeval cave towards transcendence.

With the sax and clarinet gifted to him by his sister placed in a pawnshop by his landlady, all Damo had was a broken guitar. "Sometimes I played it with three strings, but then I'm not a really good guitarist," he happily concedes. It was an international jugband language, contemporary to (but unaware of) US street folkies and many years before the stripped-down, three-string blues stylings of a Seasick Steve.

"I would improvise singing and playing with six strings, but even then I was thinking, 'Why does a guitar have six strings?'" This young hobo was clearly never intended for a conventional musical career. "It's not natural because almost everybody has five fingers," he reflects on the musical symbiosis of mind and body. "Maybe I can play on one string as well – maybe it's easier?" He'd find it wasn't the case – not that it stopped him trying.

"I was playing some kind of folk songs, but every time it was quite different." Pre-composed pieces differed in performance each time. The guitar offered a basic acoustic rhythm but no virtuoso frills. Damo Suzuki, the street singer, was forced into originality because he couldn't copy anybody else. "On the way I met a better player who knew many more songs," he says, "but with me it was necessary to vocally improvise.

"My own style was kind of Japanese music" – evolving a style out of necessity, words of his native language melded with scattered phrases picked up from English and Swedish. "It was experimental stuff, but if I wasn't getting good money in, say, a square in Oslo, Norway, then I'd set fire to my hair or things like that."

It was a time when absurdist theatre and outsider performance-art was starting to hit the streets – both of which Damo was blissfully unaware of. To him, it was just a means of grabbing the attention of passers-by. "For one month I ended up doing street theatre. There was no script, but I did it anyway because I had to make money to travel to the next station, the next point."

If his street spectacle was tolerated, it was a measure of the times. By the late sixties, the West was learning to live with the convulsions of the counterculture and psychedelia.

"My nature is that whatever comes along, I go along with it, because it's much easier to follow life than to try to create your own life." His was a philosophy based on randomness – roll the dice or better still, let your nose follow whatever is in the air that day. No stress. No goals. No compulsion.

"People were much friendlier then," he says of the hippie era, allowing himself just a grain of nostalgia. "There was not the aggressive feeling of today, not as many social problems. The rhythm of life was totally different.

"Now, life goes so quickly that many people cannot keep up with it," Damo reflects. Today, he is an uneasy participant in digital culture. "Computers and communications were introduced to our society to give people an easier life," he demurs, "but, while you may have five hundred 'friends' on the computer, you only see them via social media, you never meet these people. People say they don't have much time, but they have a few hours for all their social media. They seem not to be interested in having real physical contact with each other."

Damo occasionally issues updates on his Network activities from his website – but refuses to carry a cellphone and decries an imposter who stole his name on Facebook.

"I don't use any social media. If you see the name 'Damo Suzuki', it's not me, somebody else is doing it. Social media is not my world, which doesn't mean I'm not social. These social networks are killing your own valued time – it's not creative at all, it shortens your life, bites into your time, chains you there. 'Social' to me means 'living together', and if I can see it in front of me then I can feel it."

Insisting he has "no interest in swimming in the mainstream river" but in walking the side-streets, his faith in simple existential experience is rooted in more idealistic times: "We had no social networks, but if I went somewhere people made me very welcome. We had more real connections; it was a much purer form of contact. Maybe this is sentimentality on my part, but I love to travel to uncommercialised places and I like adventure."*

---

* "In the nineties I would travel alone with a rucksack, just like in my hippie days," Damo reflects with not a little nostalgia. "I only got to feel a culture shock in West Africa in more recent days." His account of his African travels can be found later in this book.

In his European travels, he was forging a new identity for himself – indeed, a new name. "'Damo' comes from a Japanese comic-book character popular in the mid-sixties, Marude Dameo," he explains. "'Marude' means 'absolutely'; 'Dame' means 'not good', or any kind of mistaken idea; 'O' has the meaning of a man or a boy. So I took his name because it all kind of fits together with me; it's almost like Charlie Brown. He is trying to do good things, but everything that he does is a mistake. It's quite similar to me when I was young.

"But from country to country they couldn't pronounce 'Dameo'; it got shortened to 'Damo', so I've used this name since the end of the sixties instead of my birth name, Kenji.

"Your birth name was given to you when you were born – but the people who named you cannot see your life all the way through, they are not prophets," he muses. "So if you go to a different place altogether, if you cannot stay in the same place all your life, then why not change your name also? If people have an internet address then they are often using only first names, but also they have 'Popeye', or 'Mickey Mouse', or whatever. It can carry much more character than your name at birth, when you didn't possess any influence or even your own opinion."

The freewheeling life of the street troubadour fitted the ethos of the times – a semi-vagrant existence. "I didn't earn that much money as a busker, as people were just curious to see me and ask themselves, '*Is this a boy or a girl?*' To them I was a strange creature. Mainly they were not much interested in my music; maybe to them it wasn't music at all. I was playing a broken guitar, painting on the street."

It was a lifestyle that also collided head-on with mainstream prejudices. Any kind of public spectacle could attract small throngs of bemused people, or traffic tailbacks. Cops would appear and tell the exotic vagrant to move on.

"I think it was in Kalmar that I met a friendly policeman who took his cap to collect money from the curious people standing around," Damo recalls, accentuating the positive elements of hard times. "He even invited me to dinner and to stay at his place. But it wasn't always good to be busking, many times I had problems with police; they even put me in jail in Tampere, Finland, for four hours, which cut short my busking in that country. In Copenhagen a policeman kicked my knee badly."

For all the tie-dyed romance of the era, straight society was polarised between amused acceptance and hostile paranoia. No matter how passively playful the hippies seemed, for some they were an emblem of the downfall of society – even in relatively tolerant Scandinavia.

"I performed in Danish cities like Odense, Esbjerg, Kolding, Helsingør and, of course, Copenhagen," Damo recalls of the days when, to the rest of Europe, the north seemed to be a mecca of sexual liberation. "Hundreds of hippies made a marijuana sit-in demonstration in front of the city hall. I was beginning to make love with a girl I'd met shortly before in front of a church on main street; then the police made us stop."

His sojourn to the Danish capital lasted several weeks, during which he found himself a brother protector: "a crazy Japanese guy who treated me like his young brother. Mochimaru was his name. He wore a leather jacket, Japanese carpenter's trousers and tabi shoes. He hid his eyes behind sunglasses and had rabbit teeth."

Despite his ethnic quaintness, Mochimaru would have been regarded back in Japan as a *yakuza*. "He'd also bought an imported Yamaha motorbike in a set-up box. He was a kind of guy I'd never seen before, fearless, strong, a fighter, spoke almost no English but was still able to arrange many things."

His new friend bequeathed Damo his leather jacket and ethnic clothing, "which became my style during that period. I also put a piece of fur on my head."

They were the unlikeliest team but, for a few weeks at least, inseparably close. "After Copenhagen I met him only once; then he moved to the US and I lost contact," Damo muses with faint regret, "but when I performed in NYC, many years later, I searched for him. I found out that he'd passed, but I met his wife."

Acceptance of life's inevitable changes became an aspect of the young traveller's philosophy. Movement, growth, loss – then, if you're fortunate, a chance to begin the cycle all over again. It was a stoicism more grounded in realism than any wide-eyed hippie ideals. But still, those were the times and the hippie culture was everywhere.

"In Hamburg, I lived in a commune for a few days with a German hippie couple, an Irish/German hippie couple and a Swedish hippie guy quite near to the central station," he says of the first time he hit Deutschland. "In

Bremen, a middle-aged single woman came to me while I was performing, inviting me to come to her place to stay. She meant for as long as I liked to, but I stayed for a night before quietly escaping.

"In Düsseldorf, during my performance, a Korean guy who was working in the city came to invite me to his apartment. He was really kind, and this was my first contact with Koreans." It was an amicable arrangement that belied the strange racism of many Japanese toward their eastern neighbours. It was the same cultural supremacism that allowed Imperial Japan to cut a swathe through the Far East in the years 1937–45 – but this was an aspect of his culture that the young traveller had happily left behind.*

His vagrant busker's existence made a wayward path through Germany, via Flensburg, Husum, Neumünster, Kiel, Lübeck, Hamburg, Essen, Dortmund, Düsseldorf, Bremen. Then it was over the French border to Paris, Marseille, Lyon, Toulouse, Nice, Nantes, Bordeaux, Lille, Rennes, Reims, Saint-Etienne, Toulon, Grenoble, Dijon, Clermont-Ferrand, Limoges, Metz, Rouen, Nancy, Roubaix.

"Nice is a summer resort where many people come for bathing and swimming," Damo recalls of the seemingly never-ending idyll. "I met an American guy from Pittsburgh named Donald, two boys from Ulm, Germany, and some others from different nations living together on the seashore, making living theatre for tourists escaping the hot towns, who were curious about the hippies."

It was an easy-going, sun-soaked existence, fuelled by shared baguettes, cheese and wine. "Summer was really nice at the seashore, so I stayed three days with them. I could have stayed for much longer as I wasn't in a hurry."

DAMO, FROM SHEFFIELD/*HOPES & FEARS*

I would always busk on the main street of a city. Sometimes I would get in trouble because some smaller cities, like in Sweden for instance, have narrower

---

* "If those racists were intelligent enough, they would know that Koreans in Japan have a long history," reflects Damo. "They arrived around 100AD and ploughed the Kanto Plain; by the 20th century many Japanese also had Korean blood. When I was in junior school, there was one girl who lived in a Korean hamlet; many of the schoolboys and girls were hassling her, but I could not understand why they were doing this."

thoroughfares and when there were too many people, there would be a traffic jam. Then the police would come and tell me to go elsewhere...

...Some countries had horrible police that cracked down on hippies. In Paris in July of 1969, I was just walking down the street with my broken guitar and sleeping bag and the police arrested and held me for five hours just because I had long hair.

It's easy to look back on the late sixties as a time of innocence – but it was also the aftermath of May '68, when the capital of liberty, equality and fraternity had sent its gendarmerie onto the streets, to clear Paris of student protesters. To the established order, the younger generation were not just oddly alien or 'other', they seemed positively dangerous.

"In my first visit to Paris, which is a dream city for many people, I experienced something not many people dream of: at Boulevard Saint-Michel, the police found me on the street; they said something in French which I didn't understand, then just put me in a small jail with other hippies."

As Damo was becoming painfully aware, to the gendarmes, hippies were the ultimate undesirables, fit only for hunting down. And if the home-grown variety gave offence, how much more so this strange oriental of indeterminate origin (or even gender)?

"The jail cell was something like four by four metres," he visualises his old claustrophobia, "with around eight hippies thrown in on a very hot day. The police wouldn't even give us a drop of water when some of us asked. Later they sent me to the outskirts of Paris, saying, 'Don't come back.'"

It truly was time to get out of town. He hitchhiked along the northern route towards the port of Le Havre, along which he met two teenage girls, also hitchhiking. "One of them asked me, 'Where are you going?'"

"I don't know where, I don't have any plan."

ELIZABETH MURPHY

My sister Anne and I met him while we were hitchhiking around Europe when I was about nineteen, I think – it would have been about 1968 or '69. We met Damo on the way round and back. I think we must have been in Belgium, or else in France, and we were dropped off at this point. We were on our way home and there was a boat from Le Havre to Rosslare in County Wexford. I think it still goes there, but anyway, we saw Damo.

48

He was on the road hitchhiking as well, and we used to get lifts very quickly. But I think poor Damo had been there two days without getting a lift! [laughs] So we said, "You can come in with us," because it's easier for girls to get a lift – although a lot of people used to think Damo was a girl because he had long hair, really long hair. It was a lot longer than mine. I'd say he might have been about the same age as me – about nineteen or twenty.

So he joined up with us and we got a lift, which eventually took us to Le Havre. He had met some friends from Dublin and he didn't really know where he wanted to go to. I think he was just letting things happen to him, and I don't think he had much money or anything.

So we said: "You can come with us to Ireland if you want to," and he said he'd like to see these friends who he'd met previously when he was hitchhiking. He came with us, we went on the boat and it's a very long journey – I think it's probably overnight, or even longer than that.

"So I simply went with them. They were students, sisters, introducing themselves as Elizabeth and Anne Murphy, saying, 'You can stay with us, our parents have a farm.'"

CHAPTER THREE

A 'CHINK' IN THE EMERALD ISLE

When Damo Suzuki took the ferry from Le Havre to Rosslare, he crossed from the cosmopolitanism of continental cities to the verdant foliage of a northern European backwater. Or at least that's the way the Republic of Ireland was seen then. For the best part of the year, however, New Ross, County Wexford, would be the universal traveller's new home.

ELIZABETH MURPHY

On the boat he had to fill in an entry form which said, 'What is your occupation?' As far as I remember, he put something like 'beatnik'. [laughs] His English was very bad at that time, he wasn't able to speak very much. Of course, then the authorities started – if he had just put 'student' or something like that it wouldn't have been any problem. But then we had to go and sign for him, to say that we would be responsible for him in Ireland.

That was fine, and then my dad met me and drove us to home, to our family's house in Wexford, which is about thirty miles away from the port. Wexford is a very rural county, real farming country. It produces nearly 25 per cent of the crops, it's good land. There were very few cars on the road in the fifties and sixties. Everything started changing in the sixties I suppose; the society started becoming less isolated. But people were, I would say, generally very friendly and tolerant.

The first black man I ever saw, for instance, was an American helicopter pilot doing a practice landing in a small field near New Ross, in readiness for President Kennedy's visit to the ancestral home in Dunganstown, summer 1963. He invited us children onboard; we were totally fascinated by him and the helicopter in the middle of nowhere – a surreal experience.

No one ever visited there very much; we didn't see many foreigners – very few in fact, even from Europe. Any person who was a bit different was a great novelty and people would love that.

I don't know how long Damo was in Ireland for the first time – I think it might have been up to six months. At that time, I remember, he didn't want to go back to Japan because he was very disillusioned with the pressures on him to do something. His father was an architect and they were probably quite pressurising with what he should do with his life.

I think things were expected of him that he wasn't able to give. I'm sure it's fairly typical of Japanese families. But he wanted to get away from all that, he wasn't going to conform to the things that they wanted him to conform to. He didn't want to go back to Japan at all, I think he wanted to stay around Europe.

Memory plays tricks and half-recalled memories become your own personal mythology. Today, Damo has only the vaguest recollection of who he might have intended to visit in Dublin, on his arrival on the isle of Eire. "Probably the friends were a pair I lived together with at a commune in Hamburg for a few days," he reflects through mists of time. "They were an Irish/German pair – the man was called Patrick Emmet and his wife was Sasha or something."

But there was little parallel to Euro bohemianism in this isolated setting. Instead, he found a traditional culture on the verge of change, which was both alien to and totally accepting of him.

ELIZABETH MURPHY

He went up to Dublin and met his friends, but I think they were only in bedsitters and weren't able to put him up for long. A couple of days later he arrived back again, and this old man of about seventy, seventy-five or so drove him into the yard in a Morris Minor. He said, "I found this little girl on the road [laughs] and she's lost. She gave me this address."

Of course, Damo was only able to speak very little English at that point in time, so it was funny really. He stayed with us in the house for quite a while. I was actually working in London at that time, so I had to go back to work after my trip around Europe. My other sisters were all either at school or at work. There's eight of us altogether – Barry and Eugene, my two youngest brothers, would have been at home.

He was very good at looking after the children. Damo liked children, so I think he was a kind of a babysitter, looking after Barry anyway from time to time. (Barry is fifty now.) We had a big sort of sprawling house, and there were lots of children around. Barry was only about three or four at the time; Eugene would have been about eleven or twelve. But all the rest of us were either working or at college or whatever; we'd all been in boarding schools because it's in the middle of nowhere.

A STORY FOR CHILDREN TRANSULATED* FROM AN OLD JAPANESE FAIRY TALE

DAMO of the JAPS, c/o Sweetmount House, New Ross, Co Wexford

Once upon a time, an old man and his wife, they had not got any children, they were living at [a] certain place. The old man went to the mountain for to cut fire wood. His wife went to [the] river for to wash.

A big, big peach runs down to her when his wife was washing. She picked up it. And she took [it] back to her home.

The old man cut the peach. And, just then oh! wonder! a boy came from inside of the peach. The old couple named him 'Peach Jack', a boy born from inside of the peach.

Ten years passed as dream. Peach Jack grew up a stout boy. In those days the Devils often annoyed inhabitant[s] of the village. And, Peach Jack went on an expedition of the Devils. The old man gave him a sword and his wife made clothes and dumpling of millet for him.

When Peach Jack was walking down the street. A monkey came near him and he said, "I say, Peach Jack, Peach Jack. Please give me a dumpling of millet hanging on your waist." "I'll give it to you if you come with me to go on an expedition of the Devils," said Peach Jack.

When Peach Jack and the monkey were walking down the street. A dog came near them and he said, "I say, Peach Jack, Peach Jack, please give me a dumpling of millet hanging on your waist." "I'll give it to you if you come with me to go on an expedition of the Devils," said Peach Jack.

---

* Sic – Damo's spelling of the time.

When Peach Jack and his two companions, the monkey and the dog, were walking down the street. A pheasant came near them and he said, "I say, Peach Jack, Peach Jack, please give me a dumpling of millet hanging on your waist." "I'll give it you if you come with me to go on an expedition of the Devils," said Peach Jack.

Well, Peach Jack and his companions, the monkey, dog, and pheasant made up a raft. And they went to the island where the Devils lived.

When they arrived at the Devils' island they found them celebrating and blowing their trumpets and showing their companions the lute [sic] and treasures which they had stolen from the villagers. They were dancing and drinking spirits.

"Now is our chance to overcome our enemies!" said Peach Jack. "We have the monkey to scratch, the dog to bite, the pheasant to peck and Peach Jack to lead." So in they went.

After [a] few hours, the Devils cried, "Surrender, surrender." The King of the Devils handed up treasures of diamonds, rubies, and pearls. The Devils promised never to attack or plunder from the villagers again.

Then, Peach Jack and his three pals returned home to tumultuous welcomes of people who had gathered in the village to cheer them.[*]

ELIZABETH MURPHY

Damo was very fond of my mum. I think she was kind of a substitute for him, because she was a very kind-hearted person and would encourage him to do things. She used to write to him as well and he used to write to her. He used to write to me from time to time, though not very often. "I am Damo, Japanese boy," he used to always sign his letters. He used to do this little thing with the guitar symbol – on his letters he'd always sign with this little guitar thingy.

Dad was just very hard-working – I don't suppose he noticed Damo, to be honest. He really worked such long hours that you hardly saw him except for lunch and dinner, he was out all the time. My mother didn't do any farm work herself – which was quite unusual for a farmer's wife – but there were also a lot of men working there on the farm in those days, and my two grand-uncles

---

* This is the nineteen-year-old Damo's anglicisation of the Japanese folktale of 'Peach Tarō', who here becomes Jack. His early mastery of very basic English grammar shows his keenness to learn.

living with the family. Damo was a great novelty to have around, nobody had ever seen a Japanese person in their whole life. All these fellows who used to work on the farm thought he was brilliant; they used to tease him because he was so different.

He'd always smile in his enigmatic way. One of my uncles – well he was a step-uncle really, because my grandfather married twice – lived there with us his whole life. Jimmy was a bit simpleminded but he was quite cute and cunning too. Tom Summers, this man who used to work there, was always joking with Jimmy and with Damo, egging people on to do things. Tom used to say to Damo: "Go down to the shop on Jimmy's bike and get us some bread," or whatever. So Damo used to go off somewhere on Jimmy's bike and Jimmy got quite annoyed about it [laughs]. Muttering crossly, "Has anyone seen a chink on my bike?"

Damo recalls with reverence the lady who became his Irish surrogate mother. "Mary Murphy was a kind person," he says with an abiding affection. "A few years ago, one year before she passed, I met her again after almost forty years. This was an impressive moment. 'You still have long hair, that's good,' she told me."

No longer the pitch-black of the 'little Japanese girl' regarded with bemused tolerance by the locals, the universal traveller's grey-flecked locks would echo the wire shades of the venerable Mrs Murphy. His personal philosophy of persistent change was reflected in the way his Irish family now saw him: the little oriental boy who faded out of their lives to become semi-legendary elsewhere.

"Even though she had four sons and four daughters," Damo recalls of old Mary, "she welcomed me as if I was one of her children. For a few days I worked at Murphy's Farm, Sweet Mount, as one of seven or eight helpers. Mrs Murphy, who was a lovely mother, was cooking for all those people; it was new for me to eat together with that many people." It was a kind of communal living that was natural and non-ideological, the easy camaraderie of people living off the land.

"I helped put cows into different pens and collected honey – mainly with Eugene, the third son," Damo recalls of how he became an honorary family member. "Mary may have thought I didn't have any physical power, as I'm small and thin. She didn't trust me for hard, manly work."

As an alternative, Mary found her young guest a number of jobs to cover his six-month stay: working as a hand with two different farmers, at a guesthouse and a Chinese restaurant (as an honorary 'chink').

One of the farmers, a man named Alexander, lived in a frozen time-bubble that seems representative of Ireland at the time. "He was quite a traditionalist," recalls Damo, "living in a historic house with many paintings of his ancestors and traditional furniture – even their food was traditional. His wife and daughter were cooking almost the whole day or baking bread, from soup to main course to dessert, all home-made mainly from ingredients on their own farm."

The young hand had to work early in the morning with the farmer; "it was hard physical work that, at the beginning, hurt my body all over. I hadn't worked that hard in a long time. So I had to go to bed quite early, as the others did. Another farm I worked at was owned by an English family; they gave me such hard duties that I had to keep telling myself, 'Never give up.'"

It was a discipline that would serve him well over the next couple of decades. It was, perhaps, an irony that the young Japanese who fled the strictures and traditions of his homeland should adopt the self-control of the Zen monk.

FROM DAMOSUZUKI.COM BLOG, MAY 2008
This is beginning of relationship to Murphys then I stayed there for around half year. Helping farmers, working at Chinese restaurant in Wexford... Their mother Mary treated me like if I am their real son even she had Jack, Michael, Eugene, Barry – four boys – and Elizabeth, Anne, Claire, Aideen – four girls. Since then I lost contact with them for 39 years... Until 2008, few months before Belfast show [Sunday, May 4, 2008, Cathedral Quarter Arts Festival @ Black Box], a 18 years-old-young man named Peter mailed me, saying I know you stayed at my grandmother Mary's in end sixties... I've got performance in Belfast, then after I have break for two days, so this time finally visits them in New Ross, Co. Wexford. I mailed him back. Peter arranged very-necessary meeting nearly 40 Years (!!!).

Took train Belfast-Dublin. Was journey to yesterday... was exciting to see Tom and Mary Murphy and their children. I arrived Dublin. Peter find me waiting for him, I didn't see him before, so I had no idea how he looks like. Exactly he looks like his mother Aideen: he have same curly hair. We had enough time to take bus so went to drink wine at hotel nearby. Arrived Enithcorthy after around two hours. A middle-aged man was waiting for with his car... he is Barry... Mary's youngest kid... last time I saw him he was just beginning of his life... three or four years old and having short pants curly hair in hand his puppet.

He is now running Mary's and Tom's farm. The car drive on nostalgia road, memories are replaced in my head. Arrived at the farm I spend my last teenage year. "Do you remember me?" old lady with grey hair asked me. She's Mary. She never lost her friendly face. I said, "No..." as stupid joke. Sure I can remember... It was emotional moment, for all those years, which went so quickly. Then Tom appears. Peter showed me farm place... some places I can remember, it was huge place and still it is. Walking through fields, like time trip, suddenly I was in end of sixties. Many memories come through my brain like shadow theatre [revolving lanterns] in Asia.

In the night all Mary's and Tom's boys – Jack, Michael, Eugene, Barry – joined with their wives, their daughters Claire, Eugene's daughter and boyfriend and of course Peter, the young man who arranged everything that we all had opportunity to meet for first time since almost 40 years. It was emotional moment. We were teenagers living in other situation like now. Everybody's life is very interesting how they processed and experienced all those days. Mary and Tom seemed to be very happy. I feel very thankful that I met them in my teenage period. They're all really amazing persons. We had drunk together Irish whisky and others. Talking about old days ...

Situation in Ireland is totally changed since then, yes, absolutely. When I was here, Ireland was one of most poor western European country, many Irish went out of the country to get job. Now, 21 century Ireland is one of high living standard country in Europe as good as all those rich Scandinavian countries.

ELIZABETH MURPHY

I went back to London fairly soon after that, because I was working there and I was also going to college. Then in 1970, I think he was also working for another woman – Mrs French, if I remember her name – she had a baby around that time, I think she was an older mum. My mother was in this kind of women's organisation and she was a friend of Mrs French, who was looking for someone to help her with her newborn or very young child. I think Damo went there for a few months, helping her. He was certainly very good with the children. He was learning English as well – or trying to. [laughs] He learned it quite well actually, considering he only spoke very little when I met him at first.

He was generally accepted by everyone. I don't think he ever complained about being ostracised in any way, I think he was quite perfectly happy. In fact he'd fit in with almost any society I would think, because he was a very nice, friendly person. Even if you didn't have much in common with him he was always very gentle and kind. People were attracted to him, I think; people who knew nothing about him or his culture.

I kind of got the feeling that, even though he wasn't estranged from his family, he wasn't anxious at all to go back to Japan. He hated the kind of expectations for him to do something; he had to go his own way always. He always wanted to have control over his own life as much as possible. He hated all the materialism and that sort of thing. He was a man of simple pleasures, he just liked the simple life; he didn't like people expecting him to be something that he wasn't.

He appreciated things that happened to him and he allowed himself to do whatever came his way. He was programmed against being programmed, if you know what I mean. He always wanted to be his own man, and he always was. I think he was very lucky to be able to do that.

"Work at the guesthouse wasn't so hard," recalls Damo. "Mrs French lived with her two young sons, all I had to do was the cleaning. At Wong's Restaurant, they wanted someone who looked Chinese. Michael, the owner, was a Chinese from South Africa, married to an Irish lady. First I washed the dishes, then later I cooked small, easy things, the main part of the cooking being by Michael."

In the isolation of his small room, Damo returned to his neglected painterly inclinations. His artworks that have survived over the years show a colourful collision between the pop art of the sixties and his beloved early manga, the imaginative cartoon strips of Tezuka.

"The owner liked my paintings; he allowed me to paint sometimes instead of working in the kitchen. These pictures were cartoons, pin-up ladies in the foreground and oil-painted backgrounds. I also did quite a lot of abstract oil paintings." Today, he's more inclined to dismiss his own artistic talent, but back then it was a necessary creative outlet. "During this

period I was much more interested in finding myself in my fantasy world"
– and, indeed, of enjoying fantasies of voluptuous Western girls.

ELIZABETH MURPHY

They were very busty, blonde women in profile with miniskirts – very busty.
[laughs] They were sort of caricatures really – his idealised woman with big tits!

"The background was oil paint that I used for poster colour," Damo
describes his cartoon fantasies. "I never really painted anything dark –
okay, there are many dark artists, but it's not my way to show darkness."

From his first Western sojourn to his ongoing Never-Ending Tour,
Damo's creativity has been tinged with the Technicolor surrealism of
psychedelia; ecstatic imagery that explodes in the imagination. "It has to
be something brightly shining, or to give people positive dreams. But if
you want to see darkness, you go to a graveyard" – he corrects himself
quickly, realising countless good people have their life-forces returned to
the earth. But in the world of Damo Suzuki, the imagination can only exist
as a realm of inspiration.

In the earthier realm of rural Ireland, he would return to the Murphy
family at weekends when his labours were over. "Mary Murphy took me
to some Irish dancing parties," he recalls with fondness, "even though I
was a shy person. When you drink Guinness it takes the weight from your
shoulders, so I was able to get into that atmosphere and dance."

ELIZABETH MURPHY

There was no television in our house until 1961 or 2; we didn't have electricity
even though it was a fairly big place; there was no electricity in the countryside
until the early sixties. Everything was done by hand. There were all sorts of
things going on in the local parishes – singing and dramas and so on. People
entertained themselves in a way that doesn't happen today, really.

We used to have storytellers come round as well – they were sort of semi-
tramps, you'd put them up for the night, give them a bed and board. There
were a few of those people going round the farms in the country places, 'men
of the road' I suppose you'd call them. They weren't really what we used to
call travellers or tinkers, these were fellows who just wandered round telling
stories.

It was a different kind of society altogether. Television and electricity changed everything, I suppose, but still we made all our own butter and bread and everything. Most farms were fairly self-sufficient really and there wasn't all that much imported – there was some exported farm produce, but not much. It was a fairly frugal lifestyle but still, you didn't feel it was poor. Today it probably would be regarded as poor, but the people were different, they were much hardier than they are now.

It was an Ireland where the retro-trip of The Dubliners' music still seemed contemporary to many; a fiercely alive rustic culture that hadn't changed much since the days when James Joyce put himself into exile. "I learned to love the simple ways of these people," Damo recalls now, "drinking, singing, laughing, dancing, fighting (if necessary). Then I got an idea to be a politician, to make my country more like Ireland."

In his sudden, startling burst of idealism, the young Japanese decided to return home to complete school; to take a degree in politics; to engage in a form of citizenship that had held no interest when he shook off the trappings of his native land.

DEIRDRE NUTTALL – EMAIL TO DAMO, JULY 25, 2016

Hi Damo,

I recently learned that you stayed with my grandparents in New Ross back in 1969. They were friends of the Murphy family, and I think you stayed with them when the Murphy household was full. I thought that you would like to know that my grandmother Joyce Alexander mentioned you often. Your photo is in the family photo album so you came up in conversation when the album came out. I think she was quite proud about having had a Japanese visitor at a time when there were so few Japanese in Ireland at all. She often wondered what had become of you. I found out last week when a good friend asked me if I had heard of the great artist Damo Suzuki who had spent six months in New Ross. I wondered if it was the same young Japanese man, and indeed it was. My grandmother died fourteen years ago but she would have been delighted to hear of your interesting life. My aunt Rosaleen, whom you would have met, recently found a sketchpad of yours with some of your artwork in it.

"Deirdre mentioned I was singing at weekends in the hotel," Damo responds. "I know I sometimes went to Irish dance evenings at the weekend, but

I don't think I sang. She heard this story from someone, but sometimes memories are not correct, people tell to other people what they already believe and then a new story appears. Another thing is also possible – that I forgot! Life is sometimes the *Rashomon* syndrome," he says of the classic samurai film where all the characters' memories are 'true', yet none agree on an objective reality.

DEIRDRE NUTTALL – EMAIL TO THE WRITER, DECEMBER 14, 2016

Damo came up in conversation relatively often – once or twice a year when my grandmother rooted out the family album – although she didn't know anything about him after he left Ireland. For her his visit was important in part because it challenged what her generation thought they knew about the Japanese, which they had mostly learned from war propaganda and war movies. She and my granddad thought that Damo was a lovely young man, a credit to the Japanese, and that he was too thin and should eat more potatoes.

"It was getting to be time to say goodbye to Ireland," he recalls of the departure that would last several decades. His time was drawing to a close anyway, due to the lack of a work permit. "On one of my last days, Mrs Hennessy, a friend of Mary, invited me for a farewell dinner; she was maybe in her late seventies. It was a fine evening in candlelight with some amazing food."

But it was time to leave and, in keeping with the wayfaring wanderlust of the time, the intended route would not be without deviations. Damo wanted to revisit Germany to meet up with two hippies from Ulm he'd encountered in France, right before his Irish sojourn.

"They had given me an address, but first I wanted to go back to Japan through Iran and India. I had been away from Japan for maybe two years," he muses. "I didn't have a ticket to return, but I wanted to go back suddenly." His dream of the time was to turn the rising sun a shade of emerald green.

"Ireland was such a nice country," he testifies to his lifelong affection; "the people were really friendly, they made jokes all the time and they liked everybody. They were uncomplicated people who I could trust, and these were the kind of people I really liked back in my own society in Japan."

ELIZABETH MURPHY
Mum met Damo again in the last ten years – she died in 2010. County Wexford had changed so much, at that time there was 'the Celtic Tiger' and money was flowing like nobody's business. I think it was a medieval society pulled into the 21st century almost overnight really.

FROM DAMOSUZUKI.COM BLOG, FEBRUARY 2011
Mary Murphy was a wonderful person, respectable mother of eight children... She passed away on December 6 2010, a day before my performance in Manchester.

At the performance I was thinking [of] her. I'll remember her always... my photos at my brain is clear, I can see her from end of sixties and 2008/9. I'm thinking of Tom, her husband all good things.

The dream was to cut through the bonds of duty and materialism, to overcome the *giri-ninjo* whereby obligatory duty was always expected to win out over personal inclination. It would take academic study and relentless campaigning to make this vision a reality – but the almost twenty-year-old Damo was prepared for this. For the time being at least.

"This is why I decided to take a route through Germany and then travel to Afghanistan. The only way I could get to Japan was overland." Air travel, and even the sea-cruise route that first got him to Europe, was all too expensive. "I would pass across some interesting different regions – Pune or Goa, Tibet or Kathmandu – but I just wanted to go back to my home to study."

At the end of 1969, Mrs Murphy brought him to the station; it was a farewell almost as sentimental as quitting his homeland. "After a train to Dublin, I took the ferry to Holyhead. It was windy, wet and cold, with heavy dark clouds almost touching the earth. I don't know exactly where, though it was probably while I was hitchhiking on the outskirts of Birmingham, but I got ill from the cold. I visited the hospital and they took pity on me as a lonely traveller, giving me shelter."

At the mercy of the National Health Service, the invalided Damo was allowed three days' rest, recuperation and repast. "Then I continued travelling to London, where I stayed with someone I don't remember at Shepherd's Bush for a few days, before heading to France. I took the Dover-to-Calais ferry in an angry winter sea."

The broke, bohemian traveller was carrying all his surviving paintings along with his broken guitar and rucksack. At immigration he was asked, "*Où vas-tu?*"

"????????"

The immigration officer gave up speaking in French when he saw Damo's total incomprehension. He spoke in heavily accented English until he saw the paintings: "*Qu'allez-vous à cela?* What are you going to do with this?"

Before the traveller could set up a reply, he received a pre-emptive answer. "You're going to sell this in Paris…"

He was taken to the police who, a few hours later, returned him to England via the next ferry. Back on the other side of channel, at immigration he was told, "You don't have a permit to stay in the UK. I don't know what to do with you, you were sent back from Calais…"

At that moment, Damo says, "I really thought I'd have to spend the whole of my life travelling between Dover and Calais, back and forth, back and forth."

"…Can you promise me that, tomorrow, you'll go to the Japanese embassy to ask for support to get back to your native country? Will you do this?"

"I had no better answer," he says, "it beat being stuck in the English Channel for the rest of my life."

Once through the port, Damo hitchhiked directly to London to visit Elizabeth Murphy, "to get advice and a warm place to stay if possible. No way was I going to the Japanese embassy, they'd never treat me well if they knew I had almost no money. Nor was I interested in being forced to go back home in this way, the way that Syuji had to."

ELIZABETH MURPHY

He came to London and stayed with me for a little while. I had a bedsitter in Stoke Newington and he was sleeping on the floor. I think he stayed for about three or four weeks, with me anyway. He might have had other friends around in London. Even though he was staying with me, I was going to college at that time and we didn't have that much in common. But you had to go a long time with him – Damo was very shy, he didn't talk very much and I had a boyfriend. He was just kind of sharing the room, but it was fine.

In Ireland I'm sure there would have been parties and things like that. He certainly would have liked a drink, but at that time when he was staying with me in London none of us had any money. We just barely had enough money to live on, and I'd say he was the same.

I was working in Sainsbury's every day after college, every evening and weekend, so in fact I didn't really see him all that much. Even when he was staying with me, you'd just meet him when you'd go to bed.

Elizabeth's room was close to Seven Sisters Road, in the brownstone neighbourhood of north London. "She treated me well for a month," he acknowledges, "until I made enough money to buy a railway ticket to Ulm, Germany, where my hippie friend from Nice lived."

Back in Calais again, he was now able to show the police a train ticket. "During the train journey through Belgium, where I had to change at Brussels for Cologne, a priest sat opposite me. He wanted to see my paintings but I didn't show him the pin-ups, selecting an abstract instead. As far as I can remember, he picked up one painting; I used only black and red colours and it wasn't that big a format, maybe A4 size."

"I like this… is it possible to buy it? How much is it?"

"I was surprised someone was interested in my painting, let alone prepared to pay for it. I was almost penniless, so any money was welcome."

"I don't know. It's okay with me, you can pay me as you like." Damo was given 200 deutschmarks so that he could buy something to eat at the first opportunity.

"I was always drawing like comics, not like an artist – especially when I was busking, I drew with chalk on the pavement of the street. I was also always carrying my sketchbook. Sometimes it was different, but mainly it was my comic figures.

"I painted like this as I didn't have to explain to people where I came from or what I was doing – they could see that I was travelling the globe. Besides that I made music – I'd put my cap on the floor to get some money. I made street art and I was playing music on a broken guitar."

It was also, in the spirit of the times, a way to meet likeminded people who might put a roof over his head. "I just asked them on the street if I could sleep at their place. I can look back at that time and feel that I was crazy – but in fact I was quite meek!"

At the end of the late sixties/on the cusp of the early seventies, if the meek didn't inherit the earth they might at least share a place to shack up. "There was a commune in every city I stayed in, so I'd meet a member of the commune and ask the people for a place to stay; they'd take me to their place. I lived in many different places for not more than three days. Being a nomad is something within myself," he says of a lifestyle which persists, in a different way, to this day.

The universal busker was a musician living in a musical vacuum. Constantly moving from place to place, he could rarely stop to hear any contemporary sounds. "If I arrived somewhere and met some other hippies, they might play me the Grateful Dead, The Doors, stuff like that," he concedes, "but I never bought any vinyl because it was necessary to travel with few possessions. I didn't miss it that much, and I didn't care that I was only able to listen to what people were listening to at that time – psychedelic music."

In a strange way, the young Damo was living *inside* the psychedelic culture without being a part *of* it. The same can even be said today, in his senior adulthood.*

Looking back, he acknowledges that everything came from outside of himself. "If I was staying at a commune and they had a lot of LPs, I'd ask, 'What is this that they play?' I didn't know any band names because I didn't read any newspapers, or hear any TV or radio," he recalls of his cultural isolation. "It was good that during that period, I had no information apart from what I experienced with my body and soul – because actually that is enough. My only source was when I arrived at a commune to spend a few days with some hippies and they played music.

"I'd ask them, 'What is now the hottest thing?', like a man from another planet. Whether it was interesting or not, it couldn't influence me because I didn't have any ambition to form a band. I was just living my life as a street musician, getting money for travelling and maybe tomorrow I'd get some food. But if I heard music, I just wondered why I was listening to such stuff as it really wasn't my world!"

Then, as now, Damo's travels were not propelled by musical ambition so much as existential experience and human interaction. "I was getting much more energy from travelling itself – from meeting new people to finding new cities. I was much more interested in people." It would be ever thus.

* International collaborators in the Damo Suzuki Network range from free-jazz players to heavy metal bands. He himself remains an avid listener only to classical music.

CHAPTER FOUR

GERMANY – HEIMAT, SWEET HEIMAT

When Damo Suzuki – a man synonymous to many with the backhanded label 'krautrock' – first visited Germany it was in 1968; he was *en route* from Sweden to Switzerland, just travelling to buy cigarettes. "The next time I visited Germany was in the following year, when I was busking," he recollects. "I've been living there regularly since my third visit, in 1970."

In several decades he's seen the nation pass through what was still a post-war reconstitution to the 'German economic miracle'. "If you compare every Western country with forty years before, everyone's expecting to get rich," he puts it into context. "But if I had three German marks – which is 1.5 euros – I could eat something satisfying, but today you must pay seven or eight times the amount for the same dishes."

Back then, however, he was living in a different dimension; the byways and ley lines of countercultural Europe were a pleasantly diverting route to nowhere in particular, rather than to some promised future. How disappointing, then, to turn up at an address given by his hippie friend in Ulm to find there was no room for a continental traveller.

"I met him finally, but was told I couldn't stay there as he was living with his mother and there wasn't enough space for me," recalls Damo, with his customary acceptance. "I was able to stay there for a day and, the next day, I went to a place where young people were meeting.

"Pigmatz was the name of a late-night cafeteria where I met a young Romanian girl; she liked me, taking me to the apartment where she was living with her mother and brother. I stayed there for a few days in her room."

Like the archetypal rambler in the blues rock of the day, it was always time to move on. Easy social interaction with his hippie peers in cafés or bars always contained the search for a place to stay for one night. "But if I couldn't find one I'd select a bench, or the park, or the countryside. I'd sleep outside in a farming area or somewhere. So during my busking time I was connecting with landscapes and nature quite a lot."

It was the essence of existence. No distractions. No ambitions. No bad faith. By now, Damo had connected with the non-canonical concept that life-is-art and art-is-life. "Everybody has their own stories. For me it's a natural act: everybody's usual movements and thoughts are actually art."

As he acknowledges now, this reflects the creative philosophy of conceptual artist Joseph Beuys. Raised to adulthood during the Nazi years, Beuys later rejected his fatherland's old ruthless supremacism by immersion in the counterculture. As a performance artist in the Fluxus movement, the ritualism and symbolism of his movements took him into the controversial realm of neo-mysticism.

So in 1970, the young Damo was already thinking liking a conceptual artist. How far he was aware of Beuys at the time remains a moot point – then, he was a hippie traveller; now, he is widely read and able to put his past life into cultural context.

"This may have made me able to perform in front of people without any self-consciousness," he reflects. "I'd already been thinking that 'being Damo Suzuki' is the easiest thing I can do.

"There is no special dispensation for this artist because he's a painter or something like that – actually an artist's whole life, what they're doing, how they walk, how they're dressing, everything fits together.

"It's interesting if you talk with somebody in a park, or in a pub or somewhere, somebody that you never talked with before and he has his own stories. Everybody is naked in their normal life. Many people like to create, but creativity is not coming from a desk, or from your head, or from a disc – the natural movement which you do every day is already creative. You are an artist already."

But as a more materialistic German artist* might have told him, food comes first. Damo needed to find a job, to make money, if he was to return home to Japan.

"I visited Pigmatz every day to ask people about work," he says of how things just fell into place. "A few days later, a black girl came and told me, 'In Munich they're looking for someone to play in the musical *Hair*. You have such long hair, you should try it.'"

Hair, as a musical play, remains resolutely stuck in its time. With its cast of American hippie characters and its 'Age of Aquarius' signature tune, it's seemed cheesy for decades now.** But it's still a living artefact of an era when young people were seen as decadent by their elders, for wanting to live a sexually liberal lifestyle and experiment with drugs – rather than playing kill-or-be-killed in Vietnam.

Damo, who'd already dropped out of mainstream society, decided to drop in on the producers of *Hair* in Munich. "It was a much larger city anyway," he reflects, "so it might be possible to find some other job. Munich at that time was quite dynamic, preparing for the 1972 Olympic Games. There was construction work on the underground, so some hippies were sleeping there at night, as well as in the English Garden," Munich's large public park. "I came back into the middle of hippie society again."

It was a time when much of German youth's total reaction against the horrors of mid-century nationalism could take diffuse, or extreme, forms. In the polarised late 1960s, the political magazine *Konkret* had featured both Ulrike Meinhof – the radical journalist who, when she joined Andreas Baader in the Red Army Faction, would justify the murder of not only establishment figures but their ancillary workers – and Uwe Nettelbeck, the playfully provocative manager of 'krautrock' conceptualists Faust. But the 1972 Olympics would become a victim of its times; Meinhof, who of course deplored the antisemitism of the Nazi era, would write that the slaughter of Israeli athletes by the PLO was somehow rationalised by the suffering of the Palestinian people.

---

*   Bertolt Brecht.
** The show's most uplifting musical legacy is Nina Simone's medley of its songs 'Ain't Got No/I Got Life'.

"But for years they had these kinds of international events," Damo recalls of the optimism that was also in the air, "and in the time leading up to the Olympics there was a kind of energy. Munich was in the middle of what was happening in Germany. It was a kind of boomtown for the hippies – there was one street called Leopoldstrasse and there was the Europa Café, meeting places for hippies, students and young people from everywhere, in the Schwabing area of Munich."

It was also an epicentre for the city's artistic and music scenes, where the traveller took up semi-residence. "I took breakfast there, my favourite being hamburger and baked potatoes, always finding someone to speak with; it was a nice atmosphere," he recalls with affection. "The Europa Café was an institution; you could just sit there and experience many things; you could stay as long as you wanted, it wasn't just a meeting place, it was a living place."

The laid-back life he was living wasn't suffused by the ideological extremism in the air. Damo wasn't living for politics, he was just living life – although he shared the "day-to-day attitude of making this world better".

"I was just a hippie and for me everything happened instantly," he happily admits. "I was not left- or right-wing, I was just enjoying myself.

"I was much more interested in travelling from city to city than staying for a long time in a community. I can say I was a bohemian, or a gypsy; I liked to be wandering from place to place. I didn't see any newspapers. I felt my world was where I was."

It was grassroots existentialism – but with a definite rootlessness. Whatever his affection for a city, there was still an aloofness from its cultural life when he was only likely to stay for two to three months (or two to three days). "I could not get involved in many things that were happening where I was – which probably suited me because I didn't have to take responsibility either," Damo admits.

"I took any kind of drug, I was high every day, almost forgetting to visit *Hair* to find work. The time was so nice, the weather was good, the hippies were so friendly, the city was friendly, everything went well. Why should I hurry to get a job?"

The psychedelic era is often seen as hived off into its own distinct historical compartment; the truth is that its psychoactive experiments continue into the present day, with all the positive and negative consequences that entails. Prohibition also combines with demand – just as it did back in the day – to produce bathtub substances much more dangerous than the relatively benign (if mind-blowing) LSD.

"During this time, one day I took a trip on a very powerful hallucinogen," recalls Damo, amused by his former recklessness. "I lost myself in the toilet of the café, prompting people to call the emergency services. I spent three days in hospital. I can't remember anything, but it was quite a dangerous situation according to what some hippie friends told me."

Eventually, he would manage to recall the whole purpose of his being in Munich. "There was almost no audition. I asked at an office if they had a job for me on the stage; so for them, just the fact that I was a boy with long hair was enough for them to cast me – and also, of course, I'm a pretty Asian boy!" he laughs about his tried-and-tested appeal.

Hair, as a gig for Damo Suzuki, lasted for around three months. As he puts it, "I had the longest hair in *Hair*," whereas some of the actors had to wear wigs. He was put to work learning the part of Wolf, who sang 'Sodomy' (albeit in German) – a very cheesy neo-gospel number which tries to freak out the bourgeoisie with its extolling of 'sodomy, fellatio, cunnilingus…'

"From my time begging on the streets I found my stage persona," he recalls of what was almost a non-acting role. "It didn't have any words, only dancing and sometimes shouting. It was quite an easy job – two hours on stage, one hour training for my part with one of the directors, who had vertical hair like Hendrix but was small like me."

Much of *Hair*'s notoriety among its straight audiences was due to its brief nude scene at the end of the first act. "I'm bathing and two other guys are washing my body," Damo recalls of his own part in it; "they gave me this part because my acting wasn't good enough. But my earnings were not that bad, and I stayed in one commune after another."

Damo wouldn't be the only obscure figure to break out of the show onto a wider stage. "I didn't know her really well, but the actress who took the most important part was Donna Summer*," he recalls. "And also there were

---

* Fame for Ms Summer would come in the mid-seventies with Euro-disco classics 'Love To Love You Baby' and 'I Feel Love' – on the latter, co-producer/composer Giorgio Moroder grafted her erotically breathy vocals onto post-Kraftwerk electro-sequencing.

a famous German *Schlager** singer and an opera singer involved; I don't know what they're doing now.

"Every day I was on the stage for two hours and for one hour training for my new role. So for the rest of the day I was just hanging around the café, or smoking a big joint somewhere."

For him, there was no great philosophy behind the hippie lifestyle. It was just a chance to relax and enjoy life far away from the traditional pressures he'd escaped. For now, personal and financial imperatives were not even a dot on the horizon.

"It's still the same way with my music that I'm doing now," the older Damo puts it in perspective. "I don't think about what's coming up. Instead I just keep going – if you have a plan then you have a goal. If you don't have a goal then you can go just anywhere. For me it's much freer – if I meet some kind of situation which I have to resolve, then I think in the moment about which way to go, or not. I can think about tomorrow maybe, but not ten days later."

So many decades on, the dice continues to roll. Back in the day, Damo's best friend of the time was an actor named Harry, who had one of the main parts in *Hair* as Berger. "He took me everywhere, he had good looks so he would have many girlfriends, every day a different girl, each of them an attractive hippie girl," he relives a time of ease and gentle hedonism. "We were often hanging around the English Garden, tripping or smoking marijuana."

Munich at that point had become one of the epicentres of the German counterculture. Hippies would gravitate there, some returning from their oriental pilgrimages to India. Despite his stoned hedonism, Damo couldn't fail to be aware of the political radicalism that was also in the air.

"There had been huge demonstrations in 1968 and '69: in Czechoslovakia, in Germany, in France," he recounts. "There was also a student demonstration in Japan – it was quite an interesting time everywhere.

"Today it's totally different," he acknowledges, "it is 'the folk' who are demonstrating. But I think that, at that time, people didn't have so much information and normal workers, or employees, didn't have the time to

---

* Saccharine German MOR pop, which often fitted into the endearingly corny world of the Eurovision Song Contest.

demonstrate. Only students or hippies did. The young wanted to change society and it seemed quite possible, everything was possible anywhere. We felt that everything would be changing."

But for all his easy assimilation into commune life, the young traveller didn't fit so well into the collectivist state of mind. Adrift from his native culture and travelling alone, he was always too much the individual.

"I didn't read books that challenged the social system or anything like that," Damo concedes. "But in a way I was always kind of like a punk – always against the system. Provocation is one of the sources of creativity," he insists. If his anarchic performances on the streets were a gentle form of provocation, it was only a brief matter of time before he'd realise just how far he could stir an audience.

But then Damo Suzuki always regarded himself as an anarchist – never a communist, despite the counterculture's acceptance of Marxism. To him, all dictators keep their hands clean while their underlings do the dirty work – as with the rich, religious leaders, politicians, economists, monarchies and all authorities.

As for his personal form of anarchism, Damo describes it as "without any form of violence, because violence doesn't help anything. It brings only hate. But my whole way of life is based on anarchy, as I cannot stand someone standing over people and trying to assert his power."

Well-meaning clichés about 'changing the world' receive short shrift too; finding your own way of life is far more achievable and, therefore, far more important, he contends. Only in the personal can we truly exert change.

This benign sense of scepticism extends to the hippies' embrace of Eastern religions during his youth. "Many people at that time were travelling via different routes, some went to India, some went to Morocco, and I thought, 'This is not changing anything. Because you can see how the hippies are within themselves, staying within the hippie society.' With people only having the same thoughts together, you can't change the system."

It's a realistic view of preaching to the converted. More surprising are the veteran head-tripper's reservations about the value of psychedelics. "Hippies are always smoking marijuana, or hashish, getting high for pleasure, and they believe in their visions, their hallucinations," he observes.

71

"This seems to me now to be a form of egotism. Like meditation, searching within yourself for the 'I'. Don't waste your time – without a social context you don't exist.'"

As a man who would later experience a religious epiphany, he remains scathing about the hippie fad for Eastern gurus: "If they were able to change anything, why is India still a relatively poor country and why does it still have a caste system in modern times? Why don't they even have clean canalisation? All kind of religious systems are similar," he contends, "pure-hearted people work as volunteers, the elites have Rolls-Royces, huge houses and gardens, many women and luxurious foods. It's pure capitalism, nothing to do with a living God – and it's not only Asian religions, you can see it in the Vatican, and other Western religions or sects."

With his gentle iconoclasm, it's perhaps unsurprising that Damo identifies more with the punks who followed in the mid–late 1970s than his own hippie generation: "Punks generally stayed in the city rather than retreating to the countryside; they stayed within the system, so they had much more influence on other people than the hippie movement. But generally, 'changing the world' is not that important to me; I'm only interested in being Damo Suzuki."

It wasn't long before Damo's role in *Hair* became as repetitive and demanding as any regular job. "But the pay was good – maybe two or three times the normal wage for that time (something like 1,000 marks), so I was continuing," he happily admits.

"Once I took LSD before the show started; I saw many different colours moving here and there, with me between the spaces, not able to control myself. I probably sabotaged the show. But maybe I wasn't on the stage and didn't act at all," he muses on the nature of psychedelic memory. "I don't know, I wasn't really 'in it' at the time."

It was a wholly pleasant chaos. Given the times, how many wouldn't want to continue with the lifestyle in a new urban Deutschland – where

---

* Damo: "During my trip to West Africa, I met some young development volunteers. It was nice to see them spending their youth on the search for a genuine solution." See 'African Interlude', later in this book.

long hair was seen as subversive by mainstream people, but the freaks were as freaked-out as anywhere else in Europe?

But it also meant Damo stopped gravitating home towards Japan. Life had become a blissful stasis. He had no intention of becoming a permanent cast member of the hippie musical, but neither was he looking towards anything beyond it. As for becoming part of the music scene per se, it just wasn't a consideration.

"There was a similar feeling as in Japan, because there were so many Americans, especially in Southern Germany," he says of pop culture's colonisation by WWII's victors, "and also many young German people were speaking English. The music market was American blues and English music. So there were only a few people who were trying to assert their own musical attitude."

Cue the birth of what would later be coined 'krautrock'. While the quaintly insulting term covers everything from pastoral electronica to driving motorik, among the first bands were the opaquely named Amon Düül – whose meandering folk rock found less recognition than their hippie lifestyle.

"I was in their commune for a few days," says Damo. "They had a castle where they lived in the countryside, and also one of them had an apartment on the Leopoldstrasse. All the time there were many young people there as they were very open to everybody." Very soon, the band splintered and Amon Düül II became the more creative entity. Their sax and organ-infused prog rock – on albums like *Yeti* and *Dance Of The Lemmings* – would have some fascinatingly sinister undertones, like unsettling voices dredged up from the depths of a bad acid trip.

"It was the first time I heard so-called krautrock," their communal tenant attests. "It comes from Britain, some English journalist says, 'This is krautrock,' but it's kind of a racist term.* But I heard all kinds of German

---

* Damo: "They still have this kind of stuff: if Germany plays football against England, the tabloid newspapers always look way back to the Second World War. This is not the past, so many years have gone by since the war, but a gutter-press paper like *The Sun* uses the Germans as an enemy! It's really strange, but this is why I don't deal in the word 'krautrock'. I think you can ask any kind of German musician from that time, you won't find anybody who likes the term."

music before it even existed. Amon Düül was the first, but there was also Embryo* from Munich, much earlier than I heard Can."

With the original Amon Düül, it was more a matter of appreciating their lifestyle rather than their scant recorded output. "The music itself is okay – depending on whether I'm having a good day! But in a way they were good, because they were very much into the hippie movement and not an artificial hippie band. There were many hippie bands at that time and many fakes."

As harmlessly retro as unisex long hair, tie-dye and beads seems now, in post-war Germany it was making a kind of statement. "I felt that many people were not liking their parents," the hippie traveller reminisces, "because most of them were under the regime of the Nazis and they wanted to forget about this." But there was a new orthodoxy – not goose-stepping aggression but clean-cut consumerism; the material comfort that Herbert Marcuse, the German-American 'New Left' academic, believed cushioned subtler forms of repression.

"Many people were into the American way of life at this time, but a few people were against the American system – American music, American journalism, American art. So they wanted to go against it, but not via established German art."

For Damo, it was the familiar situation of winner-takes-all, the occupying post-war power exporting their own popular culture. "Many bands from the German music scene were established around '68. These were people who wanted to create something against the system, which at the time was American culture. This was the foundation of student demonstrations at the time too."

In their melting-pot eclecticism, a little of everything could go into the mix – jazz, modern classical, primitive early electronica. But if that were all, the scene would have been no different from what the British were terming 'progressive rock'.

---

* Embryo were formed by drummers Christian Burchard and Dieter Serfas, augmented by the scraping violin undertones of Edgar Hoffman. Drawing together a similarly eclectic range of influences to Amon Düül II (if not quite with the global scope of Can), the constantly altering time signatures of their 1970 debut, *Opal*, draw a line from psychedelia to the early seventies music we now term 'prog'.

"No German bands at the time had any kind of direction, that's why they were able to create their own style," reasons Damo, "they were channelling their own information to find something totally different. They were making very German music – Kraftwerk, Neu!, but things had actually been happening from a long time before – there was a movement before the hippie time, in the beatnik time, and an orchestra called Globe Unity instead of any kind of German rock scene."

Indeed, the Globe Unity Orchestra had a virtuoso young free-jazz drummer named Jaki Liebezeit, who had since decided the open-ended strictures of jazz were no longer for him. Whatever directions the new German bands were heading in, they were taking off from the rock foundations of guitar/bass/drums.

"All of the bands had the feeling that they wanted to create their own German music: Amon Düül from Munich cannot compare with Can from Cologne, or Tangerine Dream from Berlin with Kraftwerk from Düsseldorf, they made totally different music.

"Because Germany is a federal republic, the music they created was a form of domestic culture as well as a kind of 'world music'. Anyway," Damo reasons of the krautrock label, "I've always been totally against categorising anything."

The moment when itinerant busker Kenji Suzuki – long since travelling under his *nom de plume* of Damo – entered this new musical scene came on a sunny day in April 1970. "I was shouting or singing loud (or making a 'happening', I can't remember) near the Europa Café," he testifies. "As well as being a Mecca for hippies at the time, the Schwabing was also a magnet for many artists or film actors.

"After a while, a guy with a moustache came to ask me, 'Do you have an interest to sing for our band?'"

The thin guy with the floppy 'tache and the wavy, high-browed hair looked like he might be a hip academic – a professor of philosophy or art – or maybe an underground theatre director. It just so turned out that he was a musician.

"????????"

"We have a concert tonight but ain't got no singer…"

"What kind of music you play?"

"Well… it's difficult to explain, but something else…"

"I've time tonight, I'm able to join you."

"Okay… we can meet up at soundcheck this afternoon."

As his random new acquaintance would soon find out, the moustache wearer was Holger Czukay – former student of musical experimentalist Karlheinz Stockhausen and a child of the avant-garde. Holger had been turned on to rock music by The Beatles in their psychedelic period and now, with his walrus moustache, *he* was the walrus.

"When he went back to his table there was a guy with sunglasses, sitting there enjoying his coffee: Jaki Liebezeit."

CHAPTER FIVE

THAT GERMAN BAND

The two German boho musicians – already in their early thirties by then, half a generation senior to Damo – had been having breakfast early in the afternoon. Respectively the bassist/effects man and drummer, they were perplexed by the sudden loss of their very singular vocalist. Malcolm Mooney, a black American, had returned home in a state of mental exhaustion. Picking a random performer off the street was far from the usual method of recruiting band members. But then, as everyone reading this knows, this was no conventional band.

Damo joined on a whim, as he was getting bored by the repetitiveness of performing in *Hair*. As he puts it, it was "because I did not have anything else to do. I didn't think it was my big chance or something, I just take it as it's coming. I didn't think about being a musician or any opportunity. That's not my story."

All the same, it's a story of musical history as a random game of chance. In the afternoon, Damo went to a prearranged meeting at Blow Up – a Munich 'discotheque' from the days before the word denoted 'disco' as a musical genre – a venue which regularly held live concerts and hosted a club scene, whether rock or soul.

"We were waiting outside the venue for a soundcheck," Damo recalls. "I saw two guys sunbathing outside the venue, they introduced me to them: Irmin Schmidt, Michael Karoli."

Irmin, the daddy of the band and the eldest (by a small degree over Holger), was arguably the most musically cultured: Berlin-born, bespectacled, professorial in a more stolid manner than his bandmate Czukay. A classically trained keyboardist who collided with Can's bassist as a fellow student of musical experimentalist and theoretician Stockhausen, he migrated to the far shores of rock music after a mid-sixties New York sojourn where he met minimalist composers La Monte Young and Terry Riley.

With the additional influences of the *art brut* street-rock of the early Velvet Underground and the exploded electric blues of Hendrix, Irmin as a musician was reborn. How many musical academicians would strike their keyboards with staccato karate chops?

Prior to Damo's random press-ganging into the band, Mickey Karoli was the baby – barely two years his senior. Born in Bavaria of Romanian family origins, his own musical influences were eclectic in the extreme: ethnic folk, Spanish classical, rock'n'roll, Third World esoterica all thrown into the mix. As a guitarist it made him a uniquely primitive virtuoso, whose licks could turn from feedback to faithful echoes of folk lineage in an instant.

All of which Damo was blissfully unaware of. "I met nobody with a musical instrument," he remembers with amusement. "I just didn't know what they were going to play; I didn't know what they were going to do. Actually they didn't know what I was going to do either."

If the randomness gave the whole thing an edge of danger, he'd soon realise it was in tune with the way this German band worked. "I think the soundcheck was the first time I spoke to Irmin," Damo recalls, "but I cannot remember what we talked about."

Theirs were worlds apart: academia, the avant-garde and the contemporary arts world; their new recruit was making primitive art on the street, which didn't know the parameters of gallery walls.

"I didn't know about them, so how I can begin conversation with people I don't know?" he recalls his initial bewilderment. "I didn't know these guys' music, I'd never even heard of their name.

"Can?"

But theirs was the flow he'd go with. *Hair* had become too much of a full-time job, despite the good pay. It had been too long without change; hooking up with this German band broke a period of atrophy and stasis.

JAKI LIEBEZEIT
He made music on the street – he was a street singer and guitar player. We had no singer at that time, so we had trouble finding a singer who was spontaneous enough to be with us. So we heard this guy on the street: we asked him if he wanted to try to sing with us, and he immediately came with us. The same night in Munich we had a concert, I don't remember the name of the place. He started singing there, completely free. It was good – es war gut.

We needed someone who was spontaneous enough to play the role of the 'singing superstar'; to be integrated into the group as a musician with equal rights. It was important for us at that time that all the musicians had equal rights – there was no boss. So he integrated very, very fast.

"Quite a lot of people came," Damo remembers of his first gig with Can, "maybe more than a thousand. Normally a concert would be at a nightclub with space enough for dancing, so this was quite a big place for that time.

"I didn't have any expectations. I went on the stage, which was elevated above the floor, and improvised music with the guys. It was totally random, and also it was totally equal for everybody in that we didn't have any information at all. It was good, because if I knew their sound maybe I'd try to fit together with their music, and it's not really the kind of freedom I like."

If the audience had any expectations, they were soon confounded. In the beginning they had the passive anticipation of any audience of longhairs at the beginning of the 1970s. For this was to be a 'rock concert' – wasn't it?

"But it was something crazy," he recalls, almost in disbelief so many decades later, "there was a mad audience made uncomfortable by my aggressive performance. In the beginning people were quite peacefully listening; by the middle of the song there was fighting and the place started emptying!"

The affable, shy young oriental, who'd got by on a smile and a few words when travelling northern Europe, was now transformed. Backed by clanging, repetitious drums, psych-fuzz guitar, minimally undulating bass and jabs of keyboard colour, he was transformed into a shaman whiplashing himself with his hair and gently howling at the audience. Provocation was creativity indeed.

"Many people were leaving together; maybe it was my uncomfortable style of singing that forced them. Maybe that's where the audience's aggressive energy came from and it's why they were fighting.

"*'Okay, why is there so much trouble?'* I wondered. Even the police came and asked us to stop."

In the late hippie era, when open-mindedness and tolerance was supposedly all, such a reaction was almost unheard of. Only The Stooges in the USA could elicit this level of antagonism – but they were a confrontational garage band and their singer, Iggy, frequently flipped over from aural to physical violence.*

"I was not satisfied with it myself," recalls Damo, almost bemused by his own actions, "I thought I'd ruined the show, but I didn't feel sorry or any bad feelings afterwards. I just thought, *'I cannot get the job as a singer with this band, but that's okay.'*"

It was an easy-come fatalism in tune with his random travels. But it was also wrong. Can asked Damo to extend his time with them, indefinitely for the time being. He was invited to travel to Cologne, to their Inner Space studio base, a short distance outside the city.

"I'd thought it was the end, but they were interested because they were not really a 'rock band' – they had ambition to make something else.

"Maybe my life is quite boring," he muses, once again startlingly, "the surprising moments are very few. I just take it as it comes. I don't plan anything and actually my life seems just like a movie – it just happens."

But the unforeseen sequence of events were of a part with the music, as was Damo's moment-by-moment mode of creativity. Can's own method of improvisation pre-dated his arrival, but it was no open-ended boogaloo jam. Each piece was developed over long periods of sympathetic interplaying; those that made it to permanence via the studio mixing desk would be edited, chopped down, refined. Subsequent live performances would take the improvisation further, ad infinitum.

---

* In the late 1960s/early 1970s, the young Iggy Pop's confrontational nature was mostly expressed in acts of self-harm – even when he dived into an audience, the violence would be directed back against him. That the gentle-natured Damo Suzuki once invited a similar response just by his vocalising is all the more startling.

"So I got involved in the melodies as this thing was going on," Damo explains. "At that time I was in the middle of the band. So I shared the pieces – I played my part, the melody, my singing, the lyrics."

His voice was so airily fragile that it became another instrument, reflecting the egalitarian nature of the band. Still, it could reach towards an urgent transcendence, a screaming ghost of the attack that shook that first audience. His lyrics would be semi-improvised; a quaint pidgin English with its own syntax, infused with dramatic bursts of his native accent and language.

"Suddenly I'm trying to be the singer of a band," he recalls with amusement. "It was quite easy to be in any kind of social scene, so if anybody brought something to me it was easy for me to get into it. Never think twice: *'Should I do it or should I not?'* I think always: *'I'm going to do this, we'll see what happens.'*"

But still, to join a band that already had a modest cult following in the fatherland was a gravitational jolt. He was still a stranger in a strange land.

"How they looked was from another generation," Damo recalls of their professorial bohemianism, "because I never had much of a relationship with anybody more than ten years older than me. (Actually at that time I always had a connection with somebody the same age, or a little bit younger.)

"Michael Karoli wasn't ten years older than me, so it was a little different," he says of the primitive virtuoso with the long-haired Latin looks. "But in a way he was a little bit 'old' too – he was quite studious and came from a good family, so his situation was quite a bit different.

"His is not a German name," he recalls of his long-departed friend.* "Also there is a wine called Karoli too. I don't actually know his heritage and not all Romanians are gypsies, but it could have been gypsy because he was always passionate to perform; this was a perspective quite similar to Jaki's – they wanted to play, it wasn't really a matter of the money."

After Damo's crash-bang induction at the first show, Holger inaugurated him fully by presenting him with a copy of the first Can album: *Monster Movie*. Refining its improvisational origins into self-contained tracks pitched between freeform psychedelia and hard rock, it featured the

---

* Michael Karoli died on November 17, 2001, aged fifty-three.

81

vocals of Malcolm Mooney, often raspy but always urgent and sometimes gospel-flecked.

FROM DAMOSUZUKI.COM, SEPTEMBER 2017

Holger is next to my mother, who gave me my life.

Holger gave me way to music life. If I didn't meet him that day at that time and that place, I may become a politician, a comic painter or just I'm somewhere else...

On that day in Munich he gave me Monster Movie *and* Canaxis.*

I liked both as at that time for me both were new, 'something'. In 'Boat-Woman-Song' I found fresh air and knew there're many way to make music.

Holger was indeed a pioneer for sampling, electric, house music, techno, etc. He was doing all these very long time ever since even they didn't have name.

"I didn't like its cover at all**," says Damo of Can's debut album, "but a few days before I'd bought *Grand Funk* by Grand Funk Railroad and *Monster Movie* was much more interesting to hear. I played it a few times that evening."

The cross-genre innovation of Can won out over the hard rock that belied the 'funk' in the US band's name. What was immediately clear was that, while this was a guitar/keyboards/bass/drums outfit, it could not be pinned down by generic labels of the time – whether rock, psychedelia, soul or funk.

"Holger, Irmin, Jaki and Michael were interested not in my folk songs," Damo says of the pieces he'd first performed in Sweden, "but in ethnological music. At the time there was no term like 'world music', but they were interested in Asian music or music from South America, in something new which was not part of the rock-music circus.

---

* *Canaxis 5*, named for a fictional alien planet, was recorded by Holger Czukay and Rolf Dammers in 1969, released roughly contemporary to *Monster Movie*. It married extracts of ethnic folk music to Holger's bass playing long before the term 'world music' was christened. Its painstaking approach also pre-empted his later method of utilising 'found sounds' and shortwave radio, in the years before samplers were invented.

** The cover illustration featured the Marvel Comics character Galactus – from *The Silver Surfer*, a quite trippy sci-fi comic – above a Bavarian mountain. With Marvel now a corporate entity owned by Disney, it would be impossible for such cultural appropriation to take place today.

"I cannot remember if we had other shows in Munich, but a few days later I met their manager of that period, Abi Ofarim*, at his office. The band had three possibilities for a singer at that time: one was a guy from northern Germany and then there was a female singer, Christel, both of whom had parts in the musical *Hair*."

Christel was reputedly both a technically competent vocalist and a conventional rock singer, redolent of Janis Joplin. Can's plan of the time was to combine her feminine blues style with Damo's more unrestrained wail-and-whisper. But for Christel it was no dice.

"I also think that to have a strange hippie in the band – after all, I was a Japanese with long hair – was maybe good for their visual image," reasons Damo. "So they took me in. I went two days later.

"After a while they told me that they tried many different singers – but they were too good for them, too *perfect*, that's why they didn't like them as a singer. For them it was not really to do with professionalism and singing well; they were much more interested in creating their own style."

There was at least some kind of precedent to follow: Malcolm Mooney, their departed, New York State-born vocalist, had a gospel-singing background in church but had never sung professionally; in fact he was a foreign traveller traversing Europe, whose first interest lay in visual art. In this sense, he *was* the prototype Damo Suzuki.

But there was a profound difference in delivery. On the first Can album**, from the urgent psych of 'Father Cannot Yell' to the celebrated mutant gospel of 'You Doo Right'***, Mooney sounded like a man who'd sprung out of the American urban tradition. Unlike a grand master like James Brown,

---

*   Israeli Ofarim is remembered for odd little kitsch hit 'Cinderella Rockefella', recorded with his wife Esther in 1968. Following their one-hit wonder, he restyled himself as an impresario. At the same time he was managing Can, Ofarim was handling the affairs of existentialist crooner Scott Walker, as the UK-based American's popularity declined. A relative man of mystery, Abi Ofarim was soon ousted from the lives of both acts – in Can's case by the redoubtable Hildegard Schmidt.

** Credited to 'The Can'.

*** The valedictory gospel refrain of 'You Doo Right' – 'You made a believer out of me' – made such an impression on the young Primal Scream that their early 1990s hit 'Movin' On Up' was a virtual tribute to it. But the Scream's slurred, Keef-style guitar made it a conventional rock song, whereas the insistently minimal repetition of 'You Doo Right' reached compulsively for transcendence.

however, he sounded less like he was asserting his identity than trying to escape his own skin.

"So he was very similar to me, in the same situation," reasons Damo. "I was never much interested in being a singer and I had never sung in a band before. But what I was doing was not really comparable: I'm Japanese and he's American, and also our musical interests are totally different."

JAKI LIEBEZEIT

It was a big difference – they were completely different. Malcolm Mooney came from the American gospel tradition. Black American. Damo Suzuki couldn't even speak proper English [laughs] but he sang in a strange English-sounding Japanese – there were a lot of Japanese elements in it. You cannot compare them, they both had their qualities.

"I think the special thing about this band was that each member came from a different music field," says the voice of their most celebrated era. Formal, academic, experimental, rhythmic, popular, esoteric: the four constant members cut across every conceivable musical background. Added to which would be the random expressiveness of a street performer.

"That's why it went in different directions, and that's why, after ten years, after twenty years, after thirty years, you can hear elements of punk, elements of techno music, electro music, elements of free jazz and experimental music, and all the things there were in the musical activity of the band."

If random adventures in sound came naturally to Can as a collective, it was in part inculcated by Irmin and Holger's academic training. As students of Karlheinz Stockhausen, the production of sound – outside of any discernible structure or rhythmic discipline – had been extolled by their erstwhile professor as the least compromised of acoustic forms, *musique concrète*.

"It took a little while, maybe a few months, before I thought, 'Oh, they are *academics!*'" confirms Damo, who would not have recognised this rarefied world at the time. "I don't think I ever asked but later I learned from some music paper, or something like that. For me it wasn't very important, it was just about making something that sounded like music."

For the musically trained core members, rhythm was the route out of the academic cul-de-sac. A rhythm that led to a bewildering multiplicity of choices.

"That's why we never went into special fields," reasons Damo, "like many bands just playing experimental music, or all the time playing heavy metal. We didn't have any kind of specialities, because if you have a special field then creativity is limited. But if you don't have this, you can go many different ways."

JAKI LIEBEZEIT

I have given up free jazz. [laughs] I was a free-jazz musician for not longer than two years. I thought it was hopeless music and I gave it up to do more things like Can. It doesn't mean anything. My development as a musician: I started in the school orchestra, marching music was played, and then for a short while I played dancing music. And then I changed to jazz for a while – it ended with free jazz after I changed to something with more rhythm and Can was founded.

"Maybe this kind of natural process is integral in creating something different. Because if you're already involved in music or singing professionally, then somehow you're already influenced by somebody else – singing like Joplin or Joe Cocker, or whoever." So many years on, the random performer seeks out the reason he was recruited. "That wouldn't have come together in That German Band. Also, they didn't want to have a so-called 'frontman'."

In Can mark II, the lightweight vocalese of the singer would be an equal counterpoint to, say, the motorik drive of the drums. But at other times, Damo's gently drifting voice would follow (or lead) Karoli's urgently ascending guitar lines into a screaming attack.

It was a progression from Can mark I that followed almost no direct lineage at all. Damo was selected by a process as random as that which led to the original vocalist's departure.

For years, rumours abounded as to the reasons for Malcolm Mooney leaving: his hitchhiking around Europe had been a freewheeling method of escaping Vietnam, but now he wanted to go home; he was on the edge of a nervous breakdown, as demonstrated by the legendary 'upstairs, downstairs' performance.*

"I'm sure Malcolm got sick," reasons Damo. "For one thing, he was a black person in Germany and it's not always so easy." Despite the relative liberalism of the New Germany and the influx of a Turkish immigrant community, other races remained distinct outsiders. As a long-haired Japanese of seemingly indeterminate sex, Malcolm's replacement was all too aware of this.

And then there was the particular madness of the era, where every young male American was expected to answer the call to kill for his country. "It was difficult for him, as they were trying to draft him to fight in the Vietnam War. If you've got to go to war, everybody after a while gets a kind of sickness because it's not natural to kill other people."

Damo's lifelong pacifism is as realistic as it is idealistic: even in the trauma of World War II, behavioural researchers have claimed, most conscripts never fired a shot in anger. "I'm sure many soldiers are getting sick after a while because they are normal people. If you are normal you cannot justify it in your mind to kill other people. It's not in the nature of a human being at all."

(But then, on reflection, Damo lightens up: "In the end it was the same for me too, three years together with Can was long enough. Maybe if I'd had two or three years more with them, I'd also be sick!")

In the end, these two men from vastly different areas and backgrounds were both travellers with an artistic temperament. On his return to the USA, after only fourteen months with Can, Mooney would find employment with New York City's art museums; his own naively effective artworks would later be exhibited in small galleries. Damo's individual take on pop art would replay itself in several periods of his life. Neither man struck out with the ambition of becoming a full-time performer.

"I was just trying to get money to travel back to Japan at the time, but something happened on the way," Damo reminds us. "Actually, my

---

* Malcolm Mooney often acknowledged his surroundings or the audience in his performances. At one of his final concerts with Can, he hit on the refrain 'upstairs, downstairs' while singing out to audience members on the stairway between two floors. It moved from a shout-out to a compulsion, reportedly continuing for more than an hour before a nervously exhausted Malcolm was led from the stage.

life always happens by accident: as of this moment I am still deciding by accident, so I never had the dream of being a singer – it just came."

But as of spring 1970, Damo Suzuki was rapidly inducted as the new vocalist of Can. It entailed not just a new, unplanned-for career, but a relocation and an entirely new social scene.

"The first place I stayed in Cologne was Jaki's artistic commune near to the central station for two or three weeks, on the Domstrasse. At the commune lived Gerd Dudek, an excellent jazz saxophonist."

Dudek had come from the jazz milieu that Jaki had now rejected. Indeed, both had been members of the Globe Unity Orchestra. "He was a quiet person," remembers Damo, "but when he played he exploded.

"Then there was Uwe, a TV cameraman working at WDR*," he continues sketching his social scene of the time, "who was always swimming in alcohol but often spoke philosophically in the English language, and Christine, Jaki's girlfriend, a beautiful lady who created her own fantastic dresses. She also made a huge textile decoration at Inner Space studios."**

It was in these communal surroundings that the street singer's musical references started to expand. Conducting a raid on Gerd's record collection when he was on tour, "I found some ethnic music, traditional folk music, also jazz – which inspired me. Today you could say it's called 'world music', it's eclectic and it's from all over. But before I joined Can I didn't hear this kind of music so much."

If Can be considered a 'rock' band at all, it was surely the first to abandon the 4/4 blues beat in favour of ethnological esoterica. Holger had incorporated early samples of traditional ethnic singing on his *Canaxis 5*; Jaki was fascinated by folk rhythms from Eastern Europe to North Africa.

"I think the special thing about this band was that each separate member came from a different musical field," affirms Damo. "One came from Stockhausen, one was a conductor in an orchestra, one was an

---

* One of the largest broadcasting stations in Europe.
** The epicentre of all Can activity, the Inner Space studio was originally situated a few miles outside of urban Cologne. Derived from the trippy vernacular of the time, Inner Space had also been the original name of the band – pre-Malcolm Mooney and including flautist David Johnson. It was this line-up that recorded music for the German film *Kama Sutra* – released as a double A-side single in 1968, with psychedelic phasing and dialogue samples, it was credited to Irmin Schmidt.

excellent free-jazz drummer, one was a young guitarist and I was just a hippie at that time, not intending to be a musician, just like a stone falling from the sky had hit me.

"When I came to them it was my musical beginning. This is the first time I was open to this direction. Then after, the band had their own studio and we just played improvised music; much of it is like traditional music from somewhere else. This is where it came from, because actually the only way to make music is to take it from somewhere."

As they began work on soundtrack items for a range of movies that was just as eclectic, the one band-member who knew little of the music of alien cultures was, perversely, the same guy who'd worked his way from the Far East across Europe by plucking out an improvised, intercultural folk style.

"They didn't ask me about Japanese music because they knew, at that point, much more than me," admits Damo. "I didn't know anything about it. Since I met them I opened up to interests in *koto* and other kinds of Japanese music. I didn't listen to it at that time as I was much more interested in making music for myself. I didn't have space to listen to music. There were also Japanese bands like Flower Travelling Band, but I didn't hear them," he says of the Far East's parochial attempts to emulate the West.

"I've always been doing a kind of world music – ethnic music, folk music much more than any kind of 'rock' music. It isn't actually folk music, but it's in the same way that 'folk' connects to other different kinds of music. That's the thing I like about any traditional music, for thousands of years it's been the same process. There is no final version and for me that's interesting."

As intermittent recordings started to put together the tracks that became the *Soundtracks* album, the new vocalist moved out of the communal environment into a one-room apartment on Cologne's Eintrachtstrasse that the band rented for him.

"The neighbours were all immigrants and I shared a bathroom with them," he recalls. "Almost every day I went to Plenum, a pub on Venloer Strasse where many young and middle-aged people, students, artists and musicians went; then, later in the night, I'd go to Lover's Club, a small discotheque you entered via steep stairs that led down into a cellar, when I'd no concerts or studio recordings."

It may have been the 1970s but it was early days; the decade of disillusion had yet to set in. In continental Europe the hippie scene was in full swing.

"In Plenum, I met people who invited me to stay at their place. One of them, Erick, lived in a commune with his wife, his son and some young hippies. Erick was on a bit of an India trip; he slept on the floor, had some posters of Indian gods and smelled of incense sticks. He also dressed in Indian-style clothes.

"I was able to stay there, which is where I met Stevie, who at that time was dealing, and through him I met Paul, an excellent painter who shared part of his atelier with me, which was a former church cellar. I painted my small room totally black, living by candlelight. We hung out and sometimes took trips together."

As a snapshot of the times, it's phantasmagorical. There were few taboos against dealing – at least in terms of psychedelics – as everyone, dealer and customer alike, was engaged in the great altered-states experiment. For a few people it wouldn't go well; but for most, a few positive trips were all that was needed to bring back with them a sense of life's infinite meaningfulness and beauty – the extra dimensions that mundane pressures can make us blind to.

And if Damo's black room seems like a black psychic hole from which he might not escape, well, it didn't play out that way at all. At the end of the 1960s, as the American psychedelic scene embraced various forms of the occult, an unnamed acidhead was quoted as saying you could either trip with God or the Devil. For the deepest recesses of our psyche are where humankind's deities reside. Damo would make a positive choice as to who he wanted to experience the infinite with.

During his time at Erick's commune, Damo also met Helga, his first German girlfriend. "She was an excellent painter," he reminisces, "also she was a good singer – her style was a bit of a female Marc Bolan, she was a fan of Tyrannosaurus Rex.

"She came sometimes to Inner Space studios; as far as I remember, she sang in the studio while the band was playing.

"She lived in a fantasy world," he recalls with affection. "It's a pity she didn't make it out of it, as she was very talented. At that time, I lived with her for a few months, we had together a very creative time. Both of us were painting – not much conversation."

* * *

Recording with Can would be a gradual process, from which the smorgasbord of elements suddenly created finished pieces. The relationship between the improvising/taping/editing process and live performance was asymmetrical but organic.

"At every Can concert it was really interesting," enthuses Damo of the band he rarely speaks of now, "because they didn't play pieces so much as combining improvised and composed music together. I, of course, did the singing, and I made up the words myself."

Words that were most often in English, yet couched in an other-worldly syntax that created a new language. The natural idiom of the academically unschooled traveller, assembling his mode of communication from his drifting experience.

"So there was no leader and I really liked this approach, because if there was some established group then there was always a kind of hierarchy. But there wasn't anything like this and I could always do what I like to do, creating anew."

Nonetheless, influences would inevitably feed into the band. The *Soundtracks* album was originated by Irmin – testament to his prior involvement in creating evocative contemporary (and sometimes brilliantly incongruous) musical accompaniments for Euro cinema.

"First he would see the film and it would spark his imagination," testifies Damo, "he would bring his ideas to the studio, which he actually had already before we instantly composed. On 'Spoon', we made it so quickly that my part was finished within thirty minutes or so. I made up a lyric that was inconsequential, just the same nonsense as I used to do."

If the lyric of 'Spoon' is nonsense ('Carry your moon in the afternoon / Hide your spoon she will be soon / With your fork, with your knife / Speaks your joke, she stops your life'), it's also a surreal piece of wordplay. It was the theme tune to a German TV serial (*Das Messer* – 'The Knife') adapted from a novel by British trad-crime novelist Francis Durbridge – hence knife/fork/spoon. Its psychedelic, Moog-laced tones would give the band a hit single in Germany.

But this would be later – the final track on Damo's third Can album, *Ege Bamyasi.** In 1970, as they were putting together the component parts of

---

* Named after the Turkish vegetarian delicacy featuring okra beans, the cover design carried the inherent pun of promoting a can of food. As hippie ethno-musicologists, it was also Can's way of identifying with urban Germany's largest racial minority group.

what would become *Soundtracks*, Irmin enlisted the band for *Deep End**
– a sordid yet moving black comedy set in contemporary London, written
and directed by former Polanski collaborator Jerzy Skolimowski. Set in a
seedy swimming bath, it's a tale of sexual obsession that soared in its
more surreal moments to the ascending tones of Can's 'Mother Sky'.

It was the first time that Karoli's guitar truly merged with Damo's vocal
and it's quietly mind-blowing. "When 'Mother Sky' was finished, edited
by Holger, he brought a cassette to me when I was hanging at Plenum,"
recalls Damo. "This was his sense of humour."

"Listen Damo, this is a British band!"

"It's not bad, who is it?"

"It's *your* voice…"

Can (particularly Irmin) were always adamant that they were never
influenced by the Brit bands of the era, not even early Pink Floyd or
Soft Machine at their most creative. It's a fair comment – for the Brits
too would have emphasised their own uniqueness, though theirs was a
psychedelicised take on music from the previous decade that's been
dubbed 'freeform rhythm and blues'.

For his part, Damo is keen to de-mythologise any legend behind the
music. "'Tango Whiskyman' was recorded without any special vocal booth,
sitting on the floor," he says of Can's contribution to the 1970 West German
thriller *Deadlock*. "Some guests from the US were at a table, saying, 'Such
a stupid lyric.'"

But that was self-defining: the chorus – 'I know you and where you go…
Such a stupid man'** – rises to a chest-thumping level which, to this writer
at least, evokes the *chansonnier* genre that he may have heard as a busker
on his travels through France.

As for the linking with prog rock – at least in Britain, a territory that
would be increasingly taken by Can – with contemporary bands such as
the Floyd, Damo remains sceptical. "We were categorised in so-called
'progressive rock' at that time," he acknowledges, "because neither
music journalism nor the music industry had any word for it (although

*   The other contributor to the *Deep End* soundtrack was the conventional London
     singer-songwriter Cat Stevens.
** All of Damo's lyrics for Can, as quoted here or by other sources, are approximations
     as they move in and out of recognisable English.

91

afterwards they found this 'krautrock'), but actually our music did not belong anywhere.

"That's why it's quite interesting nowadays: some hip hop musician is using 'Vitamin C' for dancing and 'Sing Swan Song', or you can even hear it in some movies: *'Oh, what is this? I can remember this song – it's my piece.'* 'Vitamin C' on the soundtrack."

Another classic from *Ege Bamyasi*, 'Vitamin C' epitomises Damo's rise from vocal tranquility to mania – losing your vitamin C being an urgent situation, when that substance was seen as a corrective to a bad trip. In 2009, Spanish filmmaker Pedro Almodovar added it to his eclectic soundtrack mix for *Broken Embraces*, a noir/'woman's picture'/comedy which used the sometimes misleading nature of memory as a plot device; in 2015, director Paul Thomas Anderson would also select it as a perfect soundtrack accompaniment to the closing scenes of *Inherent Vice*, his adaptation of Thomas Pynchon's stoner-detective novel.[*]

Less of a natural fit would be Kanye West's sampling of 'Sing Swan Song' – the sweetly melancholic *Ege Bamyasi* opener – for his 'Drunk And Hot Girls'. It displays hip hop's willingness to rifle the record racks of the past, but the artist's bling-happy vulgarity is a million light years from the Can ethos.

But Damo's memories of Can are – as with recollections of other eras of his life – informed by the society he found himself in, rather than any moment-by-moment recollection of tracks recorded in the studio.

"When I had a break I'd spend almost every day going out," he recalls with affection, "but there were only a couple of places where I was hanging out in Cologne in that period. Plenum on Venloer Strasse was one, a pub and meeting place for artists, musicians and students. Every day it was full of people; it was not that big, but when there were occasional live concerts there, jazz musicians like Han Bennink performed."

As a lifelong *bon viveur*, the compact little human being who loves to eat and drink would sustain himself in the bar on small dishes of spaghetti vongole and small glasses of Kölsch, the domestic beer of Cologne. But most of all he went to hang out at Plenum, to take comfort in its environment.

---

[*] As a complement to the original soundtrack by Jonny Greenwood of Radiohead.

Damo recalls the pub regulars: "the painter Schmidt, in black leather jacket and trousers, looking similar to Jim Morrison, with his wife also in leather with tight shirts; Marita looked a bit like Marilyn Monroe; two lesbian girls would bring pizza in the toilet and eat there; Uwe the cameraman was often there, beer in his large hand, often the only one speaking in English; then there were some guys from Floh de Cologne, a political folk band, and other interesting people."

During Damo's first year with Can, the hair-flailing, whirling dervish onstage perpetuated a romantic image of the cultural outsider. But in fact this was still his social status.

"I had a problem with the police," he recalls, "no, not with drugs – they'd found that I didn't have a permit to stay. They almost sent me back to Japan, putting me in the new Ossendorf jail. It was the influence of Karlheinz Stockhausen that helped me to stay in Germany. Holger was his student.

"I was in jail for a week: a one-man cell, with a small window, toilet and a sink to wash hands. I could hear the radio. At that time I wasn't too good at speaking German, but still I understood the report saying a Japanese singer had been placed in jail and some people were trying to help him get him out.

"This was not the first time I was in jail, but it was the longest. I was a little bit sad that I'd be sent home in this manner, but then, after help from Mr Stockhausen, I was released to continue my creative life."

In 1971, in a break between the *Tago Mago** sessions and touring, Damo recalls visiting his other favourite place of the time, Lover's Club. "A few minutes from the pub, Amon Düül II performed that night at the Keks club. Therefore Lover's didn't have many visitors, only a few people, and I'd heard the Amon Düül concert was sold out so it may have been the reason."

It was here that tragedy struck the krautrock scene. "Late in the night, someone came and informed us: 'Keks is burning!' I remembered talking to Francoise, a pretty art student from Switzerland, a few days ago. She was going to the concert. A few other people and I went there immediately. There were many people outside, including firefighters, and I heard that

* Can's third album – and their first with solely Damo as vocalist.

93

two young people were victims of the fire. One was Francoise. I cried terribly but I wasn't alone; we went to a commune and there were plenty of people upset by what happened in Keks. My tears didn't stop for the whole night."

As the youngest member of Can, Damo felt devastated by the loss of one of his peer group. His own popularity with the girls was at a peak, and he was rarely short of female company. In the latest of a series of the random events that shaped his life – indeed, the kind of events which shape everybody's lives – he'd also make the sudden acquaintance of a seventeen-year-old girl named Gitta.

"She came in the middle of the night and bedded me, stayed at my place," Damo remembers with obvious affection. "Gitta saw me on the TV and decided to meet me – maybe I was cute, I don't know," he laughs with false modesty.

Gitta was an ex-pupil of a Catholic school who was enjoying the freedom of the times. She was born on August 19, 1955 – the same day that Daiji Suzuki, Damo's father, had died; the day when his early infanthood ended.

In a short space of time, she would also become Mrs Damo Suzuki. But, as she's at pains to express here, she was very far from being any kind of 'krautrock groupie'.

GITTA SUZUKI-MOURET

I went to Cologne and there was a small pub called Plenum where Can used to hang around. I met Jaki there. Jaki brought me to his house and he was at this time together with Christina. Christina said, "Ah, no way, no way! Bring her to Damo." So he brought me to Damo and Damo said, "Sure, you can sleep here, no problem!" He was, in fact, what I imagined at this time to be a hippie, welcoming, easy-going. So I stayed there, and that's how I met him. I must say that after, Christina was my best girlfriend! [laughs]

Damo was on a big travel around the world, stayed a long time in Sweden, then travelled to Munich, met Can there and started to sing with them. I think for him it was a kind of continuing of his world travel, and it was just by luck, chance, karma, whatever you call it, that he was at this time with Can. He enjoyed having this kind of free life and he has never, ever been about money or material things! He just wanted to enjoy what he was doing.

I must confess that even though I knew a lot of the people, it was not my style of music. At this time I liked very much Deep Purple, The Who, so Can, Amon Düül, Guru Guru* was not my kind of music. My best concert I have ever been to was Chicago in Cologne, never felt an atmosphere so fantastic, and the second was Chuck Berry. I am not so rock'n'roll but he really worked hard until he made me smile.

Can's music is not my favourite. I like 'Halleluwah' and 'She Brings The Rain'** but it was not my kind of music. Frankly speaking, I know a lot of German groups and none of them I am crazy about. It was not for the music I stayed with Damo, definitely not! [laughs]

He was the youngest of Can at this time: I was seventeen by then and he was five years older than me, so he was twenty-two. Irmin and Holger were already nearly forty; Jaki was in his thirties – even Mickey, who was a bit younger, was still older than us. But we were very young and connected quite well. Damo was very uncomplicated and he was quite curious about everything – music, art, religion, philosophy – everything, you know! I was seventeen and I was in love, and he was twenty-two and he was in love. We thought, 'Yeah, we can do something completely new, completely different.' We were thinking maybe to get married one day, but not so fast.

In fact it was Hildegard*** who said, "There's no tour, there's nothing, why don't you get married so we have a little bit of publicity?" So we said, "Yeah, why not?" I must be honest: we were thinking about it but we shouldn't have

---

*   Guru Guru maintain a reputation as one of krautrock's least compromising bands. Formed by drummer Mani Neumeier, a near-contemporary of Jaki Liebezeit in the Globe Unity Orchestra, their application of free-jazz principles to rock music produced 'noise' decades in advance of it becoming an underground generic term. Enduring through the years, their most accessible music has much in common with modern ambient metal.

** 'She Brings The Rain' was a departing gift from Malcolm Mooney on the *Soundtracks* album, where the vocal tracks were unevenly divided between him and Damo – a cool, psych-tinged piece of languid jazz for the surreal SF movie *Ein großer graublauer Vogel* ('A Big Grey-Blue Bird' – or *Bottom*, to give it its dumbed-down English title!). 'Halleluwah' needs little introduction as one of Damo and Jaki's most insistently hypnotic moments on *Tago Mago* – perhaps the closest thing Can produced to an 'anthem' along with 'You Doo Right'.

*** Hildegard Schmidt has long been regarded as the official keeper of Can's flame. The wife of key member and keyboard player Irmin, she has managed the band and its music since 1971 – both during Can's heyday and after its dissolution.

married so fast. I think I should have waited till I was eighteen. It was for the law also, you know – you need the permission of your parents when you're seventeen, it was not so easy.

LETTER FROM DAMO TO THE MURPHY FAMILY OF COUNTY WEXFORD
KÖLN

6-Oct-'72

Hello Murphys! How are you?

I'm so sorry that I didn't write you for a many months. That I didn't know that my letter, which I wrote in July, didn't arrive to you. Since those days so many things happened to me and my Group.

Yes, you were in Cologne, weren't you? But, while you were here I wasn't in the town as I was in Southern Germany. It was pity that I couldn't see you. Did you enjoyed in Germany?

At the moment I'm just doing nothing at all (I meant, I have no concerts and so with my business). While we finished our recordings of new LP EGE BAMIYAGE* and finished of Can first movie** and 20 concert in England and 21 concert in Germany were fixed. At the beginning of September, Can Guitarist was carried to hospital for danger.

He got a hole in his stomach. So, we decided to not play without him till he will be able to play, I guess, beginning of New Year '73. So pity, but, it's good time to think about my self and the other people round me when I'm down. Off course it really could be success if we made tour with earning a lot of money. But, I'm to[o] young to hold a lot of money now as sometimes I feel just myself is a child. So better face it. And think for a while. Another thing is that I'm going to get married with a German girl who living with me for half a year with understanding of her parents.

And, thinking myself to be wild, while I'm young I have to try everything I can. So I might split from Group I'm staying, I don't know when. But, any 2 or 3 years' time. It's no matter of income. I would like to be a not specialist like now, just in Music world. I don't find real answer till now. But, I really like to be a business man, it's my venture I always thinking of. The Group really need me, and I'm sure we going to get a lot of money soon. But, it doesn't matter.

---

*   Sic – *Ege Bamyasi*.

**   The documentary film of Can's free concert at Cologne, February 1972.

I like to make something more independent and more freaky way. You think I've too many dream and can't get it?

But, I'd like to try. Don't like myself not try to[o] hard. Maybe it's my ego that I'd like to be out from group. But, I will, if I get an idea. As I wrote our new LP have been finished. Just wait for the day it's released. I'm going to send you one. This could be better than the other one I sent to you. So see you!

Many greetings from DAMO to everyone in your family.

GITTA SUZUKI-MOURET

We were married on November 21st, '72, at the registry office in Cologne. All was very improvised and many of our friends were there. When the person in charge of the office had seen all the visitors, he did the wedding in a very cool way. It was Christine, Jaki's girlfriend, who made the dress out of white bedsheets. After sewing a dress for me and trousers and a shirt for Damo, it was very colourfully painted afterwards in flames of black and gold. After, we went to the studio and had a bit of party. (In fact just like every day, but with more food!)*

*There was also another German group there, but really I don't remember the name any more.** They gave us for a wedding gift a tree painted in yellow! (Don't ask me, I have no idea!) Another gift was from Holger; as he is really a technical freak, he made me a mixer by himself. When I used it the first time, I got a shock!*

For all his new status as the most exotic of 'rock stars', performing with the band on live German TV shows like *Rockpalast*, Damo remained the continental traveller who still hitchhiked from place to place, or sometimes from gig to gig: "for example to a festival in Berlin. I hitchhiked from Bayern where the parents of Gitta lived, with her and our friend Ulla. At Waldbühne that day, Hawkwind were playing; the next day was our show. I wanted to see Hawkwind as I'd met them in London for the *Tago Mago* release party and had a good relationship with them, especially Lemmy."

---

*   Damo: "My memory says wedding clothes were sewed by Hannelore, my private tailor at that time. Gold/black paint I did myself."

**   Eiliff.

If 'krautrock' is sometimes known by the more palatable label of *kosmische* music, then Hawkwind was its English space-rock equivalent. Formed on the Notting Hill underground scene by guitarist Dave Brock, their driving hard rock assimilated psychedelia, whooshing electronic effects, sax playing, exotic dancing and science fiction, courtesy of authors Michael Moorcock and Robert Calvert.*

But their 1972 hit single, 'Silver Machine', would be sung by their newest arrival – bassist and biker-alike Ian 'Lemmy' Kilmister. "They had quite a similar audience to us, and also I think we had the same recording label, United Artists," reminisces Damo. "We had communicated with them, I think – or maybe it was only me. So when I went to London I stayed at Lemmy's place. But I didn't sleep, I just listened to music. Because he was really the speed king, you know," he laughs, "but he was an easy guy, not at all difficult."**

The Ladbroke Grove area that Hawkwind sprang from also popularised squattting as a late-hippie/pre-punk way of life. It was a form of anti-materialism that Damo may have found easy to identify with.

GITTA SUZUKI-MOURET

The problem with Can was we got along very well, I'm not enemies with anybody – but I know in an interview that Holger said once my dream was to get married with the most famous singer in Germany, to be rich. If I read this I just laugh, because when I arrived in Damo's flat there was nothing. There was no fridge, no TV, no bed. He was living in a two-room flat in Cologne Marienburg but it was completely empty; one room was painted completely black and the other one white. I had never seen such a flat before or after.

You know the studio of Can?*** They had these mattresses from the army which they put on the wall for the sound. Well, some of the mattresses were

---

*   Calvert also had a later stint with Hawkwind as the band's lead singer.
**   "A few years ago I performed in Wales," Damo says of a Network concert. "Nik Turner, Hawkwind's saxophonist, joined us as a Sound Carrier, and it was the first time ever I performed with him. He was still the Nik that I knew. I met Stacia, their dancer, in Japan; she came to my concert in Kumamoto, as at that time she was living in Kyoto. I also met her in Kilkenny, Ireland as well." The statuesque Stacia – who has devoted much of her life to visual art – is a fond memory to many, proving that big can be beautiful.
*** Inner Space in Weilerswist, outside Cologne.

in Damo's home – six were there as a bed, four in the kitchen as a chair which you sat on. There was a camping cooker with two plates where you could cook a little bit of food. That's it! He really had nothing.

They didn't get much money at the time – if I wanted to go shopping Damo had to call Hildegard and say I need some money, and then she'd give him like 100, 150 deutschmarks. I'd go shopping every one week, or ten days, and then he had to call again. So it was like this, he really had not even enough money to go and buy some furniture. Maybe she would have given it if he'd asked them – I don't know if he didn't ask, or it wasn't key for him, or he didn't think about it.

In fact this was also the reason why I met so many musicians. The tour group for Can at this time was sometimes Status Quo or Hawkwind. Hawkwind was a kind of hippie group, I knew from before that they were all together, living in a big house, and that's how I became friends with them. I was there living with them for the three or four weeks that Damo was on tour. So that's how I know the people from Hawkwind very well and I'm still very good friends with Stacia; I was very good friends with Lemmy, who sadly died very unexpectedly.

That's how I also met Tetsu*, who was starting to play bass with Free and then he became a bass player with Rod Stewart. We spent six weeks with Tetsu and he welcomed us. It's also the reason why I cannot see baked beans and eggs any more in my life from that day, because I had to make them every morning for breakfast for him!

I remember several years ago when Damo was in Japan for a tour – he called me and said, "Hey Gitta, I met Tetsu!" There was also Stomu Yamashta**, and then there were Michiko*** and Yoko in London. (Lemmy stayed with my girlfriend Yoko when he was kicked out from Hawkwind.) We always kept contact – Michiko, I think, later sang with Holger, they made some concerts or records. In

---

*   Tetsu Yamauchi, the bassist who replaced Andy Fraser in Free and Ronnie Lane in The Faces.
** Yamashta's music of the time combined traditional Japanese percussion with Western progressive rock. His seventies band Go featured Steve Winwood on vocals and Klaus Schulze, the ex-Tangerine Dream/Ash Ra Tempel electronica composer.
*** Michiko Nakao was at the time the partner of Brian Eno. Still then a member of Roxy Music, the future ambient composer/record producer introduced Michiko to his friends Can – with whom she recorded some vocal tracks in the period before Damo's departure.

Can, Irmin, Hildegard and Holger always had contact with very famous people, very influential people, and I was the one who'd always run with anybody else [laughs], who in fact were much nicer than the so-called famous people.

As Damo was very moody, I remember a concert in England (I forgot where) when he sent me to get him a roasted chicken: then he sat on stage, with his back to the audience; all the Can members played and he was eating his chicken.

We travelled all together in a car with seven seats, and it was very tiring. I remember one time, a big German music paper asked about the text of one of Can's songs and we tried for hours to find out what Damo was singing. When we asked him, he always answered, "I don't remember!"

ELIZABETH MURPHY

After that time in London when he had come to stay with me when he came back from Ireland, Damo went off to Germany. And then I must have seen him a couple of times after that, because he used to write and say he was getting on well – he was kind of an itinerant musician with Can.

He came to London from time to time. I remember going to The Rainbow to see Can – I think that was the first concert when I went to see him actually play or sing. That must have been about 1970 I would say, and he had given me tickets I think. I used to go to college near there, the North London Polytechnic was fairly nearby.

I'm not really into music – it's not something that resonates with me. I wasn't into Hawkwind or any of that crowd, but he often spoke of them and I can see that Can were of the same ilk, if you like. [laughs]

I remember before they even came on stage, for about half an hour or so, there was this very loud, booming pendulum sort of thing that was hypnotic. In fact it was so loud that I got this most splitting headache, and I never get a headache in my life. I had to leave, to go out of the hall.

*I went back a bit later and Damo was standing there, but his face was covered with his hair. He wouldn't show his face ever, it was like a shroud of hair over his face. He was very shy, I would say – well he used to be, anyway. But later, when I saw him in a hall at Portobello Road he was on his own, very confident.**

---

* Elizabeth is referring latterly to a Damo Suzuki's Network gig, decades after he left Can.

LETTER FROM DAMO TO THE MURPHY FAMILY
27-Nov-'72
Dear Murphys

Thank you very much for your letter, and a couple of weeks before when I went to London I met Elizabeth. I was in London for a couple of reasons, for promotion of forthcoming new LP which is already out in England and our first movies.* I had a room in Regent Palace Hotel, really on middle of the town, Piccadilly. I stayed there for only 5 or 6 days. Wake up and went to United Artists record and in the night I went to pub or Indian restaurant and just walking around. Terrible thing was all pub is closed at 11:30 in the night. (In Germany pub is open till 2:00 in the morning – in Berlin it's open for 24 hours.) Even subway is stopped at 12:00 or something, it's hard to understand while London is one of biggest town in the world. As I told, I met Elizabeth one day with John**, they seemed very well, Elizabeth got our new LP and I hope you can hear sometimes when she get back to Ireland. A week before, I got a marriage with one I've been living with for a long time. So DAMO isn't a single boy anymore! (bit sad?)

I'm going to see you again. I'm always wishing so, but, didn't get time and when I have time there is no money left it's horrible...

Our group going to back on the road again. I hope before Christmas you know, if I don't have any gigs for a long time it's almost dying for me. Get so nervous and I feel so aggressive. I began to paint again, but, this time it's a bit different I draw comic with my style without any story on human just a comic DAMO make! See you and give love to people I know...

DAMO

As Can became an increasingly cultish live act in Britain, so Damo cemented his own friendship with musicians on the London scene – including fellow Japanese expatriate Tetsu, who he'd also met at the *Tago Mago* launch party.

"We had many similarities," he recalls, "but Tetsu had much more musical experience. He belonged before to a band called Samurais who

---

*   Damo seems to be referring to the promotional videos of the day, which would have been just live footage.
**   Elizabeth's partner of the time.

played most of Asia and maybe Europe too at that time, maybe in the mid-sixties. He treated me a like a young brother. We understood each other quite well at that time, because we were the only two persons from Japan in Europe, in the musical field."*

But still, as the memories of ex-wife Gitta suggest, the mantle of 'stardom' didn't sit so easily on such slender shoulders.

"I don't know how many times, maybe twice I toured England at that time and I was getting twitchy," Damo admits. "It was not to my taste. It's much nicer to live as an unknown person, who are much more interesting people than those 'stars'. Everywhere those people go, everybody's watching and asking for autographs, or taking photos together. I do it now but these are not the kind of things that I wanted."

Still, the creative process of working with Can had yet to lose its shine. For Damo, this was the be-all and end-all: "how to work together with the other guys in the band; how we created a process and made an end result. I never wanted to be a special person, unlike some other kinds of people. Sometimes I dressed like a special person," he admits, "but it was my personal art to dress like that at that time."

In fact, his stylistic flamboyance was of its time – for this was a period when even some underground bands took on the appearance of the more commercial glam-rockers, flamboyance verging on androgyny. It was also a time when the attitude of the music papers toward Can was one of near-reverence.

"The press in Britain appeared very serious to me," he says, with perhaps some lingering bemusement. "But I actually met no interest at that time, because there was a spokesman – Irmin Schmidt or Michael Karoli – who spoke a thousand times better than me in English. So I didn't have any interviews at that time. I just didn't enjoy it. I was sitting there behind them with a stony face."

'Stony' as in reefered-up, at a time when a little bit of hash could still get you a few months in prison. "You know, if you are totally stoned you don't speak so much. At first I wasn't so interested to talk to people about

---

* Damo: "Still I have a little bit of contact with him: in 2014 I performed two or three times with Tetsu in Japan."

music – maybe I didn't even know anything about music. So there is not so much documentation of me at that time."

The man who speaks to us here remained an enigma for many, many years.

For the most part, Damo's memories of the Can era are the details of his personal, day-to-day life. It's these little building blocks that are, he would assert, so much more important than being 'a singer in a rock'n'roll band'.

LETTER FROM DAMO TO THE MURPHY FAMILY

27-Jan-'73

Hellow Murphys!

and Happy New Year!

   I must say very sorry that I didn't write you for so long time. I'm little bit lazy now for looking for our new place to live. Tomorrow I'm going to see a house which might be good for us which has 5 rooms, 2 bath room, 3 WC, garage and garden.

   Thank you very much for your gift!

   We have now a dog with us we call her 'PoPo' and it's nice to have such a[n] animal. Because you can wake up quiet early and go for a walk, to bank of the Rhein.

   We have a bit concerts at the moment. So, I have to tell you that I go to England again. 15th Feb we play first gig in Manchester. And London we play on 18th Feb at 'Rainbow'. We going to stay England till the end of March with 20 or little bit more concerts. And after that if I have time and money I might visit you for a week or some days.

   Did you hear any of my songs from new LP? Did you like it? 'Hellow' from my wife.

   Remember me to everybody in your family. Have a good new year!

   With Love

   Damo.

   PS. I write you more longer letters when I get time soon as possible.

"In '72/'73 we had a small black dog we named Popo – 'bottom' in English, but that of a small child," he sentimentally recalls of the time before Gitta and he had kids. "We got her from an animal shelter. They say a dog is similar to its owner, but I don't know if Popo resembled me or Gitta. She was a happy dog, always shaking her popo and playing her tail like an excited violin player with a bow."

But they were to hit the kind of trauma that regularly afflicts pet owners: "Once she ran under a tram and we thought, 'Shit, she's dead!' We searched for her after the tram had gone, but we found no dying dog there. Two weeks later she came back; she was waiting outside our entrance door. It's so strange, because we were living on the fourth floor at that time. How could she remember? She was a very special dog."

When he's pushed, though, Damo can remember life with That German Band he didn't speak about for years.

"Can didn't give that many performances," he recalls of that same early-to-mid-seventies period, "mainly we spent the time in Inner Space studios. Until the *Tago Mago* period this was in an old castle*; from *Ege Bamyasi* it was in an old cinema.

"We did endless sessions, the tapes were always running. Sometimes I went there just for a game of chess with Irmin, even while the others were playing. Our chess playing got on Holger's nerves sometimes while he was working his duties as sound engineer, watching us very critically.

"People ask me often if I played any musical instruments in Can, so I'll tell you that you can find me playing mandolin at the beginning of 'Peking O' and 'Aumgn'."

The most radical tracks on *Tago Mago* – in itself possibly the most radical double-album to be defined under the catchall 'popular music' – were sonic experiments that swallowed the listener whole.

Damo's repetitively gentle pickings can be heard below Irmin's neo-gothic organ stabs before his aeriated vocals turn into screams. The whole of the band creates a sound mesh from which it's impossible to escape, what we'd now term a soundscape but clearly infected by acid psychosis.

(The fact that the title 'Aumgn' seems to be a conflation of occultist Aleister Crowley's *The Rituals Of The Elements: Autumn Equinox* compounds its psychic potency. For Damo, though, it would later become an issue.)

---

* Schloss Nörvenich.

"Also, I once played guitar at a school theatre where we were scheduled to perform for a few days. It was in my very early period with them," he says of the early transition between street and stage performer.

"Michael came so late that day – he was never exactly on time anyway – that the performance had to start. So I took his guitar, played a few chords and sang 'Full Moon On The Highway' for the first time. This piece I used to sing when I was a busker."

As close as Can got to head-on rock'n'roll with the driving repetition of the title, 'Full Moon' would make the band repertoire in the Damo era but not be recorded till after.*

"'Mushroom' was originally played by Jaki and I, with our road manager at that time, Roy, on guitar. Irmin and Michael weren't there; Holger, as usual, was busy working on technical effects; so we just recorded it after we decided to play as we were."

At a concise four minutes eight seconds, 'Mushroom' is a psilocybin apocalypse in miniature that anticipates both punk and electro. Its refrain, 'I was born / I was dead', would also prove personally significant for its singer.

"I started to sing 'Sing Swan Song' before the rest of Can developed it. I also made the seashore sound in 'Future Days', by bubbling water with a pipe.

"Sometimes someone had a good idea, like the explosion of the bomb between 'Mushroom' and 'Oh Yeah'. It was Irmin and Holger who brought a small firework, exploded it and recorded it. It happens for a few seconds. This recording, arranged by Holger, is the super-slow version; this is how an atom bomb was made at Inner Space."

This is how That German Band made a sonic attack that blew apart the components of modern music, then pieced it all back together again in startling order. This is how an unassuming busker stood at the heart of it and played an oft-unacknowledged role.

---

* Included on *Landed*, the first full post-Damo album, it featured vocals by Michael Karoli. The composition credit was the usual band conglomerate – but without citing Damo's contribution to the lyric.

GITTA SUZUKI-MOURET

At the beginning it was exciting for me to go with him to the studio. But after a while it's quite boring. They did a lot of music, hours and hours. Sometimes very serious, sometimes it was a lot of fun. Sometimes it was hours of waiting, because of technical problems. The most famous phrase of Holger: "Ich habs Gleich!" (I'll have it in a second.) This second sometimes took hours.

The studio was an old cinema, very big but with a little garden, and the cinema was in the back of a local pub. The pub owner had a giant, fat German Shepherd, she was soooo fat that the body reached nearly to the ground and she frightened everybody. The only one who got along with Senta (that was her name) was Holger.

When Holger did technical stuff, always one of them started to play acoustic music and the others followed. I have to say that this kind of music I liked much more! It was a jazz mix, which was often very good, and I regret that they did not put one of these pieces on the records.

JAKI LIEBEZEIT

All the things we did, they just happened. There was never anything written. We never wrote anything so that's why we had our studio at the time, to make improvements in the studio. So all the songs we made just happened. Sometimes we had to repeat them a couple of times until we were satisfied. But the ideas, they were all developed together by all members of the group. 'Mushroom' is one of my favourite things.

DOMINIK VON SENGER
Guitarist, The Damo Suzuki Band/Damo Suzuki's Network

The first time I heard Can I was really angry! I didn't like them. I thought, 'How can they be so famous and can't remember a track?' For me this was a lot of mistakes! [laughs] *It was too much. Also I thought, 'They're only famous because the people who supplied their PA equipment (called Farfisa) support the band, so they have some possibilities – me, nooooo, I don't. If I played like them I wouldn't even be allowed by my neighbours to practise.'* [laughs]

But somehow in Cologne there were not so many musicians, and not so many bands, and one would always meet the other one day. This was very important for musical development because Cologne was like a place in a very optimal state. If people from all over the world came you would meet them and every musician in Cologne itself would meet, famous or not. We all knew each other.

So I came to know Can, and with my school band I played the same concerts – of course before them, at a school or an art show. But we'd meet, we'd play the same show! It didn't matter that I knew them, but someday I liked them because they helped me with my equipment and I felt, 'They're the same freaks as us!' [laughs]

This was before Damo, and also when Reebop Kwaku Bah and Rosko [Gee] came in the band instead of Damo. But I didn't get to meet him at that time – I remember seeing Damo but we didn't meet. The roadies for Can knew me before.

LUCA GIOVANARDI
'Sound Carrier', Damo Suzuki's Network/guitar and electronics, Julie's Haircut
I was born in '74, so I wouldn't have been able to listen to it when it was happening! [laughs] But that music, I think it is classic. When I say 'classic', a classic will always be contemporary music. Beethoven is classic because when you listen to the 14th Piano Sonata, for example, that will always be contemporary. Everybody will understand that – maybe not in any culture, but as long as Western civilisation goes on, anybody can understand that's a great piece of music. The same thing goes with Can's music, I think.

A lot of it has to do with the fact that it's not so much thought-out – I mean it's so fresh, because it's basically improvisational music so it's something that's a documentation of the moment. It's really something that is springing out from human beings in a room together. If you do that today, or in '69, or in '71, that freshness will remain untouched, I think. And if you listen to their recordings today they can be as influential, maybe even more now. Because you can recognise patterns in their music that may have been incorporated into the popular music of the last thirty years – maybe even by people who never listened to them. I think it's one of the most influential bands ever, like The Velvet Underground – it's something so basic, the idea is never going to go away.

We're talking about over twenty years before the word 'crossover' came out, but that's what they were doing. They were listening to African music,

107

Asian music, music from the world, and curating that in what was a very firmly German/European kind of mentality. But I think of all the German bands of the period, they were maybe the one that really incorporated all those different elements in their music.

When people think about what we call now 'krautrock', maybe the main element that springs to mind is the so-called motorik beat – the one that's, for example, at the basis of 'Hallogallo' by Neu!, that's what they call the 'long line', this continuous, hypnotic beat going on with all this stuff floating around it. Can did that, if you think of a song like 'Mother Sky' – that's motorik beat going on there, but it's so much more than that. It's really impossible to think that's just one band in there.

Everything they did was so influential on what happened after that. If you think about electronic music, for example, it owes a whole lot of influence to that approach. Because you get the clock pattern, the loop repeating itself, the sequence repeated obsessively. But you also get the improvisational stuff, which is a core element of electronic music as well. I think if you listen to British bands like Primal Scream, it's quite obvious that they listened to that stuff and learned from it a lot.

KENICHI IWASA
'Sound Carrier', Damo Suzuki's Network/founder, Krautrock Karaoke
Damo's quite a difficult person isn't he? He never talks about Can. I've tried many, many times when we're really, really drunk or stoned. And he'll talk about them a bit but I asked him once, "How did you record 'Future Days'?" Just one song. And he's like, "Just one microphone in a room," and I'm like, "Okay!"

He sings a song, so that's why I asked him about 'Future Days':* did you write the song, the lyrics and stuff, beforehand, and he said it's all improvised. I was like, "That's bullshit!" [laughs] It sounds like it's written before, prepared.

---

* 'Future Days' is one of Damo's favourite Can tracks, as well as being one of his last. The deceptively simple truism of the lyric – 'All you're gonna do for all that you do / Is all you're gonna do all' – is an existential truism that plays in an almost dubwise groove.

CHAPTER SIX

CANNED

In the early 1970s, the visual persona of the era's rock star briefly merged the look of the hairy hippie with the style of the flamboyant dandy. As poppy, sub-three-minute truncations of the rock sound were played by glam-rock* bands in glitter eye-shadow, Mick Jagger got with the times by morphing into a version of Turner, the androgynously decadent character he'd played in the film *Performance*. The lamb-voiced folkie of the Brit underground band Tyrannosaurus Rex hit the charts as the feather-boaed bopping elf of the rockier T. Rex.

Even underground bands could don a little satin and velvet, in keeping with sartorial liberation. But then Damo Suzuki had always invited comment with his looks. The 'is that a girl or a boy?' bemusement of straight onlookers when he played the streets could be played up to the hilt now he was a performer on a wider stage. With a little help from his designer friends anyway.

"My costume on the stage was entirely designed by myself," he confirms, still with a little pride. "I had a tailor, Hannelore, who was the wife of my friend, the excellent painter Mani Löwe, and was normally sewing only ladies' dresses." But as young Brit singer-songwriter David Bowie pointed

---

* As with many other rock subgenres – i.e. heavy metal or punk – glam rock's label was slightly retrospective, not coined when it first hit the scene.

out, at the time of his early seventies classic *The Man Who Sold The World*, dresses weren't just for ladies any more.

"It was part of my creativity during that period," Damo says of a time when self-reinvention could be as provocative as the music. "I had enough involvement to make what I thought looked best. I gave her the design before: 'This must be like this,' which I'd drawn. Then I went to look for textiles, materials, and brought it to her so she made it within one week.

"I had quite a dress thing at that time; some people may remember the half-red and half-pink costume at Can's Free Concert.* In 1972, I even wore a sleeveless, orange dress whilst walking on the street with my future wife. In the same year we had a public show at WDR. After the show was Q&A time; one guy in the audience was interested to know my breast, waist and hip sizes; he really seemed to think I was a girl, or it may have been an ironic question – I don't know," Damo shrugs with amusement.

ELIZABETH MURPHY

*I met him around '71 too:** and he had his first wife, I think Gitta was her name, and they were staying at the Strand Palace or the Regent Palace Hotel. That's where I met him and he had these fabulous platform shoes, very shiny and very glittery; I remember being very impressed because they were about four inches high. He was suddenly much taller! You remember those wooden clogs that were very fashionable in the early seventies? I used to have them and Damo used to borrow them to give himself an extra couple of inches height.*

"If you're young you need things like that to gain attention, I think," reflects the senior bohemian now, "even when I later became a salaryman at a Japanese company, I designed my suits and went often to Thailand for tailoring as they were quite cheap. I designed a few silk suits coloured in pink or green, but when I got old I lost interest in that sort of thing."

---

* February 3, 1972, to a 10,000-capacity crowd at the Cologne Sporthalle. Filmed for a 50-minute documentary, the band was supported by circus performers.

** This was more likely the latter half of 1972 – see Damo's letters to the Murphys in the previous chapter. After so many years, memory plays these kinds of tricks on all of us.

Now, in the 21st century, the gaudy flamboyance of the early 1970s is of its period, dandyish but dated. Now, with an international network of randomly interacting musicians, music is all.

"I don't need it now. I've enough experience in my life," Damo waves away the superficialities. "But ever since I was a teenager I had an interest in original designed clothes. I dressed in flowered trousers and my knee-length boots were handmade. Some people have asked me if I still have those fancy clothes I wore on stage, as they'd like to buy them, but I don't have them any more. I don't know where they've gone."

The clothes may have vanished into that same mysterious black hole where all the time goes. For a section of the audience that listened to Can attentively, they were only window dressing anyway. To not a few, their wide frame of sonic reference numbered them among the bands whose label demanded you take them seriously: progressive rock.

"We played a big concert after we had a hit with 'Spoon' [in 1971], probably at the Stadium in Aachen," recalls Damo. "That is where I heard Pink Floyd, Procol Harum, some of the big names at that time. I don't think Can was ever in the same direction as Pink Floyd, which was much more British. Maybe it's much more like Hawkwind, because they played quite similarly to German rock. I think Pink Floyd was much more formal. I didn't hear that much of them, I think I had one LP: *Atom Heart Mother*, that was all, and I didn't listen to it much. I don't have it now."

Back in the day, Damo was more in tune with hard funk than he was with what we'd now call prog rock.* "James Brown was for a long time my favourite!" he testifies like a soul brother. "For me, two performers had a really great band or orchestra: one of them was the James Brown Orchestra; the other was Captain Beefheart's Magic Band."

Two uncompromising pioneers of where post-R&B music might have headed in the late sixties/early seventies; two one-off individuals ruling the bands who played their hard-edged rhythms with a harder rod of iron than any classical conductor. "Those two are the only music I can listen to all the time; I could not have listened to another band for forty or fifty years."

---

* Given the band's eclecticism and Jaki's love of hard-driving rhythm, this is probably equally true of the other Can members.

Can and Beefheart. Beefheart and Can. They're a potent shared passion for many music-heads that go together as naturally as rhythm and blues and surrealism – a seemingly disparate mix that were made for each other.

"You cannot really categorise Captain Beefheart *or* Can," affirms Damo, "it doesn't belong anywhere. It's not soul music, it's not classic rock music. You cannot put Captain Beefheart under blues, it's not really jazz. You cannot put both bands anywhere else. That's why his fans and our fans were similar."

Under his Beefheart persona, white R&B musician Don Van Vliet steered his various Magic Bands towards wildly electric shores, via the surreal freeform classic *Trout Mask Replica* and out the other side. By the time the good Captain quit music in the early 1980s, in favour of creating primitive expressionist paintings in the desert, he was still far ahead of any post-punk innovator.*

"If I listen to Don Van Vliet's music I don't think about the lyrics**," says Damo of the vocals that, to him, are a decoration of the beat. "I listen to music as a complete thing. If this thing has a groove then I really like it, I don't listen to any kind of message. Because music itself is actually the message, it doesn't need it."

This is an area where the writer takes issue: Beefheart's words were an imagistic slideshow that enhanced the beat. They coloured it less with literal meaning than with a kind of poetry *concrète* where the meaning was the sound that it made.

"But, unfortunately, because he's a singer he must make some kind of text," concedes Damo, "because everybody else in the world who creates songs must have lyrics. I don't think this is wrong," he muses, "it's okay – but it's not my way, lyrics are not so important.

---

*   The final Magic Band guitarist, Gary Lucas, would become a friend and occasional collaborator of Damo in the new millennial era of Damo Suzuki's Network.

**   From DamoSuzuki.com: "*December 17 2010, Don Van Vliet passed away. He and his Magic Band was the band from 60/70s [I] still like to hear from that period others I've no interest at all. We lost one of most innovative and original artist in modern music world. Captain forever!!!*" Take a look at Van Vliet's appearance around the time of *Blue Jeans And Moonbeams/The Old Grey Whistle Test* performance of 'Upon The My Oh My' on YouTube, then see the photo of Damo with his hat and Beefheartian hand gestures. The affection is clear to see.

"In every painting there is always a message behind it. But when I make my music there is already a message behind it – the process is also the message and I don't need anything else."

Music as pure expression which doesn't need verbalising – indeed, as a random expression which avoids too much pre-planning or any intellectualising – is the mainstay of the man. In its method, it first took root in his time with the collective he refers back to as 'That German Band'.

"Many people still regard me as 'progressive rock'," he says of people's need for labels, "not only the young people coming to the concerts or playing together with me but my generation, somebody fifty or sixty years old. They lived in the same time as me, the same period, so they come to the concerts too.

"But 'prog rock' is not really my kind of thing. I listen only to classical music now, but the industry pushed that music I think. It's an epoch, but I'm not so interested to look back to the sixties, or seventies, or eighties. It's not my interest; it's not my work."

SIMON TORSSELL LERIN
Experimental musician/archivist of Damo's time in Sweden
Damo's old Swedish girlfriend's name is Birgitta, but her nickname, which Damo took on, is Gittan. We started to talk to her and she invited us to come to her place. So we went there and then she found this box in the attic where she had kept all these letters that Damo had sent to her. They had been friends when he'd stayed there, and she'd saved all the letters he had sent: I think the first one was from '69 and the last one was from '72 – he wrote about fifteen letters and he was talking about some of the Can recordings, like Tago Mago; he told her about early concerts with Can in Germany. It was really funny to read it today because it was written in '70, '71: "We performed together with some English bands yesterday evening – one was called Black Sabbath, another one was called Pink Floyd, and yeah, they were quite good." (Hawkwind I know about – Fat Mattress was another band. Maybe it was some festival or something they played together in Germany.)

I was very interested in how Can were working with the studio equipment and how Holger Czukay was recording their improvised thing, how they were jamming and recording the songs, how he built the songs in that way and how he was using the studio with the early albums. That was something else really other than just doing songs.

113

In the letters Damo wrote it was quite interesting, because he wrote that he wanted to create this network with instant composing and improvised music. He already wrote that then. He told her that he was tired of recording in the studio, that he didn't like it and that he wanted to record only live music or improvised music. Some of these ideas that are in the Network now, he already had them even back then.

LETTER FROM DAMO TO THE MURPHY FAMILY

Niesenberg 5-June-'73
Dear Murphys

Thanks very much for your letter which I received on 23rd of May. At the moment I'm in holiday. But, quiet board* by many bad things happened. Last Tuesday, our bathroom burned and this was my first experience to see my place in fire. At the moment we're looking for a new flat in town (I've many problems with human who owns this country house and I should get out of this place till the end of June). It's really hard to get a flat here, specially if you're foreigner and musician with long hair (anyway I don't have long hair anymore – I cutted very short).

Well, surely we go to Japan, 10 days later on 15th June from Frankfurt by air plane. We got very cheap charter flight.

My brother is not sure that he come to Europe this year for his studying about Law. He said that he much better stay in university till next spring and after he will come. Because if he like to stay in Europe he can go to university here without any trouble. First thing he should do is but finish 2nd year in university.

So, I'll go to Japan very soon . . . Many greeting to the people! See you and take care.

With Love
Damo

GITTA SUZUKI-MOURET

Hildegard paid Damo (and me) for the trip to Japan to make some connections for concerts and with the record company. We had been there for three weeks and stayed in the house of his mother. He was happy to see his family after many years. When we returned to Germany, everything was as usual.

---

* Sic – Damo's spelling of the time.

114

HIROFUMI SUZUKI
I was expecting he will form band in Europe as he brought with himself guitar and saxophone, I never thought he become person release records. Simply I thought he is a great brother. I listened into Tago Mago *he sent me. When he came back to Japan, happened to watch a late-night programme at the part German Evening. There was a scene where German strip theatre was showing and stripper was dancing on Can's 'Spoon', I was surprised.*

I went to Germany for the first time in 1973, I think when Future Days *recording was over. He brought me to the studio and met the members of Can. When I [went] back to Japan I can remember that I received the master tape of* Future Days *and delivered it to a Japanese record company.*

NAOMUNE ANZAI
Sound designer/Damo Suzuki's Network
After Can released their first two or three albums, they came to Japan and were released on a Japanese label. They were not popular at all – only the really core fans of the prog rock bought them. My friend was one of them and he introduced me: "There is a band called Can which is really interesting, and their vocalist is a Japanese!" I was interested and listened to them, and they were totally different from the other prog rock kind of thing.

I think I first heard Can when I left high school, or when I first went into uni – so I was around nineteen years old or something. I'm almost sure the first album I heard was Ege Bamyasi *– of course this is one of my favourites. They were totally unique but I heard that less than a hundred copies had sold in Japan, or something like that. At this time they were really, really a cult band, so later on I didn't expect they would become this huge. But I liked the original structure and the basic idea of the songs, and I was really inspired by them.*

JONATHAN LAMASTER
Ex-bassist/violinist of Cul de Sac/Damo Suzuki's Network
Oh man, I think Can's importance is huge! I'm no musicologist or anything (though I'd like to play one on TV!), but I think they definitely had an impact on British bands even at that time – Hawkwind, that sort of early metal scene that was happening in the UK, they were certainly aware, and I think Can was getting decent distribution. So arguably they had some influence there, and they certainly had some distribution in the United States as well.

I just know that they have gone on to be hugely influential: you hear their music now in commercials, and there was a recent TV show called The Get Down *about the history of hip hop in Brooklyn and Queens, it's on HBO or Netflix – I can't remember if it's 'Vitamin C' but a couple of songs from Ege Bamyasi, and those guys were sampling it, a couple of hip-hop guys were sampling from Can and Kraftwerk. There was definitely an interesting influence if you consider young American DJs like Grandmaster Flash had found these records which were not mainstream, to say the least. But those guys were digging through record bins and finding these interesting records.*

That motorik beat that Jaki Liebezeit has, or Klaus Dinger*, it's perfect for electronic music. There's a foundation of electro in there and Detroit techno. A lot of that stuff I think was influenced by not only what Can was doing, but Neu! and Kraftwerk and all of those bands. If you consider how huge hip hop is, if that music played even some small part in inspiring those early DJs then that's massive.

If we're talking pure minimalist rhythm, then 'Doko E' is one of the more uncompromising tracks recorded by Damo-era Can. Salvaged from the early seventies, it would wind up on the compelling selection of oddments that was the *Limited Edition* LP – by which time the band had lost their unique Japanese vocalist.

"I never wrote a lyric for 'Doko E' before we played it, I was just singing it as we improvised," Damo confirms of his usual method. But in its stripped-down repetitious compulsiveness, this carried a native's lament for his now little-seen homeland and its toxin belching-factories. When translated from his native language, the slogan 'Discover Japan!' could be detected – ironically taken from the TV and radio tourism commercials he heard on his return.

---

*   The late, mercurial Klaus Dinger remains one of the krautrock pioneers, alongside the individual members of Can. Whilst playing drums for the early, analogue version of Kraftwerk, he teamed up with Michael Rother on guitar to form the duo Neu!. As nurtured by catalyst producer/engineer Conny Plank at his KlingKlang studio, Neu!'s driving, minimalist motorik would take years for its influence to be felt – by which time, the duo had long since split. Dinger switched to vocals/guitar to form La Düsseldorf, a less uncompromising refinement of the German scene's spatial sonics.

116

"It's an interesting piece," he agrees, "it was '71* and it's kind of hip hop – although actual hip hop came maybe ten years later, or maybe free-style hip hop or hip hop-punk. It's almost like The Kinks' 'All Day And All Of The Night'," he says of the drumbeat's repetition – though it's more redolent of the acoustic proto-rap of The Last Poets. (If that's a Kinks riff then it's a loosely broken-backed version.)

"'Doko E' is quite a strange piece with mainly drums on it, not much else happens," Damo concurs of its post-folk atmosphere. "The lyric was in Japanese. It was talking about all the poison and pollution. In '71, when I went back to Japan, I found it had lost the brightness I always had in my head. It was really dirty everywhere; even schoolboys got lost going to school in the smog. It was really poisoned."

The land he had been so keen to depart had remained an idyllic picture postcard memory. On his return, the industrial evidence of Japan's gradual rise up the economic league table implanted a less romantic image.

"Everywhere that you go to in Japan now is quite clean," Damo says of his periodic returns over the intervening decades, "but now it is also poisoned by radioactivity." In the wake of north-eastern Japan's earthquake of March 2011, the meltdown disasters at Fukushima Daiichi and its sister power plants belied the whole idea of nuclear power as 'clean energy'. The visible evidence of a poisoned environment only added to the traveller's feeling of estrangement from his roots.

"If I go to Japan I am not really happy to be there," he says with regret. "I feel sad because corrupt politicians like to build many nuclear power plants so that they can trade with other countries via the big Japanese electric company.

"I had this same feeling at that time with 'Doko E'. I was happy to come back to Germany – but I was always happy there with the Germans anyway. It could have been anywhere – Spain, France, Britain and so on – in Western Europe; as long as it was not in Japan, I was happy to work there.

"As for the cleanness on the street, if I went for a walk in the park I saw much dogshit," he restates his sense of disaffection. "Nowadays I have much doubt about many things, but still I can live in Germany."

* 'Doko E' was recorded in 1971 but not issued until 1974.

"I cannot live in Japan for many reasons; one of the most important is that many of the people living in Japan are frightened, so they are doing what the government is saying: 'Don't make any demonstrations,' as any political demonstrator is taken to be a communist."

With his lack of faith in ruthless ideology, only a fool could accuse Damo of being any kind of communist. But in terms of human freedom he's a fundamentalist. When he left Yokohama for Europe, it was endless horizons he was seeking; he sought escape from the overarching conformism and stifling sense of duty that prevailed in his homeland.

"Compared with Western politicians, Japanese politicians never enjoyed their youth," he reflects, "never went to parties, never smoked a joint or whatever. They're hardliners, and I never want to befriend such people. They're all in the system and if you're in the system you're just a robot, not able to search out your own worth.

"I don't like to be influenced by anything except The Bible," says the man from a Shinto-Buddhist culture, who knew little of the Christian gospels before he headed west. "So nobody can force me to do something like any other people. It's my life, and creativity originates in one's own experience. Any kind of art that people create must be a parallel to the artist themselves. Otherwise it's not their essence, it's just a fantasy and that is not so interesting. Real experience is what an artist must have: talk about it, or do it, then open your door."

Christianity came into Damo Suzuki's life by way of a psychedelic epiphany. The more he tripped on acid, the more he perceived a spiritual light, as his senses broke down to their component parts and then reconstituted themselves.

"Since 1972 I'd been interested," he says of his gradual immersion in The Bible, "studying it with Jehovah's Witnesses. Like many young people I was searching for my own truth.

"At the beginning of the seventies, when I joined the band I didn't have any idea about spiritual things. I didn't read any of The Bible at that time, I was never interested in any religions at all. So I was in a different sphere, I was influenced a lot by drugs.

"If you take a lot of drugs you have hallucinations; if you have hallucinations then you develop a philosophy." As so many did in the psychedelic era. Many trusting young people believed what middle-aged acid evangelists like Leary and Kesey told them – that shared psychedelic experiences would lead to universal brotherhood, bringing an end to humankind's warlike impulses.

More esoteric trippers might follow a reactionary anti-hippie like Mel Lyman, who'd played bluegrass at the Newport Folk Festival when Dylan went electric but founded a creed of pessimistic conformism after tripping out. Or they might go totally out on a limb and get into the acid fascism of Charlie Manson, who claimed Hitler was Christ reborn and what we deem 'good' or 'evil' were just labels applied by straight society.

Damo wasn't buying into any such egotistical bullshit. His first lysergic-tinged visions of Christ may have glimpsed a figure familiar to those brought up in the Christian tradition, but it was one that was exotic and largely unknown to a Far Eastern traveller. The fisher of men. The saviour of souls.

"This was maybe part of my spiritual thing at that time, but it wasn't so deep," he admits. "Just my own ideas and my own answers. It was maybe the beginning of this. I also began to doubt whether I should stay in music.

"Nowadays I'm reading The Bible every day, but that began in 1971 when I met Gitta, my future wife, whose mother is a Jehovah's Witness. Their world seemed to be believing in The Bible." Their bright-eyed fundamentalism appealed – as did the esoteric adoption of the name Jehovah, a derivation of the old Hebrew Yahweh, which also gave the Rastafarians their Jah.

"I found the truth somewhere else," Damo says of his present-day spirituality. "I am not really interested in any church and organisation. I like to find the real truth, which is starting from The Bible – not influenced by American-established organisations."

But back in the day, learning about Christian theology was a new avenue of exploration for the traveller. "If you're living in Europe, it's actually quite important to know about religion based on The Bible. Because all history, if you go back, is to do with religion. If you visit a truly interesting place then one of the main attractions is the church."

It was a window opened for him by his mother-in-law – not, he insists, by his less spiritually devoted wife of the time.

GITTA SUZUKI-MOURET

Damo asked about Christians and said he wanted to read The Bible from the beginning to the end. Which in fact is not the Catholic way, it's more the Jehovah's Witness way. So he met a Japanese Jehovah's Witness who did this with him and he started to be very interested in The Bible. (This was a while after he left Can.)

I think he took it much more seriously than me. If he does something he studies it 120 per cent. I still see him sitting in front of his table for hours and hours and hours, reading The Bible and making notes, and I said, "My God!" Because we have grown up in this so we don't think so deeply or so much – for us it's something like watching a TV series. You know what it is but in fact you don't know really.

For him it was new, so he went really into it and he asked me questions I could not reply to, even though I am a Christian. Whenever he does something he does it with a lot of passion. He went into it so deeply, I said, "Give it a break!" For me it was already too much.

"Irmin was reading Aleister Crowley," Damo reflects of his latter period with Can, in 1973. "Michael was into horoscopes. Jaki has always been interested in magic. If you're beginning to believe in The Bible, all these things they were doing just seem like the total opposite."

Some rock musicians of the time saw Crowley as Jaki did[*], who'd inspired Can to name probably their greatest album after the Balearic isle of Tagomago – once one of the legendary occultist's European refuges.[**] To them he was an esoteric synthesist of religions whose philosophy offered up the ultimate libertarian credo: 'Do what thou will shall be the whole of the law.'[***]

---

[*]   Led Zeppelin guitarist Jimmy Page is the most celebrated rock Crowleyite, to the extent that he bought the Great Beast's old manor, Boleskine House, close to Loch Ness.

[**] Pre-Can, Jaki had endured a tumultuous session with celebrated trumpet player and hopeless junkie Chet Baker on Tagomago. It seems to have been one of the factors that led to him giving up jazz.

[***] As Jaki told this book's writer shortly before his death: *"I know Aleister Crowley, but actually I'm a friend of him too! He said some good things, but some of it doesn't mean anything."*

But to Damo, a gently questing soul seeking the light, Crowley's addition of the biblical beast 666, from the Book of Revelations, to his retinue of ancient Egyptian gods must have been all too palpably dark.

GHOST STORY BY DAMO SUZUKI

A few months before I left Can ... I saw a ghost of an old Japanese woman.

It was a summer night. Even though it was hot outside, our flat was cool; we didn't feel the outside temperature. In the middle of the night, I woke up from sleep as I felt something. Opening my eyes, I saw a small old Japanese woman in a kimono standing beside the bed (a futon on the floor). She was just staring at me without any living motion. I wanted to ask her, "Why are you here?" I wanted to say, "You don't have the right to just come to our bedroom" ... but my voice didn't appear, I couldn't make any words come out. I covered my head with the blanket and decided to wait a bit. My body was shaking from fear, getting hard and cold.

I slowly take off my blanket to check if she is still standing there.

She is still staring at me.

I cover myself again, this time in much more fear.

My wife was sleeping deep and peaceful beside me, as if she knew nothing of someone standing just beside our bed.

For almost half an hour it was the same procedure: I open the blanket, she is standing, staring ... I cover my head ... Suddenly, sleepiness captures me and I fall down deep.

Woke up the next morning ... late, already near to noon. I found the window was open. (Even in summer, it was not necessary to open.) Under the window it was wet...

"Also I was isolated," he recalls of the time. "I felt frustrated during that period. I was not so much into it, feeling that we were getting too popular. On the street many people noticed my face. At that time I was not so comfortable with it; I wasn't so proud about what I was doing or interested in what I was going to do. I wasn't so interested in being a pop star; I'm still not."

What he saw as his marginalisation within the band and his increasing alienation outside of it became too potent a mix to ignore. The end finally came at the Inner Space studio in October 1973.

121

"I'd come back from Japan, where I'd been visiting my family," Damo recounts.* "There was a WDR TV team preparing for a documentary. I was quite alone in my vocal booth. I was feeling bored, what with everything taking place over so many hours; I may have shouted or maybe not. I took my microphone and amplifier and went back home by hitchhiking (at the time I didn't have a driving licence)."

JAKI LIEBEZEIT

Damo was disturbed by his wife and the Jehovah's Witnesses. He left with no warning. It was because of his wife that he left the group. Her family insisted Damo became a Jehovah's Witness. They probably washed his brain and told him not to be a hippie any more. After a while he saw it was a big mistake he made.

For one day we tried to keep him there, to hold him, but he had changed his mind completely, he was brainwashed by the Witnesses. Through the day it was quite funny, we had quite an argument – but I couldn't talk to him, he was through with being a hippie and all that.

*It was a catastrophe for us that Damo left the band. We never recovered completely from when he left us. It was really the biggest catastrophe that Malcolm Mooney left – then the same thing happened with Damo Suzuki. After that we never found a singer again – we tried some people but it didn't work.***

GITTA SUZUKI-MOURET

I know sometimes they were very happy about what they did; some days they were not so happy. But it was a jolt when he came back home and said, "I quit

---

*   Can never played in Japan, despite efforts to interest the national music scene in their unique native-born vocalist.

**   In the months and years that followed Damo's departure, Can experimented with a range of vocal line-ups. They included Michael and Irmin dividing up the vocals, as on their 1976 Euro-disco hit 'I Want More'; a one-off gig with celebrated US folk-rock singer (and doomed heroin addict) Tim Hardin; several months in 1976 fronted by Malaysian vocalist Thaiaga Raj Raja Ratnam; the latter was followed by a stint with English hard-rock singer Michael Cousins, who left after a German tour and quickly faded into obscurity. The most successful variation was the assimilation of the Afro-Caribbean contingent of British band Traffic, bassist Rosko Gee (who supplanted Holger Czukay on bass) and percussionist Reebop Kwaku Baah (who spontaneously became an occasional vocalist), in late '76/early '77. But this was short-lived, and Gee's unfamiliarity with the Can collective ethos pre-empted the group's disbandment.

with Can, I never go back there." I thought, 'Wait a few days and somebody will call,' or, 'Somebody will pass by. He'll go back in a few days, it's just another mood,' or something like this. I didn't think it was so serious, because at this time they started to be really successful. But Damo was never, ever a money or material person. No.

There were always two groups: it was always Irmin and Mickey; because Mickey really didn't have to worry about anything, he had rich parents. Contrary to what they say that they were all equal, Irmin and Hildegard were always the boss; Holger was the technician and, frankly speaking, Jaki was just happy to play drums – he didn't want anything else than to play drums.

I don't know if Damo felt isolated, it might have been the age difference – it must have been something really, really big because he never, ever played with them again after then.

As Gitta expresses, and as Damo concedes, his wife was left entirely in the dark about his reasons for quitting.* As for himself, he'd come to a turn in the road which he had no inclination to retrace.

"The next day they wanted me to give back the microphone and amplifier," he confirms. "That was it; they didn't discuss it or even try to meet me. This was the end of my period with them.

"I'd been thinking all the time about this for a few months. Because the chemistry wasn't so good, and also they were quite old at that time already – I was the youngest, although Karoli, the guitarist, was only two years older than me. The other people were ten to twelve years older.

"Anyway, I cannot say we were good friends," he reasons. Neither was there any enmity – just a gulf in terms of culture and experience. "We just came together for the same purpose, to create music, but many things had happened. I had a small group of friends but they were mainly nothing to do with music, people around my age of twenty-two-to-twenty-three years old. That's why it was easy to get together with them, I needed space to breathe."

* Gitta remains hurt that she is sometimes scapegoated for the split in Can. Jaki's belief that Damo's Jehovah's Witness faith played a major role in his leaving was obviously well founded – but, as we have seen, his faith was not a diktat imposed by his wife.

After three years as vocalist of the most brilliantly idiosyncratic rock group of their time, the break was clean.

"I wanted to do something else," Damo explains simply. "I wanted to follow The Bible. If you make a decision to go another way, many things will come together to create a reason to escape or to quit. Everything came together.

"Nobody from the band ever tried to communicate with me, so I was sure the time had come to leave. I stayed a few more months in Cologne and then moved to Düsseldorf, walking on into a new life in a new city."

While he felt few ties of friendship at the time, the camaraderie with Jaki would later be re-established. But this would be a time post-Can, when the ground had shifted for both of them. Even so, Damo's former bandmate retained his own singular view of the life that lay in wait for their ex-vocalist – informed at least in part, it seems, by his own regret at the fracturing of relations.

JAKI LIEBEZEIT

He had a bad time after that. He had to work in the street-building business. He went to work making the surface of streets for maybe two or three years. It was a very hard time for him. So he was completely in the hands of these people. They changed his mind, I think, they wanted him to leave the group; we all wanted to hold him in the group.

He said goodbye to the Jehovah's Witnesses after a while and was divorced from his wife. And he got really ill – he had to stay in hospital and needed blood transfusion, but the Jehovah's Witnesses forbid transfusions. After that he said goodbye to them.*

"Brainwash..." Damo reflects on Jaki's words. By the time he came to read them, his old comrade in rhythm had departed this earth. He muses not in hurt but in sober reflection.

"Anyhow, everybody has been brainwashed since birth. It may be from parents, tradition, religion, nationalism... people who believe God exists; people who don't believe God exists.

---

* This is Jaki's personal overview of what happened to his bandmate in the subsequent years. As we will see in the next chapter, the reality was rather more complex.

"A human being's ability to find truth is limited and may not be achievable at all. Our vision is limited, our possibility of riding with time is limited.

"One man's perspective is 'right' because he believes that his opponent's perspective is 'wrong'; he believes too strongly that the universal perspective of human beings is that God doesn't exist. But there are many ways to see these things, whether with conscious thought or not.

"Some believe in the Big Bang, that suddenly this world appeared out of nowhere. Look around, brother – everywhere you see the higher mathematics system. Do you think this appeared in one moment?

"Jaki thought I'd been brainwashed because I'd become a Jehovah's Witness. Now, I'm not one of them.

"I'm a person trying to understand the 'why' of any matter; I need time to find answers because I need to get involved in it. For me answers can only come from experience; there can be no truth without personal involvement. If you know already the answer before you search for it, does that not come from brainwashing too?"

CHAPTER SEVEN

I WAS BORN, I WAS DEAD

Düsseldorf, a distance of forty kilometres from Cologne, is traditionally Germany's industrial heartland. To anyone who'd regarded Damo Suzuki as a fixture in the now burgeoningly diverse krautrock scene, it was not the obvious location for him to uproot and head to with his young wife.*

"My life changed altogether," he acknowledges. "No more travelling, just staying on and working as normal people do.

"Düsseldorf is the centre of industry but much more of an office city, also quite famous for fashions. It is the most expensive city in Germany and the population is about half the size of Cologne – Cologne has a bit more than one million."

As the capital of the North Rhine-Westphalia region, Düsseldorf was also attracting one of the largest Japanese migrant populations in Europe. Which is not to say that it's a 'Little Tokyo' – as many corporate and industrial workers only migrate on a temporary basis for several years, Damo estimates that the city itself contains a Japanese community of perhaps eight thousand.

---

* Düsseldorf could boast of the seminal motorik duo Neu! at the time. However, they were far less visible in popular culture than Can, who appeared with some regularity on TV. The minor irony about the wider krautrock scene, of course, is that it didn't receive much attention from the 'krauts' themselves.

"It has a population of half a million, so eight thousand is almost 2 per cent of the population," he emphasises, "it's quite a lot. Also there are some other cities nearby where they are also living, so let's say altogether ten thousand Japanese."

GITTA SUZUKI-MOURET

Before, we lived with Mickey [Karoli] in a small house in the countryside [outside Cologne]. In fact when Damo quit Can I was already working, and then we moved to Düsseldorf. He had difficulty because he didn't speak German very well at all and he had difficulty finding a job, so it was for me to work for our living. In the end he was lucky because at this time Düsseldorf was the biggest Japanese colony. We thought maybe there is a chance that he can find a job there more easily and this was certainly the case.

We moved to Düsseldorf, to a friend's. It was summer or autumn [of 1974], and we lived there four or five weeks. We were trying to find a small apartment for us and after we found this I was already working, because we had to pay the apartment fee and everything. As he'd stopped with Can the payment was finished now. I could find a job easier. At the time my English was a little bit better than now, so I found a job as a secretary at a Japanese company.

They were very happy to find somebody who spoke English and German. In fact I was very lucky to find a job like this which was also good pay, and after a while Damo found a job in a hotel and we did get along very well. It was not so urgent because I had a nice-paid job. So I said: "Take your time and do what you want."

"Düsseldorf is also a totally different musical city to Cologne," observes Damo. "Cologne has much more tradition, beginning in the early sixties with new jazz; there was an orchestra called Globe Unity which played free jazz*, but also there was Stockhausen and electronic music. Düsseldorf was much more into visual art; there was an academy where one of the teachers was Joseph Beuys, one of the leading German artists."

Beuys, centrally involved with the Fluxus performance artists who included a pre-Lennon Yoko Ono, had taught a sculptor class at the

---

* Globe Unity, as we have seen, was also the training ground for a pre-Can Jaki Liebezeit.

127

Düsseldorf Academy of Art. While he was from a cultured Teutonic background that included classical piano and cello training, some of his students adapted the art-as-provocation (or perhaps art-as-a-laugh) ethos of Fluxus for the art-school band PISSOFF. Reputedly more provocation than music, they pre-dated the later punk-rock scene – as well as Damo's unconscious audience baiting in his early Can performances.

In terms of an actual music scene, Damo refers us back to the bands which echoed Düsseldorf's industry via their sounds – just as Howlin' Wolf had assimilated the USA's smokestacks into a lyric and The Stooges seemed to incorporate the thump and grind of Detroit's car plants. Working way outside of the American blues tradition, Neu!'s motorik pulsed and drove ever forward; the mekanik of Kraftwerk had progressed way beyond its neo-psychedelic roots, to celebrate the modern world of technology.

Music, however, was not part of the Suzuki family's agenda in 1974. For the sake of stability, Damo was seeking to reinvent himself as a working man. He would also find himself a member of an expatriate working community for the first time.

"Back then it wasn't like today," he reminisces, "where on every corner you can find people from Asia. When I'd left Japan it was not so secure in its economic prospects, maybe twenty-first or twenty-second in the economic table. Now Japan is not as affluent as it was, but it's still maybe in the economic top five or top seven.

"Nowadays, around Düsseldorf they have 240 Japanese companies and a Buddhist temple, a Japanese school, even a Japanese nightclub, Japanese barber, Japanese beauty salon, Japanese bookshop and a fair amount of Japanese restaurants, of course; you can live like you are in Japan. Now they even have a 'Japanese Week', with Japanese fireworks, in the summer that brings a million people to the capital of NRW."

But in 1974, Damo was still a member of a small (if visible) ethnic minority. As he admits, finding a job wasn't easy at first. "I'd learned nothing as a profession," he concedes. "But, a few months later, I found a job at a business hotel near the central station. The hotel was mainly used by Japanese companies, so the owner of the hotel thought it'd be good to have Japanese-speaking personnel."

It was a modest little place with about forty rooms and a breakfast lounge. As a night porter, he was working alone from 9 p.m. until 7 a.m.

"I'd talk to the guests and give them their key, prepare breakfast, serve drinks when needed; sometimes it was nice to speak, but some guests were too arrogant or unfriendly. Still," he shrugs, "you had to be friendly and patient."

As a business hub, Düsseldorf was frequently the host of industrial expos. "Those days were really busy; guests came back late into the night, some drunk after visiting Altstadt, which is proud of being the longest bar mile in the world." None of whom had the slightest conception they were being served by a former musical performer, rapidly becoming a lost-in-action legend.

"Some days there were almost no visitors in the hotel, but still I had to be there as I was getting paid for it." On such nights, it must have earned the cliché 'graveyard shift'.

The job lasted a little short of a year, before economic necessity brought it to an end. "A year later, my wife got pregnant," he recalls. "I had to leave the hotel and find a better-paid job." The days of being a footloose traveller, leaving every decision to chance, were over for now.

"I was married for fourteen years," he underlines. "I was the father of a family and I was much more interested in life itself. If you must earn money for the family it's totally different than if you are living alone.

"Fortunately, a friend of ours informed me of a new vacancy for a street worker, because you could get better money. My son, Martin, was born in '75 and I had to support my family, so I went out to work on the roads, fetching stones and laying pavements.

"I have three sons now: the oldest is in his early forties; the second son is at the end of his thirties; the youngest one is in his middle twenties."

GITTA SUZUKI-MOURET
Martin was born the 13th of February '75. My second son was born when Damo worked in a Japanese company – because I remember they sent me a huge bouquet of flowers – the 25th of October '77. There's two-and-a-half years' difference between Martin and Mirko.

The exigencies of heavy labour in the street are obvious. This was a small, thin guy who hadn't been trusted to perform heavy farm-work by his Irish hosts in the late sixties. In the intervening years, he'd given some physically demonstrative performances but had hoisted nothing heavier than his own slender frame onstage.

"I'm a small person and not a muscleman," Damo reasserts the obvious. "At first they were sceptical at the deep construction company. They thought I'd stay only a few days and give up, or they may have thought I was a student and would do the job short-term. It was a hard physical job: digging a hole and arranging the tubing for electric wire, water pipes, gas pipes and telephone lines."

To coin a cultural cliché, Damo adapted to heavy labour with the commitment of a samurai – except that the samurai class had rather starved than submit to the shame of manual labour. But here, in 1970s Europe, the Japanese expat had no such reservations. He put his back so far into digging holes that he won an upgrade.

"After that, they arranged for me to work as a pavement layer," he recalls with a small note of triumph. The work remained hard but it had its benefits. "I was much freer then; I worked piecework, starting early; when enough was done for a day I finished anytime I liked. I also knew how to work with migrant workers, from Yugoslavia, Turkey, etcetera."

GITTA SUZUKI-MOURET

I must say he wanted to work. He's not one of these people who enjoy being a couch potato. He always wanted to work even if he didn't like the work. At the beginning the hotel job was okay, it was something new, but after a while he wanted to do something different. It was very hard work, but I think he was most happy at this time.

It's very strange but he never talked to anybody about this except for my mother, and he said: "You know what?" He made the pavements and it was really hard. "I go there in the morning, I do my work; I start out at five o'clock and I see ten metres, fifteen metres, and it's what I did – I'm very proud." He really loved it.

He loved to do something and at the end to say: "I did it." And maybe also this physical work gave him a nice tiredness, you know?

"It was a hard time, but it wasn't a bad time," Damo emphasises. Being a conventional working man had saved the day: there was a regular wage; health insurance and taxes paid; the mishaps and injury that come so easily to physical labour were avoided; he never got sick. In fact, he seems to regard the sinew-straining experience with something like nostalgia.

"In summertime, during the week, I drank a lot of beers but I was able to finish my work. I always had it in my mind: *'I've responsibility, I've a wife and a small kid.'*

"But wintertime was hard," he recalls. "It wasn't only the coldness, if there was frost I couldn't work, which meant no income. I'd get only winter money, which wouldn't last long. You cannot get that much money as a street-worker – it's quite dependent on the weather."

Yet still, the positive memory remains: "It wasn't so bad because I could train my body. It was hard work because I used to wake up at four or five o'clock, but I had already done my work by two or three o'clock in the afternoon in the summer. But in the winter I was doing less hours so life was quite hard."

As Damo reiterates, Düsseldorf was only a short distance from Cologne – "but people didn't know me so much and weren't expecting the former singer of a band to be working as a street-worker. So I was good to work at anything."

It was also the height of his ten-year devotion to the Jehovah's Witness faith. "It was actually good to have a religion because it was the foundation of my life," he reflects. After years of footloose hedonism, a transition to self-denial was eased not so much by the Japanese tradition of *giri-ninjo* as by the ethos of sacrifice in Christianity.

The street-paving work continued for two years. Then, in 1977, Gitta gave birth to their second son, Mirko. Funds were about to get tight again, but the Suzuki family would be aided by a Nipponese inclination to give employment to their own, rather than the indigenous *gaijin*.

As Damo recalls: "A Japanese businessman asked me (in Japanese), seeing me working on the street: 'Do you have interest to work in Japanese company?'

"What kind of company is it? Do you think I'm able to do job? I don't have any experience as office worker..."

"We're selling measuring tools and instruments, you can try if you like."

GITTA SUZUKI-MOURET
He was very happy at this time but he didn't stay so long at the street-building job, because the new job was much better paying. I think he earned double at

the beginning; at the end he really earned a lot though. Plus they made him department manager of spare parts. He had a quite good position and salary at this time.

Visiting the company several days later, Damo saw there was already a core (solely Japanese) staff in place. "The boss of the company, a cousin of the founder who was really quiet but seemed to be a nice man, asked me, 'Do you have a driving licence? As our company is on outskirts of Neuss, you need a car.'"

"No, I don't have licence..."

"If you like to make lessons, we'll pay you money and you can pay us back, anytime you want."

He didn't need to be asked twice. It seemed to solve all financial problems for the Suzuki family in one hit. "Okay, I'll go to driving school..."

"This Japanese businessman had asked me because I could speak a bit of English and a bit of German," explains Damo. "I think they needed to have someone like me as it's just so practical."

While Kraftwerk, Düsseldorf's most famous sons, created rigidly danceable electro-paeans to the technological age, krautrock's lost son found himself living in the brave new utilitarian dream.

His new employer was a manufacturer of industrial measuring equipment: "So we had micrometers, microscopes, 3D measuring machines, things like this. You could measure things by micron – precision measuring instruments. I was in the department of service aftercare, serving spare parts and having contact with customers.

"It was quite normal office work," concedes Damo. "I'm not a specialist in one thing but I can do many kinds of work. In having a job I learned so many things – like having respect for other people, working quickly, so it wasn't such a bad period."

Indeed, his tenure amounted to almost a full working life. "I stayed with this company for twenty-six years (!!!)," he writes, with a sense of disbelief at his rebirth as a salaryman. "At first I was developing catalogues and leaflets, making panels for measuring instruments for display at exhibitions. After that I had a job as a serviceman, selling spare parts in a small department on the telephone, also delivering by post and packet service.

"Any type of job I get, I take it very seriously. Twenty-six years was too long to stay there, but time goes so quickly and I was promised a rosy future."

He was also finding it educative of how workaday society functions. As an expatriate son, he was sometimes the guide to his native land for groups of visiting businessmen. At one point, he went to Japan with about thirty company associates from Italy and Switzerland: "It was really hard to travel with such an amount of people. Swiss people speak English and German, so I didn't have much problem, but many of the Italian dealers spoke only Italian. Still I had to communicate with them for two weeks long, visiting our factories and doing all the tourist things.

"One day an Italian told me he wanted to see rush hour in Tokyo, with employees of the station pushing passengers onto the train: 'I'd like to see with my own eyes.' So I went with a few of them to satisfy their curiosity.*

"Another time, a few of the older dealers wanted to go to a strip club in Kyoto, but they wanted to leave already after twenty minutes. I don't know if I believed them, but they said the strip show was too hard-core for them and they didn't feel good about staying any longer, maybe because of their blood pressure.

"On another day, a dealer from Switzerland got sick and totally run down; I even had to take him to hospital. He said he was so weak, but the doctor couldn't find anything wrong. He was almost crying and holding my hand, saying, 'Send my mother my love when I have to leave...'

"This guy later begged off the trip, since he was very pale and quiet. I heard he even wrote a last will and testament. But once all his travelling was over and shortly after he got back home, he got better and better.

"Was he missing the Alps?" the seasoned traveller whimsically muses. "Can you get homesick at that age?"

In its own way, Damo was finding the salaryman lifestyle almost as stimulating as his time as a performer. In fact, a version of the glammed-up early seventies singer persisted into his office career.

---

* "I have to say no Italians were lost in that train, which was my good fortune," quips Damo of the daily spectacle of Japanese workers condensed like sardines into subway trains.

"I went to Japan for the company a few times," he recalls. "At every plant and office I visited I received a special welcome, as I had long hair and – more strangely, from their point of view – I had boots with skeleton paint on them. As you may know, in some places in Japan you have to take off your shoes, so some even looked at my boots with fear: 'Who own these boots with the skull head?'"

It was the shade of a singer who'd once inspired disquiet not by his appearance (though it was unusual enough), but by the strangeness of his delivery. Yet the musical iconoclast had long since vanished from the scene. It would take a life-changing experience to draw him back towards it.

Damo recalls the period in the early 1980s when he first realised something was very wrong. It was a ghost of the past, and also a long foreshadowing of things to come.

"At that time I was working really hard because I had so many things to do in the Japanese company," he recounts. "The lower part of my stomach was starting to ache, and I was getting periodic pain. To begin with, maybe every fifteen minutes came this pain; then it started getting shorter: every five minutes I had pain. Also I had blood in my stools – the doctor found this and so he had to operate."

He speaks matter-of-factly of it now, but at the time a diagnosis of colon cancer must have carried a mortal shudder. The disease evoked a sad family history and an echo of bereavement.

"One of the reasons for getting cancer is stress," Damo opines, "and also eating too much red meat, like beef. But in my case, I'm sure if you are getting stressed you don't have that much time to take food. I think that was the reason why I got ill the first time – or maybe it's DNA from my father."

Daiji Suzuki had died from the same ailment in 1955, when his son was only five years old. He was thirty-eight; now his son, afflicted by the same disease, was five years younger than that.

"At that time medical techniques were not as good as today," acknowledges Damo. "That is why he got sick and died at that time. The doctor says one of the reasons for cancer is DNA, but I don't know really," he muses aloud. "Because the doctor studies at university and the school of medicine; in nature there are many good things but many doctors believe only in the school of medicine."

He leans towards homeopathy because, in the spiritual belief system of Damo Suzuki, God and nature are one. But for now, he would have to entrust his life to medical science.

GITTA SUZUKI-MOURET

It was terrible. He said he had a pain – but you know, if somebody tells you he has pain you think he ate something wrong. But he started to feel badder and badder, then I said I'd make an appointment at the doctor. Then the doctor couldn't find anything; she said: "Okay, let's make a blood test." They knew the value of haemoglobin is normally around 16–18 for men; for a woman it's 14–16. His one was 7, so the doctor said: "No, there's something wrong."

He was losing blood so she put him in the hospital. In the hospital they checked but they didn't find it out, and he had pain. So they put the camera in the throat, going down-down-down-down, and they didn't find anything. When they put the camera in from the back they didn't find anything, and this they did every three days.

In fact the cancer was in the guts, exactly where seven metres stopped and the one metre at the end started. It was in the part where they hardly could find it. It was a bit like a tennis ball. It was why he was losing blood all the time and his haemoglobin was down.

"It was 1983 when my life first came under attack," Damo remembers sombrely. "I had to undergo surgery and for almost half a year was not able to work. It was really serious. I had two small sons and had to face this judgement at the young age of thirty-three. I wanted to stay strong, but my tears didn't stop when I was in alone in the hospital. The faces of my sons would come and go through my brain. I was so sorry for them in case I had to leave."

Added to the trauma was the danger of potentially life-saving surgery, with only a partial success rate. "In the last moment before surgery I was almost crying because I thought I wasn't going to survive. My wife and my children, how would they live? The only source of support for our lives was me.

"At that time I thought of many things in my head, because before surgery the doctor's assistant, or the nurse, gave me a paper to sign. All the responsibility was on my side. When I signed my name at this moment I was really upset."

Damo recognises how such a near-death experience can realign someone's path. "Many people who survive after dangerous surgery change their life, I am sure, because their whole life could have gone with a slip of the knife."

His course was no easier to chart, because, as a Jehovah's Witness, his faith would not allow the mercy of transfusions from another's blood. "It was painful," he acknowledges, "although you cannot fully feel anything because you're under anaesthetic.

"At that time I had two operations, because the first surgery was not good enough and so the second operation had to explore my body. Two or three days later I had surgery again in the same place. The first time, the doctor had said my possibility of survival was maybe 60 per cent; the second time he said it was less than 20 per cent. But I survived."

GITTA SUZUKI-MOURET

They operated on him and it was a heavy operation. He was in intensive care and I visited him with the children; the children were very small – eight and six at this time. The next day I came back and they said: "Oh, he's back in the normal room, he's no more in intensive care." So you think: 'Wow! Better now, no?'

No, far off. I went with the children, one on the left, one on the right, and said: "We go see Papa now!" We knocked at the door and at the same time his doctor, and another three or four doctors, came out. The doctor said to the professor: "This is his wife," and the professor was so upset because Damo had told him: "I don't want any blood transfusion."

The professor told me: "Your husband is going to die tonight. So if you want to make peace with him, or if you have something to tell him, then tell him now." I vomited immediately on his sheet, which made him even more upset.

I got a girlfriend to pick up the children; I go in Damo's room and find him there with very high fever. I said: "My God, what's wrong?" He said: "It looks like after the operation my haemoglobin was down to 2.6," which was really life-endangering. He knew. He said: "Be nice with my children; all will be fine.

Don't worry if I die." He was sure he was going to die. *I was there all the night; they had to operate again because inside everything was reopened. And he survived.*

But I asked the doctor one time before he left the hospital: "Do I have to take care of any diet? Do I have to give special food or anything?" And the doctor said: "No. He will have only seven years maximum to live. Enjoy his last seven years." He has passed already thirty years.

Rising from the drugged mists of the second operation, Damo recounts his gradual return to consciousness: "From the anaesthesia I was coming slowly back to reality; my sight was covered with fog, but behind that I could see light. This light came closer and closer, until I was able to see a beautiful world... I'd survived. This felt like the happiest moment of my life.

"I think that every patient that survives a big operation feels lucky that they got a new life. This is an ever-so-beautiful moment – in my eyes the sun was shining and I could live this life again, I could see again my children and my wife.

"This cannot compare with any happiness that I had before. When my first kid was born I was not there, but when my second son was born I was with my wife. The moment he came into our life was also a very special moment – but at this moment you feel free to cry, that kind of happiness. So it's very difficult, but I think that many people who survive surgery know this is a moment when everything is open for you and it feels like every word is a welcome to you."

There was everything to live for again. And there was a lost world of creativity to regain.

CHAPTER EIGHT

DIE DÜSSELDORF

As the fug of near-death cleared from Damo's head, so a clarity of spiritual vision replaced it. The creed which demanded a percentage both of his leisure time and his working wage was losing its persuasiveness. Up until 1983, he'd been devoted enough to decline a blood transfusion as he faced a crucial life-saving operation. Within two years, however, the faith began to seem like a more worldly enterprise – all too worldly.

"After a while I found many things that didn't fit together with The Bible," he reflects, "because the Jehovah's Witnesses are using *their own* Bible.

"Also I didn't like the organisation, which is based in Brooklyn, USA. Everybody was meeting people door to door, and of course they were not paying them any money." The path to righteousness, it seemed, carried the taint of commercial exploitation. "You can see many religions believing in a different kind of God: the people leading the organisation are using people who have good faith.

"You can also see *Watchtower*, the magazine of the Jehovah's Witnesses, and it's mostly sold at houses door to door." The religion's house magazine persists in print form, though – as with all faiths in the 21st century – it's now supplemented by online material at lesser cost to the devotee.

"So each issue they sell 25,000,000 copies [internationally] – they have their own printing press and everybody is working gratis. House-to-house preachers pay the same price for *Watchtower* that they sell it to people for. So where is all this money going actually?"

Damo ponders, with healthy scepticism, on the tax-free status of worldwide religions. The profit margin that transcends the spirit world sits squarely in the here and now.

"The founder of the Jehovah's Witnesses, Charles Taze Russell, came from the Freemasons and his grave is at Pittsburgh, where it carries Freemasons' signs." With his suspicion of established institutions, the former Witness shares the unease of many with masonic ritual and power structures.

"It's strange to me, and after a while I found there were many things I should not support. Many things I had believed in had so many question marks."

None of which negated his liking and respect for individual Jehovah's Witnesses. But they were the faith's foot-soldiers; banging on doors and making a heartfelt sales pitch for what they saw as the path to salvation. The systemic structure was, as with all things, in the hands of an elite – the dominant 5 per cent who exert their influence over all earthly enterprise.[*]

"But you can say that in any company or country only a few people are making so much money by using other people almost as slaves. This kind of mechanism is always part of our history."

Hierarchical structures were anathema to the Eastern wanderer who left a strictly ordered society behind. A devoutly unorthodox Christian to the present day, Damo's conception of Christ is of a free thinker sent to release humankind from its material shackles.

"But if God exists, which I really believe, then there shouldn't be any kind of material aspects," he insists. "You can see many Bhagwans, or Protestant preachers, with many people working for them as a front – some of the Hindu gurus in India have twenty-five Rolls-Royces or huge grounds, people at a higher level are using people who believe, the people who go into the church or temple give everything to these organisations."

For him, it's a game he walked away from in the mid-eighties. "If you're in the middle of the stream you cannot see anything," he describes his

---

[*] For case histories of how a dominant 5 per cent of members influence all social groups, read the theories of the late psychologist Abraham Maslow (as echoed in the work of pop-philosopher Colin Wilson).

shift of perspective, "but once you're out you see that many things you were believing in are not the right way to God.

"I don't know how many people are really believing in The Bible or God," Damo muses with mild regret. "I think it's not so many."

In his awakening from near-death, Damo felt the rekindling of a fire he hadn't experienced for a long time. "I decided I must live my life much more freely. I must do everything which brings me happiness for my body and soul. I must do something that I was searching for. I was longing to do something that I really liked to do, or I *loved* to do."

But how? There was now time, in the sense that he was prescribed a convalescent period of six months before he could return to work. What remained was to find a way back.

"After I'd left Can in 1973, I kept away from the music scene for eleven years," Damo recaps. "I'd made a break from music and I hadn't heard so much. In fact I wasn't interested, so it wasn't bothering me – for me, it was easier to quit everything to do with music, or music-making. I just switched it off. I wanted to go a different way to survive. That was much more important for me."

What repaired the disconnection was the return of an old friend. Lemmy – long since fired from Hawkwind for getting busted for 'the wrong kind of drugs' – had kept going as the frontman and bassist of Motörhead, named after the Hawkwind song he wrote to celebrate his speed habit. The hard-rock trio lost the *kosmische* elements of his old band, taking their sound back to the greasy nuts and bolts of basic rock'n'roll. But the boys were back in town.

"So in the eighties we still had a kind of contact and Lemmy played Düsseldorf, where I was living at the time," Damo recalls, still with a sense of wonder at re-entering the rock ferment. "'Tonight we play at Philips Halle,' which was a really big place. He wanted to show us a small aeroplane on the stage.* It was the first time I'd been to a concert in a long time."

---

* Lemmy was a leather-clad contradiction. A working-class Brit who voted for Margaret Thatcher's plutocrats, he later migrated to LA because 'the spivs' (Mrs T's pet corporate sharks) had taken over. A child of the 1960s counterculture, he took his penchant for biker Nazi chic to its conclusion with a model of the Heinkel bomber plane as a stage prop.

GITTA SUZUKI-MOURET

In the late seventies up to the eighties, it was me always who picked Motörhead up from the airport and brought them to the hotels. Lemmy was so nice, he was so funny, he said he couldn't believe how successful he was. I remember one time we went to a concert and he said: "Gitta, I really did it, I'm really famous now." And I said: "Come on…" He said: "Wait, I'll show you," and he opened the curtain of the concert. Everybody went: "Yee-aah! Lemmy! Lemmy!" He said: "D'ya see?" [laughs] But he was still nice, he was still the same as when I met him forty-odd years ago, he didn't change at all. He was just lovely.

"This was the last I saw of Lemmy," Damo quietly laments. "I didn't have any further connection.

"I don't know, maybe I should write to him or something because he seems to be quite sick now," he muses. "At the last concert he played only ten minutes or something like that. After that he said on the stage, 'I can't play any more.' He really looks like an old man."*

The next gig he attended would be the antithesis of Motörhead's oil-stained biker rock. Kraftwerk played a hometown show in Düsseldorf, but by now Damo's interest in them had waned.

"As far as I can remember, I was quite disappointed; not only was it not my kind of music, somehow it was quite boring because they were trying to be robots and it's not my thing."

In the mid-eighties, Florian Schneider, Ralf Hütter and their electro-percussionists had made a shtick of the automaton image first seen on their 1978 album *The Man-Machine* – which would be further refined over the years until they sent their robot simulacrums to play 'live' onstage.** But, for all his distaste at their dehumanised image, Damo shared their affection for Fritz Lang's 1927 epic futurist movie, *Metropolis* – although the influence would later play out with him in a more experimental form.

* Due to the long composition period of this book, Damo's comment dates from the autumn of 2015. Lemmy would die of prostate cancer and congestive heart failure in Los Angeles, on December 28, 2015, aged seventy. At this time, Damo was preparing to enter hospital in February 2016 for life-saving cancer surgery.

** Kraftwerk's 'robots' would actually be more akin to remote-controlled mannequins.

"At the beginning of Kraftwerk I liked them a lot more because they had a real drummer, Klaus Dinger," he recalls of their early, neo-psychedelic period. "Klaus once visited us at Can's studio, at the end of the eighties.*

"I also had a little contact with Thomas Dinger, Klaus's brother. We were improvising music in his cellar. The Dinger brothers played as La Düsseldorf and I like their music too," Damo says of the crystalline electronic rock Bowie once claimed would be the music of the 1980s, with Thomas on drums as Klaus switched to a frontman role. "Unfortunately, both have already died."**

While there were later, temporary mergings of La Düsseldorf with Klaus's influential first band, Neu!, it's the original Neu! line-up of Dinger and Michael Rother that Damo looks back on with fondness.

"If you hear Neu! it's quite mono music, quite simple," he says of its drivingly hypnotic repetition. "Many young bands today, playing in Europe or America, are playing 'krautrock' – mainly sounding not like Kraftwerk or other bands but Neu!".

But when Can's lost vocalist engaged with the music scene again, it was on a more universal level.

"If you experience near-death and come back to life, you feel differently, your perspective is so altered," he describes his path back to a different existence. "Once you've been between dying and living, if you're in a coma for a long time and you survive, then you're just happy to be alive again. And I thought at this stage of my life: *'Before I die, I'd like to make music again'* – but with a different attitude and to create a different thing, not working together with a record company or any kind of concert management. I just wanted to make it by myself."

The next engagement with modern music would be in July 1984, by which point Damo had to some degree recovered. "I went to a one-day festival in Cologne. At that time I was living in Düsseldorf, but I came here***

---

*   By this point, Damo had reunited with ex-Can drummer Jaki Liebezeit in The Damo Suzuki Band – see next chapter.

**   The quiet but glammed-up Thomas predeceased his elder brother on April 9, 2002; the mercurial Klaus followed on March 21, 2008. Both had periods of intensely heavy drinking throughout their lives (supplemented in Klaus's case by heavy use of weed and acid).

***   In subsequent years, Damo returned to Cologne as a resident.

and I saw Jimmy Cliff and quite a famous American band from that time, Talking Heads – and also one Swiss guy, Andreas Vollenweider, who played the harp."*

Cliff is the veteran reggae singer who could uplift even low-budget crime movie *The Harder They Come*. Talking Heads had travelled from Eno-produced art-rockers with a funk edge to one of the world's quirkier singles-chart acts at that time.

"For me I wasn't so much into the music," clarifies Damo, "but it was the atmosphere. Music came into my body and I decided I should make it again, in a different way – this time from the heart and not working within the industry.

"I've survived, so I have to enjoy my life; at the same time I have to share this feeling with other people – the feeling of freeing myself from any authority and establishment influence. That was why I joined a German underground band who'd all been friends at the same school."

DOMINIK VON SENGER
Guitarist, Phantom Band

Now if I go a long, long time back, Damo was off the music. When he left Can he was away. I saw him coming back into the Inner Space studio, making two songs, playing guitar alone and getting Jaki to play. Jaki said: "Okay, for two tracks I can let him come." We helped him and what did he do? He wanted to make two tracks for Grand Prix Eurovision – the biggest commercial song contest, and he made two songs to take part in that; one was 'I'm sitting in between the shell' or something. Later I think it was a step up, coming back to real art. In between I don't understand, but it might be part of coming into it again.

So I saw him coming into the studio where we were working on Phantom Band. The first time I played with Damo, it was the first time Damo sang after Can before an audience, when he started to come back – it was a concert with Phantom Band. My first major experience of him was this concert, which I have a cassette from. He was convinced to make music again, because he was out of it – he'd married, he had children with this woman, they were religious or something. Then one day he came back. He made a friendship with us and

---

* Vollenweider is generally referred to as a 'New Age' harpist.

we convinced him to have fun enjoying music. Just do it – it was no big deal, you know, it was really friendship.

But the Phantom Band was only Jaki, Helmut Zerlett (keyboards) and myself. The singer [at the one-off gig] was Damo and the roadie from Can – he was like a soldier and he was making the cables, he made sure that the Can studio would work. And sometimes this guy would sing – one time at Damo's comeback! [laughs] But he didn't join Phantom Band – no, no, no, there was another guy called Shelly Ancel.*

Phantom Band was named after side two of electronic systems composer Terry Riley's seminal *A Rainbow In Curved Air***, with its repetitive structures and shape-shifting tones. By the time the *Nowhere* LP was released in 1984, on Can's Spoon label, the influences of Neu! and La Düsseldorf could be heard, overlaid with Ancel's spoken American vocals. But Damo was just a passing collaborator. His new musical home would be found elsewhere.

"Somewhere in the city of Cologne I met members of Dunkelziffer," he acknowledges, "probably Stefan (drummer) and Jumpy (synth) in '84. They were familiar with Can, and they communicated personally with the members – particularly Jaki Liebezeit, because they shared rehearsal space in the same building. It is quite a similar story to how I joined The Can. They asked 'if you like to come to our rehearsal at Stollwerck?'"

This time, he would find the generation gap lay in the other direction. The line-up was also completed by Dominik von Senger on guitar, moonlighting from Phantom Band.

"Dunkelziffer's meaning is 'unknown number', it's 'countless'," Damo explains of the German band name. But its meaning carried negative undertones he was less comfortable with. "Maybe some bad thing has happened so you cannot account for it. The proverbial meaning has dark connotations like when a bunch of people are dying in an accident, or a number of people are still missing. I am not fond of this word," he admits. "Dunkelziffer is an unknown count; no limit. 'Dunkel' is dark and 'ziffer' is numbers."

---

*   The vocalist on Phantom Band's self-titled 1980 debut album was Rosko Gee, ex-Can (post-Damo line-up) and Traffic. Ancel replaced him later.
**   'Poppy Nogood And The Phantom Band', 1969.

My father – I guess in Japan Rail uniform. I know him only from tales told by older family members.
©THE SUZUKI FAMILY.

Little Damo in kindergarten uniform, marching with pals through the bush.
©THE SUZUKI FAMILY.

Hirofumi and I. As you can see, my younger brother Hiro was very dominant and funny when we were young.
©THE SUZUKI FAMILY.

My sister Hiroko and I. She was employed at a bank, which had a residence for employees in Kirigamine. In the summertime Hiroko invited Hirofumi and I to spend a few days there.
©THE SUZUKI FAMILY.

Me and my mum, Kimie. The most conservative part of the body is the stomach: my mother wasn't a kitchen queen, but still my taste is brainwashed by her philosophy of food. ©THE SUZUKI FAMILY.

At Sweetmount, New Ross, County Wexford, Ireland – with Barry Murphy at his family's farm. ©THE MURPHY FAMILY.

In my busking-time outfit, Copenhagen 1969. The clothes were a gift from Mochimaru, who treated me like a young brother, and I was carrying a broken guitar. ©DAMO SUZUKI.

At MacMurrough with John Alexander (left) and Daniel Salès, a student from Paris. Rosaleen, John's cousin, who had long dark hair, said John's mother thought her parents very strange to let her sit topless with two young fellows – she thought I was Rosaleen! ©THE ALEXANDER FAMILY

In Can's Inner Space Studio.

At my wedding to Gitta. In the background is Cologne Cathedral, but it's a miniature model.

A few months before my departure… Jaki, Irmin, Holger, me and Michael.

Turtles have short legs? Irmin, Jaki, Michael, Uli (Can's road manager) and Holger are behind me.
©PICTURE ALLIANCE/JACQUES BREUER

Malcolm Mooney (the original singer of Can) and I performed on the same stage in Manchester and London, 2007. This was taken at the London show.
©GERALD JENKINS.

Boots Are Not Made For Walking right way up … and upside down. ©DAMO SUZUKI.

Strangely, when I painted this the phrase *Junk Food* was not popular. The pusher comes out of the opium flower to give an injection to the food (egg burger).
©DAMO SUZUKI.

DOMINIK VON SENGER
Guitarist, Dunkelziffer

To me, this name Dunkelziffer was made under circumstances when we didn't know who was in the band. We really didn't want to make names – it was planned that we put no names in there. But the meaning was the music is important, not the musicians, and 'Dunkelziffer' in German means it's not known how big the number is. If you say it's 20 per cent, 'Dunkelziffer' is a dark number, maybe it's 40 per cent, but you don't know how many. It's left in the dark, and this is what was meant by the musicians in the first instance – meaning: 'It's not important who this band is – it's the music, please listen to the music. We all work in music' – it's this workers' idea we were putting out.

Dunkelziffer's drummer, Stefan Krachten, would die in 2014. The rest of the band comprised Dominik, keyboard player Matthias Keul, female bassist Rike Gratt, percussionists Reiner Linke and Olek Gelba, and saxophonist Wolfgang Schubert.

"At the begining there was also Helmut 'Jumpy' Zerlett, synth player, but he left," explains Damo. "Sometimes other people came into the band, but mainly there were seven people altogether while I was involved."

Dunkelziffer was a fixture of the local music scene. "Stollwerck was a former chocolate factory in the southern part of Cologne, now used for creative space by artists and bands. In 1983, young people had taken over the place for an indefinite period. There were many spaces that were used as an atelier, rehearsal rooms for bands and a big hall for events, etcetera. Jaki Liebezeit also used the space for his projects Drums Off Chaos and Phantom Band.

"A punk club was opened every Monday from midnight. During this time at Stollwerck I performed concerts with both Phantom Band and Dunkelziffer. With Dunkelziffer I would release two LPs, one single and one EP on the label 45 (Fünfundvierzig), which was run by Piet Manns."

Damo's vocals were often at their lightest and most ethereal with Dunkelziffer. Listen to trilling lost-love lament 'Sunday Morning' on *In The Night*, the first of their albums where he took the vocals. Compared with the lower growl of Rosko Gee – ex-Traffic/Can/Phantom Band, still then a recurring figure on the German music scene – who had preceded him,

Damo's vocals could take Dunkelziffer over to the poppier side of jazz-rock fusion.

"They were all seven or eight years younger than me. As the name of the band is 'unknown number', sometimes in live concerts there were five people, at other times there were seven or maybe more, it was really countless. So I joined them as a singer for a few years."

The productions were eighties-clean, incorporating different musical styles without managing to achieve the wild hybrids that Can had. "Maybe you can say it was a kind of garage rock," muses Damo. "We really didn't have a kind of special direction, but they were young people and at that time reggae was quite popular. We performed a kind of reggae sometimes – but I'm not a reggae singer so I did something else."

Indeed, a lighter form of reggae (in terms of both sonic content and skin tone) had set a template for (mostly white) pop bands to have crossover hits by the early eighties – from The Police's early singles to a piece of cheese-flavoured bubblegum like The Art Company's 'Susanna'. To this we can add Dunkelziffer's hit single, 'I See Your Smile'. Watch the band's German TV performance on YouTube and witness a rare creature – Damo Suzuki as a Euro-pop star, relatively short-haired and adhering to the three-minute pop format.

"I don't listen to reggae that much," he demurs, "because for me the songs are always quite the same. If I hear rap it all sounds the same to me; the same thing with heavy metal – every guitarist plays similarly, moving similarly on the stage.

"So for me it is the same feeling as the beginning of rock'n'roll: Chuck Berry and others all sounded quite the same at that time. Everybody played three chords, the same riffs, the same kind of guitar solo. Some of it is good, but I'm not particularly interested in picking up my style of playing from this kind of music – or let's say I have no idea!"

As for how Damo's own future music would evolve, 'I See Your Smile' set a perfect negative template for what would *not* happen.

DOMINIK VON SENGER
Guitarist, Dunkelziffer
When he joined the band he was complete and he was so fantastically professional like no other. He was so disciplined and aware – very, very

important always, no matter how far we go. It really was Damo who forced it in another direction. It was him making and recording songs.

I can't tell you if he likes more reggae, or likes more soul, more funk. When the band went in those directions it was with a smiling face, because in a way we'd say reggae guitar rhythm is a regular beat, it's like a beating guitar – um-cha, um-cha, um-cha, um-chaa! I personally like reggae music very much, I *like so much music very much, and at that time I was not worrying that it goes in those directions.*

This time, music could walk hand in hand with Damo's new status as a corporate salaryman. "I even did a tour," he explains. "In Germany at that time, I could get thirty days' holiday at any time of year excluding Saturdays and Sundays, plus national holidays, so I had plenty of time to tour and make music. For instance, in Hamburg I played a concert up to about one o'clock, returned in the car and by seven or eight o'clock was working at the company."

Dunkelziffer offered a new musical environment that was, at the same time, a comfortable fit. "Because they were younger than me they had a different idea of the music, and also they were kind of a collective – that means nobody is the composer so everybody's composing stuff together. How they made music was totally similar to The Can; I created my part, the vocal melody and lyric."

It would also occupy three years of Damo's intermittent musical career – as much time as he'd spent with Can. "It was mainly a local scene, but a minimum of every two or three weeks or so we had a concert, because we'd captured the chocolate factory, they had a big hall with a capacity of maybe 800 to 1,000 people.

"We invited other bands from Düsseldorf, Cologne and nearby cities, and made a festival quite often in the so-called underground. I could work with my Japanese company and the music together. It was really good because I didn't like to limit myself to only a musical life. Besides which, I had a family so I had to manage to work somewhere else also – though by this time I was already divorced."

In fact it was in 1986 – the year after Damo had contributed vocals to *Dunkelziffer III*, another two sides of seductively sax-laced fusion rock – that he and Gitta had parted. They had stayed together through the Can years, through the early years of integration into the workaday world, and through medical crisis and near-death. As so often happens, the experiences that urged them to stick together at the time would finally wrench them apart.

The boys would stay with Gitta, but maintain regular contact with their father. As Damo describes him, the eldest, Martin, stayed longest with his mother, with whom he was always close. Now, he works in a hospital, as a logistical administrator; but back in the day, he and his younger brother were part of the burgeoning skater culture.

MARTIN SUZUKI

My name is Martin Akinari Suzuki. I was born on the morning of February 13, 1975. I like all kinds of sport, especially soccer and fitness. Before I did also skateboarding and snowboarding.

The first memories of my family life were in moving from Düsseldorf Oberkassel to Düsseldorf Heerdt. I remember the house was under construction. After that I remember jogging with my father, who was also a sportsman. I was really little at this time, must have been six years old (four years at time of moving).

I had a really lovely childhood. We lived at the blocked end of a street, so there were no moving cars; there was a cemetery in a big field, so we also had a lot of space to play outside. We built jump ramps for skateboarding – it was great.

When we were young (my brother and me – Mirko is my younger brother; Marco is my half-brother – same father, different mother), my father spent a lot of time with us. But sometimes my mother told me that he is out on a business trip to different countries. For me it was not like he is a musician and making concerts. I only knew that he had a lot of musician friends in Cologne, where we also sometimes joined in and tried to play instruments like the drums or other stuff. So really, at that young age, I didn't recognise that. He worked a lot but maybe I was too young to see that.

Of course, you see what your parents do and you do it also. I really also believe in God and that He is the creator of the endless universe, and this had a big influence on what I see as my meaning of life. But at the time when my parents divorced, the communication between my father and me on religion was nearly '0'.

He changed and lived life like a musician, so it was not possible to see him every day. It also changed my life. My brother and me visited him sometimes for the weekend and we did family things: playing cards, visiting the zoo in Cologne. I remember we played roulette (for fun) and he was not motivated to play, so he put all his money on the 36. My brother and me shouted after him, "That's not okay, you will finish this game!" and were upset. But he stayed at this number and told us that was his choice, so we accepted it.

And then the 36 came in. That was really funny.

We grew up with my mother, and I think for children where the parents are divorced it's not so easy. I was twelve years old at the time. But they did well. They didn't speak bad of each other and it was all okay.

Sometimes at weekends we slept at my father's home in Cologne. The only boring thing was to travel by train. My father didn't have a car, and sometimes my mother didn't have the time to drive us there. But this was the time when it was safer for people to travel.

We also did a big Asian trip when I was aged twelve (I think). Our stops were Japan and Bangkok, so we visited our family. It was great to get to know them.

But I didn't recognise that my father had been a musician for Can. I was not so enthusiastic about music. At this time I was a skateboarder and we were listening to hard stuff like Anthrax. I think we grew up with this, so it's not like, 'Boom! Your father makes music.' I only remember he worked for a Japanese company, and he made a lot of overtime to get additional days off to travel and make music. It was okay for me, but I never saw him on the stage. I was too young to know what it was, and also I never saw any other concerts at this time.

I think music is his life, and if you feel this then it's what you must do. And if you get ill like my father, and think you may die but you survive, then in the time of illness you think of what makes you happy. So he started again with his music and resumed contact with all his musician friends. I think he was born for it.

Sometimes we saw him on TV in Stadtgarten. I liked the Dunkelziffer songs 'You Make Me Happy' and 'I See Your Smile' – they were great and they made me happy.

Now, it's also funny to hear Can's 'Sing Swan Song' on Kanye West's 'Drunk And Hot Girls'. It makes me proud that stars actually sample my father's music with Can.

149

Damo describes his second son, Mirko, as a fiercely independent figure who mirrors his own individuality. He first left his family to live alone at the precociously young age of fourteen or fifteen. As his father puts it: "He was working as a printer and was already old enough to look after himself.

"He became later a skateboarder. He had four or five different sponsors, so he didn't have to pay for skateboards, clothing or shoes. He went to film skateboarding in Gran Canaria, LA and Rio for *Skateboarder* magazine – he travelled only for skateboarding. It's not a bad way to travel when you're young."

Now in his early forties, Mirko has adapted to the passing of time. Forced to give up skating due to damaged knee cartilage, he works as a digital graphic designer. "He develops board games and also makes designs for industrial product packaging," says his father, with the same quiet pride that applies to all of his sons. "He did the covers of the double CDs *Metaphysical Transfer* and *Suomi** for me."

MIRKO SUZUKI

My name is Mirko Akira Suzuki and I was born in October of 1977 (in Düsseldorf, Germany). I have a lot of memories of family vacations – my father tried to go on vacation with us every year. So we were in Thailand, Japan, Greece, Spain, Portugal and a lot more countries… it was cool to see so many different cultures and people.

I never remember him hanging around or being lazy. I always knew he was into that music stuff, but I never realised he was that important for some musicians. There are still some people my age (or younger) asking me if he is my father. To be honest, I never really listened to his music. I grew up listening to rap music. It started with The Beastie Boys, Run DMC and Public Enemy, and switched to Big L, Tupac, Ice Cube, Das EFX, Alkaholiks…

I was staying in my mom's house because that was my hood and all my friends were living in that area. I always kept contact with my dad, too. We ain't living that typical family life and usually we never had that strong

* CD releases from 2001 and 2006 respectively, they originate from the two different sides of Damo Suzuki's Network. *Metaphysical Transfer* comprises semi-improvised tracks played by a regular band line-up; *Suomi* is a double album of recording from Damo's noughties Finnish tour, backed by 'Sound Carriers' – albeit musicians who'd become familiar to him, having performed with them several times.

contact like it is in other families, but when someone has problems we always stick together. I believe in God and I always give my best to be a nice person, but I don't belong to any religious organisation.

GITTA SUZUKI-MOURET

Now I think, the more I know and the more I hear, that people who have a certain genius may be a little bit crazy and difficult. Everyone thinks that Damo is a very influential singer, but I think he had a genius for painting. I think he could have been a second Dali, you know – he is a really, really good painter. It's amazing, and so detailed. It's what my family, my son and me, regret a lot: he said no, at the moment he was not in the mood. But when we were married, I gave him every freedom to do it – also after he worked, he wanted to go back to the music and I had no problem with this.

"In my time with Can, in the early 1970s, I did many paintings," confirms Damo. "I have a few at home, some copies of them anyway. I painted so many but I don't know where they are now, because I was moving from one place to another. Many things were lost on the way. Maybe I gave them to someone else, but I cannot remember because I used to travel with a guitar, a sleeping bag and only essential stuff. It would have been too heavy to carry paintings all the time. I was always creating something new in my own style, because I never studied art."

Take a look at the painting *Junk Food*, as reproduced in this book. It's a vivid piece of self-schooled pop art: a malevolent larva erupts from an opium poppy to inject smack into an egg burger with a distinctly unhappy cartoon face. It's like a subversion of *Alice In Wonderland* surrealism by the underground comix cartoonists of the late sixties/early seventies – except that Damo's painting is in the deepest hues, rather than black-and-white pencil primitivism.

"Bad food is fast food, industrial food," he says of the sentiment behind the piece. "Everywhere you go in the world you can taste the same taste, hamburgers, and it's all the same product because no food company has a good philosophy. Food is another kind of energy, but this is a bad energy. Because there are always people buying this there will always be slaves to this kind of food who never stop to eat, that's why it's called junk food. Because you become like a junkie.

"It's not so different from bad drugs, you are always a slave of this company who are selling this food. But if you go to a place near to the sea or near to the mountain, they are using only local products. There is much more energy from organic things, you will always get a better energy."

In 1986, much was changing as much else also stayed the same. Although Damo wasn't aware of it, he was reaching the end of his time with Dunkelziffer. It had been a happy musical environment for a while, but recurring ideas and creative desires – principally, the dream ideal of creating a pure form of improvised music at random – was starting to hold sway again.

DOMINIK VON SENGER
Guitarist, Dunkelziffer
I was really curious, because he was talking always about improvisations, composing in the moment, making rules, how to react together out of the moment, going on stage without any preparation and making a cue-less plan for people to play together ten years along, you know?

It didn't really work on any of the tracks that actually happened. Some tracks just stop and then the next one starts – I don't know why they stop, maybe it's just more amusing to have a little break that way. It was really strange how Damo recalled some of the words – indeed, 'words' – and some of the musicians as well repeated what was in the last concert, if it was some great idea.

I was very curious in talking about revolutionary freestyle – repeating a track and making songs, and this really happened when we worked on songs with Damo – a lot of them maybe two hours long. But suddenly we couldn't escape the rules and the rules took over.

We made more spontaneous recordings as well, and concerts, but not that much. But when it came to studio recordings, we really made records with music that was very spontaneous. In the beginning there may have been more practice before, but later it was freestyle. But we could still play it again – it was a genius kind of style!

By the mid-1980s, a new generation of 'underground' musicians had come to maturity, who revered Damo as an iconic figure with Can. The clashing gentleness and wildness of his delivery, the suddenness of his departure from the music scene, the fact that hardly anyone knew what had become of him over the past decade, all served to cement his legend. But, as a number of the new guard would soon find, he was no longer some kind of missing-in-action icon but a flesh-and-blood figure reintegrating into modern music – often in the least predictable manner.

CHAPTER NINE

I AM DAMO SUZUKI

"Any musician always thinks back to past days," reflects Damo. "They have to get some influence from somewhere."

For him, however, the music of any particular era has always been a component of the time, not the overriding factor: "the music is parallel to the lifestyle; the lifestyle is what you feel absolutely comfortable with, your natural flow free from doubt. Music (or art in general) and the foods you take every day are all connected to the tastes that build up your personality."

As anyone who's read thus far knows, however, it'd be naive to expect Damo to live in a nostalgic reverie that looks back to the golden era of krautrock – no matter how creative that period was.

"I still listen to classical music," he confirms. "Prokofiev, Rachmaninov, Mozart or Beethoven: they influenced me in a way, though I'm not a classical musician, but I feel good if I hear classical music. It makes me feel stable and comfortable."

But as he well knew, by the 1980s, much of what was interesting in modern music had followed the previous decade's primitive garage-rock explosion of punk. Many of the bands – loosely termed the 'post-punk' generation, many of whom appeared to detest each other and the music they played – were adding different sonic textures to their rock primitivism. Traces of psychedelia, dub reggae – and, of course, the motorik of krautrock.

"Those punk musicians who may have been influenced by Can treated it as a form of research," Damo opines. "I heard from somebody that Johnny Rotten wanted to be a singer with Can, but I don't know if it's true."*

As he says, for the creatively inclined there's always a natural curiosity about the creativity of earlier times. "For me it's quite normal and it's not really surprising. But the surprise came in 1985, when Mark E. Smith wrote 'I Am Damo Suzuki'."

For over forty years, the late MES was the acerbic whippet dynamo at the centre of garage band The Fall. Often lumped in with punk, The Fall augmented their insistently catchy riffs with influences from rockabilly, Beefheart, dub, the darker side of post-psychedelia – and a certain German band too.

The ultimate namecheck to Damo came on The Fall's 1985 LP, *This Nation's Saving Grace*. Its skeletal yet oddly familiar riff was overladen with wordsmith Smith's trademark northern English surrealism.

"The moment I saw this I thought, *'There must be another Damo Suzuki,'*" recalls Damo in amusement. "That same year, The Fall had a concert in Bonn; after the show I had a conversation with Mark E. and his wife Brix in their hotel room until early morning. I told them I thought their song was really good fun. He wrote quite a good lyric, which is based in part on my past life and quotes a Can song called 'Oh Yeah'."

On the original *Tago Mago* track, the band's gently urgent riff perfectly matches Damo as he builds from his serene delivery to a whelping scream. His allusive, almost-but-not-quite English lyric sits on the edge of sexual intimacy. MES took the 'Oh Yeah' riff and overrode it with a speed-freak surrealist tribute to Can and Damo himself while throwing in an oblique reference to Fritz Leiber, one of a number of supernatural horror authors who also obsessed him.

"It's quite amazing what he made out of it," praises the man himself, "if I listen to 'I Am Damo Suzuki', I think that Mark E. Smith is the *real* Damo

---

* Given the young John Lydon's affection for *Tago Mago*, it's almost certainly true. It was only when The Sex Pistols fell apart and he stepped aside from their mutated Chuck Berry riffs that the influence of Can's elastic eclecticism could be heard, in the early recordings of his band Public Image Ltd.

Suzuki." Given how personal an obsession Can were to him, for a while Smith may have felt that way himself. Damo, after all, had been just a rumour, a faint outline of legend, for a long time.*

But now, in the mid-eighties, a change of life had allowed him to gradually rematerialise into popular culture – as, indeed, had the band that granted him his mystique in the first place.

"Can contacted me when they made a kind of reunion," Damo confirms. "I think it was in '86 or '87.

"They asked me if I could join to make one album: one side would be Malcolm Mooney singing and the other side me, but I said no because I'm not so interested to go back to past days. For me, it's simply that anything that is finished is finished."

The resulting album, *Rite Time*, would have to be recorded without him. Sessions would begin at the end of 1986 (although it wouldn't ultimately see release until early '89). It's an underrated disc that carries a lineage fractured only by the arrival of digital recording technology – and, indeed, by the smoother sounds the band had fallen in and out of since Damo's departure.

Malcolm, it has to be said, made a seamless return. His mature voice was by now both deeper and smoother. On a track like 'Below This Level' he managed to strengthen the Can-Beefheart parallels without really trying – albeit the more accessible Captain B of the mid-seventies, before The Magic Band went out in a final blaze of surreal glory. It plays today like an eighties form of mutant jazz-rock – what sophisticates like Steely Dan

---

* An unpredictable trouper till the end, the irascible MES succumbed to lung and kidney cancer on January 24, 2018. On May 12 of that year, the remaining Fall members became Damo's Sound Carriers at a gig at the White Hotel in Salford. Michelle Heighway was there to film it for *Energy*, her crowd-funded documentary on our mutual subject. "Having this Damo gig," reflected guitarist Pete Greenway, brought back "some of the great times we were having with Mark, and some of the last times I talked to Mark, we were listening to the old Can records. They were his favourite LPs, he played them on vinyl." All the remaining quartet agreed that taking cues from Damo was similar to working with the departed Fallmeister: "This is what we used to do with Mark, it was the same thing really – Mark'd never do the same vocal twice, it would be different every show. It's great to play with people who can do that, I think people like that are quite unique – so that's what we did with Damo."

might have done if they'd laid off of the cocaine and stopped thinking in such linear terms.

What it resembles *least* is Damo-era Can.

DOMINIK VON SENGER
Guitarist, Dunkelziffer

I was good friends with all of The Can before this happened. The guitar player [Michael Karoli] came to my place and we knew each other. I became very close to him, and I used his equipment to record and play in Inner Space, I could use all his stuff.

But for every member of Can I was surprised, because everyone didn't want it!* [laughs] Hildegard Schmidt, the manager, I think she did a lot of work to make that possible, she really forced it. Hildegard was a very big power in Can. She was very important, the manager and wife of Irmin Schmidt, who I really love – though I never played with him, I'm really sorry about that. But his wife has so much to do with sustaining Can – fantastic work, very strict and very strong.

I met her several times – once on this film about Can that these Austrian guys made.** We were in the studio with Dunkelziffer, Damo and Jaki [Liebezeit]; I took my guitar for the film crew – funnily enough I knew the guys – you could put it in glass and it looked like the light would glide over my strings. You couldn't see the bridge on the guitar neck, but you could put it on the camera and the glass on the bridge would hit you in the eye! It looked great so they filmed it, but then Hildegard Schmidt came: "I don't want that in my film! This is Can – I don't want to promote Cologne!" [laughs]

"I think Michael, Jaki, Holger and Irmin had always been in contact, because these four people were the real members of Can," Damo says without ego or envy. "Malcolm and me were not really members; we'd been only a short time with them, so we were kind of seasonal workers. I don't know how Malcolm was thinking about it, but for me it wasn't such a heavy-duty thing. It was only three years, so it's not such a long time.

---

*   The late 1980s Can reformation.
**   *Rite Time Special.*

"I think that the past just keeps on repeating, and I try to avoid this because I was a member of Can for not even 5 per cent of my life. Why should I walk back to the past? It's almost against the flow of time. Time is like a river flowing in only one direction, which one day meets the ocean.

"Okay, there were reunions of many bands from the seventies, but it's not my world," he gently dismisses. "People like to see them at sixty or seventy years old; they like to see the originals, as the younger generation didn't experience them in real time."

The band reunions of the last twenty years have often been fuelled by a sense of time running out – literally in the case of The Stooges, who boasted with their album title that they were ready to die. But in other cases, regular reunions have become a predictable commercial treadmill. How many times have The Rolling Stones gone out on the road in their dotage, congratulating themselves that they're still doing the same thing they did as young men (when their surly faux-rebel image could be played more convincingly)?

"For me it's like a kind of tourism," Damo explains. "It's like they're taking a photo of a bridge in this village and they're happy about this. There is the old monument, which is the old band, but the social backgrounds in the seventies were totally different.

"In the mid-sixties some English band was singing how they would like to 'die before I get old', but they've already got old and fifty years on they are still singing the same piece!"

Indeed, in the late sixties/early seventies, Pete Townshend of The Who was compulsively trying to push back the boundaries of mainstream rock – sometimes it worked, as when he assimilated the electro-minimalist style of early Can influence Terry Riley into a breast-thumping ballad.* By the early 1980s, he split The Who due to what he saw as their irrelevance; now he plays nostalgic tours with the band's vocalist, bereft of their dynamic, long-dead rhythm section.

"Nowadays everybody's getting much, much older than before," observes Damo of the old 'die young' ethos. "Before, you had maybe fifty years or so, now the attitude is to keep healthy: maybe by fitness in the gym, or eating organic food. Things have totally changed and you

---

* 'Baba O'Riley'.

cannot believe any word of the sixties in the 21st century. For me it's like a souvenir, nothing else. The musical world must change every time.

"Now, with Damo Suzuki's Network*, I've found a way to communicate with people all over the world who I've never met before and create music together for the moment. This makes me much freer, because music itself can create freedom in time and space.

"Time itself is always moving, always changing. Why I should go back to forty, forty-five years before and do the same thing, playing the same pieces three hundred, four hundred, five hundred times like a cover version of myself? It's impossible for me to do it because time always moves towards something new. This is the great fortune I have had, because I never worked in this way. Never!"

Back in 1986, Damo had already reached the same length of tenure with Dunkelziffer that he had with Can. At that time, he ran into his predecessor with the latter band on a trip to Canada.

"We understood each other quite well. He is now living in Calgary, married to an art director. Also we shared a stage twice in England, at concerts in Manchester and London. Malcolm played and then I performed; we were the two Can singers and it kind of showed."

But this would be in future days – in the era of Damo Suzuki's Network.

FROM DAMOSUZUKI.COM

April 6 2007 (Friday) UK Manchester @Night And Day
Last time I performed here was just a half year ago. It's kind of home address whenever I perform in Manchester.

*This time very special... Double feature show with first singer of Can Malcolm Mooney. Didn't see him for around 20 years. He seems to be OK, he was so friendly and nice person still and he sung a couple of Can tracks for his fans. Then my set with Jay the ever sound carrier in Manchester and this time with his brother Ben on drums and other local sound carriers. Andy Hall who wrote original Can Book, also Jono and Sandra** visited the show.*

---

*   As we will see, Damo Suzuki's Network began as a band in the late 1990s. By 2003, it had metamorphosed into a never-ending tour with random groupings of musicians – many of whom Damo had never met up to that point.

**   Jono and Sandra Podmore – respectively, Hildegard and Irmin Schmidt's son-in-law (aka electronic musician Kumo) and daughter.

"In three years with Can I made four LPs," reflects Damo, contrasting it with the Network era. "It's quite an ironic situation, because today I cannot make one LP a year. For me, honestly, I say it's quite boring. In fact I'd much more like to have concerts every day than to work for one LP, with maybe five or six pieces. Instead I like to perform one piece for two hours, and it's a nice thing in that moment."

It's this improvisational ethos that reputedly led the Schmidts (in latter years) to cite him as the keeper of the Can flame. The lineage is clear – but in some senses Damo goes a little further.

"It's a totally different world," he insists. "Because if you are working on an LP then you have always a structure. If you improvise then you are going to edit this piece, and you have many different moments. If you are playing live then sometimes it's not coming – so we keep on going and going.

"But I like the energy flow between the audience and the Sound Carriers on the stage. This is why I'm saying I'm not just making music. I'm trying to find – or maybe I've found it, I don't know – *something else*.

"Maybe it's a new representation of art but I'm not so involved in only musical things. It's something to do much more with the space we share with the audience, and within this space we create something: the audience have a special moment together with us. They are paying their entrance but also, much more importantly, they are spending their time with us.

"In fact, a few times before, some concertgoers got really angry because I didn't sing songs that they know. What they don't accept is that I'm still living, not staying the same all the time like this memory they have of me in their brain.

"'What is this strange guy on the stage singing?' This is the kind of attention I get, because what I sing doesn't have any meaning – sometimes it does but mainly not, because it's not so important for me to stand on the stage and give some message. This message, one week later or one month later, will be changed and my experience will be changed also."

For some people, however, randomly evolving, free-pulsing music is redolent only of a particular era of their youth. It's as if modern music stopped developing when a particular band broke up, or when they themselves stopped paying attention.

"In Australia a few years ago," explains Damo, "a rich man asked me if I was interested in going on tour with the original members of Can. He would provide enough money that I could live well for the rest of my life."

It was the kind of motivation that fuelled the reunion craze. A last chance. A last time. A final breath.

"But I said, 'No, I don't disturb my philosophy of life just for some funny paper.' He was quite upset as he wanted to see the original Can with Damo Suzuki (even though Michael Karoli had passed already at that time)."

It's almost inconceivable that many veteran vocalists would pass up such an offer. But for Damo, who had already declined a reunion with Can in the eighties, it seems only natural.

By the time of the latter offer, he'd set out on his never-ending Network tour. Australia was one of several geographic regions where he'd forged contacts, connections, camaraderies. It was also where he'd hear a welcome anecdote.

"One guy told a friend: 'I don't know Can, but I know Damo Suzuki,'" he recalls almost with a sense of wonderment.

"That made my day as I don't look back to days past. This guy was trusting in what I'm doing now. If somebody knows Damo Suzuki more than Can, it's a good thing. I gain much motivation for my mission."

Long before the Never-Ending Tour that became his personal mission, Damo took a step to re-establish himself – not just as a musical performer but as an individual person; an entity that existed in name, as well as in spirit.

When he founded The Damo Suzuki Band, he was also reuniting with his old Can comrade, Jaki Liebezeit. "Dunkelziffer didn't like my idea to start another band," he shrugs. "They wanted to have me as their exclusive singer and for me not to have any side project. But it's an old, old story," he says of the classic 'musical differences' ego schism.

"I had a good relationship with them and other musicians at that time too. So I established my first band – I wanted to make it my own special band. After a while Dunkelziffer found an attractive lady singer and made some vinyls and so on."

161

DOMINIK VON SENGER
Guitarist, Dunkelziffer

When I lived in Cologne – Brüsseler Platz, which is now a very 'in' place – he moved there from Düsseldorf, where he lived and worked, he lived there in a room. It was like a Wohngemeinschaft – some place like a commune, there were workers, students. He lived there for some time and it was funny: there was some Japanese guy who was a cook in the best Japanese restaurant. Damo put him in there after he moved out – this Japanese cook took over. [laughs] This was prophetic!

Dunkelziffer stopped. Damo became more troubled, and I was finding out that all the time he was working in the factory* in Düsseldorf. He was a worker: I lived with him in the same apartment and in the morning sometimes his car didn't start, but I expected him to come to practice and concerts.

Now I can see how much work that was. He kind of didn't sleep. When he started with music he was a worker in the factory; in the afternoon and at the weekend, or on holidays from the company, he could do something else – do more music. So he was a worker and it was a long year: now I'm in the same situation and I see: 'Oh, this must have been so exhausting!' In the morning, going to Düsseldorf from Cologne on the train and doing it every night, it was so hard for him. Now I feel so sorry, I understand him so much because it's happening to me now.

But he would very much like discipline, and in the end it was very hard – I encouraged him lots of times to go home. Because a lot of times he didn't like it when people were arguing; he was not so much into the way it was going. He wanted very much to go away, but I convinced him for one or two albums still to go on. But one day I couldn't do it any more – he was already so free in his conclusion to go on following his ideas, no matter whatever happens.

The last album without Damo** was not heavy, not at all. And Damo at that time I don't think was ready for it really – he liked a song very much that I played with real heavy guitar, called 'Watch Out For The Professor' or something [sings ominous power chords], which he thought was great!

---

*   As we've seen, Damo was actually a departmental manager at a company that made measuring instruments. Dominik may be projecting some of his own circumstances of the past two decades onto the situation.

** *Songs For Everyone* (1989), with jazzy female vocalist Irene Lorenz.

JAKI LIEBEZEIT

After Can was finished I tried something with some people called Phantom Band; they made three records but they didn't sell and there were only a few live concerts. So after a while they gave up.

In The Damo Suzuki Band we never tried to do things like Can. No, no, no, no – but all the musicians were equal. That's what I still do today when I play with other people. I'm on the same level as other musicians I work with, even if they are unknown people. I will share the money with them equally and never be the boss. It's important for me. It was the same with Can – I think there are only a few bands that work like that.*

DOMINIK VON SENGER
Guitarist, The Damo Suzuki Band

It wasn't like Dunkelziffer ends and The Damo Suzuki Band starts, there was a development, it was natural. Because there were some old people coming from Can, Jaki and Damo, an all-star combination of the scene. We take only four musicians, we can't take everyone, and it starts by making a German tour. The management was very important – because we never had management, even today. This manager called Micki Pick, he put a tour together and he put effort into it. It worked. We made tours of Germany for some years, every year. Good concerts, good clubs, everything was okay. I was so happy that Jaki and Matthias and myself could make The Damo Suzuki Band – it was like an all-star band from this family, you know? We'd go on tour again making very free music, but on a very high level professionally. Jaki was the best drummer ever; Damo was the most fantastic singer; Matthias was our keyboard player; I had all my freedom to do whatever – it could have been fantastic then but I wasn't that good. I really tried my best and I enjoyed it – I learned so much at that time.

---

* When the writer spoke with Jaki, a short time before his death, he was keen to stress the importance of his Drums Off Chaos project for the past thirty years: *"It's not a commercial thing at all,"* but it was clearly central to his life. He also spoke of his contribution to the book *The Drum Thing* (Prestel 2016): *"It contains pictures and short interviews with I guess 100 drummers by this Irish woman called Deirdre O'Callaghan. It's a very interesting book and I was lucky to be included."* Given the universal esteem that the motorik metronome was held in, both his enthusiasm and his humility were touching.

The Damo Suzuki Band spanned from late 1986 to 1990. Matthias Keul on keyboards and Dominik on guitar were co-opted from Dunkelziffer. Then of course there was a drummer from another time and space who just wanted to keep drumming.

"This was to be a touring band, because I was not so interested in making a record in the studio. I just wanted an all-improv band," recalls Damo of how his long-term longing for freeform freedom was starting to shape up.

There was one other criterion for what otherwise might have passed as a conventional four-man band line-up – no bass player, at Jaki Liebezeit's insistence. It was his late-Can disaffection with the stringed half of a rhythm section that caused friction with old bandmate Holger*, which may have led to Czukay largely abandoning the instrument in Can's latter days. But by the mid-1980s it had hardened into a rule.

"He meant that bass was not that important now because he could make it with the drums," says the man who gave Jaki's latest band its name. "After a while I understood what he was doing – without bass guitar you can take it up into the air; with bass you are on the ground. And also the amplifiers on the bass never sounded good.

"In fact the bass as an instrument in musical history is no older than 100 years. You hear any traditional music, it has no use for the bass. So it's not really necessary to have bass guitar; it's more for the idea of musicians learning to score notes and anyway, keyboards have bass functions."

JAKI LIEBEZEIT
*Usually I don't need bass players. [laughs] Because with drums and bass I always have problems. There are very few exceptions: there are only very few bass players in the world I can accept – one of them is Jah Wobble, you might know him.** For*

---

* There is a famous anecdote that describes Jaki chasing Holger Czukay with a hatchet! In his defence, Jaki insisted he'd never have hurt Holger if he'd caught him.

** Jah Wobble, the east London-born bassist and multi-instrumentalist formerly known as John Wardle, first came to the fore with Public Image Ltd. With John Lydon (aka Johnny Rotten) on vocals, their *Metal Box* is (alongside The Fall) the finest emblem of Can's influence on the more creative post-punk bands. But Wobble's undulating bass went beyond Holger Czukay's less demonstrative rhythms, treating it as a dubwise lead instrument. Having worked with a bewilderingly eclectic range of musicians throughout his career, he continues touring with his Invaders Of The Heart.

nearly thirty years I've played a lot with him in England, and he's one of the few bass players I can play with. The reason is he plays it like a musical instrument and not like a bass. Most bass players think they only have to play deep – what bass means for them is to play on the deep 'C' all the time. There are only a few who think they can play the bass like a musical instrument, a saxophone or whatever – Jah Wobble is one of them. Another one is Rosko Gee.* I can work with people like that.

DOMINIK VON SENGER
Guitarist, The Damo Suzuki Band

In The Damo Suzuki Band we had no bassist. We don't need a bassist and Jaki says: "Don't worry – The Doors they have also no bassist!" He didn't like bass because the bass always destroyed the bass drum. Bass players are never good for Jaki, he hates bass players. But Holger Czukay played a Fender Mustang bass (in Can), which is a small bass which means it doesn't go so far down in frequency.

We made a lot of CDs – in a CD box but taken from the mixer, which really shows the energy. Whatever Jaki played was very advanced drumming, the most sophisticated drums I can listen to. In The Damo Suzuki Band Jaki made his biggest technical performance. No one knows but it was a highlight – it was great in Can but there he'd really go into it. And after it he stopped playing a drum kit: he plays self-built little drums, sitting in a little shell Indian-style.

If hypnotic repetition was the driver of classic krautrock, then The Damo Suzuki Band brought the same ethos into the crystalline era of digital sound mixing. Damo's vocals had deepened pleasingly by this time, a fore-echo of the primal growl that can be heard in concert today – singing in the invented language that might contain scraps of German and Japanese, but abandons the quaint cod-English of the Can days.

For all his own reservations about his ability at the time, Dominik's guitar lines were clean and spiky – a trebly framework for a band with no bass player. Matthias's keyboard playing merged with the guitar in

---

* Rosko supplanted Holger as bassist in Can, when the latter switched over entirely to radio and sound effects.

its insistent yet gentle electronic repetition. All were driven along by the human metronome, with his subtly unshowy diversions around the beat.

"Jaki is kind of a *worker*," emphasises Damo. "He thinks a drummer is not like a musician, it's something else, a working man. I think he's still training eight hours a day.*

"So I recruited Jaki because if I needed drums I wanted somebody good, so that we could improvise together – and also he was in the Stollwerck neighbourhood.

"Our philosophy was quite similar," he underlines, "*nobody controls music.*"

Regular tours were made of Germany and Austria. While Damo was insistent that his band were not going to be cooped up in the studio, there is a recorded output taken directly from the mixing desk. As for his notion that Can belonged firmly in the past, listen to their first album, *Vernissage* (a French term for a private exhibition), and hear the metallically funky 'Don't Forget Ya Job' medley, occupying the whole of side one – with its snatches of 'Halleluwah' and 'Mushroom'.

But then, the vocalist might argue, the past was being put in its place. Besides being the leader of a band, these days he was most definitely a man with a job.**

"I had something like 100 days when I could do something I liked to do," he says, toting up the holidays and free time in lieu of overtime he could work up. "So we did some tours and I was quite happy about this, because on the one hand I could get regular income; on the other hand I could do the things I love to do."

But nothing comes without a price. "Let's say I performed in Hamburg at a concert until one o'clock, driving back to Cologne and then working

---

*   Damo's description of Jaki was obviously made prior to his passing. But it's believed that he kept up his dedication to his (now modified and compact) drum kit to the end.

**   Damo: "Before, I performed some songs from my heyday (as you might say) – unplanned, we didn't have a running-order at all. It was my period with The Damo Suzuki Band and the very early stages of Damo Suzuki's Network; the reason was that I performed with Jaki/Michael. Since I performed with random Sound Carriers I won't do it, even when some band played a Can-like piece to get me to sing a song from my 'heyday'."

with the company without sleep," Damo describes his routine of the time. "I don't know how I did it, but there were many days like this.

"Maybe at that time I had a kind of power, and maybe the opportunity to do both things gave me much more energy. But I was able to do this and during this time also I made a US tour, and later a tour of Japan (both with Damo Suzuki's Network), when I was an employee of a Japanese company."

DOMINIK VON SENGER
Guitarist, The Damo Suzuki Band
One year after another, we had the opportunity to make German tours – the clubs here and there around Germany – that made people think, 'Aha!' They sang the songs, they knew the words – Damo really hooked up again on some things. We had some songs, it worked and people really sang with it. We were an explosive free band – but people sang with it, between the most spontaneous stuff.

Back in 1986, we played in a very big place in West Berlin at that time – really it was The Damo Suzuki-Jaki Liebezeit Band, and this was one of our biggest concerts. I remember playing one note the whole track long in one timing and didn't make any other note. All the time the same. It was monotonous: where you start, you finish it the same. There was no break and for me, it was the first time for the band to see me doing something like that. But there were some people in the audience who realised that too, and because of that they made a cassette recording where it's only one channel.

These kinds of experiments, which every musician made, were always at work. To me it was a feeling of pure music, being a pure musician. It's not about how you look, how you are dressed, if you have a show, we could do without PA – Damo would sing with a poster, you know, he'd roll a poster and make it like a megaphone. *

We called it 'latest news': if you go to the concert, in the last five minutes before you go on it might change your idea of the whole thing and your approach, because it was always the most up to date. In the concert, if

---

* "I can remember this at one concert with Phantom Band at The Basement, Cologne," clarifies Damo. "Phantom Band didn't have a singer that day, so they didn't prepare vocal equipment. I took off a poster from the wall, rolled it and used it as a megaphone/microphone."

someone looked very nice it might change the entire music. It's always the latest, it's always on 'now'.

We did a song called 'The Latest News'. We only named it because we felt like that – we experienced it, it was coming to us this way because we lived like that. If I go to the Can studio every day, every day I feel different, and the way you feel is the way you play. And you feel differently every day.

GITTA SUZUKI-MOURET

At the beginning he did the music aside to being a salaryman. He did it on the weekend with old friends, and then after we got divorced he still worked for a few years as a salaryman and making music aside. He took his holiday to make tours, and at the end he quit his job and made only music. But then he started to say: "I don't want any more material things. All that I have is two suitcases and that's it" – he didn't want to have any kind of possessions. He had an apartment, he had a musical instrument collection – I think he gave it all away or he sold it.

DOMINIK VON SENGER
Guitarist, The Damo Suzuki Band

He had a lot of trouble; he was fighting very much Jaki, because Jaki's school is very, very, very hard. I call it the Can Tooth – 'Tooth' is in German how you make cars go on the road whether they're official or not; on the musical road, whether it's closed or not, Jaki said in that circumstance you have to go over it, to learn. On the tours, always there were flip-outs – stopping the tour, it was chaotic, all this stuff. We were not really peaceful.

I went out of the band in Munich – I quit, jumped out of the car, having no money at all. I went to the central station and ate at a workers' café. I stopped: "This is too much for me." Suddenly I met some people in Munich who knew me, it was a place where those guys played. They were waiting and laughing, and I had to go. [laughs]

This was really a hard time, it was not easy at all. Those two big Can guys and the two Dunkelziffer guys, it was too hot, it made stress. To me it was a clash of generations. I also had that argument with Jaki at the time – a very, very big argument about generations: "I can't be like you, you are fifteen, seventeen years ahead! I never will overtake you, you are too much advanced – you always have to deal with a younger guy who doesn't have all

168

the seventeen years in which you learned." He was very angry, he said: "There is no argument, not at all!" He was older and had made something fantastic, and he was right – but me too! [laughs]

In 1990, The Damo Suzuki Band was drawing toward its natural close. In lasting into a fourth year, it had already extended beyond the time spent in both Can and Dunkelziffer. But its finite nature was not immediately apparent. Today, it's still possible to find online an impressive piece of demo footage shot that year by documentary filmmaker Astrid Heibach. There's a beautifully clean urgency to the sound and Damo himself looks like the fuller-faced elder brother of the airily-toned Can singer.

Astrid would, for a while, be a significant other in his life. She would also bear him his third son, Marco, who today is an aspiring filmmaker. Having been through film school, he has trained in editing and sound design, and worked on some soundtracks. His vocation obviously owes much to his mother's influence – though it's perhaps not too fanciful to wonder if he shares his father's love of working in the moment.

ASTRID HEIBACH

The first time I saw Damo Suzuki on stage was on the occasion of the Can free concert at the Cologne Sporthalle, February 4, 1972. Damo, in his pink and red velvet overall, was dancing and swaying to the music by Jaki, Michael, Irmin and Holger. He created ecstatic effects with his vocal techniques and seemed to go into a kind of trance. The stage show I liked a lot, including varieté *attractions like a juggler with bottles, tennis balls or umbrellas, and an older musician playing solo on a singing saw while acrobats were performing floor exercises.*

In 1990 I saw Damo on stage for the second time, in a concert by The Damo Suzuki Band. Instead of the two-coloured overall, he wore a white shirt and tie. But his performance was similar to that in 1972. At that time I was editing my movie, which I shot in the United States a year before.* I asked Damo if he had music which I could use for a dreamlike scene. He provided a soundtrack,

---

* *I Did It* (1990). The music was already recorded by Damo and not specially composed. Later, *The Gallerist* (2007) featured music by Damo Suzuki's Network/French Doctors. The films were shown at exhibitions and video festivals.

which he had produced together with Nils Kristiansen. I was able to show him more of my work and we talked a lot about Japan, where I spent two months in 1982.

Mine and Damo's son, Marco Akari, was born in 1991 in Cologne. At the age of fifteen he joined Damo on his Never-Ending Tour through Japan to film the concerts of the Network. Later, Marco combined the influences of his parents in his studies. He is expecting to receive his bachelor degree in Digital Film Arts/Editing Picture & Sound at the Internationale Filmschule, Cologne.

Damo has always cultivated an attitude against any kind of establishment or authority. His life is a balancing act and he finds freedom through his music. That's why his healing process, which has been ongoing since 2014*, is just another balancing act, which he will master soon in order to continue his Never-Ending Tour.

MARCO HEIBACH

I was born on the 12th of May nineteen hundred and ninety-one, in Cologne. I lived together with my parents until I was five – and then they split up. So I basically went to live with my mum most of the time, went to school and grew up in Cologne.

I studied editing pictures, I finished my studies in 2016, and after that I started to work as a freelance sound designer, film editor and composer. After I graduated, I started a small video production company. We're focused on post-production, but recently started to do more in-house productions of fictional and non-fictional films or music videos – basically everything that's handed to us. And if we get the free time, we like to experiment.

I wanted to do something different from what my parents were doing. I was basically a very computer-orientated kid, I would say that when I grew up I was a little bit of a geek. I wanted to do something with computers, but not in a technological way – I found out in school that I'm not the best programmer. Then I found the creative part of the computer – which is like editing, creating sounds, creating digital images, stuff like that. So that kind of led me.

When I was younger and when I graduated from school, I never wanted to do something that is close to what my parents do. But somehow, I don't know

---

* As we will see, Damo's illness has recurred in more recent years.

how, I ended up doing exactly a mix of what both my parents are doing. So that's a twist I didn't expect.

My father is a musician who creates a certain atmosphere onstage, puts people into a certain vibe or mood during his composition – I was never like that, that outgoing, I was more shy to present my works to the world onstage. So actually I started playing in a band, but after that I felt that maybe I can like take control of everything, every instrument – so that's when I started to compose music mostly on the computer.

I lived together with my father in the band years – it was interesting, [but] it was different after that. We always stayed in contact and I was seeing him quite a lot – but of course when he was on tour or something like that, I wouldn't see him for a while.

I can remember my dad always making music and always doing what he's doing now – in my perspective that never changed. Myself I'm listening to hip hop mostly. But I grew up with my father's music – or listening to him listening to classical music. Because his own musical tastes were, to me, either his own music or classical. And maybe that was also one point when I was grabbing like a part of his attitude.

I can say for me my father was never untouchable. I'd always experienced that he didn't treat somebody different because he had a certain background. For me the equality in his behaviour was always normal, I never felt awkwardness or any uncomfortable feeling in that. I would say also there was always more positive than negative experiences connected to anything that he did.

Sometimes seeing him on the stage is like a strange moment, but I can also say that since I got a little bit older I started to feel proud about what my father did. I would say in my younger days I was a little bit more against everything that he did! [laughs] It was maybe like a rebellious teenager thing. Because when you're a teenager, you have that kind of rebellious, not unhealthy but not very nice way of seeing your parents.

"After The Damo Suzuki Band, for a few months I had every second Thursday a session at the pub Ruin, at its cellar in Cologne," remarks Damo of the music career that was shortly to go into hiatus. "The project was called Damo Suzuki & Friends. One regular member on drums was Thomas Hopf (Yellow Sunshine Explosion): later, I invited him for a US tour

171

as a member of Damo Suzuki's Network (with Michael Karoli), as my other Sound Carriers were changing. Also under this project name we performed in other places too.

"A bit later I was making music with Thomas Dinger and Nils Kristiansen; the project was called 1A Düsseldorf.* We did only one concert at Königsallee, in the middle of Düsseldorf. We were mainly playing just for ourselves at the cellar of Thomas's house."

But mostly, the nineties would constitute a creative break for Damo which lasted almost eight years. It was at the end of this period that The Damo Suzuki Band – which had previously followed a 'no recordings' policy – had their semi-improvised sound captured on disc.

"In 1997 Piet Manns listened to some of this material and wanted to release it from his label, as he'd released Dunkelziffer before," he confirms. In the event, *Vernissage*, with its intricate hand-drawn cover, would be issued on a label called (pre-emptively) Damo's Network, in a collaboration with Manns, proprietor of small independent label Fünfundvierzig. This would be followed by *P.R.O.M.I.S.E.*, a seven-CD box-set archive of selected band performances.

"The CD covers of *P.R.O.M.I.S.E.* were accused by some people of sexism!" says Damo of its tinged composite images of a naked woman in motion, hiding her face. As ever, he has an idiosyncratic interpretation. "They had the seven different colours of the rainbow as a motif. The rainbow was meant to be HOPE (God's promise to Noah)."

But these were now commemorative works – no longer a project in motion itself.

"The Damo Suzuki Band were kind of my friends," he acknowledges, drawing a contrast between then and now. "I knew them all, so it was a little bit different to Damo Suzuki's Network. Because now I am performing with people that I never met before – afterwards they are my friends, but at the time we've only just met. If you know the members of the band you know the chemistry, and the chemistry flows quite easily because you know them. But now I am doing a different thing, much more of an adventure.

---

* An obvious play on La Düsseldorf, the band in which Thomas had joined with his brother, the mercurial Klaus.

"At The Damo Suzuki Band live performances I occasionally recorded them, because it has much more meaning for an instant composer – it's really live and we cannot play in a studio to machines, because there's no audience and music is communication. Communication is not only between the musician's brain and the recording that is one day going to be released. I'm not so interested in working in this way; 90 per cent of the bands are doing this, but a lot of our music now is the audience – that is Damo Suzuki's Network.

"Because it's played live on the stage, now we're creating the concert together with the audience feedback. They come without knowing anything – except that Damo Suzuki is playing, and maybe some unknown local Sound Carriers are also there. Also it's different every time – we don't 'cover' ourselves, in the musical field we're just the opposite."

ALEXANDER SCHÖNERT
Yellow Sunshine Explosion / Jelly Planet

When I was ten, twelve, fourteen, I don't know how old, I was into heavy metal, I wanted to sound like Jimi Hendrix and Metallica. All these bands here in my hometown of Dortmund, in West Germany, wanted to sound like somebody – like Red Hot Chili Peppers, Rage Against The Machine, whatever, all the idols we have. The same with me. But when I got into Can – when I was eighteen, nineteen, smoking pot instead of drinking beer and stuff like that – I developed self-consciousness and wanted not to be a cheap copy of American and English music, I wanted to be a German musician.

It was a good opportunity to play this kind of 'krautrock': repetitive, typical German, straight and let's say 'disciplined' stuff. It's a good term, krautrock, it's a German thing and not an American or English thing – though it's an English term because of the world war, and because we all just eat sauerkraut! [laughs] It's fun, I like it!

I think the most important thing that we learned from, for example, Jaki Liebezeit or the Neu! drummer, Klaus Dinger, is that they always played the same rhythm to give some kind of trance feeling, some kind of meditative repetition. It might be a good idea as a guitarist to follow this and to have a nice line that develops continuously, and you repeat it and repeat it until after a while the saliva slips out of your mouth! [laughs] If you're lucky!

173

I slipped into this well-known psychedelic sixties rock band from Dortmund called Yellow Sunshine Explosion – they decided, 'We don't play songs any more, we just go on stage and jam spontaneously,' and they invited me. Then we had this gig together with Damo at a little festival, I guess it was in 1988, and Damo played together with Jaki Liebezeit and Dominik von Senger. Before it was called the Damo Suzuki Network it was The Damo Suzuki Band.

We went to Cologne, it's just one hour from my town, and we were complete Can fans at the beginning of our twenties. We went to this gig and that was the first time I saw Damo live. We had a gig as a support band, before Damo – and he watched us, and he liked us very much, and he asked us: "I'm a bit bored with my band. Your band was so funny and you seem to be nice guys – can I visit you in Dortmund?"

The next weekend he came with his car and a case of beer, and he slept there. We smoked a lot; there were many, many hours of rehearsing and it was so nice, it was the start of him inviting us: "I've got a gig here, maybe the whole band will come? Or just you Alex – come with me to the Japan tour, to the US tour if you like," and so on. There was always a colourful mixture of musicians and many, many gigs since then.

He wants to be this individual singer Damo Suzuki, who was only from '70–'73 in Can, it's a very short amount of time. He never stopped playing music with different musicians, but for them Damo Suzuki is the Can singer and they're all Can fans. It's all played in the tradition of Can, in this kind of 'I'm not an egomaniac asshole playing solos all the night – we're just in the middle of a machine that works together to bring it all to a nice result.'

I think most of the hundreds of musicians Damo played with in the last twenty years have this idea. In the name of Can, in the name of krautrock: it would be cheesy if there's a blues band playing 12-bar blues shit. I like blues but it's not Damo's thing, I guess. It must be spontaneous, you cannot rehearse with him, you cannot have a soundcheck with him and say: "Hey, this sounds nice, let's do it the same!" He would say: "No, no, let's make it new!" And that's the thing.

"The feeling that is in music is what I was actually searching for after my surgery," testifies Damo of the late eighties period that pre-dated the Network. "It had so much impact – it's not the actual music itself, but still I didn't think I'd be making music. It was a stronger thing, the energy. I

174

wanted to have this energy, to create something and to extend myself further."

Energy is, in his definition, not just a byword for vitality or stamina. It is the life-force itself.

But in the aftermath of Damo Suzuki & Friends*, 'energy' would equate not so much with musical creativity as with another chance to wander the globe.

---

* The fortnightly live sessions that ran for two years after The Damo Suzuki Band – see above.

CHAPTER TEN

AFRICAN INTERLUDE

BY DAMO SUZUKI

In my life, two times I've made a so-called creative break for many years. (Also almost three years of forced holiday at the moment.)

From 1973 to 1984 and 1993 to 1997, I placed distance between my life and music. I didn't have any problem with this; in fact, music is not the very best thing in this world. Sure, music-making is one of the interesting things, but something behind it is more interesting: music is the tool to explain, let's say, passion, the longing and willing for it to last forever. I don't miss music that much if I have time to open up and enjoy the essence behind it.

'Adventure' is the word – sometimes I like to spend my time recklessly. It shouldn't have to be a geographical approach; in a way, every day we have space for adventure. At the beginning of the nineties I had this feeling: I had to travel to where I'd never been and go alone with a rucksack... the awakening of a romantic? Or a flashback to my teenage travel?

In the eighties and nineties, I had quite a few good African friends in Cologne, mainly musicians. They were quite happy people, smiling, surprising, optimistic figures. When they were most surprising (and they always seemed to be surprising) was when they made a loud 'ouh' in very high tones.

This is one of the reasons that brought me to West Africa; flying from Europe, I was in almost the same timezone. I also liked music from Mali (I began to hear Oumou Sangaré around this time), and it must have been in the middle of summer – how I imagined African life to be!

Mainly, Western tourists go there in the November to January period as the weather is quite bearable for them. In February it is not possible because of Harmattan, dry and dusty wind from the Sahara over West Africa. Sometimes you may not see even ten metres in front of you, it's really impossible to walk. Also, in the rainy season (European summertime) it is impossible to travel because of swarms of attacking mosquitoes.

For a long time I didn't have this kind of adventure. I was travelling mainly in Western countries and South-East Asia, where many tourists go, and to places for my performances. Those countries have long been open to visitors, they have good financial resources and you can find information in tourist guidebooks, it's easy to get.

No, I wanted to avoid going to such places. It seemed more worthwhile to spend my time and money on my own experience, not to visit famous buildings or take photos of nature as an alibi for tourism. I wanted to go for adventure!

There is another reason I wanted to take a trip to West Africa. Musically it's an interesting space: jazz, blues, samba, Cuban, gospel, etc. A heavy part of the Western music we hear today has roots in West Africa, brought by slaves.

Well, there were many interesting reasons to go for this trip. I took my first visit to West Africa one month in the March/April period of 1993. The plan was to visit Mali, Burkina Faso and Guinea (Conakry), all former French colonies. Even though I didn't understand French, it didn't matter. Anyway, it's much more interesting to travel to a country where I don't understand a bit of the language, it's part of an adventure, isn't it? To have difficulties adds meaning to my life, I love it.

The gateway to Bamako is Charles de Gaulle Airport; there were few Western tourists, instead there were stylish African ladies in their traditional costume, African gentleman with light-coloured suits without neckties and gold watches on their arm. Africa began here, so I felt like everybody else at the very beginning of a holiday – a simply childish, happy moment. As I expected, the flight was not full at all.

BAMAKO, MALI

In transit via Accra, I arrive at Aéroport International de Bamako-Sénou early afternoon. At immigration, everybody is in a hurry, running. I take an immigration form from the table. Gosh… it's all written in French. Every passenger is passing me.

I told a customs officer I didn't understand what was on the paper. He kindly said I should wait until all passengers were ready for immigration. As I was the last passenger, he filled out my paper.

Then he said: "I took time to help you, do you have some money for me?"

"What???" I thought he wanted to help me from kindness. I said, "I don't have any CFA francs." (In fact, I didn't want to pay the money he wanted for his service… he is paid as an officer and is making money for his pocket? I just don't agree with it.)

Then he asked me if I needed a ride to Bamako. I said no (he wanted more money, I was sure). The bank was not even open and the aeroplane arrived only a few times a day. *'So what shall I do?'* I wondered. *'I don't have domestic currency.'* Well, I had to find any solution. There must be a bus or something to Bamako, possibly I can pay in French francs.

Just a few steps out of the airport: "Gâteau, gâteau!" Six or seven young boys, not even teenage, follow me. They need some sweets? I don't know French at all – they may need food, drinks or money. It doesn't matter, I don't have domestic currency so I'm not able to buy.

I thought it better to just ignore them. If you give one thing to one boy then you have to give to all of them, and they may bring another group of gâteau boys who were playing around there… it's endless. So I ignored. This is good if you don't understand the language, you can act very natural.

The officer followed me and brought me to a taxi stand, still not believing I'd no domestic currency. I'd French francs but not coins. I explained to the driver and asked if this was okay. Before I finished talking he agreed; within the smile in his eyes, I could see already the fancy paper shining.

Anyway, I was quite tired and stressed by what had happened until now. I was in a hurry to move. I threw my rucksack on the backseat and myself into the cab – which is not possible for you to imagine as a vehicle, it was scrap, no use outside of a museum. It was probably more than thirty years old, it seemed ready to break down in the next second. There were some other cabs but this one actually looked better than the others, so I took it, as the driver also understood a bit of English.

The way to Bamako wasn't so far, maybe ten kilometres or so. Driving in the dusty streets, even at crazy speeds, it still took around half an hour or more. I didn't have any sense of time, it was like I was stoned.

Listen! You have to take every second day a malaria tablet that is very strong, you're feeling stoned... you should take them from two weeks before the start of your journey, during travel and also two weeks after too. It has side effects, damages the liver. So this is the reason I don't travel to countries where I have to take this tablet nowadays. Anyway, I'm much older than that time; I was fresh as a fish at the time of this trip.

So I'd been stoned before I started this travelling; the heat of the African summer made me feel more high. I didn't terminate anywhere in Bamako, I didn't have any address to reach; the driver took me to Grand Marche, one of the markets that seemed to be in the centre of the city. I was stoned on my first journey to black Africa; it didn't make any sense to make trouble with the driver over the taxi charge. I paid two or three times more than I expected, he got what he wanted. The main thing is that I arrived at my first destination.

Grand Marche is huge, but easy to miss (even if you don't have any place to go particularly). The market is one of most interesting places all over the world: people are there, you feel the atmosphere, 'Life' is there. It gives so much information: the smells of living, the standards of living, etc. At the marketplace I was also followed by 'gâteau' kids, this is normal for travellers here. I was almost every day surrounded by young kids.

Well, what I have to do now, for sure, is find accommodation for tonight without paying CFA. I'd like to take a shower, then get something to eat... that's the very natural flow as a newly arrived tourist in this kind of temperature. I'm so wet from this heat, surely over 45°c in the shade, I need to relax.

I found a pension not far from Grand Marche: no window, the room was dark (therefore cool) even in daylight, the old main ventilator on the ceiling faltering and shaking. Bed came with a thin textile – I don't know the last time they changed the bed sheet – and a bucket with water. That's all. There wasn't even any floor, it was feet directly to ground.

Sure, there are some hotels for Western tourists with something near to Western standards. But I'm not just a low-budget traveller, I like to experience a country's standards. If I'm in Africa, I like to live like everyday Africans! I don't like to behave like a colonist with filled pockets.

Went to the toilet which was separated outside; you wash your ass with water in a plastic teapot after you finish your product. Then I went to eat. There is a café for the military which even tourists like me can use; I ordered an ice-cold beer (yes, there is!). There were few local people who came to try to take conversation with me. Seems that it wasn't so often that Asian people came here.

I was in quite a good mood after almost a day without speaking with people. Opposite this military bar was a restaurant; they didn't have a menu card but they spoke something in French. I wanted to eat something with rice, which they understood; it wasn't long to wait before the man brought me a meal – it was quite a huge amount, not possible to eat alone, probably for four people, so spontaneously I invited some men to eat, drink and talk together at a table placed on the street.

We had enough to eat. It was my first meal in Africa, rice, vegetables and dried meat in one pot – and the good thing was I could pay in francs in these places. I went to bed quite early and easily as I had to digest much information, stoned from malaria tablets and the heat around me. The room was warm but cooler than outside; the ventilator shook and made noise and melted away. I fell down in a deep sleep.

Next morning I went again to the market to look around shops and some interesting domestic goods, after taking breakfast with lemon tea and a baguette. Everything I saw was exotic and I felt a culture shock: second-hand glasses, clothes from Europe, probably for some organisation to help Africa connected with the Goodwill people. These wares were making money?

Some kids are following me, like yesterday: "Gâteau, gâteau!" Kids are marching everywhere I go, they don't go away; I stay like my shadow. I tolerate them, treat it as accompanying music, then I don't feel bothered.

"Avez-vous besoin d'un guide?" First he spoke in French as I stood there not understanding. "Do you need a guide?" He was a smart young man, but for what did I need a guide? I came here for adventure, but in a poor country like this there's a bunch of men looking for spontaneous jobs as tourist guides.

I say, "Sorry, I don't need a guide, I like to get into people here." He is still hanging around me. He might have enough time and curiosity to talk. He introduces himself as Sergey; it's a Russian name, not African, but people here have quite often European names.

"I'm a singer, I've interest to research this country, this is my first trip to black Africa."

"Oh, I'm singer too," his answer came before I finished my sentence.

"What kind of music you're singing?"

"Originally I came from Senegal, I'm African reggae singer."

If you find some similarity then it's easy to communicate. He was a nice-looking guy, which made him seem trustworthy. In his eyes I found something sympathetic.

"Can I help you anything?"

I didn't change to domestic money, I paid everything until now with French francs. So I asked him to go with me to change my money to domestic CFA, like 300 or 400 francs.

It took many minutes to receive this amount of money in CFA. It was really astonishing, I got an amount of paper money back that left me feeling like a millionaire. As the currency there is low and people don't use much paper money of any value, I put all those bundles in my rucksack. In Mali, people are getting around US$2 average for a day job, so as you can imagine, I'm now cash-rich.

(During all my travels this bundle of money didn't get any less, as every day I could live on such a low amount.)

We hang around in the city, I invite him to eat and drink. We're getting friendly, we're on a similar level, there are many things to talk about, this and that. Then I remember that I didn't book accommodation for tonight as I wasn't so happy with the room last night.

"Do you know any hotel? But not in Western style – I'm in Africa, I'd like to live like African."

Sergey replied: "I've good idea, I have small cabin at outskirts of the city. If you like you can stay there, of course I don't ask you for money. I can stay at my girlfriend, no problem, but it's in ghetto."

He understood that I liked to live like an African while in Africa.

In Africa, sunset comes suddenly. The sun was up in the sky, the next moment it fell down and suddenly it became completely dark.

Sergey brought me to the ghetto, across the city of Bamako. In the darkness I could see only people's eyes; it's a scary feeling if you see only their eyes, partly yellow, some of them red.

I don't know how long I walked with him. It felt like quite a long time as many eyes in the air were watching me, some of them following me. In darkness only dull moonshine helped me to walk in front. I was unable to see my footsteps, it was so dark. All the way along we didn't have any electric light. If I didn't take care, I'd drop into the ridge.

There was a really dull light at the ghetto. We passed a small, open-roofed textile factory, then entered one space where four small houses were standing. In the middle was a small garden. Sergey showed me his cabin. It was around 6 p.m. There was actually nothing inside, only naked ground. I brought my sleeping bag, and also mosquito nets.

I set them up and went out to the garden. Sergey was speaking with a woman carrying her baby on her back. A boy around fifteen years old was studying mathematics under really dull light. Living in such a poor ghetto, he was willing to study even under a naked bulb, probably only 40w or less. He was studying for his future – and yes, it impressed me.

Sergey prepared mint tea, which is very common in Africa. (I enjoyed this in Morocco a few years later too.) Fresh mint leaves and gunpowder tea mix with much sugar; the teapot flows into a glass; repeat this many times until the tea gets enough foam. This is a kind of ceremony, an African hospitality ritual, and it's really good drinking it in that heat. Tradition has wisdom.

When later Sergey went to his girlfriend, I went to the cabin. Later, one of the women of the neighbourhood brought me food: baguette, salad in milk sauce and Lipton tea with a friendly, shy, smiling face. I wasn't expecting it; Sergey arranged for her to bring food.

I stayed at his cabin for three days; every morning one of the women brought me breakfast and every evening a small snack. I was really pleased by his kindness and the friendly housewives who tried to communicate with me. I didn't expect this; I was almost crying for happiness. Now I was in the middle of African life.

The first night there I fell into a deep sleep very soon. I was tired not only from the baking sun but from all the information, which was too much. I felt it with my body and soul very intensely, but I was happy.

I woke up quite early with some interesting music going on around me. But first I heard flying mosquitoes making noise outside the nets, then a small group of lizards parading on the tinplate roof around 4 a.m. Then, a few minutes later, the singing of a prayer from a mosque at sunrise followed.

Mali is an Islamic country. This voice came with the morning fresh air; then, at around 5 a.m., housewives were cleaning the garden with tree branches and cleaning their teeth with tree bark. Suddenly all those sounds were mixing; it was incredibly interesting. My ear was deeply curious to catch them.

After the breakfast one of the housewives brought, I went to sleep again. I was sure I'd crushed a malaria tablet, but I was so stoned from yesterday. My brain didn't allow me to begin the day.

In the afternoon, I woke up and wanted to go to daily work... or rather I wanted to go to the toilet, my stomach seemed to be having trouble. "Where is toilet?" I asked one of the women. She brought me a plastic teapot with water and took me to a communal latrine (with all four families sharing).

It was in the backyard of this small commune, outside, covered all around with a low wall. In the middle of it was a low basin with a hole; I had to make my product there. It was okay when I sat down as no one could see, but if I stood at that basin just about anybody on the street was able to see me.

I was probably the first Japanese or foreigner there in this ghetto; small children were very curious about this guy from Mars. While I was trying to sit on the basin, kids were watching me. In such a situation I was not able to make my daily duty. So I got back to my cabin and later went to the city with a bit of stomach trouble – even though I was able to finish dinner. Next day I went to a museum that was closed; I asked the caretaker if I could use the WC. After I finished I felt really fresh and my stomach pain was gone.

But it was really nice to stay there, in the middle of African social life. They're always so friendly, smiling even though they don't have much. They gave me positive energy for sure.

SEGOU, MALI

Next stop was Segou. I took a full public bus for 235 kilometres north-east of Bamako.

Segou has still many French colonial-style buildings. The size of the city is about one tenth of Bamako (population 1.5 million); it was so quiet there and very clean. I wanted to arrange some African-style accommodation, but instead I found Hotel France – a European hotel with its own shower room. It's very important that at any time I can take a shower. I thought and decided, *'It's really hot. Without even one hour for a short shower and lie-down, it's not possible to go out.'* My motivation was that if I don't go out, I miss something.

Early in the morning or at night it was possible go out. Like any other city in Mali, young kids kept coming: "Gâteau, gâteau!" At the hotel reception, I got quite close to a guy working there called Frank, as he spoke English. He invited me to his place, a real African living space on the ground, and I asked him if we could eat traditional West African food.

On some parts of my journey, I asked people to cook home-made food; generally, they were happy they didn't have to buy, this strange figure from another planet was paying for all ingredients from the market. That was enough for a big family of fifteen people or so.

No, please don't misunderstand, this is playing like I'm a supporter of colonialism... I just wanted to experience African life, eat together, drink together with them.

Frank said his cousin could cook really well. We went to the market, bought what she needed. For a few hours we relaxed at Frank's place, taking a shower, staying in the shade, watching the stylish ladies walking very slowly but elegantly outside.

It was the very best decision, his cousin was an excellent chef... it was yummy, the best food I ever had on this West African journey. What she cooked was Senegalese food for weddings; as far as I can remember it's called *zame*.

It's a rice dish with eggplant, some vegetables, fresh local fish from the River Niger and salad. They don't have many cooking tools, it's all done in one big pot. First put enough peanut oil (this is very common in this part of West Africa) into the pan. Fry fresh fish until it has a crispy skin; put on another dish, then comes a whole eggplant into the pan; then carrot and cabbage in the same oil. Stir-fried vegetables are on another plate, keep them warm. Then fry rice adding tomato, tomato ketchup and small slivers of chives. When rice is ready, put fish and vegetables in pot again. Serve all together. Side dish is salad in milk sauce (this I had so often on my journey). Be sure to eat it with your hands.

Frank's cabin had a coolness that shut out hot air from outside. I was in the middle of the cabin watching people walk by. Actually, you didn't have to travel that much; just stay at one point and watch people. It's a culture shock anyway. It was like Warhol's twenty-four-hour Manhattan movie – but this was not boring, it was in the middle of a heatwave and the smells of a hot summer.

Next day I walked down to the Niger. On the way I heard percussion sounds coming from one cabin. I looked inside out of my insatiable curiosity. Two young percussionists were playing their *djembe*: they'd made their instrument themselves, as local musicians usually do there.

Frank and I went together to the bank of the Niger, to see the sunset. I felt I was in the middle of West Africa; it was an amazing feeling, far away from civilisation, watching the sunset from the banks of a huge river. African rhythms always bring some people from somewhere and a party begins.

This trip, I didn't make any plans, just staying at a place as long as I liked. It's not necessary to travel to all parts of a country and anyway, my flight back to Europe was from Conakry, Guinea. I should be there at least on departure day, but if I travelled this way I'd miss Burkina Faso...

Travel in Africa is better if you don't plan anything, improvising every day. People there have the talent of improvising, so no hurry, walk don't run. Every day is a new movie; without planning it, something happens and you just live with the time flow. For example, if you take the bush taxi, generally they won't start exactly on time, they wait until all seats are filled up.

Imagine any light van, filled up with twelve, thirteen people plus luggage – sometimes a passenger even brings a living animal. You go to the bush taxi office, ask for the schedule to your desired direction. I come back to the office at the scheduled time; they say I should come back three hours later; then I come again three hours later, they may say I should go back in another two or three hours. If you are lucky, six hours later than scheduled is relatively good. Once I waited more than fifteen hours, but it's okay... it's my holiday, why should I get stressed? Everything is totally different, any situation I can enjoy.

When the long-awaited bush taxi starts, probably a half-hour later, it will break down. The taxi is thirty, forty years old, its floor has holes like Emmental cheese. In Europe, they'd never get licences to drive it because of the calculable danger.

Generally, they have a driver and co-driver – or pilot and co-pilot. With this almost broken-down old vehicle, they drive crazy – like F1 drivers, left to right, right to left to avoid getting into holes in the road. If the tyre gets into deep sand and it's not possible to get out, then it's time for the co-pilot to proudly take his shovel or any tools to free the tyre. If this is not solved, all passengers have to get out of the vehicle and push it until it's free to move. The pilot is also very flexible; when he had trouble with some small spare parts once, he saw my Swiss army knife: "Lend me your knife!" He disappeared for fifteen minutes in the bush, came back with handmade spare parts and our journey was safe to continue.

There's a nightclub in Segou, I went there out of curiosity. There were many dandy guys and attractive, well-dressed ladies; I was the only guy with wet, sandy, smelly T-shirts. They moved elegantly, dancing to the local music and sipping long drinks.

I met two French guys in Segou; you don't see many tourists from another continent, so I wanted to get information on the places I'd be going to in a few days. They both had beautiful local girlfriends so I had to leave them alone. French people with l'amour are everywhere, it may be their trademark or in their DNA or something.

During my stay, I found postcards of Segou. I bought eight cards to send to my friend, but strangely, none of them arrived. They may have been of interest to someone who was collecting foreign-language postcards.

DJENNÉ, MALI

On arrival, I was already quite stressed with the locals. They were forcing me to let one of them be my tourist guide. They were being naughty and extortionate: "If you don't take me as guide something will happen to you today." How they were saying it was aggressive, I felt danger and other visitors there felt the same.

We all went quickly from one place to another, followed by local people and many small kids. They were saying I cannot see this interesting place without a guide. I met three Germans and a Japanese tourist having the same problem; so we were forced to have a guide, not only for this place but even for a few days in Dogon.

Even if you don't know Djenné, you may know the very famous clay-built Great Mosque that became a World Heritage site. The whole city is made out of clay and it's a labyrinth. Once you get into it you may lose your orientation. This city is worth seeing even if people are pushing you, forcing you to take them as a guide with the threat of violence.

I stayed for a few hours then went directly to Dogon. It was the shortest stay on this trip, a very interesting place but the atmosphere wasn't as good as the villages.

Nowadays there are many World Heritage subjects, but I'm not interested in UNESCO's choice. It's almost like Michelin stars to me. People visit there as they have the stamp of World Heritage, it's mainstream and in a way manipulative. Human activity is everywhere interesting, it's not necessary to be guided from somewhere. This kind of automatism makes me queasy. I can find interesting places by myself, just like I can find interesting food.

So, from now on, we were two Japanese and three Germans guided by a local guy. He knew I liked to smoke ganja and was interested in other local goods. On the journey with him I had much contact with Dogon people, I have to say. This was also the first and last time I travelled with a few people together; it made for another experience.

The three Germans came from Düsseldorf; they were all the same age, went to the same school, two males and one female. The nature of three people travelling is that one is always spokesman of the group and the others follow. They were all like German people I knew from home. (Once my friend Tommy, a Sound Carrier from LA, said to me at Venice Beach: "Damo, you know how to find German men here? They have shorts on and black socks!")

The spokesman was a scientist researching the hearts of flies in Bonn for a couple of years. The Japanese guy was a world traveller, crisscrossing the planet from the West – he had been to North and South America, Europe, now he was visiting Africa. He'd been already three years on the road.

DOGON, MALI
Dogon is probably one of the reasons tourists from Western countries visit Mali. This is an amazing place; we visited a few villages in five days.

It's also on a plateau which it is only possible to walk by foot. The African guide and German trio walked so quickly, as if they had a different compass. I was always at the back. One good thing with this domestic guide guy is that he connected us to local folk and brought us to some attractions like village music-fest evenings.

But I'm able to do all these things and arrange them alone. At that point I didn't have any responsibility for it, so I just enjoyed a bit of group travelling.

We had accommodation in cabins; mainly I slept on the roof. I climbed on special stairs with steps made out of a tree. On the roof is the best place to sleep in this area; in the middle of the night it's still red heat, but quite smooth.

Watching the sky is a festival of stars. You may never see that many stars, it's a kind of traffic jam; in civilisation, lights shut stars out of the night sky. It was really amazing to see stars and to think about the many things that had happened on this trip, for example. I also thought about my family as I followed the direction of a star; the future; the past; fantasy visions. Suddenly, the night curtain brought me to deep sleep. Waking up on the roof, it was beautiful to see the sun come up.

I like to sleep outside; my friend Tommy wondered why I slept always in his garden while I was in LA. But, strangely, I'm not fond of camping. My life is not always well balanced!

Unfortunately, I didn't notice where I was in this beautiful, amazing experience at Dogon. It might be because I was travelling *en bloc*, with a group of people. In a way, if I travel alone I'm much more concentrated, feel all things intensely, everything comes direct.

We drank African beer from a kora vessel passed by locals; it's weak, warm beer (there is no refrigerator, not even electricity) but good under hot sun like this. The action radius is limited in West Africa: between eleven and four it's not good to move, better to stay quiet under a tree or find some shadow; 45°c in the shade is the temperature, you have to change T-shirts every three hours, it's really getting wet, sweat is pouring. If you find a bucket of water it's an incredibly fresh feeling.

All over Mali, every day is a pure new experience, a culture shock. Dogon people are living like hundreds of years ago. Their community is still the system of ancient times. It's always the oldest that decides the fortunes of the village, then there are a few older men who support him. Their economy is agriculture and domesticated animals.

One day we visited an Animist priest.

He was living in the middle of a cliff, he just came down to the village once a year for a ceremony. In his holy place there were a few ropes hanging from the top of the cliff, I could also see many holes there. When he felt it was time to rest forever, he'd choose one of those holes and climb there to lay down in peace. There were a few tools to make sacrifice; an old, wooden, curved puppet figure; a place to make fire. All things here were quite mystical and magical, so I didn't really get into it.

In West Africa, you don't meet old people who live to be eighty or something. Life expectancy is low, something like the middle forties when I was there at the beginning of the nineties. So in cases where I gave my age they treated me so well and respectfully, giving me their hand to shake.

One night was really horrible, like I felt I was freezing in a hot pan.

There are some places where you may find ruins of buildings from the French colonial period; one night we slept in the garden of this French-style ruin with another group of tourists. In the middle of the night I felt I had to go to the toilet; one French guy had just done his duties and came out with a candle in his hand. "This direction is toilet," he explained. So I went into a huge room with a pot in the middle.

The room was dark even in the moonlight. I entered and then I heard a strange sound, as if my feet were crushing something. I sat on the pot in candlelight. Then I saw the room fill up with thousands (really, thousands!) of cockroaches; no space was free.

I recognised I was crushing these ugly insects, now I could see them in the candlelight. I just ran out of that spot quickly, but really quickly. My feet were shaking with the ugly feeling that came from the floor. It was really awful!

I had no more feeling that I wanted to produce anything. It was suddenly really freezing on a hot night.

Dogon is such an amazing place, a very special place. Village people live in ancient times, with no stress. If it's too hot in the middle of the day, they just rest under the tree, drink mint tea, talk about this and that. They're talking only about their own experience. Everybody has enough time, the community works really well, nobody bothers anybody.

MOPTI, MALI

We spent a few hours walking to Bandiagara to take the bush taxi to our next stop, Mopti. Mopti is reached by the Niger and Bani rivers. Its main parts are on three islands, therefore they are called the 'Venice of Mali'. It's quite a lively city, with as much atmosphere of African life as you can imagine.

I said goodbye to the three Germans and one Japanese. I was interested to go to Timbuktu, like their plan, and they asked me to come. But there's no road to Timbuktu, you have to use a canoe to get there and it takes one week. One week each to get there and back to Mopti would lose two weeks of my adventure.

Timbuktu is kind of a dream. I decided I'd go there one time, but from Fes in Morocco to Timbuktu by camel riding across the Sahara, on an all-inclusive trip for forty-eight days.

I also wanted to go back to a lone traveller's life again, I like to experience very special moments on my own. Anyway, if I went to Timbuktu, I'd not be able to take a flight back to Europe from Conakry and my vacation would be over. Unfortunately, I'd only fourteen days more for my first adventure in West Africa.

Mopti is traditionally inhabited by the Bozo, fishing folk. The market there is amazing. There are tons of dried fishes that smell strong in the open air.

I met two teenaged local boys who were so kind as to guide me and even gave me a place to stay. I stayed in Mopti for two days. It was amazing. The boys were respectful and so welcoming; they were happy to be together with this strange figure from Europe (or Asia). They were also happy to share, saying, "Whatever you need, we can prepare things for you."

One of the boys was named Sabo; his parents seemed to be rich as he had a light motorbike and his family had a TV. (Imagine, at that time only 2,000 TVs existed all over Mali!) His brother made handicraft, making interesting wooden masks for tourists. (I bought two of them as souvenirs.) On my leaving day, they brought me to the bus station; they were there until my bus went down on the horizon, two young African boys under a big, grilling sun.

190

I went back directly to Bamako via Segou to set off for Guinea. At a village where I had to stay for a few hours for connecting, I saw football games on an empty square; national teams from different countries but also teams of refugees. At this point, I didn't know about refugees. Later I recognised, sadly, that neighbouring countries like Sierra Leone and Liberia have been in crisis for many generations. But it was good just to watch the amateur games, to kill time waiting for bus connections.

I waited only three hours at Bamako bus station to change bus for Kourémalé, the border village to Guinea. Arriving shortly before midnight, there were only a few people wanting to cross the border. Unfortunately, the border office was closed: "You can go this way, and you can find place to rest yourself until office is open." You had to wait until 7 a.m. the next morning.

Everything here was in darkness, just moonlight or starlight. I walked forward and then I stepped on something. 'Something' cried loudly to the sky, as if in pain.

I was shocked, taking a few steps backward. Some sheep had awoken from a deep sleep and ran spontaneously in any direction. They were surprised, but I guess I was surprised more as I didn't expect animals sleeping peacefully on the borderline.

After this shock, I arrived at an old house where I was going to lay myself on the floor. Already there was a guy there. "Can I sleep here?" "Just anywhere you like." At this moment he put his mattress on the floor. I found a place closer to the outside.

I was really tired from the long bus and bush-taxi trip, it was a long way from Mopti to here. It didn't take many minutes to fall into a deep sleep.

I slept really well. I wanted to lie for longer but already the sun had been up for a few hours, so it was better to begin my next steps to my next destination. My next surprise came when I put my sleeping bag into my rucksack, then a very curious mantis showed his face. It seems that while I slept in this space, he slept in my bag.

SIGUIRI, GUINEA

Not much time to wait, I got a stamp on my passport. (There were only a few people.)

I've quite often a huge appetite whether I'm travelling or at home. First I took a short walk to the village to change my francs to GNF (Guinean francs) at a tiny exchange office ('office' is not really the word), then I'd get to satisfy my stomach. It's an easy thing to find places to eat: just go in the direction the smells come from, then my walk will be lighter.

A dish full of rice and cooked vegetables looked and tasted like mangold. I found a place to sit down where local people enjoyed their breakfast; some ordered baguette and sheep's milk. I just had Evian, it was enough. Food wasn't that bad for the start of the day, it gave me energy. But it was a huge portion.

Today's goal was Siguiri. Went to the village centre to book a bush taxi for the morning: "Please come back in two hours."

So I just walked around, and found myself quite dirty from the sand and sweat of the last few days. I asked one guy who was working in his small backyard if I could have a bucket of water to use for showering. He was kind enough to send me to his shower space. From early morning the sun is g-r-i-l-l-i-n-g, so the freshness of the water was really fantastic!

I still had enough time, so I decided to make a product on the field. This scene was watched by the village policeman. He called me to come to the police office as soon as I finished my duties.

At the office there were dozens of questions, but mainly the police wanted a 'passing fee'. I explained I paid enough for a visa fee in Germany, so why did I have to pay extra? "We need passing fee paid through every village in this country." In fact it's not that much money for us, but for people working there, getting less than US$2 a day in value, it makes a difference. Anyway, this money will be in the pocket of the police.

Mali and Guinea (Conakry) are French-speaking countries, but even so I was communicating with them. They were speaking French and I was answering with English, but I'd been travelling these French-speaking countries for a few weeks so I understood. If you have plenty of time for conversation, you come to this point.

I was even able to discuss customs with the police. Amazing! But I didn't have that much time to argue, I had an appointment at the bush taxi... I just took the easy way and paid the money they asked.

It was a heat-grilled village; there were a few people walking very slowly, many sat and resting under the shade. I reached the bush-taxi office. "Please come in three hours, we have still enough seats free." So I had to wait again. Things go like this, you have to be patient. Bush taxi is a business; if they cannot fill every seat their takings are low.

I took the bush taxi on this journey many times; it was mainly a light van, normally for five or six passengers in our part of the world. But these bush taxis fit twelve to thirteen passengers tight. Many come from tiny villages in the middle of nowhere, not even on the map, so they have a huge sack to carry, they bought something in the bigger village or they're bringing some goods themselves. All luggage goes on the roof of taxis or finds a place underfoot. Sometimes you can even find a living animal like a goat on the roof.

It's crazy tight. 'Uncomfortable' is not the word – it sounds too comfortable compared with this situation! Many people sit shoulder to shoulder, knee to knee, for hours of driving. One's bottom is on someone else's knee. On a hot and dusty road, everybody smells from endlessly pouring sweat. This situation, the loud cassettes of highlife music and Bob Marley, the hero of the Third World... this is pure West Africa to me. It's easy to bring this situation to mind even now. I can smell it, I can conjure the exact visions, it's my first Africa trip and I can imagine it.

I was able to take the bush taxi eight hours later than its original departure time. You have to have enough time. There are always some curiosities, even in a small village.

This day I passed many villages; the first bush-taxi stop was at a police office. (Gosh, so many police in this country!) Pay another pass fee. It's really stressful.

Then I reached the bank of the Niger River. I bought a ferry ticket, then a militarily-dressed guy with a machine gun came to me and asked for a pass fee. I don't know exactly how much I'd paid already. I said: "I passed many villages, I paid enough money, I'm not intend to pay..."

Then he came very much closer and pointed at me with his machine gun. I almost pissed my trousers. He took all my local money, just changed this morning, from my pocket. It was good luck that I'd bought my ferry ticket already. The rest of my currency in francs I'd hidden deep in my rucksack. But I'd no local currency and there was no bank either here or in the next village.

Anyway, I ate my baguette and drank Evian before reaching the opposite side of the river. There I saw an old guy sitting with domestic musical instruments. He was blind. I asked him if he could play music for me to forget this bad experience, as I love Africa; I had to forget this bad thing had happened.

He understood what I said, took his musical instrument (not a kora, something else with bass strings on it) and began to play and sing with his beautiful, deep, bass voice. His voice got naturally deeper and deeper but it wasn't disturbing, just free space.

Then came many women who were washing clothes in the river and began to sing with him; then many kids who were playing in the water came and sang. They made circles around the blind singer and me. I was in the middle of a circle with at least fifty people singing for me!

I tell you, this moment was the best concert I've ever experienced. It was an incredible, emotional scene I'll never forget in my life. At that moment I felt the warmth of people from every direction.

Then I went to the next bush-taxi station, deciding to pay in francs. All those people followed me to the bush taxi; fortunately, I wouldn't wait so long. I suppose that, as Siguiri is a city, many passengers were going in this direction.

On the way to Siguiri, the bush taxi had a problem. Curious policemen came and looked at me, a very strange person from another planet – especially a beautiful police lady who wanted to show me her karate technique. I've never been interested in fighting sports so I just avoided her, but the lady police officer was, in a way, charming.

In Siguiri I stayed only for sleep, then went to...

KANKAN, GUINEA

Kankan is the third biggest city in Guinea. I don't know why I stayed there for three days. Maybe the name of the city seemed friendly. I didn't have much information for this trip, so where I stayed and where I'd go just came from the feeling of the moment.

In the last stage of travel from Siguiri, fortunately, friendly soldiers drove me up to Kankan. My accommodation was quite near to their military base. Whenever I walked in front of the base some soldiers waved their hands.

They recommended me to stay at a kind of pension; it had enough space for me, maybe more than enough. It was the largest room I had on this trip so far, with a window I could open in the middle of the night for a bit of coolness. In the middle of the room I put a mosquito net on the bed. On the ceiling was a lazy ventilator, but it still helped.

The guy running this accommodation was a friendly person who spoke a bit of English; he also worked as an open-air bartender and as a cook grilling meat and fish. He was just everywhere. He knew much information about the city, where the girls were, also where to find a kora maker.

Under a tree would be my special place for the next few days. Late at night, people would slowly arrive there; some were in military clothes, some seemed to belong to high society – beautiful ladies in costume. It was not boring, even if it was on the outskirts of the city. Some interesting people came there to talk and to enjoy the grill and beer. The nights were long. Even though I wasn't part of it, I had an amazing three days there watching them. You were just dropped in the middle of what was happening, watching a living movie in cyclorama. (You know this cinema style?) Everybody made interesting gestures and actions; it was probably a good place to study character, it's a pity I'm not a screenwriter.

As with everywhere I had been on this trip, highlife music made people dance and laugh. It was party time. Of course I talked to some girls there – but they were so young, mainly teenagers.

On the last day I ordered a kora, to get it ready to send to Germany. (I got this safely after two months, by the way.)

KANKAN – KOUROUSSA – MAMOU – KINDIA, GUINEA

There is no choice of route from Kankan to Conakry by bus. It may take a whole day or more; it's around 500 kilometres in distance and it was my last stage of this trip. The traffic office couldn't really give an arrival time. At this point I felt delay was normal; I'm patient enough, no stress, it doesn't matter how long it takes to reach my destination.

Travel by bus was still the most uncomfortable, but air and rail were often not trustworthy here so I'd no other way. On the bus there were no seat reservations and everybody had much luggage as usual. It started slow, not even getting that much faster later; the road was not asphalted and was in a terrible condition.

As I said before, the African sun seems to drop down so quickly. We'd drive for a few hours and stop at some village; the passengers would get something to eat and a cold drink due to the heat; mainly they didn't bring their own food, they'd buy at the stop.

Everywhere on this trip I experienced very special moments: housewives selling home-made foods; children asking you to buy something like a toy car handmade out of a can. A small village is busy when the bus arrives.

I spend two nights travelling on the bus. It wasn't comfortable, my bottom was sore. But still, I was not bored as I had an attractive teenage girl travelling to Conakry on the seat beside me. With hand gestures, we could understand each other well.

The bus trip was quite dangerous, even when driving slowly. Mountain after mountain, up and down, up and down, on such narrow roads without asphalt. When a car came from the front we had to find space, back up or crawl forward, losing time again.

Two hours before arrival, I saw a very beautiful and peaceful landscape. It was the most dreamlike image I'd ever seen, I still have it in my head after so many years. There were intensely coloured lights; many trees; here and there were small houses. It's very difficult to explain with words. I've travelled more than enough in my life, yet still this landscape was fantastic. I was really happy to be there, this place and its view had never been in any tourist guidebook or photo book. It was really a pleasure to find a place like this, part of Fouta Djallon – a small village I cannot find on any map.

CONAKRY, GUINEA
Now I can see the Atlantic Ocean. The bus enters Conakry at the top of the peninsula. It's the end of a long bus trip.

I'll stay here a few days, then my first West African trip is over. It's the second biggest city on my trip after Bamako, with a million and a half inhabitants, many European buildings and Western-style hotels. I arrange for myself African-style accommodation near the marketplace.

(I cannot remember its name, there are many markets in Conakry. I like markets everywhere, they're living places, meeting places, with fresh products from the locals.)

I found a group of men wearing tricot at the hotel, I asked at reception who they were.

"They're national football team from Botswana, they're here for African cup qualification."

"When is the match?"

"Tomorrow."

As a huge football fan, I have to go to an African stadium one time to see it. *I have to go there!* So I've a plan for tomorrow already.

That night I went near to the beach road where musicians meet, a small bar and grill recommended by the hotel personnel. Two petrol cans were used for the grill, with a nice smoky smell to create atmosphere.

A few musicians talk of their experiences abroad. The sun is setting on the horizon. I'm watching them and enjoying one of the last days of my first trip to West Africa. Drinking beer and eating meat on a pike. The tiredness of two days on a hard bus trip slowly melts away.

I took the same breakfast as usual, French bread and mint tea with much sugar, creamy mango. Walked around to enjoy the breeze of the Atlantic.

In the afternoon, I went to the match: Guinea vs. Botswana. There were many people at the front square of Stade du 28 Septembre. Even on the masts there were a few crazy football fans hanging.

The capacity of the stadium is not huge, probably around 25,000. Many people had no ticket, some tried to break in or climb the entrance. Police were hitting people, dragging them to the truck. It was almost like a war there. As a foreigner, you could not believe it was reality.

Many people ran away from the police. It was hard to get inside, but a service guy at the entrance looked at me and signalled me to come to him. The stadium was really filled up tight with fans. When I got to my place, the match had already begun ten minutes ago. It was exciting to see that amount of black people at once, all crazy about football; when the home team shot for the goal, many fans threw plastic sacks with drinking water. Everybody was getting wet.

The home team won three-nil or something. I'm not sure as, as much as I was excited to see all these crazy football fans, I'm small so I couldn't see the game itself. But it didn't matter. I knew they were playing football and that people were crazy for it.

The atmosphere of the stadium; the police demonstrating their power. What I saw was real.

On the last day I just relaxed and looked back on my first journey to West Africa. Walking through the marketplace, I saw European companies and hotel buildings which were too modern for this place. In the breeze at the beachside, I already had plans to come to West Africa, maybe Mali, again… I'd see in the very near future.

I remember someone said: "If you go once to the Sahara you'll never get out of it, you'll go back again and again…" I think this is true; the Sahara is such an amazing place, the biggest space in the world, even from another planet you can see it.

The Sahara has different faces, different colours, depending on where you stand. I'm in love with the Sahara, the most amazing place I've ever been.

CHAPTER ELEVEN

AFRICAN INTERLUDE II

BY DAMO SUZUKI

After you eat tasty food, you like to taste it again. This is that same feeling. Once you've been in the Sahara you passionately want to get back again, you've got to taste it again. Sahara is calling.

Since my last time in Mali, a year ago, my love of the Sahara never cooled down. Flashbacks were not seldom. The Sahara is beautiful, the greatest spot on this planet, and it's not just a tourist attraction. It's a wise old man... it showed me the depth of life.

So, was I planning my adventure? No, it didn't take much time to find a destination; I wanted to go where not many people go and not much information is available. In fact, Mauritania had only 2,000 visitors a year(!!!). I purchased a map but there wasn't much showing, just yellow sand, huge empty spaces, countable dots (towns) and few roads. The emptiest map I ever owned.

Situated next to my beloved Mali, its western neighbour Mauritania had a magical name. It was just calling to me.

In March/April of the year 1994, I spent about three weeks travelling around one quarter of Mauritania. On departure day in the morning, Marco, my youngest son, who'd be three in a month, looked at me as if he was seeing a stranger. The traveller stood there in his 'safari look': desert boots and small rucksack. He never saw me like this before; maybe he already knew I was going for an adventure.

NOUAKCHOTT

After five and a half hours of flight from busy Charles de Gaulle, I arrived in Nouakchott late afternoon, a totally unknown city of an unknown country. It was exciting.

It was twenty minutes of driving by bush taxi (condition/comfort were the same as the last trip to Mali/Guinea). I'd planned nothing, I just intended to go and get into whatever may happen, only avoiding one thing: I wouldn't go to the northern territory; I'd heard of violent riots (by people fighting to get back their own lands) for many years against Algerian and Moroccan soldiers in western Sahara. Neighbouring countries in northern Mauritania were in a state of anarchy, not controllable.

North of Mauritania, the Arab-Berbers were dominant; in the southern part lived mainly black people. There were often fights between both ethnic groups. The country was not a peaceful place, they even still had slavery in the north. All the information I had about it was rather negative.

Nouakchott is an artificial new city, chosen as the capital (it's between the port town Nouadhibou and the capital city of Senegal, Dakar) for strategic reasons during the French colonial period. The city's population was exploding; there were many refugees from small local wars and drought. Probably the most famous spot in this city of a million population was the mosque, a gift from Saudi Arabia. Mauritania is a strict Islamic country.

The first night I stayed at a hotel in the city centre. There was a dirty window (it had probably gone years with no cleaning); a curtain with small holes (probably insect bites) hanging listless; a naked, poor-quality lamp at 20w; a slow and noisy ventilator on the ceiling, occasionally malfunctioning. Bedsheets were used hundreds of times without washing, leaving the multi-mixed smells of hundreds of guests before me. On the carpet there were stains from drinks and cigarettes. So, you may imagine sleeping in this space.

Eeekkk…

But I couldn't sleep outside; the police here may have been strict and you didn't know the danger – you may become a victim of robbery or worse.

Strangely, I had a good, deep sleep, probably from the heat and tiredness of the trip, or malaria tablets. Early in the morning I went to market for breakfast: small baguette and coffee with much milk and sugar, like my last West African trip. People were very curious (it's not surprising), some wanted to try to communicate with me despite the language barrier. As the country is not a tourist attraction, visiting this place is still very interesting.

I met a young guy who understood English; he also understood that I like to be close to life inside a country, so he brought me to his family house not far from the bazaar. His was not a poor family: they had enough space, their small ventilator was working, they had electricity. (Strangely though, I didn't meet him any more.)

There were few family members; no one else spoke English. Even so, they were very curious to try to understand me. They had enough time, I had enough time.

Papa was the name of a pretty three-year-old boy with big, shining, beautiful eyes; he liked me so much that, even when I was taking a nap (it's necessary – it's really, really hot, even the air was melting like ice cream), he came under my thin bedsheets and slept by my side during my stay at this house.

His mother was very young; she showed me her fingers when I asked her age. (Twenty-two?) And she was a really beautiful lady, she could have been a photo model in every Western country. She had a good body posture (generally, ladies from Africa have a fine posture as they carry things on their head), beautiful oval face and smoothly black skin. If I'd had a model agency or something similar, I'd have brought her to Germany. Her husband was working in the US, she explained with gestures. She and her mother-in-law cooked food that was to my taste: Arabic food, slowly cooked. Eating here was similar to eating Arabic food (in the north), Senegalese food (in the south) or a fusion of both.

After three days hanging around, enjoying living together with a Mauritanian family, the curiosity of the traveller won out against a comfortable life. But I could have stayed there, and I was very thankful for their hospitality.

NOUADHIBOU

The second biggest city is Nouadhibou, an industrial port town and centre of fishing on the peninsula. The distance from the capital Nouakchott is around 480 km. But there is no road between; expect desert road that might be dangerous, as tyres sink easily in deep sand.

Another transport possibility is to take the beach shore, drive at midnight as the tide is at its minimum for three hours. I have to say I was lucky to take a drive on the beach, as I experienced an unforgettable time. A few Jeeps made a queue, waiting for ebb tide. Then they gave it gas. Every Jeep seemed to be happy finally to move after a long wait.

The left side is dark – the mysterious Atlantic Ocean in moonlight; the right side is the endless Sahara. Riding by the ocean in the deepest night you may feel fear, imagining an enormous, unknown animal lying beneath you, and the next moment this animal may move.

It's amazing at this time of the day, cool breeze from the ocean brings the temperature down to 15°c. In the day it's 45°c in shadow and more; in the middle of the night you need a sweater, sleeping on sand you need a blanket to cover you.

When a tyre gets deep in sand then every male passenger pushes and shovels till it's free. Strangely, from a Western perspective, even in this situation females don't lend their hands to help us, just watch men fighting with sand. After several times freeing tyres, every male passenger is suddenly part of a well-trained team.

Sleep a few hours on sand. Much fresher than in the heat. But still longing to see the sun.

After a few days' stay in Nouadhibou, I ate the main dish at the local restaurant – grilled fish from the port. Arab-Berbers in the north take their main meal in the night, black people in the south at midday.

While I was walking through the city to the railway station, seven to ten small kids threw stones at me from a distance. They never saw a human being like me? An old man shouted at them to stop.

From here, I started my trip to the middle of the Sahara.

NOUADHIBOU – CHOUM

For the next 450 km I took the longest train in the world: four locomotives and 2 km-long wagons (200 wagons). Can you imagine? It's an endless train to the horizon.

It's the only railway in Mauritania. This stretch was built to carry iron ore from the last station, M'Haoudat, to the port town, totalling more than 700 km through Northern Sahara. From these 200 wagons, just the last one is used for passengers. The rest are all open-roof cargo wagons.

While I bought a ticket, some just climbed up onto the cargo wagons, which were empty, having just brought iron ore from the mine. People got into the passenger wagon from every direction, it was an anarchic situation, total chaos; everybody wanted to find as quickly as possible the very best space, but with no seat, just a space to sit on the floor.

If I'd known I just had to climb up to the cargo wagon, I might not have paid and pretended to be a blind passenger. In the passenger wagon, passengers were sitting tight (*really* tight) next to each other; it was also very hot, as the heat mixed with body temperatures. You felt like you were in a sauna. Everybody was sweating like crazy and it made a stinky smell.

Even in this situation, someone was making tea (this is a kind of ritual everywhere in the Sahara region: gunpowder tea + mint + much sugar). Incredible. The windows were so small, round like in a U-boat, but if you opened them sand dust soon came in. This was also the first time since the airport I'd seen some white people. About a dozen French girl scouts were using their spring holiday to exchange with Mauritanian young people.

After while I got a bad feeling and I needed a place to lay down. It may have come from heat in the wagon or the smell of people (I'm sure I was smelling horrible too). It was difficult to breathe, my throat was dry and even worse, I was getting hungry. (I didn't prepare any food.)

I asked the conductor if there was a comfortable place for me to rest. I didn't feel good and I thought the situation was hopeless, but he kindly gave me a place in the conductor's room... the seat had too many holes for me to be able to sit, but still I was very thankful that I now had space. This kindly guy even shared with me his lunch, slow-cooked meat and rice that he proudly said was made by his wife.

You know, life is amazing when you're treated so kindly, even though you don't share any communicable language but can still understand each other. It's a beautiful thing when you didn't expect this kind of situation. Love is spending time with each other, sharing and enjoying the moment together.

The longest train in the world goes very slowly sometimes, down to 20 km/h. It was a long, long trip. That was fine – I didn't have an inclination to ride to the last station, altogether almost 700 km at this snail's pace.

I bought a ticket to Choum, which is a bit more than midway to M'Haoudat. Normal passengers are probably only able to take a ride to Zouérat; the two stations that come after are only for mine workers. Anyway, after Choum on the trans-Saharan trading route, trains go into the non-self-governing-territory of Western Sahara for a while.

I was probably toasting in the passenger wagon for more than eight hours. Here and there, there were stations that were not like stations: no platform, just a few passengers setting off in the middle of nowhere... you could see the endless sand ocean, no villages visible. All those people had to walk miles and miles under the melting sun. I wondered how people could live in such a place with no name on the map, and probably no one to visit them; no green, just endless sand.

After this we arrived at Choum, very close to the border of Western Sahara. This place had a railway station, if you can call it that: in front of the station were twenty huts, waiting rooms for passenger, a few shops and bush taxis going in every direction. Except for this there was nothing, from desert to horizon. Most passengers got out here.

ATAR

It was not long to wait for the bush taxi to start; I saw one of the passengers who used the train, a man very curiously looking at me from under his sunglasses. He communicated with me: "Was I going to Atar? Did I like Mauritania? What did I intend to do here?"

There are so few tourists that he might never have seen an Asian like me in his life. He introduced himself as working for the military, responsible for transportation facilities logistics (I guess he had a good post there); on his break he was going to Ouadane, 180 km east. He asked me if I'd drive with him to Atar.

"No worries, I pay all your expenses."

So, a relatively comfortable trip; we'd be the only two passengers to our next stop, Atar. Before the war of independence it was the largest city in the land – and the junction to every part of Mauritania.

"Do you have place to stay?"

"No, I haven't, I'll look for accommodation..."

"Then you can stay by me, I've my wife and family there." He said he had four wives in different part of Mauritania.

This kind of offer I never say NO to. Why should I? The most important thing in travel, its purpose, is to get close to domestic life – to live together with indigenous people.

His parents also lived at his place; it had a typical Arabic dining room with sitting cushions, a water pipe, colourful carpet and small windows. (Some houses have no windows at all in this area to protect them from sand dust.)

A young black boy (probably a slave) served us that famous green powder (mint tea) with much sugar, dates and some sweets. Some curious neighbours appeared, to sit together with the family and I. But there were no women in the dining room.

Three days went quite fast; in this heat there wasn't much possibility of doing anything anyway. A few men were just hanging around like me, under the shade; some were discussing their God, some paid no attention, in their own world somewhere.

The military officer asked me if I'd come to Oudane to visit his other wife and stay there for another few days, then to Chinguetti. He'd already made my plan for the next few days.

OUDANE

In Oudane, you feel much deeper into the Sahara. There are ruins, there seem to be no complete houses left. His house was (to my eyes) also a ruin.

The space I slept in was half outside, without a roof but with a blanket in case I got too cold in the night. I carried my body up there with a small rucksack and some bottles of water; every day tired, all the time tired (stoned?).

After dinner with the neighbourhood (again, only men, no females), everybody was in a good mood. Someone said, "There is a festival, we should go there."

In such a place as this, with no attractions at all? Festival? Music? It attracted not only adults but children, everybody.

"Damo, do you like to join us?" asked Mr Officer.

"I'm so… tired. I like to relax now, lay here, watch stars and moon in night sky…"

Travelling this way was filling me with information that I need to be sometimes freed from. If you're in such a situation you need for a while silence. Until now there was too much information; now, I could hear, see and feel with body and soul.

All the people were gone, I was alone in the roofless ruin's dining room. Enjoying the deep sky, bright stars, thinking about this and that... falling asleep.

The festival starts, I can hear music. Fantastic music, man! A singer and guitar duo, the guitarist plays like Hendrix. Wooh! ...in the middle of the Sahara, fantastic blues... Sahara blues.

Now I am ashamed that I didn't go there with my friends. I hear in the clear sky living blues that captures the whole surroundings; the voice swimming in the air attended by crazy guitar playing. It's a natural psychedelic experience. Everything is surreal, peerless, bringing me to another world. In a foreign country, alone at a house I've known only for a few days, in a state of nature, the soundtrack fits perfectly.

CHINGUETTI

Way back in the direction of Atar is the eighth Islamic pilgrimage site, Chinguetti. This place is really like a picture, you may imagine a fairy tale Sahara. Waving desert. Date trees. Caravans. Camels – hundreds of camels, I never saw any amount of camels like this.

One might even imagine packages of American cigarettes.

This time, our accommodation (I'm still travelling together with Mr Officer) is on the other side of the old town with the mosque. Between huge spaces for trading caravans and camels, the whole place is coloured light brown and red.

Each of us has an Arabian-style room with a small window, one of the most comfortable sleeping places in the last few days. The wife of the owner actually runs this as a hotel; she has a pretty, photogenic daughter, very shy at first. Her young brother is always hiding himself tight behind her as if both are one person. Their mother reminds me of Isabelle Adjani – dark hair, sympathetic face, not big.

We meet again that group of French girl scouts from the train, they are staying at the same accommodation. I don't know if there is another place to stay, there are not many travellers here – but it's getting like we've known each other for many years. It's a traveller's feeling if you see someone again on your path. (Very long ago, I met one African guy in three different parts of Europe within one short period.)

We took a walk together through this part of town. Every girl wanted a photo of herself riding on a camel, this arrogant, lazy animal. Next morning, the girls went east.

A man talked to me at the corner of the street, he made me stressed. He was of course a Muslim but very fanatical, non-stop talking about his God in a very aggressive way, to get me into his religion.

It's not comfortable if someone takes a conservative view like this, believing deeply in his religion but not accepting any other opinion. Everything was against Western manners, customs, culture, even though he wasn't there he knew it was all awful, all against his God.

It's not a good situation at all, but you must never get aggressive. This is quite a problem when I visit Islamic countries, which have very interesting culture and history. Still, you cannot escape as nobody will support you if you walk away from Muslim preachers, who will only get more aggressive.

Mr Officer was dressing up in his boubou*; until now I didn't see him in Arabian costume.

"Where you going?"

"Today is Friday, I go for prayer in mosque."

I was curious, I'd never been inside a mosque. I thought it was surely too shameful to ask if I could attend with him. But he himself said if I had interest I should come along, it might be boring to stay in the hotel alone.

I don't know from where he got it, but he handed me a white boubou: "Wear this." At the same time he looked at my white cap, Sahara jacket, T-shirt, white safari shorts and light-brown desert boots – the prototype of the safari look – critically, up to down, his whole face saying, *'No, no, with this costume you never get into mosque.'*

He showed me how to wear a boubou. After a while he asked me: "What will be your name? You must have name sound Arabic."

Within a second: "What about Sinbad?"

Sinbad was born. We went through hundreds of camels to the entrance of the mosque. The male congregation all watched me very curiously.

Mr Officer was introducing me (it seemed he had good relationships) to many people. Mainly they were relatively friendly, though many were watching from far behind. I was feeling like everybody was watching me.

* The long, baggy robe worn by both sexes in West Africa.

After dawn, walking through the desert was not a bad idea – it was a little cooler, of course, with the boubou making it much more airy. Now, I was quite integrated with this costume – and the name 'Sinbad'.

I said farewell to Mr Officer. We'd travelled together a week; he paid everything during this seven days and brought me close to traditional life and local society. I gave back the boubou to him.

"No, I don't need, you can take it home, it's my gift."

He also brought me two bottles of water, dry dates, Mauritanian bread, dried meat, etc. It was enough for a few days. We hugged: "See you sometime."

TERJIT

I rode on the bush taxi back to Atar on the only road that exists, changing vehicles to get to Terjit, which is not directly on the trans-Saharan Road. Terjit was 45 km away, with the last 12 km without asphalt; on the map it's a street, but actually this is a huge, wide space surrounded by plateaus – with 30–40 cm-tall trees here and there, taking up just a small amount of space in a sea of sand.

I didn't know about Terjit, I came here without a plan as it was the earliest destination when I arrived at the bush-taxi stop in Atar. It wasn't really filled up; some passengers went out in the middle of nowhere.

You don't find some names on a map, there were many place like this. Mainly, the smallest point on a map has a population of a few thousand; it may be possible some places don't even have names. At both sides of the bumpy road were plateaus; it would be a good location for western movies, I wouldn't have been surprised if a bunch of Red Indians had shown up.

Then I saw some green space, which I hadn't seen for quite a long time.

"Oasis? It must be oasis." I answered my own question. It was amazing to see, especially as I'd never seen an oasis before.

The bush taxi's last stop was here; I was the only one at the end of the travelling. There were date trees and muddy water. I don't know the size but the oasis was quite huge, not small like I'd imagined.

It was late afternoon and some others were there: Arabs, French tourists, altogether around fifteen people. It seemed to be a touristy place.

I took my place in front of a hut just before the creek. It was dinner time. I stuck my feet in low, warm water. From the plateau, it trickled down from a few small waterfalls between green ivy.

Oh man, this is an *oasis*. Life is there: ivy, date plants. I spring into the water, it's not deep, just knee-high. It still brings you up fresh.

An indigenous Arabic family were on excursion, relaxing, their small cassette radio groaning with their tribal tunes. It wasn't loud, it fitted absolutely as a soundtrack mixed with the conversation of four or five young French tourists.

Time is stopping, it's a 3D postcard; all the scene is like a dream. One group after another slowly disappears, with silence taking over by sunset. All of a sudden... I'm alone.

I've enough food for three days, so I don't have to leave here. Also, there is no possibility of transfer. But... how can I get out of here? Is there any way to get a bush taxi in a place like this?

I have questions but, like always, I'll see whatever comes along.

Now it's very silent. You can see the night sky clearly. I stand up in the windless air carefully, seeing my feet in moonlight... just hoping no animal appears and surprises me.

I hear a soft waterfall sound, taking this direction through dates, dates, dates... There I see a pond, behind it is a small waterfall surrounded by (of course) date plants.

It's so beautiful. I take off all my clothes to spring into the pond. It's refreshing, just feeling so good after the heat of Mauritania, without hope of rainfall.

Small insects are rushing to escape from the noise I produce. I climb a low waterfall, walking through low-table land beside the creek. I'm in the middle of nature, the moon and me, all the world seems to have left me alone here. For the next two days I meet no one.

I leave after three days.

In the late morning there's no possibility to find a transfer. I decide to walk, it's just 12 km or something to the main street. It's doable.

It's already in heat, the liquid from my body drying fast. The sky is baking me, the sun is burning, making me blind. I begin feeling bad before I've even made half of this stretch.

Foam is running out of my mouth. My sight is not clear...

I still have the strength to bring my head into the shade of a small half-metre tree.

After a while a scrap pickup shows up on the horizon, spitting sand dust. I put all my power into getting their attention, so they can see me.

They stop, a man comes out and carries me to the pickup, with many barrels of water. I drink and drink. It was a really serious situation…

The car terminates at Atar, so I get our to hitchhike; there's no alternative.

AKJOUJT

There is no town except Akjoujt between Atar and Nouakchott on the asphalt road for 450 km distance: point 200 km to Atar, 250 km to Nouakchott. Copper and gold mines are the economic powerpoint of this town, with a population of a few thousand.

I found a space at a hut under tin roofs. Next morning, I took breakfast standing: slow-cooked meat and rice. This was my last station before I got back to Nouakchott.

The result of this trip was around 1,800 km total distance; riding on the longest train in the world; probably the hottest place I've visited (I didn't bring a thermometer, but I'd guess on many days it was more than 45°c in the shade); finding an oasis; a near-death experience.

It was very interesting to visit an unknown country like Mauritania. It gave me lots of motivation and power. I may make this kind of trip again.

What will be next?

Where shall I go?

Even though in this period I didn't make music, I was travelling. There are hundreds of people who've travelled to all the countries in the world. I'm sure I won't make it and I'm not intending to do this. But there are surely many interesting places, even if I haven't been to half of them.

Now I have a feeling I may go back to places I loved, see friends again, and that I'd like to know their culture deeper. Travel is the best thing you can do with money (also without it); all the experience you gain on a trip cannot be exchanged for anything in this world.

CHAPTER TWELVE

NETWORKING

The return to music came in 1997, with a return 'home' – except this was a place Damo Suzuki only rarely visited, which he now considered an almost exotic locale. "Occasionally I'd go there as a holiday but not very often," he reminisces. "I'd been taking my creative break from 1992–1997, I hadn't made any kind of music. But because I got an offer – 'Why don't you play in Japan?' – I got involved in music again."

In fact he'd never performed in Japan before – not even during the heyday of Can. Nor did he have a band any more. This new chapter was going to require a new group of participants.

"I had a lot of contact at the end of the nineties with Michael Karoli," confirms Damo. "I wanted to have some special guitarist who does not just sound like how a guitarist should. He had a very special sound, but the main thing is that he was willing to go to Japan for the first time.

"I'd already found a promoter who'd like to organise three concerts but I didn't have any band, so I put an instant band together. I thought it'd be a good idea to invite Karoli and he said, 'Yes, without a doubt,' he'd come.

"I think at that time he was ill," he reflects on the first (and youngest) member of Can to be lost to us. "He had it already in Japan, this sickness, because at that time he had already a skinhead. His illness was brain cancer or something like this, so he had to cut off his hair – but at this time it wasn't a heavy period, it was quite an early stage of his sickness."

211

In the years since the late 1980s Can reunion, Mickey Karoli had been rendered invisible. There had been no live gigs to follow the *Rite Time* album; he remained musically active but only in the most private way, ensconced in his studio.

"He was playing lead guitar," Damo recalls of seeing him again for the first time in years. "We met a short time before for rehearsal – rehearsing not set 'pieces', but he seemed to really enjoy it and was happy to be together with us."

By now, the organic flow that had passed from Can to The Damo Suzuki Band – in the sense of playing improvised pieces that could be edited and refined, in order to play again in a similar form on stage – was reaching a wide-open sea. The new repertoire was to be self-contained one-offs; crystallising in the spur of the moment, never to be repeated.

"I think at that moment this was the stuff he wanted to make," affirms his old bandmate of Michael, "so he could play live again instead of working in the studio. He had his own studio in France, but what he really wanted was live performance. So maybe it was a great moment [for him] when I asked him to join to play live."

The Japanese dates were the effective debut of Damo Suzuki's Network. "I wanted to make a very special concert so I played three dates. Each entrance ticket got you a live CD of the night. Each CD was limited to 500 copies, because we performed in a 500-person capacity venue. I played a concert that finished the next day, then I painted a very big painting and cut it all into 500 different parts. So everybody who came to this concert had a CD with a different cover – also with a photo of the complete painting."*

The ex-Can guitarist aside, the original Network comprised Mani Neumeier from Guru Guru on drums; Mandjao Fati, a bass player from Guinea-Bissau; and Matthias Keul, late of Dunkelziffer and The Damo Suzuki Band, on keyboards. "I think Mandjao is five years younger than me," recalls Damo, "he quite looks like me, small and thin, so he's kind of my twin brother. And so we made an instant band. Michael toured with us for three concerts." It was one week only, two concerts in Tokyo and one in

---

* It would be made more widely available in 2000/2001: respectively *JPN ULTD Vol. 1* and *2*, on the Damo's Network CD label.

Osaka. It could have been a total one-off – but life would take a different turn.

HIROFUMI SUZUKI

I live in the northern part of Japan. Sometimes, my brother arrange concert here and visit my house. He treat me good. Sometimes he cook for us as he is good at cooking. When I meet him after long time no see, I wish to have this time forever.

I think I went to concert about three times. It's a long performance but it's caught up in the sound whirlpool and the feeling of time is gone. Tuneful voice quality also increased comfort. I don't know the feeling of the audience, I guess they like Damo of today too as getting power and energy from him. I think that I'm most pleased with Japan's Sound Carriers. Because they can stand on the same stage with krautrock legend.

"Before he left, Michael had one of his last concerts with me*," muses Damo. "I had quite an interesting time together with him, but he was quite ill at that time.

"He died in 2001, the 17th of November. Before that, I think in August or September, we made an appearance at a festival. So after that he was already in the hospital, and he was not allowed to go out. The doctor didn't allow him, but he came to the concert with his mask for breathing. Because he was just happy to perform, and it was quite important for him. I said to him, 'This could be our last concert' – or maybe it was his next-to-last concert, I'm not sure."

The past may be way behind him, but Damo recognises the uniqueness of the man he'd brought back into his own musical fold. "I met Karoli in 1970," he reconfirms, revisiting a random explosion of brilliance. "At this time there were not so many of his style of guitarist – but if you were together with him for a long while then you could hear his tastes, so it's the kind of thing where you need a bit of time to listen to it.

"Not at the first moment – you may say: 'Oh, what is he playing?' Maybe some people say it was primitive, but I never did because at that time I was also searching for something new.

* In New York City – see Alexander Schönert's recollection.

213

"It was good to perform together with Karoli because he was also of the same generation. It's quite interesting to have such a person who is creative enough to find their own style. Because this was also in the same period that I was searching for something too, you know. I was just starting in this professional band but I was not really a good singer, so I had to find some other way, to do something else."

It was this fusing of disparate elements – virtuoso and street performer, from ethereal to cacophonic in a few breaths – that gave Damo-era Can its power. "I wasn't really a musician," he acknowledges. "I'm still not like a musician. I've never tried to be a musician – I'm just trying to be Damo Suzuki and that's enough for me. There are millions of singers who are singing better than me, technically. But only I'm Damo Suzuki. For me it's enough to create my stuff rather than trying to be somebody else."

It was an attitude that fermented back in the day, when he'd found himself suddenly recruited by a quartet of long-haired German bohos. Virtuosity was not a consideration.

"I was always listening to hear somebody who was just freaking out and doing something that I never heard. Other things are for people who just like to listen to the music. I'm not so interested in listening to music – I like musicians who are giving me a great time, but not *with the music*.

"It is the things that are behind the music that are maybe a kind of passion. So if he has a passion behind his musical playing, to me it doesn't matter if he has a good technique or bad technique – to me there is not a good or bad musician. It's dependent on my tastes, which fits together with my musical interests."

In Damo's estimation, his late friend's strength was "a guitar melody that doesn't really sound like a guitar". It was the belief of noted Can-head Julian Cope, for example, that Mickey K's spatial tones were informed by the Turkish ethno-music to be heard in urban Germany.

"Hear the solo part of 'Mother Sky' from 1970," reminds Damo. "Karoli made a very special, detailed solo you cannot compare with anybody else, 'good' or 'bad'.

"Hendrix was special too, but he was kind of based on blues guitar and Karoli wasn't so much. I think everybody was trying to be somebody who could play really good blues guitar – it's always easier to copy anybody else because you can hear it already. It's not so innovative a musical instrument. You can make so many different sounds with effects and things, but still a guitar sounds like a guitar."*

ALEXANDER SCHÖNERT
Guitarist, Jelly Planet / Damo Suzuki's Network

It was about twenty years ago that I formed Jelly Planet, and because I don't want to sound like a metal guitarist, or my friends when they play in bands, I found these three guys from other musical 'homes' – like funk, jazz, classical music. We built this together and it was the early nineties, so it was a very good era for doing this kind of crossover thing. After a while we mixed all these different styles together and it was kind of 'psychedelic space rock', we called it – but after a while we said it's krautrock. Because they liked it when we played in Netherlands, or Italy, or somewhere besides Germany – in Germany nobody knows krautrock!

I think I've played with Damo almost a hundred times. He sometimes invited me: "Come to the tour to Japan", "to Croatia", "to America", "to Spain". With Jelly Planet maybe it was five gigs with the whole band, but the drummer sometimes.

(I've had another band for fifteen years, it's called Frankenstein's Ballet – the drummer is the reason I got to know Damo, he was the drummer of Yellow Sunshine Explosion.)

He refers to the actual music he's listening to in a very clever way. He always sings in the way you should sing in this kind of moment – if we go like punk rockers, or like death metal, which sometimes happens, he is like: "Rrraaarrr!", screams like a pig. If we play on a very, very low level you might hear a needle falling down, he is whispering all the time.

---

* "Okay, Gary Lucas, when he is playing solo, can make sounds like a hundred people playing, it's really interesting with echo and stuff like that," Damo says of his sometime collaborator in the Network. With a resumé that stretches from Captain Beefheart's final Magic Band to joint recording with Peter Hammill (ex-Van der Graaf Generator, one of British rock's great innovators), Lucas deserves mention in the same breath as Karoli. "Nowadays I think many more people are playing music with the laptop than the guitar," observes Damo. "But still the guitar is still quite often the beginning of everything. It's just quite difficult to find a really good guitarist."

People come to me after the gig: "Can I have the CD of the third song that was played?" "There is no song!" "Can I have the playlist?" "There is no playlist! It's [in] the moment." "But they sounded like songs!"

Because Damo is so sensitive and clever, so experienced after all these years, he never tells you something – never tells you, 'Okay, the next song should be fast,' or slow, or anything, he just points to somebody: "You start with the next piece." Otherwise they would discuss on stage and it would take too long. But he never says anything and his style is many styles, so he can scream, he can whisper, he can sing melodically, he can sing bizarre. I don't know many singers who are able to do this.

It's so funny that some Can-heads wrote lyrics on the internet and Damo is reading this and he's laughing, because it's got nothing to do with what he was singing. Because he sings nothing: in the early seventies with Can sometimes it reminded you of an English word, but we have these new recordings of Jelly Planet and Damo Suzuki – it's not English, it's not German, it's not Japanese. He said it's "the language of the Stone Age" – prehistoric stuff, you know!

We performed in Greenwich Village, New York* – it was Michael Karoli on guitar, it was me on guitar, and Gary Lucas who formerly played with Captain Beefheart. We played for five hours. There was one short break but altogether it was five hours. It was so orgiastic and it was typical Damo – you cannot do it with another singer, it's very hard to find somebody else to have so many ideas over such a long amount of time.

So many gigs come to my mind. He's spontaneous: for example in Helsinki, Finland, we had a very nice support band and he loved them so much that he told them: "When we play just join us – so we are not five, we are ten musicians on stage. Let's just do it!" And they did it and it was so nice.

Even at big festivals he's always experimental and he's always very professional, and besides the musical thing Damo is always very fair to the others: he shares all the fucking money, he's very nice, he's never an angry person and he's always cool. He says: "It's very late and I want to go to sleep!" and I say to him: "No, no, there's a party on the next block!" "Okay, let's go there!" It's fun to be with him on tour. He loves to eat very well – and me too!

---

* Damo: "Alex is telling of Damo Suzuki & Friends, an early stage of the Network project. Now, we make very long pieces – as long as we like."

216

JONATHAN LAMASTER
Cul de Sac (bass guitar, violin)/Damo Suzuki's Network

There is a famous British journalist called Simon Reynolds, and he coined a term in his review of Cul de Sac's first album, which came out in 1991 and it's called ECIM. (I was not on that record but I was a big fan of the band around that time.) He did a review of ECIM, which is 'mice' spelled backwards, and he coined the term 'post-rock'. It's a blend of certainly krautrock elements, while the guitarist, Glenn Jones, is a real devotee of John Fahey.*

So he started the band along with Robin Amos, who's an analogue synthesizer player – really steeped in krautrock, Hawkwind, Can. Both of them agreed that Can was the greatest rock'n'roll band, certainly out of Europe. So that was a pretty distinct element for what Cul de Sac was doing even back then.

The original drummer from that band, Chris Guttmacher, left the Boston area and went to California to work for Amoeba Records after the first album, he was one of the buyers there. He was out in California for twenty years or so and Damo had done a couple of tours of the West Coast. A couple of those tours I think Michael Karoli was there with him, and also a guitarist who I have recorded with and played with in Russia, Alex Schönert, who was in a band called Jelly Planet with the drummer Jens Küchenthal. One of those tours I think came out of Seattle; it was around that time that Chris Guttmacher met Damo.

Chris had given Damo some Cul de Sac recordings and Damo just kind of sat on them, I don't think he listened to them. He's funny, I don't think he listens to a lot of rock'n'roll, he listens to classical music. So he sat on those recordings for a while and then he wanted to do a US tour in 2002, and he pulled out these recordings that people had given him on previous tours of the US. He found these Cul de Sac records and reached out to us via the contact information on the records. Lo and behold, we get this email from Damo which was very funny – something like: "I don't know if you know who I am..." Well, if you listened to our music you'd know we absolutely knew who Damo was! We were all extremely excited for him to reach out to us and say: "I'm looking for some bands to play with and tour with, to back me up." The

---

* Classic American steel-string guitarist and musical primitivist.

rest is history: we did a tour in 2002 of the United States and Canada, and that's how I first met Damo.

I was tasked with picking Damo up from the airport, when he first flew in, and he stayed with me at my house where Cul de Sac actually did some recording – the soundtrack we did for a Roger Corman movie called The Strangler's Wife was recorded in my old living room. I picked up Damo from the airport, he stayed with me for a couple of days prior to the tour and we got to know each other as friends, hung out and cooked and just had a great time, we instantly kinda connected.

And so I think I did about fifty to sixty performances with Damo and Cul de Sac on various tours, and then probably an equal amount with him, just myself, on other tours. The first tour I did on my own – and with the then drummer of Cul de Sac, John Proudman – was I think a UK tour in the late summer of 2002, after that US tour. I remember we played at The Garage in London with Circle, and we played and hung out with Justin Patten from a band called Now – which is still around. He's been involved in the Kosmische Club, which does a lot of krautrock events. Then there was Dominik von Senger the guitar player.

So that was the beginning, you know: Damo is doing these tours with Cul de Sac but then he's inviting me to do some tours as well. So after that UK tour, in the November of 2002 I went over to Russia and Finland with him. And then out of that tour came a live recording which is on YouTube: I Was Born, I Was Dead, you'll find the entire DVD that's been cut up into the individual songs. When we were in Finland a double CD came out of that, just called Suomi (Finland). Just a really, really great period of my life.

I'll go on record as saying that when Cul de Sac was first working with him, and this started to happen less and less as time went on, some of the stuff he did with Can would emerge in what we were doing. I know that 'Mushroom Head', at least once if not a couple of times he might find himself there. 'Mother Sky' a couple of times – some of the more well-known Damo contributions for Can showed up. That was earlier on, probably 2002–3. Subsequent tours and outings I've done with him, I don't recall that happening. I think there's a connection of course. I also think that anyone who's heard that music can't help but be influenced by it in some way. If they think, 'Omigod, I'm gonna play with Damo Suzuki,' what are they gonna do? They're gonna listen to those records! And so some of that is, I'm sure, gonna creep in.

DOMINIK VON SENGER
Guitarist, Damo Suzuki's Network

And then this brings us into a little gap – I made a lot of contacts and I played guitar for one year for a famous band in Germany: big festivals, a lot of money, and became a big name in the so-called mainstream – but not really. So it was the absolute opposite of the serious Stockhausen music scene – and we absolutely hated it.

Then I met Buddy Miles, from Jimi Hendrix's Band of Gypsys, and we became friends in Cologne. This was top secret; in the night, when Jaki [Liebezeit] left the rehearsal room, I sneaked in with Buddy and he played Jaki's drums. We made day-long sessions one year and the next, and then we didn't meet again. He gave me a guitar from Jimi Hendrix and it made some magical soul.

Then, after that, the period came when I stopped everything. When I was younger I was playing with Karlheinz Stockhausen's trumpet player; earlier, I lent Patti Smith my guitar before she became famous, in an art gallery in Cologne. I was so much into all those situations.

I went away from Cologne to the countryside and stopped making music. I tried to get papers, I tried to be a legal person, to work. I married a very enthusiastic wife, she threw me out for being mad. Not for my ideas, but because I was like a cow that had eaten all the grass. [laughs]

I became a worker after being a musician, in really hard jobs – when I was seventeen, eighteen, I learned a job, but then I became a musician. This time, twenty years ago, I had to start work again – so there's no more inspiration growing and you spent your time only on music. The whole world is music, so you miss out on almost all the other things. Which includes being a legal person, knowing how hard it is to earn 50 euros. Because if you're in music, maybe you have no food for days or you make a lot of money. It's going up and down, up and down, and in the downtime I found a lot of inspiration. So the next step is you get older and it's getting harder to get all this downtime.

Then after one year I unpacked my guitar – someone called me on the telephone and it was Damo. No other friends from all my career; it was Damo who called me. He said: "Dominik, do you like to come to Japan on a tour?" I said: "Damo, I just started a job, they will not give me holidays and my passport is not ready. I can't. Thank you."

And one year later he called again – no one called that year, only Damo. And he said: "Dominik, it's another year, you like to come?" And I said: "This time I'm ready." Okay, and then it happened that I came back into the music world. And he invited me to Japan.

It was very nice, I took my guitar and I was so astonished in Japan. So many people came and so many people liked what I played, and Damo was like always! It all meant nothing: I became a worker, I dropped off, I changed my life, I had a complete hard time, whatever. He was like always, this was very normal for him. He was so warm. He took me away and talked to me, and really invited me to understand something – but what, he didn't say! [laughs]

The band was put together by Damo, his choice of people: Tommy Grenas from the Farflung band in Los Angeles; a guy from Africa, Carlos; then there was a guitar player, Alex, from Dortmund in Germany, like heavy-metal style; there was a drummer, Nicole, she was a French-American girl from Neuwied, Germany. This was a really fantastic mixture.

I'd go with Damo from Cologne but we'd all meet there in Japan, for a week or ten days. People all over Japan were very enthusiastic about my playing. I was really astonished, because I stopped practising! [laughs] The more experimentally I played, the more they liked it. I really enjoyed that so much, it gave me so much that I thought: 'Well, you're not mad, you were wrong – the world around is mad!' [laughs] I felt at home with my music in Japan, very much so, and then this helped me over another year of working.

And the next year Damo called me again: so one year, next year, another year. And then after, the bass player from that Japan tour, Tommy Grenas, invited Damo and myself to go on a tour from Los Angeles to Vancouver in a row, one after the other – San Francisco, all the places, all the West Coast. I took another of my factory holidays and left home to go with Damo on this tour with the car, staying in Los Angeles for some days, playing the first concert there. Damo and I weren't allowed to go to Canada; we almost got arrested. [laughs] We paid a lot of money to make one concert in Canada and had to go back to Los Angeles on the road – from Vancouver to Los Angeles in one go in the car, like forty-eight hours. And if you came on holiday from a factory in Germany, you had only ten days! [laughs] This was so great, so fantastic – it was really great musicians from Los Angeles. We made a CD there, we made a CD in Japan – all of this is on CD, both are documented.*

---

* *Odyssey* (2000)/*Metaphysical Transfer* (2001).

I still didn't come back to my hometown of Cologne. And Damo called me again – he said: "England!" and we made the England tour. This time it was two musicians from America, drummer and bass or violin, and myself and Damo. The England tour was also great. I took a picture at The Garage with Damo in front before the concert, this was the opening of the tour. I took the photo and I like this very, very much: he's so lonely on the big street before people come, and after the soundcheck is done there's a little gap, you get into your own preparation for what's coming. This picture really shows it: 'but where am I, me, myself?' [laughs]

JONATHAN LAMASTER
Cul de Sac (bass guitar, violin)/Damo Suzuki's Network

And then Cul de Sac did a European tour with Damo. We would perform our set of instrumental music, usually forty-five minutes or something, and then we would back Damo for two, three hours, however long. It worked, really great fun. We ended up doing two tours of Europe with him, and then on a third tour we hung out with him and played with him in the UK: we had Portishead's road manager, Chizz, and they kindly lent us their van, and we did a show with Damo in Bristol I think. But that was pretty much the end of Cul de Sac playing with Damo. We did a live record, I think it came out in 2005. It was one or two songs from our first North American tour with Damo – the very first track on it is called 'Cambridge', and those are the very first notes that Cul de Sac ever played or I ever played with Damo. We thought it was important to have it on there because it was just a magical moment. The record is called Abhayamudra, *which is a mouthful.**

Went to Russia with him a separate time – or actually we both played at a festival, he was there but I don't think we got to perform with him. But, I got to go to Japan with him, played a couple of gigs that were super fun – we stayed in Zama, at his brother's house; I think his mother was still living at the time, she was late eighties, early nineties. I'm going to say that was 2006.

There were two different bands that we played with each night I think: this guy Keiichi (Mandog is his stage name) and then the guy from Captain Trip Records***, the founder of that label, was on one of those gigs. So I've not*

---

*   Abhayamudra *comprises two live discs, one recorded in 2002, the second in 2003*
**   Ken Matsutani, founder of Japan's most eclectic independent label.

only had the experience of playing different bands with Damo, backing him, but also with totally disparate players. I remember Ghost* might have sat in on a song, but I know it was The UFO Club in Koenji. I remember listening to minimalist music with them before the show, they were really into American minimalist composers. I've heard him play with various musicians and participated in playing with various musicians; it's just fascinating how he can apply his aesthetic to pretty much any scenario. So we had some amazing times and saw that transition from 'I'm bringing the band with me' to 'I'm just gonna show up and play with new performers every single time.'

*   Veteran Japanese underground rock band, active from 1984–2014.

CHAPTER THIRTEEN

CARRYING THE SOUND

The early years of the new millennium saw a full-on return to music-making. By 2003, Damo had been working for twenty-six years at his Japanese corporate employer in Neuss, near Düsseldorf. Leaving his job meant that music would become a fuller occupation than it had been since the Can years. It might have been termed 'early retirement', but it was no such mutual arrangement. "For me, it was a decision that it was no longer worth staying there," he says of his break with the workaday world, "forced to live without my freedom.

"At that point I was always making music," he reflects, "together with my friends who I'd known already for a few years. But at that point I thought I could communicate much more directly with the audience by playing only with ever-changing domestic 'Sound Carriers'."

It was a culmination of the Damo Suzuki's Network concept. Up to that point it had been a band – albeit one with an amorphous line-up. But in the back of its founder's mind it was not a career structure based on permanent personnel. It had been gestating since the early days of improvising in Can's Inner Space studio.

Its originator expresses the concept without any grand theorising: "Whether you decide to go this way or that way, I cannot actually force anybody and neither should I try. But a platform for artistic communication is always good.

"Since 2003, I've got together generally with musicians I've never met before and never performed with," he reaffirms. "So it's totally different."

According to Damo, what finally forced his dream into being was not strictly musical, but historical. The culmination of apocalyptic events; of extreme reaction pitted against extreme reaction; of a 'you're either with us or against us' stance that demanded all the world, in the post-9/11 tumult, subscribe to some form of violence on either side of the war of cultures.

"For political reasons I was against the USA," he states without reservation. It sounds like the old leftist/anti-imperialist reflex that condemned American adventurism whilst cutting some slack for its ideological opponents. But his closeness to the creative fringes of US popular culture remained.*

"Before 2001 there were not so many violent things happening everywhere," Damo contends. "There was terrorism," he concedes, "but it wasn't like worldwide terrorists."

Instead, the aftermath of the 9/11 attacks and the subsequent 'War on Terror' seemed to bear out the old aphorism (oft attributed to Confucius): 'Before embarking on a journey of revenge, dig two graves' – one for your opponent and one for yourself, as the cycle of violence will be self-perpetuating.

For Damo, this was not overt preaching. (As we've seen, he fights shy of the 'messages' prevalent in mainstream rock music.) In his conception, it was a personal war against the brutalism born of one individual (or organisation, or nation) being blind and deaf to the life experiences of another, and of the oppressed or disenfranchised party becoming hostile in their reaction.

"I wanted to adopt a political attitude not only in music," he explains, "I wanted to oppose all violence in this world – which means not only war, there is much violence at home, violence at the office, violence at school, violence everywhere because there is not so much communication. Communication is the way in which you respect and understand other people.

---

* Just check the sheer number of American musicians Damo has played with since the formation of the Network.

"That is why I use music as a weapon against any kind of violence, and this started from 19th March 2003, at the time that the Iraq war began. I decided to perform together with different kinds of musicians I never met before. If possible, from there on I would always perform with local Sound Carriers."

DOMINIK VON SENGER
Guitarist, Damo Suzuki's Network/solo artist
Meanwhile... I found a computer in a garbage can. I put it on and now I've got internet. So I got into internet and found something which brings us back to what it was before – before Damo. Someone played something for me, a record which was a very long time ago, and I answered their email: "Hey, can we mix this tune?" I said: "Well that's very old, I haven't got the tapes." I looked for the tapes, it took me one year.

It was my first solo album, a track called 'No Name', and then I found the tapes were not existing any more. It was a very big production, finished in London in a studio, and those 24 tracks were gone, they were too old. So they said: "Come on, record it again!" I said: "What? How can I record a track again? This is from eighties, very early."* So then I did that – took another year with some musicians here from the countryside. At the end of production I got invited to come to New York: I finished this track and it came out with a company making DJ records. So suddenly I came into a new situation – and at the same time Damo decided: 'I'm not touring with the band any more, I tour alone.'

The main thing I experienced with Damo: first of all I went on tour with three or four people; then I was with him alone, meeting all the other people; then he went alone. And now it's all the other people and Damo – every day other people. It's very investigative – like in the early days, we'd always say: "We're investigating." It was like passing water from one mouth into the other, passing it back again and again. It's not like digging for gold – if you just try it, something will be left, you know, and that is the way.

---

* 'No Name' appeared on Dominik's first solo album – prosaically titled *The First* – in 1983. By the time the re-recorded and remixed versions came out as an EP, it would be 2009.

The more you play with other people and travel around, and the more we make combinations, the more we investigate to a point of total purity, to find out what has nothing to do with all these complications, the easy way to find out whatever we want to find. [laughs] Yes!

I really felt with him that I enjoyed it. But later, the more I played with him, there comes a point when you say: "Omigod, Damo, Damo, I can't do it any more!" My friends became a problem because they couldn't stand it any more, and I think you can't hear Damo every day. But my friends had to hear me every day – when they came to my place I'd play tapes and it became like always: for musicians, a singer is a problem. [laughs] First of all comes the part of being famous; second, they always get on your nerves! For myself, I like very much instrumentals – I like to sing myself sometimes, but I'm very shy and I only sing if it's necessary.

When the Network passed from being a band line-up to random ensembles playing freeform rock music (or, as Damo would have it, making non-verbal communication), it became not so much a musical system as a way of life.

"It's really the best way of making music," claims the man himself, with some satisfaction, "because you don't know before the concert how you will react to the Sound Carriers, or how the audience will react. We just communicate in the moment. This is the very beginning of communication and it is how I've wanted to work ever since.

"Sure, not everything in life is like this," he concedes. "But if you are creative enough then you can create something living, fresh, honest. You will feel much freer because you are not forced to do things; you merely open your mind and create. It's the best way to find yourself: a kind of philosophy of how a human being can exist in this world.

"Whether you believe in a god or not, I personally believe that God created human beings to decide for themselves: to act freely.* So what the Sound Carriers are doing on the stage reflects how they feel at that moment; the audience are also starting from zero and so they find it much easier to communicate with us, because it's not programmed at all. We are in the same room and travelling to another space together."

---

* "Without hurting anybody," qualifies Damo – ever the pacifist anarchist.

LUCA GIOVANARDI
Guitar, keyboards, bass, electronics – Julie's Haircut/Damo Suzuki's Network

They tell me Julie's Haircut is actually a silly name for English-speaking people! When we started out we actually wrote songs in English. So we wanted a name that sounded English and we had a girl back then in the band. I'm not sure why but we liked the way the word 'haircut' sounded. [laughs] Over the years we've made up all kinds of stories about how the name came up – it was quite randomly chosen. So we've been active for many years.

We got in touch with Damo when the band decided we were actually done with writing 'traditional songs', the traditional structure and lyrics. It was about 2004/5. We released our first three albums basically between 1999 and 2003. We had a germ of improvisational rock, but the improvisations were within the structure of traditional rock songs. Then we'd done all we felt we could do in that realm, so we decided to move towards more experimental stuff. We did this album called After Dark My Sweet *in 2006, and that was all based on improvisations in the studio. That was basically later edited and restructured, and that is how we do records since then.*

In those years around 2004/5/6, we really fell in love with Can's music and we really wanted to incorporate that kind of improvisation theme into our own music – maybe gradually. Let's say the traditional structure of a song is verse-chorus-bridge-solo. We really decided to drop it out, we were not interested in that any more. The music of Can, and of other German bands of the period actually, was moving us in that direction. So we found that Damo was still travelling around doing this Network thing, and we said: "Maybe that's the best call – to learn how to do that and then maybe grow up as a band, and grow up as musicians ourselves, understand the methods of it and incorporate it into our own music."

We had some fellow musicians in Italy who had experiences with Damo, and Damo is not a difficult person to get in touch with! [laughs] He's a very, very open person – you write an email to him and you know he'll get back to you. We did our first improvised show in 2006 in Italy with him as a band. And then we did another one in 2007, in Modena – it was Damo and Sonic Boom together. (Sonic Boom – who goes by the name of Peter Kember – was one of the guys in Spacemen Three, he co-produced with us our fourth album.) It was a fun night, we had a great time. But we continued this relationship with Damo.

We never played any more shows with him and the whole band together, while I played many, many shows with him and other musicians, coming from other experiences. And I must say it was even cooler – I found out that it's much better when you do these improv nights, when you haven't rehearsed, to have musicians that you've never played with before. The music seems to spring with much more efficiency. I have to thank Damo for this because he gave me the opportunity to test it. Probably I'd never even get the idea to do something like that.

Damo likes to say he creates within the time and space of the moment – he uses this phrase a lot. He is in fact very, very focused on what he does. I must say I'm really a sucker for that. My own music too has moved further and further down the years towards that kind of feeling. The improvisational side has taken up a big chunk of what we do at the moment. That's completely thanks to him and the experiences we've shared. Sometimes he came to Italy and I put on shows for him, and I couldn't play or maybe I didn't like to play because I wanted to see it from the outside. I had the chance to put together the bands for this stuff – maybe picking different musicians that I liked, I was curious about seeing what these people could do together on stage and I only had the chance to do that because Damo was around.

It's really some kind of magical stuff going on there. How can I use the word 'magic', how can I say it in a very traditional way? If you understand about the history of alchemy, it's basically science and magic together. That's a lot to do with what's going on onstage with Damo. Really, I don't want to sound too cheesy, but there's a telepathy going on among musicians on a good night.

And Damo himself really has the kind of magnetic personality to help these things spring out. He's like a catalyser for this thing. Even musicians may be a bit shy in doing something like that because they're not used to it and it's not about technical skills. It's about the way a musician thinks. I've heard not-so-good musicians being perfectly in focus on a night like that. While I've seen technically very skilled musicians kind of scared away from it. Because what's being asked of you is to completely let yourself go and to listen to what is going on. Most of the time musicians are kind of focused on themselves, there's a lot of total personality going on in bands. While when you are doing these nights of improvisation with him, you really learn that the main thing is not playing so much but listening to what is going on. That what you do is completely in service of the music itself and you don't need to show off, you really need to be in service of the music that is being created in that moment. It's really, really fascinating to know that what is going on there is not happening again ever. And it's something completely unique. I totally understand why Damo is not keen to enter the studio and do recorded music, because that's against the idea of music that he has at the moment.

What you have to understand is that for him it's not as much about music as it is about people. For quite a few years he's loved to meet people, that's what he's always looking for. And he's conscious enough that the music will come. If the people are interesting and he gets interested in the people, a kind of human relationship starts out and the music will come for itself. That's his belief and I must say it's mine as well now! [laughs] He's convinced me about that, because it happens every night.

Another thing you have to understand about Damo, which is not so common among musicians, is that when you put on a show in some city, some town, he always prefers not to go into a hotel. He always asks if possible if he can stay as a guest in someone's house. He likes to get to know people, he's very curious about people and he likes to live in people's houses, when he's around.

So every time he's come to Italy he's been a very welcome guest in my house. And that's actually when he presented me with some of his solo music, solo concerts that he recorded. I don't think that the first time we played together I'd ever heard anything he'd done outside of Can actually. I don't think I'd ever heard any of his solo recordings before.

I'm not sure he ever really changed his method of doing music, you know? What is changed is the band that's backing him. Because with lyrics, even back in the day, I'm not sure he used to write down something before entering the studio, I don't think so. What he does now, he doesn't use lyrics any more most of the time. He's really interested in the sound of his voice and he can do a lot with it – it's really amazing sometimes. He can do this growl sound – sometimes when we play together he goes into that, he doesn't do it a lot but I'm blown away when he does it! I think the sound is what interests him.

He uses words sometimes – English words, German words, maybe sometimes Japanese words – but most of the time he doesn't even use words. I think what his focus is really about is the sound of syllables. I'm pretty sure that if you listen to the Can songs, sometimes you can recognise some phrases – yes, there are sentences in there, words saying something! [laughs] Maybe the grammar there is wrong! He couldn't care less about that, because what's important for him is the sound of that. And so if two syllables make the right sound when next to each other, he will use that completely regardless of the meaning.

He imitates instrument sounds with his voice – I'm not sure if he's aware of that, I think he is – but really when you play with him sometimes it's like having a saxophone onstage. And it's him! He can pass from a very high register to this growling sound, it's like having Coltrane playing sax with you onstage but it's not. [laughs] Maybe in his mind it's a kind of concrete poetry, but I think it's something else as well. I don't think he likes to consciously think about that so much. He really likes to let things flow as they go.

When you talk about Damo, he's something close to a family member now. I have pictures of him holding my little daughter when she was born. When he comes to Italy, even if we don't play together, or always when we meet up, he sleeps here for one night, he comes visit. We were due in Europe with Julie's Haircut in January 2015, for example; he was ill at that moment and we went to visit him at his place. So we meet many times even if it's not for music now.

All the members of Julie's Haircut have been Sound Carriers with him outside of the band. For example, one night I might be playing guitar and we would have a different drummer and a saxophone player, maybe a keyboardist, who comes from different experiences. Because it's much, much more interesting.

Playing with him and the band – I would do it again, but I found that less adventurous. Maybe because we know each other so well inside of the band that we're used to improvising together. And so it's less surprising for us, and it's not surprising enough for you. So I did many, many more shows with him and other musicians than I did with Julie's Haircut.

What we're doing now is so freeform, because it's so little based on actual composition and it relies so much on improvisation springing up out of the moment in the studio, that even though what we do is not completely improvised, it's kind of a mixture: the method we use is basically what Miles Davis was doing in the late sixties with Teo Macero.* What we do is very, very long improvisations, and then we take maybe a twenty-minute piece of music

---

* Luca: "Teo Macero was the producer/sound technician on those Davis recordings with Wayne Shorter when he was tenor saxophonist, and immediately after he left the band. Macero was the guy that actually made all the edits on the tapes, 'building' the structure of the songs after they were recorded as long improvisations."

and we kind of edit it, pick out the good bits and kind of shorten it. It's like making vinegar in a way, you have to extract the quintessence! [laughs]

So doing these improvisations, even when writing our music, is of course very, very much influenced by what Damo does and what we've been doing with him. That's of course a very strong influence for us, and also now in Reggio Emilia, Italy, where I live, we have a collective of musicians called Arzán, which is not a band – we've done shows with six musicians, up to thirty-five musicians, a big orchestra, a rock orchestra maybe, four drummers, ten guitars, stuff like that. This thing was put together by me and several other guys, including Olivier Manchion from Ulan Bator, which is a French band; he's been working with Damo for many years as well. This stuff we do now with Arzán is complete improvisation. Sometimes we can decide a very, very simple pattern to follow but with no specific instructions to the musicians, so there is much improvisation. This comes out of all these years' experience with Damo.

He's quite unique. But at the same time I think he created a bunch of musicians spread all over the world that are now doing what he does. It's something that is probably more common in other genres of music, like jazz music. In rock music it's something quite unheard of. But there's one guy that really travels the world around and has no fear at all in entering a stage with completely unknown musicians. Just saying, "Let's make music now," and being fascinated by something that is going to happen just once in this room – because that's what's happening with this improvisation.

That is also why I'm not really a fan of his recordings as a solo artist – because you only get half of it. What Damo is doing has to be experienced live. You have to be in that same room in that same moment. I have been listening to recordings of our shows with him and it was nothing even close to the emotion you get in the room. So I think the importance of what he's doing is in that.

Also you have to understand that we kind of take recorded music for granted in some way, we've been growing up with recorded music. If you think about it, it's something quite new – recorded music? Humanity's been doing music for ages, since the Iron Age, but we started recording it only in the twentieth century.

What Damo is doing now is really getting music back to its basics. Back to the Iron Age, let's say! [laughs] People playing instruments in a room and people who are listening to it: the people who are experiencing it are as much *a part of it as the musicians. It's a complete feedback from the audience to the stage. I could watch a guy in the face as I'm playing, and that guy is going to be a huge influence on the next note I'm playing. Because I don't know where I'm going while I'm doing it, I'm improvising. Whatever happens around me in the moment is going to be an influence on what I'm doing onstage. Even the place you're playing in is going to be a huge influence on how the night is going to come out, the room, the space, what you're looking at – if you're playing with your eyes closed or if you're looking at something. Everything is going to be an influence on what you're playing in that moment, and that is so fascinating.*

It could be scary sometimes as well, if you're not used to it, but if you go past that scary element in there, you're going to find out it's so fulfilling and so fascinating.

DAMOSUZUKI.COM BLOG
January 19 2008 Saturday
Damo Suzuki with Nazim Communale (Piano), Francesco Donadello (Drums), Enrico Fontanelli (Synth, Electronics), Luca Giovanardi (Guitar, Electronics), Olivier Manchion (Bass), Jukka Reverberi (Guitar, Electronics), Luca Rossi (Bass) and Giulio C. Vetrone (Guitar)
@ Calamita

Last night I stayed at Luca and Ricci in Reggio.

Today's performance at Cavriago is few cat step from Reggio Emilia.

I woke up quite late, it was already noon. Ricci wrote note that she will come and pick me up as both has appointment with Luca's parents. They made appointment at the restaurant which is closer to both. I was once there at that amazing restaurant, that time mother of Luca invited us. His parents were already there I see Mr Giovanardi, the world businessman for first time. Food here is really great… I forget the name of the place… I have to ask Luca next time I see… maybe end of this year. After the lunch Luca brought me to Olivier, with whom we release half of double CD HollyAris*, he is calm French smart guy married with Italian lady… he really looks like French with his big nose settle in middle of face. Once I said to him or joke he is as Jean Paul Belmondo…

---

* Live CD set of Network performances in LA, 2005.

"For me it is not so much a matter of musical or technological possibilities," says the man who lends the Network his name. "The form is not so important. The machine is not making music – the human being is making music, so all mistakes are allowed because it's normal.

"I don't like to make this a platform for dictatorship; this is why I don't talk about music before or after the concert." As enthusiastic as his Network collaborators are about the end result, to him it's the process that's most important – the singer, not the song, to evoke an old cliché.

"All people really need to have their own life and to maintain a distance from the system," insists Damo. It seems maybe incongruous for a guy who was a Japanese salaryman for twenty-six years to express anti-corporate/anti-establishment sentiments. But then, with much experience of the working world on his shoulders, perhaps he knows better than most how vital it is to find small pockets of freedom, moments in time not filled with obligation and responsibility.

"I've been staying in Cologne for quite a long time now," Damo concedes of a full-time residence that stretches back to the eighties. "But still my feeling is that I can connect with somebody somewhere different." Again, it's the process of travelling from place to place, of switching between culturally and geographically separate groups of Sound Carriers, that stimulates him as much as the onstage product.

"My early bohemian life may extend only from my time in Sweden to touring in Can – maybe two or three years of travelling altogether. But I still think that I'm a 'spiritual bohemian' and I've always travelled when I had the time."

In that sense, what he would christen his Never-Ending Tour has been a way of returning to the travels of his youth; of maintaining the life of the worldwide wanderer.

NAOMUNE ANZAI
Sound designer/Damo Suzuki's Network
I was born in 1962. I started my career as a synthesizer programmer in the seventies and eighties. I became a professional musician in the mid-eighties just working on the synthesizers, and then became a more professional keyboard player. Also I made a studio for my work – for making a soundtrack for a film, a demo for my friend's band and things like that. So I became a

recording engineer in that studio – that was around 1990. I was doing that till about 2000. Then I moved [from Japan] to Melbourne, Australia, in 2002; because I was not known at all over here I could see it was not a great idea to promote myself as a musician from the start, I thought it was easier to promote myself as an engineer, so it became more a full-time engineer-producer situation at the Rancho Cumbo studio.

After that time I met Damo in Melbourne. I was a big fan of Can as a teenager, so I was quite happy to meet him and since then I've worked with him many times. After the nineties, Can became kind of famous with DJs and in the creative world; in Japan it shaped up like that. So when I came here I saw a flyer: 'Damo Suzuki at The Corner Hotel'. It was about 2003/04. The Corner Hotel has an 800 capacity and is a very well-respected venue in Melbourne, so Damo was kind of a VIP.

I didn't know he was that well known outside Japan – so I was very interested because I didn't expect to see Damo's gig in Australia. I got a ticket and went in, but I went in early because I knew some person at the Corner Hotel. I thought I may get a chance to see him and talk to him, but actually he just came out with the band to have a drink. So I just introduced myself and bought him a beer... then I bought him one again!

From 2003–2010 or 11, Damo was here every summer (summer in Australia/winter in Germany). He was staying for about a couple of months, so I had a chance to meet him every year. Because I was working at venues in Melbourne, I took care of his concerts many times.

Almost every time he was here, Damo has invited me to have dinner with him because he's a great chef. I remember the first time my family and I invited him to dinner, he made avocado soup. It was amazingly good! I think that the last time he was here I asked for his recipe to make it, but he didn't really remember. I think he is improvising his cooking, but his food is always great!

In February 2007, we had a big gig dedicated to Damo in Melbourne. I knew what he was going to do, as I'd seen him three or four times before that. There was a double-band situation on the stage – like lots and lots of musicians onstage. I set up my mixing desk beside my synthesizer and I was playing while I was mixing, so I made an entire recording of that gig. That was probably the biggest contribution I made: on February 1, 2007, at the venue called the Rob Roy Hotel. There was an original sound – synthesizers, Network *members – and we made a double CD just for Damo. He didn't refuse to but we didn't have a chance to release it. But it's quite well made, so if I get a chance to talk with some label guys I'm happy to release it.*

I was a keyboard player at that gig – all the other times I was working as a sound mixer. Every time I've mixed him to take care of his sound, the members on the stage are a different line-up. He doesn't usually repeat. It's interesting – it's sometimes more like a jazz-improvisation type of musician, sometimes electronic musicians and sometimes heavy doom music – lead guitar, drums and bassist style. So it's always different.

He is always acting like a conductor with his voice. I can understand how good the gig was for him by the way he's feeling after the first set or the second set. If he wants to keep going more and more then it's a very good situation; if he is not feeling very good then he doesn't keep going. So it's always the length of the show but it's unpredictable, we can never expect how long it will go. Sometimes he keeps going till the venue says: "You have to stop, we have to close."

In Melbourne around 2006 or 2007, there was a big boom in experimental music, soundscape, post-rock, all of those things. So the audience was really keen to see Damo as a master of that type of music. And the musicians jamming on stage were very keen to see Damo as a conductor and where he leads their music and where they're going with Damo's kind of sound.

FROM DAMOSUZUKI.COM BLOG
January 25 2007 (Thursday) Australia Melbourne Hi Fi Bar
Damo Suzuki with Edmond Ammendola (Bass), Tony Buck (Drums), Ollie Olsen (Keyboards), Nick Seymour (Bass) and Davey Williams (Drums)

Melbourne is my winter home and stay here around a month sometimes more as Tim* and Sally, my Australian family invite me to stay at their residence in middle of city. It's usual I relax here and charge my battery for next coming Never Ending Tour since 2004.

Hi Fi bar is near from Tim and Sally's residence. So, I can reach within a couple of minutes to there. The venue is too huge for my kinda music.

---

* Tim Peach has for a long time acted as Damo's host, promoter and photographer in Australia. Some of his photos from the last two decades can be seen in the picture section.

This time with three drums, two basses, saxophone and guitarist. As you can see in my list of sound carriers missing names of Saxophonist, Guitarist and another Drummer... In Melbourne I perform quite a lot. Most place I perform is Tokyo with much distance to second place London, then Melbourne. Melbourne is four million city and second biggest city in Australia, but for art and music take a place of capital city and living many artists and musicians. Quite often second biggest city of land is art metropole not biggest one: Montreal, Osaka, Barcelona, Cork, etc...

Anyway audience lost in space. But, music was OK... Band was fantastic. Even my friend haircutter Katsu told me this was my best performance he saw.

NAOMUNE ANZAI
'Noiser'/Damo Suzuki's Network

It looks like he doesn't care what kind of jam the musicians are on, or what kind of music his voice is on. If he likes something in it, if he finds something inspiring in it, his voice can be inspired even more and it seems to affect the audience more. He's always at the centre of what is happening, and he translates those musicians' progression into one music when he's feeling inspired.

When it's not going really well, we can hear it's separate, Damo's voice and the musicians' sound, it's not really as one. There may be a progression but it doesn't feel like one tune. But when it's going well, of course there's no rehearsal, no preparation, it's just happening, and when he's well inspired the music that is coming out through Damo is a complicated tune and a really attractive one.

I'm not really familiar with the recent Japanese music scene – for the last thirteen years I've been living here in Melbourne. But as far as I know from other musicians in Japan, and also as far as I know before I left there, there was no big scene for experimental music, alternative music or any indie kind of music in the market. So actually Damo is not as big in Japan as overseas.

Of course, Acid Mothers Temple and those bands are well known by underground music fans. But they don't have any media to expose them to 'normal' people, like outside of underground music society. So because of the lack of media, it's quite hard to make that kind of thing big in Japan.

Recently, every time I worked with some experimental guys, alternative guys, who are well known, like …And You Will Know Us By The Trail Of Dead, when I told them I know Acid Mothers Temple and Damo Suzuki, they said: "Wow! You know them personally? That's great." That's the same response I got from the American death-metal band Isis. Yet these are things I'd never expect if I'd stayed in Japan; he is well known by people who later became quite big musicians in any part of the world, except for Japan.

He is actually from the region very close to my hometown, as later I got to know, about fifty kilometres from downtown Tokyo. It's big in summer for the workers from Tokyo. I think that the most recent time he came here I didn't have a chance to work for him. I met him and had dinner, but I was on tour with other musicians and Damo's tour schedule and my schedule was not really matched. That's the last time I met him, just before Damo stopped touring here.* I'm really hoping he will come back and tour again. But if not, I'm happy to come if he has a show in Germany.

DAMOSUZUKI.COM BLOG
Melbourne, Australia
March 8 2008 Saturday
Damo Suzuki with T.B.I.
@ the Old Bar

I have a Japanese young sound carrier friend called Yuki, he learns Japanese Religion in University, is living since around 15 years in Mel… since when he was 15 years old. So, he has much Aussie mentality than Japanese from my perspective. He organised this concert and this is second time I perform with him. The venue is a pub musicians come and meet.

Mel has much Asian people… around place I live (it's also very close to Chinatown) you can imagine like Vancouver, sometimes you cannot realise you're in Mel… could be in Hong Kong or Singapore or somewhere in Asia. There are three Japanese papers, one of them my other sound carrier friend, Nao, is writing about music in Australia and he is expert on keyboard and wrote some books about that music instrument, also he has studio and record shop, is living really middle of music scene. And he will make sound

---

* By Naomune's reckoning, by the time Damo's illness recurred in 2014 he may not have been back to Australia for about three years.

engineering tonight. Nao is a perfectionist. Sometimes he is DJing as well. Man of many faces in good sense. Both my friends I mentioned are very good in speak English and knows lots about Aussie mentalities, society and whatever. They live without any handicap here at down under where tornadoes go other way around than Northern Hemisphere.

So, if I have performance some Japanese young people come, I don't know if they enjoy my music.

After the show the guy run the venue presented me their T-shirt. T-shirt, I have quite a lot at home. Every set I need one. I sweat quite a lot.

Believe me or not, I lose average four to five kg after every show. So, take liquid is very important to [go] back to my normal weight. Before it was beer, but now I try to drink just water or if I go to eat then I take noodle soup sort of things to cover my lost substance.

DAMOSUZUKI.COM BLOG, LATE 2008

Year is nearly closed to the end...

This year was very exciting year for me.

In October, I became a grandfather for Lucy, ¼ German, Japanese, Mexican, Puerto Rico. She is sweet and all those years with my three sons, a bit of light and sweet dreams, flowers, puppets...

I as grandpa, can you imagine? I have more motivation and kind of more responsibility that is good. I have to live long...

CHAPTER FOURTEEN

JAPAN – A SLIGHT RETURN

If life progresses in random cycles, then the international Network gigs of the mid-noughties brought their main man to a geographical full circle. Having begun the Network with a band line-up put together to play his homeland, Damo began to forge closer links with Japanese musicians. Among these was an old friend and rock veteran – Tetsu Yamauchi, formerly the boozy bassist of Rod Stewart's legendarily hedonistic Faces, now retired from the music industry.

"Maybe the middle of 2005, I had a concert in Yokohama and he was living quite near," explains Damo. "Kamakura is maybe only twenty-two kilometres west of Yokohama.

"This was the first time ever I performed with him, even though I knew him for such a long time. He's making music but not so often. He's older, he has one kid, he's married and living in a temple somewhere."

Having renounced rock music as unsuited to a man of his age, Tetsu was – perhaps surprisingly – making occasional forays to its wildest Eastern shores. He would sometimes play with Keiji Haino, the veteran Japanese guitarist and progenitor of the underground subgenre now known simply as 'noise'.

In the West, the noise scene could denote the most disturbing elements of industrial music or so-called 'power electronics'. But with Haino it came to mean something more fundamental, a return of the classic rock guitar/bass/drums line-up to its essential electric state.

The most recognisable starting point might be Lou Reed's *Metal Machine Music* – four sides of loosely structured guitar feedback and discord, trashed by critics back in 1975, latterly acclaimed as a classic and performed as a chamber symphony by the Zeitkratzer ensemble. But Haino's own music sometimes goes way beyond this*, into realms of confrontation and unlistenability where he's not so much playing guitar feedback as manually abusing his instrument.

But then there's Fushitsusha, his sublime band format which started as an electronic duo and later became a power trio. 'Power' is the operative word here – the violence of the rock riff is distilled to its grinding, thudding essence, with vocals that sound to the non-Japanese speaker like they're screaming their way out of a cultural straitjacket (though they could be saying anything, of course). It's as if Black Sabbath, back during their invention of heavy metal, had discarded all blues licks in favour of all-out aural and emotional assault.

"I performed with Keiji Haino as well as some of the other noisemakers," acknowledges Damo, unfazed by their audio violence. After his debut Japanese gigs in 1997, "after another five years or so I performed with young Japanese artists. At that time I found that Japan was actually not such a bad place for music, many young Japanese musicians were creating something different to European or Western musicians. That's why Japanese noise music is getting quite popular all over the world.

"I'm talking from my side of music, my area, but they're making far better music than forty years before, when I left Japan," Damo acclaims with mild amazement. "Many young kids have a feeling for free creativity. This is a good thing even when it's something I don't like, because they're trying to do something outside of mainstream Japanese pop."

As he notes, in Tokyo today there are as many as up to 400 live music venues – possibly as great a number as any city in the world. It's a prescription for diversity, as the tastes of such a modern metropolis can't be limited to saccharine (if sometimes borderline porno) J-pop, or reworked Western rock clichés. In the post-modern manner of current music, it's also a cue for genre boundaries to melt into and contaminate (or catalyse) each other.

* At least to the delicate ears of the writer.

240

Outside of the brutality of pure noise, his own J-music collaborators in the 21st century have included Keiichi Miyashita – whose ambient guitar playing touches on the sonic spaces of jazz and the multiple dimensions of psychedelia – and Acid Mothers Temple, whose fluctuating line-ups* and lysergic multitracking give the lie to Japan as a nation of programmed conformists, with guitar lines that soar above gravity and evoke Robert Fripp in his early 'Frippertronics' period. By his own admission, all are the children of an evolving underground scene which, in his decades-long absence, Damo was neither part of nor witness to.

"Maybe it was boredom with what took place before," he reflects. "I think the same thing happened in Germany in '68 with so-called 'krautrock'. Nothing in Japan happened, I think, for thirty, forty years, and so later, some people found something special, some power that is working against the trend. That is how they got the energy to do this."

Other artists to whom Damo gives a namecheck include Masonna, aka extreme noise veteran Yamazaki Maso: "his concerts are only three minutes while he makes a soundcheck for one hour. He makes noise, some of the loudest, for one hour in his preparation soundcheck." It's hard to believe the classical music enthusiast could endure the cacophonous Masonna for long – but as with many of his own Sound Carriers, it's the concept of creative freedom which excites, rather than the end product itself.

"I've also played twice with an opening band called Hijōkaidan, who are the pioneers of Japanese noise music." Indeed, their live performances, with an edge of machine noise, can make Fushitsusha sound like easy listening. "They have two members working as the managers of a big Japanese company**, and if they give a concert they make it *really loud* – they are actually the loudest noise band in Japan. After they played it created all kinds of problems, as the audience's ears were already ringing. It's not easy to perform after them."

As far as the Network's Sound Carriers go, the Japanoise artists and Nipponese neo-psychedelicists serve the same purpose as any other

---

* From the mothership Acid Mothers Temple & The Melting Paraiso U.F.O. to Acid Mothers Gong, a merger with veterans of the UK psychedelic scene.

** Band co-founder Jojo Hiroshige also runs the Japanese experimental label Alchemy Records.

accompanying musicians: Damo's randomly composed vocals can erupt from within their sounds like a primal growl, or float ethereally above them. The affinity with Japan's pop avant-garde is there – but this is something that's developed over a different time and space, while he was living as a European performer.

At least once, a parallel has been drawn with his fellow expatriate Yoko Ono – a contemporary of Joseph Beuys in the Fluxus movement and an avant-garde pop performer before such things became hip. "I've also listened to Yoko Ono's music for a short time before *Plastic Ono Band* and things like that," he says of her disconcerting early mewlings*, "but it's not really for me. I think she's improvised with a lot of different people too** – I can say the same thing but it's not my world!"

MARCO HEIBACH

I was onstage in some concerts. I wasn't in the centre of the stage but at the back somewhere, and was like experiencing the atmosphere that was created in the moment. When I was young, I also filmed some of my dad's concerts – not in a professional way. I had a camera and it was like the most natural thing to do – anyway, I was there. His music was interesting, but I wouldn't say it was my type of music because I grew up in a different generation. So I would say I understand, not the emotions, but the energy he wants to transport to the audience. Of course it differs with the musicians he's playing with – because of each band and each location, each one is a very different concert. The only constant was my father, and maybe it was like a different view to watch him through the camera, to see him there onstage.

I think I was a bit too young for finding my roots there or something like that, because for me the language barrier was also quite big. When I was younger I tried to learn Japanese in a school, but I didn't really fit into the

---

* After performing with Lennon, her husband, in the Plastic Ono Band, Yoko's *Approximately Infinite Universe* (1973) was an infinitely more digestible mix of psych-rock and soft-pedalled feminism. Artists as unlikely as kitsch-rockers The B-52s have cited its underrated appeal.

** Plastic Ono Band performances over the past decade or so have featured the participation of everyone from benign, ex-Sonic Youth guitar experimentalist Thurston Moore to confrontational filmmaker Vincent Gallo. The guitar playing of son Sean Lennon is a constant.

school because I didn't really talk any Japanese at home. All the kids were talking Japanese and learning the written language – I was the only kid not speaking it and then I was put into one class with one other guy! I felt a little bit excluded so I stopped learning Japanese.

So when I went to Japan the language barrier was really quite big for me – I couldn't really talk to the people and most of the people couldn't talk any English.* Most of the signs back then were totally in Japanese, so if I'd been alone back then I wouldn't have any idea of where to go. So I can say from my perspective, at least for the first part of the travelling I saw Japan like a tourist. The first time I felt different about this was when I met my uncle Hirofumi in Hokkaido.

He was like a janitor in a school – we actually slept in the school because the school had holidays, then he made us some rooms, made us some beds there. It was a good feeling, because I got to know my cousin, Shu-He. The moments when it really felt different were when we met family and stayed with them for a while – for a dinner, or just to visit them for a few hours. This wasn't like my experience on the coach, where I was getting a very touristic view.

There was one situation that was very interesting for me, when we met an actual fan of him: he was a dentist and he was really coming to his concerts a lot. At some point before we travelled there, my father became friends with him.** A very decent guy – he let us sleep at his home, his wife made the beds and cooked us a meal. This was also a very nice experience, but as a guest – not like a cultural experience you have by yourself.

There are a lot of memories. I'm not really sure about the location of where he played – we were travelling. I wasn't actually so aware of where we are, in which city, but there was one concert where he was playing with two drummers – which was very interesting for me. I never saw two drummers onstage at the same time, really like accompanying each other and filling the other's blank spaces. This was a part of the concert that I was really interested in, and then his concert with Marble Sheep*** – because we knew

---

*   Even for Marco, as a German citizen, English is the common tongue.
**   Takazou, Damo's dentist friend.
***   The Japanese psych band formed by Ken Matsutani, founder of Captain Trip Records.

the band, we knew the people, this was a very interesting, very fun event for me.

There was one quite weird and funny concert for me, because I was a little bit too young, I'd never experienced people who made noise music before, in this very noisy way! There was one guy on the stage who had a microphone connected to a lot of effects pedals. He held the microphone in his hand and banged it against his head because he liked the noise! This was a moment when I was very confused.

Also, at one location before the concert actually started, my father invited all the musicians to dinner. During the dinner you could see some of the musicians started to get more and more nervous, because the time was passing and they didn't even have a soundcheck, they didn't even prepare their instruments. You could really feel the nervousness!

It was a very interesting moment, because my father was like very relaxed and not even bothered by them being nervous. Then they went on stage and some of the musicians could feel the vibe and be confident again in their abilities. But I would say there was like a moment where some of them questioned their abilities and were scared, and this was interesting for me, because I think this actual moment describes a lot of the feelings that are going on when people go onstage to improvise music.

Of course I see a lot of the randomness, but I think it's also a very big part of his personality that makes it, his character and his ability to focus on the attention from the stage. Which not everybody has – I say this as a person who doesn't really like to be on a stage. I viewed this from a spectator's perspective.

I know his concept and his central idea is that all the musicians and all the elements should have equal part in the music, and there's not one lead singer or lead instrument that's leading all the way to everything – it's like an equal element. That's the way I would say I understand his motivation.

KEIICHI MIYASHITA
Guitar musician, aka Mandog/Damo Suzuki's Network
Around 1980, when I was ten years old, new wave and electro became established in Japan. It awakened in me an interest in this kind of music. I got a small analogue synthesizer in 1983, but, as I was more influenced by rock, after a short time I changed to guitar. After two years I connected to

modern jazz, like Miles Davis; at the age of sixteen I became conscious of improvisation. At that time I listened to free jazz, but I was much influenced by old-style bebop and swing-style jazz, and also by different Western and Eastern music.

In 1999, I received a self-recorded live cassette of Damo Suzuki's Network In Kyoto from my future wife, a short time after I met her for the very first time. At that time I didn't know about Damo. In Japan there is the category of 'progressive rock', Damo and Can were categorised in this way. When I started to play guitar I heard all the major songs of progressive rock groups, but I didn't have any interest in it as its musical expression seemed exaggerated. I didn't have time for listening to so-called progressive rock. However, when I listened to the cassette tape of Damo's concert, it was different from the preconceived image of progressive rock I had and it felt very cool.

In 1999, I was naturally drawn to things like instant composing; I found Damo was already doing this, which helped to clarify his image for me. And I started wondering: 'What is Damo doing nowadays?' I found his website and sent mail to him. Surprisingly, I received a response from him a few days later. Email exchanges started from this time on.

Our exchanges weren't so much talking about music, instead it was, 'This and that food tastes good,' or, 'I've experienced this and that today.' This had been continuing for a while, then one day Damo wrote: "Do you have any interest to join Damo Suzuki's Network West Coast tour?"

I was really surprised, as Damo didn't know my guitar playing and yet he invited me to join. In the summer of 2002, I met Damo for the first time on the outskirts of Los Angeles. Our last concert in Hollywood became a CD, Hollyaris. I performed with him in USA, Japan, Germany, South Korea and UK, around fifty concerts together.

Instant composing with Damo began very naturally; we were not playing written notes, therefore each time was different according to the Sound Carriers and Damo's reaction. Instant composing is effected by joining up the Sound Carriers' musical backgrounds and their ideas. It will be different with each combination. When I play with Damo, he gives me the freedom of musical adventure.

There were many memorable concerts, one of them in Cologne, 2005. Damo and I joined Grundwasser, the band of the guitarist Dominik von Senger, who *was also in The Damo Suzuki Band and Dunkelziffer. When the concert began to heat up, the performance became transcendent. I got much more into it, the audience became like a wave, I felt I could get into a spaceship and fly somewhere... such was the energy I felt.*

I feel that Damo is a shaman. His vocals are Damo bushi* (or maybe 'Damoese', whatever). It sounds like a musical instrument but it's a human voice; sometimes like a saxophone, sometimes like percussion.

For me, Damo is a European musician. Music created with Damo surely has some psychedelic element, but it doesn't happen by saying: "Let's play psychedelic!" It's something similar to seeing a landscape, flower or plant in nature and finding something psychedelic in it. I say that at that moment we are creating music outside of any categorisation.

In 2004 Damo came to Japan, where Makoto Kawabata organised a show with Acid Mothers Temple in Nagoya. Two years before, in 2002, Damo Suzuki's Network had performed at the San Juan Islands festival; it was a project joined by Daevid Allen and Gilli Smyth of Gong**, and Kawabata's group. Since this time I have kept in contact with Kawabata.

MAKOTO KAWABATA
Guitarist, Acid Mothers Temple/Damo Suzuki's Network
I learnt to play guitar totally by myself. So i spent four years finding so-called 'regular tuning'... i played with my tuning fork then. Also i practised with the TV at that time. I improvised in C minor and i was always thinking: 'If there is my space in this music, what should i play?' So i played with the announcers speaking over it.

---

*   Keiichi Miyashita: "In Traditional Japanese folk song, a type of vocal ornamentation called 'kobushi' is used. I used the words 'Damo bushi' as a unique singing method for Damo."

**   Gong are an often unsung oddity in the history of rock music. As much an ever-changing hippie/countercultural community as a band, they were formed by Australian beatnik and ex-Soft Machine guitarist Allen and his longtime partner, Ms Smyth, in Paris in 1967 – having evolved from the UK's Cambridge scene. Self-styled 'pothead pixies' in their early days, their music was a sometimes engaging mix of trippy improvisation, free jazz and English whimsy. Daevid Allen died in March 2015, aged seventy-seven; Gilli Smyth followed him into the cosmos in August 2016, aged eighty-three. At Allen's request, Gong has kept going in yet another permutation.

I discovered 'krautrock' during my high-school to university-student period, late seventies to mid eighties. It was no influence on my guitar playing, 'coz then i especially loved (still do now!) Popol Vuh, Tangerine Dream and Cluster*... they don't have so much guitar playing. But i didn't get any influence from Japanese sixties and seventies rock. I always believed their music was just copies of Western music. If someone said Flower Traveling Band was great, were they sure FTB was better than Led Zeppelin? I'm sure it wasn't, even if FTB was the best group in Japan at that time.**

Acid Mothers Temple had something like that in our past which we called the Soul Collective, but it's over now for many reasons. Now, we are smaller though we have a much stronger creative relationship. Unfortunately i'm not like Daevid Allen of Gong, not such a heavenly, friendly, open-minded person, so i can't create and keep a great network like Gong going.*** Also we are not native English speakers, we have many problems of communication with Western people still.

But i believe in music. Music can be shared by anyone who needs it. The relationship with people was only music for us, not words... even in the band we have never talked about music, 'coz i need musicians who can understand what we should play in each moment by improvisation. We don't need any words about music, just listening and playing.

---

*   The three bands that some claimed made 'krautrock' synonymous with electronica or ambient music. Performing as Popul Vuh, the late Florian Fricke's meditative, devotional soundtracks offered an atmospheric counterpoint to the obsessive mania depicted in Werner Herzog's early films – particularly his nightmarish classics *Aguirre, Wrath Of God* (1972) and *Nosferatu The Vampyre* (1979). Edgar Froese, the composer synonymous with Tangerine Dream, detached his internalised synthesizer pieces from any form of driving rhythm; the airy (and sometimes eerie) tones of his *Zeit* ('Time', 1972) were once thought to be a path for rock's evolution, in the days before punk took it all back to year zero. Hans-Joachim Roedelius and Dieter Moebius had conducted many sonic experiments before their epochal looping and distortion of traditional analogue instruments in Cluster; it's unlikely that the ambient music of onetime collaborator Brian Eno would have developed in the same way without their influence.

**   See *Japrocksampler: How The Post-War Japanese Blew Their Minds On Rock'N'Roll* by Julian Cope (Bloomsbury, 2007) for an effusive account of Flower Travelling Band and their contemporaries.

***   The collaboration between the two musical collectives is preserved on a live album: *Acid Mothers Gong Live Tokyo* (2006, Voiceprint).

I met Damo for the first time at the festival on the island of San Juan. Damo played before us; we played as Guru And Zero (Daevid Allen + Cotton Casino + Makoto Kawabata). The first time i collaborated with him was in Japan; after that we toured in both Korea and Japan. I went to see Damo in Osaka; when he saw me he asked: "Mako-chan, do you bring your guitar?" "What? I came here just as an audience, also as your friend." But he said to me: "You should bring your guitar and play together tonight!"

Next time in Osaka, i played with him at the same venue. Also i had a solo show at a different venue the next day. I asked Damo: "What will you do tomorrow?" He said: "Just day off." I asked him: "Can you play with me, 'coz i have a solo show in Osaka?" He said: "Of course! Yes!" Always we were like this.

Sometimes we were in the same city, then Damo joined with AMT, even at All Tomorrow's Parties one time. Damo and i toured in Ireland and the UK.

DAMOSUZUKI.COM BLOG
December 7 2008 (Sunday)
UK London @Bardens Boudoir
Damo Suzuki with Makoto Kawabata (guitar)

We arrived London, had hours to relax… This performance is remarkable as the club owner thought Makoto and I perform as duet and didn't invite sound carriers at all, even not guitar amplifier for Makoto… Anyhow we managed two members of Kits, an Australian band from Melbourne, now based in London, joined us spontaneously (I will meet them in two months in Melbourne) and Glyn, the flute player. I sat at merchandising spot, Shingai from Noisette said me hello, but I didn't recognise her as she changed a lot. (Another hairstyle!) She joined Network performance in Aberdeen a couple of year before.

All members of Bo Ningen, London-based Japanese band. Everybody of the band is so skinny… like sticks ('Bo' in Japanese), 'Ningen' means human being. You can imagine four (young) Japanese John Cooper Clarkes…

It was short and nice trip with Makoto, an excellent guitarist. He said some days before, he is getting taste of creating time and space of the moment with ever-changing local sound carriers, unfortunately it was too short…

MAKOTO KAWABATA
Acid Mothers Temple/Damo Suzuki's Network

I remember that London show. We had a trio as a support band, they were like a punk band. I proposed to Damo that we should play as just a duo, 'coz it was the final show of the tour and we had no other chance to play, but Damo said we should play with them.

Then i asked them to collaborate with us; they were surprised and said to me they hadn't played any improvisation. Also they didn't know what improvised music is... so i explained, and we decided on some simple signs for playing. I don't remember what the music was that we played... hahaha... i just remember they played almost the same riff and beat all the time, very minimal. Maybe it was a good experience for Damo.

I don't know the correct word for it so i say that all of my music has come from 'my cosmos'. I wanna be just like a radio tuner to catch the music and play it to people. Then i don't need any personality or my own expression... i need to play only 'pure' sounds from my cosmos. Even when i played with Damo, i could hear music from my cosmos in each moment. I'm sure music can teach me what i should play – even sound, colour, i have to reproduce exactly – then i look for how i can get this sound, and choose effects then too.

I don't need to seek. Music knows everything already, we should hear it and reproduce exactly. That's all for me. Any personality or expression just prevents me reproducing music from my cosmos. I don't know what Damo is seeking, but i believe we run towards the same place even by different routings.

DAMOSUZUKI.COM BLOG
Kokubunji, Japan
March 15 2008 Saturday
(First Set) Damo Suzuki with Varunk: Love (Fretless), Nozaki Masahito (Drums)
(Second Set) Damo Suzuki with Fujikake Masataka (Drums), Hiroshi Higo (Bass), Shinya Kojima (Guitar) and Munenori Takada (Turntable)
@ Morgana

My dentist friend Takazou and his wife Yuu picked us up from Narita airport. Fortunately they have day off. Both work hard at their own dental house.

Elke[*] has come from another terminal also she is first time in Japan, she took a bit time. It was rainy day through Tokyo to Hino, where Keiichi and Kiku live took four hours drive. Trafic jam and hard rain took so long. When we arrived there we were quite hungry, drop Yuu at their place. Normally when I arrive I go to Japanese food restaurant at airport... they have many restaurants... this I really like from Narita Airport, you have many choices not in food style and also restaurants. Anyway today we didn't go there instead went to so-called family restaurant. This is chain restaurant, but if you sort out like Mac-something you are wrong. Most of family restaurant is not fast food here. They make fresh and assortment is huge. Look at menu they have, it shows measurement of calorie. We went tonight to place called Tonden – this is my favourite family restaurant. They bring fresh fish from Hokkaido, Northern Island, every day and every three months they change menu and they have some speciality of the season...

Love-San is sound carrier friend and he arranged this show... that means he will perform tonight too. Varunk is two-piece band, Love-san plays fretless bass with Nozaki, the drummer. Fujikake is the drummer having trio project with my sound carrier friend Keiichi (Mandog), Higo is quiet nice guy plays bass. If you travel around the world you find always somebody similar to your friend. Higo remains me of Mandjao, my African sound carrier friend (also play bass) lives in Cologne. They both don't speak that much, but always smiling. Someone told me Higo made first Japanese indie label.

After performance, we go to Uchiage – a kind of after-performance party with sound carriers. Uchiage will happen at Izakaya, a kind of pub with sake assortment and have to order small dishes of foods, which is very delicious... I like this place. Izakaya is just everywhere... like German has every corner pub, Izakaya, you can find every corner. I love this way to drink alcohol... and I think healthy, eat and drink combination.

SIMON TORSSELL LERIN
Musical partner of Bettina Hvidevold Hystad/guitarist, Damo Suzuki's Network
When we first saw him I didn't know so much about the Network shows. I listened to Can and I had also heard an album he made with Omar Rodríguez-

---

[*] Elke Morsbach, Damo's partner of many years – see concluding chapters.

López, from The Mars Volta.* I think that album might have been my first encounter with Damo singing.*

I was quite interested but I didn't know really what to expect. He performed with these two young guys from Osaka, these young Japanese guys that were eighteen years old or something. I was quite surprised by that because they were inexperienced and I thought that was an interesting aspect to the Network, because not all of the musicians were really professional, some were just beginners, and some were really professional.

By my experience, when we've been travelling with him and seeing a lot of shows, and sometimes performing with him as well, my impression is that sometimes the music's really good and sometimes the tempo's slow but it seems like the audience have been really into it. Sometimes it's not always great, but anyway it seems like it's opened new ideas for people in the audience, so I think it's been quite effective – depending on what aspect you're looking at it from.

The first time I played with him, that was in Japan also** and I hadn't really performed improvised music live before in front of an audience. I was used to playing with bands on more rehearsed music – I just came as an audience member, and Damo asked me if I wanted to play because they had some extra guitars laying around: "Do you want to join, do you want to play tonight?" I was not prepared at all for it, so the first time it was kind of a bit scary and shocking for me as well. The Japanese bass player and drummer really improvised a lot, but they'd also played together a lot so I was kind of out! [laughs] They knew each other really well, and I didn't know them at all, so it was quite difficult for me but

---

*   Rodríguez-López was guitarist and sound designer for The Mars Volta – a band that embraced the taboo term 'progressive' out of desire to move their music forward by assimilating different styles. Certainly, *Please Heat This Eventually*, his 2007 12″ EP with Damo, carries elements of freakbeat, free jazz, even dub. The thirteen-minute title track was recorded live at Gebäude 9, Cologne, on November 14, 2005, later edited by Omar Rodríguez-López in the studio. There's a depth and urgency to Damo's vocal that you'll still hear in live performance now, particularly in the alliterative repetition of words/sounds like 'way'/'ways'/'wise', which seem to mean both everything and nothing.

**   The concerts for which he returned to Japan to celebrate his sixtieth birthday in 2010 – see footnotes for Chapter Two.

really fun also. Then that really started me kind of playing my own improvised music.

I think I've played with Damo maybe seven or eight times now and each time it's been with different people. Bettina has been with me as well – she wasn't there the first time but, for all the other shows, she was the only one who's been there for all of them. But otherwise it's been different musicians each time. I think it's really interesting to meet the different musicians that we've played with because we all try to talk to each other a little bit before the shows: some people have played more rehearsed music, so we always try to have a little bit of a plan or a structure, but Damo is always saying he doesn't want us to talk, he doesn't want us to have any structure! [laughs]

But some shows have been really, really great – one of the really interesting shows was this thing we did two or three years ago maybe at the Red Bull Music Academy in Tokyo. They had this weekend where Damo created a seven-and-a-half-hour improvisation by twenty musicians! Some of the performers were playing traditional Japanese instruments, some traditional drums from Japan, and then in the background you had twenty-year-old noise musicians and Keiji Haino played guitar, who was also in his sixties. It was a very interesting mix of musicians, because some were more noise musicians and some were playing like funk bass or some traditional instruments, it was a real mix of sounds! At some points it was very good – because it was seven hours some people had to rest, but it was good.

I was playing with a few different noise-rock bands in Norway and Sweden. I was working with ambient music and improvisational music, so that's why I was interested in Damo's Network because it's improvisation music. Now I have put a musical project together with Bettina, who was also playing with Damo. We perform together, we work with pre-recordings, and ambient music and electronic rock as well.

Bettina wasn't a musician before she met Damo. We met in art school and she had been working with this art project, like relational art, so she was interested in how he invited these different musicians and the first meeting was on stage. But during this time she also started to perform with musicians as well – synthesizer stuff and pre-recordings. She's done some live sampling of Damo's vocals when we were performing with him.

DAMOSUZUKI.COM BLOG
March 29 2008 (Saturday) Japan Kumamoto Django
Damo Suzuki with Ishiatama-Zizo: Katsunori Akutagawa (Guitar), Tetsuya Akune (Guitar), Yuji Takagi (Bass) and Toshiro Usui (Drums)

We took breakfast nearby at shopping mall which looks like standard US shopping mall with all these ugly fast foods, but in Japan you can find still some interesting things to eat... after we drove to Usuki-city (which is impossible to read in Japanese Kanji letter: Chinese letter equally) famous for old Buddha figures from ancient Japan. From six century, very first time Buddhism enter to Japan. I'm not Buddhist, but I'm very interested in history. Also I wanted to go out of the city to nature... Such old Buddha figures smells of 1,500 years. This time in Japan I found many things. So, I decided to travel top to bottom of Japan one day... I will make it in year 2010. I discovered Japan. This is the land where I was born and grow up... I should have known better. Can remember, one foreigner artist said Japan is so small country, but in this tiny space you can find many interesting things, culture, foods, locale to locale so different, every inch you can find something curious...

Travel to Kumamoto is better with bus than take train. So, beautiful landscapes through Aso national park. Aso is very famous for its volcano tourism. I was there once when I was a schoolboy. Bus reached Kumamoto a bit late. At bus terminal, three members of Ishiatama-Zizo (Ishiatama means stone head, Jizo is kind of Buddha figure which is not that huge, standing quiet on path, you can find it in China and Japan but not in India).

Akutagawa is contact person, who organise alternative music performances in this local city Kumamoto, normally run his record shop. Kumamoto has one of three most beautiful castle in Japan beside Sendai and Himeji called Kumamoto-jō – also there is Aso national park, Amakusa, a bunch of islands as touristy attraction. Historically very heavyweight in Japanese history and supporter of new Japan system at end of Syogun period. Foods here are famous: basashi horsemeat sashimi. We had much time to soundcheck, so I wanted to go to eat and taste this basashi... Sure I can eat it in Tokyo as well. But look, when I saw dish friendly old woman brought no compare to Tokyo's tiny slice, here they serve much wide slice and taste better... yummy. And this could be local horsemeat. Mainly Japanese import horsemeat come from Australia... basashi you can get in Tokyo must be imported goods... anyway I have to research. It fits really good with uronhai (uron tea, rice schnapps mix which is my favourite drink in Japan)... Good food and good drink... What I need more...? Just good performance will be done!!!

Stacia once was dancer of Hawkwind in seventies, now she is visual artist staying in Kyoto for a while; visited me this performance from such a distance by train she said she took something like five hours or so. So, this is first time I saw her since early seventies. She contacted me as she was flying from Dublin to Berlin, seat beside her was one of my Irish sound carrier friend... again such a small world we are living in!! ...isn't it nice? ...

Day is shorter also it's in March. Went to Kumamoto-jō. This castle is really amazing and huger than I thought. It's strong looking. There was not that much tourist... it was too late and we couldn't get enter Tenshukaku (castle tower). We walk through park, you can feel silence of souls who lived here and fight against enemies.

FRANCESCO DI LORETO
Director, *Neverending* (2015) – a documentary film about Damo Suzuki
Several years ago I saw a concert of Damo Suzuki's music here in Milan, and I was a big fan of Can's music especially. So I had made several music documentaries – one of them about Robert Wyatt* – and I tell him about my project. I think he was very honoured about that. So I tell him about the places I will be shooting, and I start to contact him when he is travelling and making concerts.

Little by little it starts to take shape, take form. I make two or three interviews – one of them is in the shop of Xabier Iriondo, who is a musician.** We start to make a real project: I have some interviews, some concerts, I am making my documentary – then I go to Lüneburg and Würzburg for concerts two years later. Every year I shoot four or five hours. Then in 2012 I applied to go with him to Japan.

We started July 10, 2012 – I was with my assistant Samantha [Vecchiattini], we were only a little crew because it was quite expensive, so we are two people. But it was a really nice period and a nice experience to make with him. To know him better, you know – because we stayed for maybe fifteen, sixteen days, travelling together every day, staying in the same hotel. It was

---

*   *Robert Wyatt: Little Red Robin Hood (1998).*
**   Guitarist of Italian band Afterhours.

interesting for me for my film, to combine music, travelling and food together. The three points of my documentary.

I am happy about that because Japan is his birth country. We organised together the trip. He didn't have a telephone number [laughs], so we met in a hotel in Tokyo. Yes, it was an appointment, but we need sometimes to check by telephone – he came, luckily. He refused to carry telephone – I don't know why! He uses very well email or Skype or technological stuff, but not telephone.

And then we start for maybe a fifteen-day trip in Japan. He makes some concerts with Sound Carriers in different places – we have one in Sapporo, one in Tsurugashima and the last one was in Asahikawa. Two concerts were in Tokyo and two were in Hokkaido, the island in the north. We travelled a lot together. He was a good guide for us in Japan.

He brought us to knowing something about the food of Japan, which for me was new because I knew only sushi or sashimi, something like that, which now is very popular in Italy too. He likes food very much, so he's very interested in it. He brought us plates of special foods from several parts of Japan, from the south to the north. We discovered several dishes which were really interesting to me, because I opened my mind to Japanese food. Now I discovered that they have a really, really large range of things to eat.

I start with his preparation of food. Throughout the film, Damo is sometimes in the kitchen cooking something – for me, for my friends, for the Sound Carriers. So of course I ate many things – he's a good cook.

I met his brothers in Sapporo – we stayed together for one hour, then I left him to his brothers and his family because it was a little bit private. He told me about his mother, and his uncle was an origami maker.

From 2010, he rediscovered Japan – he was thinking about Japanese things and he tried to be closer to the origin of his life. He was happy to play with Japanese guys because he felt more close to the people. His idea of energy in the music worked better, I think, with Japanese people who were close to him, of his culture. He plays with people of every part of the world, he's very open to every culture. But I think at the end, Japanese culture is his culture.

DAMOSUZUKI.COM BLOG, MID-FEBRUARY 2011

Well... I was travelling in Japan, Australia, Malaysia, UK and Spain... since middle of August 2010.

I live here in Europe since end of sixties, so, one day I thought of to discover Japan, where I was born and grow up, from top north to bottom south, all through Japan islands... around 3,000 km length.

So, finally I've done. Even I don't think it was great idea to see everywhere so superficial. (I won't do it again.)

World around trip is easy thing, you don't have to visit all countries on this planet. Just you choose one of both direction westbound or eastbound. Also there are some flight companies offer World Around Trip for not that expensive.

Definition of Japan around-trip is to visit all prefectures (we have 47 prefectures).

Only pass all those prefecture and not stay for a while is really, really superficial and I'm not interested to make record like shortest around Japan trip or so.

So, I put a rule, every prefecture at least to walk 400 metres.

Result is around a bit less than 15,000 kilometres by train, four times with airplane and some part with bus (and taxi).

I will report this later one day.

I collected many experiences, find good and critical things, taste everywhere fantastic foods, enjoyed nice view, culture, landscapes...

Now, I know much more about that pretty land.

Me as a Kabuki actor? No, this was a gag for a Damo Suzuki Band poster. On it were written names of band members in Japanese calligraphy: 蛇毛鈴木= Damo Suzuki / 邪鬼愛時= Jaki Liebezeit.
©HEINZ KASTROP.

The Damo Suzuki Band: Matthias, me, Dominik at back, Jaki at front.

"Sinbad" in Chinguetti, Mauritania
©DAMO SUZUKI.

Julie's Haircut visited me between surgeries in 2015, on the way to their next performance. Left to right: Azzurra Fragale, Claudio Cuoghi, Andrea Scarfone, Ulisse Tramalloni, me, Nicola Caleffi, Andrea Rovacchi and Luca Giovanardi. ©ELKE MORSBACH.

Dominik von Senger on guitar; the other guitarist you can see in the background is Mandog (Keiichi Miyashita).
©DOMINIK VON SENGER.

With Jelly Planet at All Tomorrow's Parties, Camber Sands, 2005. Left to right: Jens Küchenthal, Alex Schönert, Felix A. Gutierrez, me and Stephan Hendricks. ©GERALD JENKINS.

My mum, Chihiro (baby daughter of Hiro), me, Haruna (daughter of my older brother Isamu) and my lovely, funny sister Hiroko. ©THE SUZUKI FAMILY.

Kids are getting taller and bigger and fathers are getting smaller and older ... Marco – Martin (front) – Mirko with their old man. ©GERALD JENKINS.

Poster for *Neverending* (2015) – a documentary film by Francesco di Loreto. ©FRANCESCO DI LORETO.

Elke and I ride the escalator to Tate Modern, London. ©GERALD JENKINS.

I'm so thankful to Sally Fethers (and her partner Tim Peach) – all the way from Melbourne to visit me and give me motivation while I was in hospital, 2014. ©TIM PEACH.

Fake Fall: the fake Mark E, centre, with the last formation of The Fall (now Imperial Wax) in Manchester 2018. Left to right: Kieron Melling, Simon 'Ding' Archer, Dave Spurr and Pete Greenway.
©MICHELLE HEIGHWAY, from her film *ENERGY*.

Recently, Hiro sent this portrait of me drawn by him.
©HIROFUMI SUZUKI.

DAMO SUZUKI

SANTIAGO MOTORIZADO NIÑO ELEFANTE

DOCTORA MUERTE CHATRAN CHATRAN

FONEZ

ROTENAPELS!

MUSICALIZA AMITO

ENSAMBLE PUPORA!

MARTES 12
DE DICIEMBRE

PJE AGUSTÍN PÉREZ 99

PARAGUAY

MERCADO PARALELO DE EMOCIONES

PARASONICA

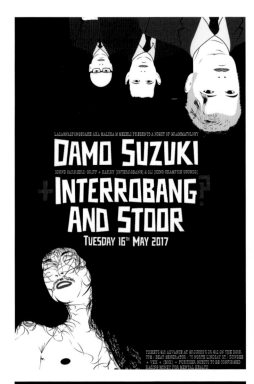

CHAPTER FIFTEEN

NEVER ENDING I

"I don't really know how many concerts I've done as a Network project," says Damo of his Never-Ending Tour. But before the sickness that plagued the first half of his life recurred, he estimates it at between eighty and a hundred concerts per year from the early days of the new millennium to halfway through 2014. Of course, the international locations differed wildly – as did the circumstances.

"Sometimes I performed with forty people altogether – forty people but thirty-five singers," he laughs. "Some concerts I performed together with three bands on the same stage, so I did three sets with three different bands: each of them is on average five people so with everyone there I performed together with fifteen people. So I think I performed with well over 7,000 people anyway, but I'm not so interested to be in the *Guinness Book of Records*."*

From the early days of the Network, one gig that sticks securely in his mind was arranged by ex-Magic Band guitarist Gary Lucas** at the Knitting Factory, Brooklyn, in 2002. "It was my birthday and I didn't tell anybody," Damo remembers with some affection. "But Gary knew somehow and

---

*   "Interested in Guinness, yes!" quips the onetime honorary Irishman. "Records, no."
**   The ever-inventive guitarist's live activities have ranged from a symposium on his erstwhile captain, the late great Beefheart, to live scores for classic black-and-white horror movies of the early cinema.

played the 'Happy Birthday' melody on the guitar, and the audience were singing too. Knitting Factory made me a small cake with a candle on it!"

But the main engine driver remained the flow of communication between performers and audience – non-verbal, random, intuitive. Communication in its most instinctive form.

His impetus for changing the Network from a band structure to a worldwide pickup of random 'Sound Carriers' was, Damo insists, the events of March 19, 2003: when the USA and its 'coalition of the willing'* began bombardment of Iraq in the second Gulf War, despite street protests against the war by millions of citizens all over the world.

"If there was communication it wouldn't happen," Damo asserts, "but war always has to do with profit or the military industry." We may also say that if the military industrial complex wasn't so adept at manipulating its own citizenry, then indeed war might never happen. But Damo finds hope in how distrust in established media channels (or establishment disinformation) is growing, with scepticism about governmental power as almost a new orthodoxy.

"Almost half of US citizens do not believe that 9/11 happened like the mainstream media broadcast it," he insists, "they will never believe the US government of that period.** So what I've wanted to do ever since that time, when I arrived at John F. Kennedy Airport, is communicate to the people. Music is a weapon against violence."

To fully grasp what Damo means, we need to agree at least that international warfare becomes easiest to wage when the populace are psychologically conditioned. In short, his crusade for communication is also a counterwar against control. It's this, he stresses, that makes the traditional role of the 'rock frontman' redundant in Damo Suzuki's Network.

"This is not really my way to live, to have a plan that is easy to control," he explains of his refusal to dictate either the melody or duration of his music. "Many people are controlling themselves too much, maybe they don't realise that they are being controlled by the system as well."

In this sense, the open-ended musical fusion of the Network has a direct lineage from Can. But it is also its antithesis.

---

*   Principally the UK.
**   For Damo's own beliefs about the war of information, see penultimate chapters.

"Last time I went on an American music website about my last release, which is only one piece, one CD, seventy-six minutes[*]," laughs Damo, "this reporter said, 'This must be one of the longest pieces ever released.' But for me it's really quite difficult, I really don't like to cut it. I'm not so interested in editing, because if you edit this instant composing you are losing something already.

"The interesting thing in instant composing is the dramaturgy, each minute is different from the last but everything is connecting together. This is how it begins and how it grows – everything is coming together and I cannot edit it, because then instead of seventy-six minutes it exists only as fifteen minutes. Maybe some people like to make it this way, but not with my stuff." It's a conscious rejection of the editing processes that condensed improvisation to self-contained tracks, back at the Inner Space studio.

Initially, any recordings of live events were issued on Damo's own Network CD label. But as the Never-Ending Tour traversed more countries and embraced ever greater numbers of collaborators, he became more open to licensing material in the region in which it was recorded.

"We released one CD which I performed together with a band from Tel Aviv, Israel.[**] So they promised to do the record cover in the Hebrew language; I wanted it to have a local taste and all the titles to be written in the local language.

"So if I perform in France everything is written in French, and if I perform in Japan it's all written in Japanese. If I'm cooking I'm using all local products; if I make a release I like to release it as local product."

Not only the music but the management method are soundbombs, aimed at a traditional music industry which now only supports its highest-grossing artists. Everything is arranged by the artist himself from the

---

[*]   *Floating Element* (Cleopatra Records, 2013) – Damo Suzuki's Network with The Elysium Quartet. Recorded live in 2007 at the Purcell Room, Queen Elizabeth Hall, London, this four vinyl sides of freeform composition features the prominent contribution of the 'nonclassical' (i.e. contemporary experimental) string quartet formed at London's Trinity College of Music. "No standard rock formation," confirms Damo, "instead I performed together with classical instrumentation like a violin, viola, piano and so on."

[**] *Live At The OzenBar Tel Aviv* (Third Ear, 2014) – Damo Suzuki & Tree, recorded 9/2/14. A sort of energised freakbeat of the most open-ended kind.

ground up, bearing the costs of flying economy class to almost any geographical region in the world. But as the ethos of random composing established itself, the choice of collaborators was often delegated to others.

"Mainly the Sound Carriers were curated by local promoters," confirms Damo, "because they know much better than me about the local music scene, and also I don't have to be bothered by financial things. According to his opinions and tastes he can arrange the Sound Carriers.

"If there is one person who performs with me again, there are another four or five new persons. I needed to go in another direction," he says of his personal ethic, "not only in terms of music but in terms of experience. If someone needs to have this experience again I'm happy about this – but I'm not so interested to perform with the same persons at the same place that I've already done before. It's the kind of sentimentality I really don't like."

Its creator stresses that the Network experience is exactly that: as experiential as it is musical. "You should be there and listen, or feel with your body this moment," he insists, "then you can tell other people – because it's really your own experience. So this is why in Damo Suzuki's Network there are no repetitions." He qualifies this, in case it sounds like the band are not allowed to get into a groove: "No repetition of the Sound Carriers; the venue is always different – sometimes we go to a big place, sometimes small clubs."

As Damo is at pains to emphasise, this is not 'product' that he's pushing; despite being the force at the centre, he's less concerned with selling himself as a performer than in propagandising for a grassroots form of creativity which (much like life) leaves itself way open to chance.

"I may be going from place A to B, or somewhere in between. What is most important is that you are moving, and if you are moving then there is always energy. With the Network I'm not doing it alone, I'm doing it with five or six, sometimes more, Sound Carriers together. We are moving from point A to B together and the audience is feeling our music within a trance – this is how the Network sound is."

The Network themselves were now random collaborators, who might co-exist with Damo in one particular time and space only, before moving back to their own lives. But the earlier friends and collaborators had played a vital role and might occasionally reappear.

DOMINIK VON SENGER
Guitarist, Grundwasser / Damo Suzuki's Network

I feel that we all like to sing. Even an instrumental concert should have singing – even if it's only two seconds, it should have a solid singing part. If you're singing it's the first instrument – before my guitar, before a flute, singing is what a mother gives a child. Singing is physically what comes from my throat, and there must be a way of making a difference between noise and emotional noise.

I think singing starts in a very basic way – there's no mathematics, there's no notes and it's the first instrument. On the scale, every other instrument has to be behind it. If it's electrified it has to be behind it: if it's the drums, if it's a wooden thing where you press the air, these all help it. But the voice itself is really so true, it comes from the body, from the person, and there's nothing that helps it. It's really the first natural thing to work with, so this is a five-star instrument. [laughs] This is the only five-star instrument!

Personally I like my music more neutral, having nothing to do with styles – but this came much later with me. It's not really like making spontaneous music as a law. Myself, I love very much to make music that is really ruled by mathematics, which makes it a must to play it because it is there. It is there. It's like a diamond or ornament or something that comes from dividing a circle into halves, a half into a quarter, a quarter into five pieces, and then finding out that this is a natural process if you work with numbers, or with time, or from sums or geometrics, which is a must for the human mind.

Which in music is the same. It makes a difference between noise and music: if you have noise it's [hissing feedback sound]; if you have music then it's [hissing feedback sound divided by rhythm]. If you have some information in between which has order, which has some ornament, something strange happens. Before you hear it, it only unnerves you; if you have shortwave radio like Holger Czukay, and you search around, you stick on someplace when you hear, 'too-too... too-too... too... too-too... too-too-too... too' – ah, there's a signal! There is something in the order, what is that? And even if it's moving, there's some order, some geometry, some repeat of form, and this is where music starts from. It comes from making some other thing than noise – between noise and music.

It's not free jazz, it's structure-free music. It means composing in the moment, which means every individual has as much as everyone can to interact with each other. It's very basic and very true. This is really what's happening now with Damo. He really pushes it to a point, and when I see the videos, I know Damo – we call it 'creating in time and space', you know? This is what it means: creating in the moment. Maybe I'm not the same, I see it my way, but I can understand him absolutely.

Today he talks a lot about energy, energy – I really understand what he means. I think he is kind of secretive, Damo – always deeply secret. If he opens up something it's always nice. I was called a 'guitar philosopher' thirty years ago, they wrote that about me – because I thought about all the aspects of a note, of a rhythm. Between chaos and music, it can go on for years! [laughs] But then with Damo he's so different – but we connect so much, there's a big part where we connect.

The random musical form of most Network gigs over the last decade and a half became a statement in itself. "Whether it fits together with a noisemaker, ambient musicians or something else," says Damo, "I don't differentiate between the music, so there is my 'message' – it's okay, I can make any kind of music."

In terms of the events that meet with their ringmaster's approval, it's the unlikeliest of combinations. "My opening band in São Paulo, Brazil, was arranged by the local promoter," he recalls. "They thought it could be interesting if the supporting band was a military orchestra; it was a thirty- or forty-piece and it was a total contrast. We were maybe twelve Sound Carriers on the stage, and this venue was totally different to any kind of venue where I'd performed. In the middle of the audience was the stage; the audience was separated on the left side and the right side. So we performed showing only one side of our faces; we made a kind of ring where everyone was standing around it while we performed in the circle; I was standing in the middle.

"The orchestra was not improvising at all; the interesting thing is that they played totally loose. They sounded like they were drinking much sugar schnapps and they were playing marching band music from New Orleans. It was not perfect but it made for a great contrast; not really like a formal military orchestra playing at all. It was somehow funny, but they were also serious; it fitted well with my Network concerts, it was a total mix."

In the capital city of Chile, Santiago, "One guy, Carlos Reinoso, a member of the Sound Carriers, was dancing on the floor of the stage; then afterwards almost a hundred people came onto the floor of the stage and we didn't have any space. Everybody wanted to sing with me, so that was too much and I just gave them the microphone and went in front of this concert hall. I was selling CDs during their playing," Damo recalls with amusement.

It's sometimes the special nature of an event, rather than the music itself, which defines the moment. "I performed together with disabled people in Croydon, outer London," he says. "It was put together by two music teachers. These two were also a part of the Sound Carriers and the other four were disabled people.

"We had a really nice time together; they brought their families with them and all their friends came to the concert. It was a really special moment, because music is healing people; even if only for a short time, they were really, really happy. For them it may be an unforgettable moment. For me it is very, very important to create this space."

The randomly experimental nature of Network gigs naturally attracts its share of extreme or abrasively-styled musicians. "Sometimes I get together with the noisemakers," confirms Damo, "which is not really a loud noise, more of a 'small noise'. I was playing with four noisemakers and didn't have any ideas – so I ran many times into the hall with the audience – I was running and running and running to make some kind of happening, or escaping. I'm not always making music," he confirms wryly.

"So different formations like that happened. I was really happy that every time I performed it changed. I'd never get bored and every day there is always something I can learn. It's like soul food to have this experience."

Experience, rather than music, remains the key to Damo's personal philosophy. Whatever the Sound Carriers may carry away from the experience is purely personal. There is no didactic element, no desired outcome: freedom of personal choice is all. The man at the centre of the Network sees his working methods as a platform for developing the powers of the individual – but how those powers manifest is something he neither wishes to nor is able to control.

"I am still looking for my identity," he confirms of the never-ending process. "In a way, I can also say I am still travelling all the time*, because your situation is always changing between what you were as a child and what you are now.

"You listen to different music too. If you always have just the same tastes – which I don't believe everybody does – then you cease to develop in yourself. Otherwise, you can go in a bad way or a good way, but still you are changing.

"For quite some time I didn't listen to pop music, because I was doing other work. But as you get older your perspective may widen; you have choices, your options do not really diminish. It's part of why travelling is so important – it is not only geographical, at home you can travel also. If you read an interesting book then you can widen your perspective; travel can be internal."

As we will see, for a period travelling had to become a purely internalised, imaginative process for Damo. But then, like the method by which he measures time – in tune with that of an astrophysicist, perhaps – it is a relative concept.

"This may seem very strange to say, but I'm not really creating something. Because this is instant composing, 'now' does not actually exist – if I say 'now', it has already passed. There is only the past and the future, there is no 'now' and I don't think about the time going by or the hours passed, I have to work in this moment."

At this stage, he saw a return to the Never-Ending Tour as essential to recovering health – rather than as a desired outcome of his recuperation. It was also a return to a state of happiness: "I'm happy to know new people and to create fresh, organic and pure music."

JONATHAN LAMASTER
Bass guitar/violin, ex-Cul de Sac/Damo Suzuki's Network
When Cul de Sac first started working with Damo, everything was improvised, nothing was written down. However, in the course of a tour you really get to know each other and each other's signals. Damo really puts out a lot of not

---

* This comment was made at a time when Damo was incapacitated by illness and in stasis.

264

only energy – I don't wanna be too touchy-feely or too metaphysical, but he does put out a lot of that – but there are also certain cues, physical cues, as well as musical cues that he makes that you start to learn after a while. But certainly, even before we started playing together, when the band got together with Damo when he first got off the airplane, we talked about his philosophy and his ideas about creating time and space. He doesn't like the term – or at least at that time didn't like the term – 'improvisation', he preferred to call it 'spontaneous composition'.

I come from not only a rock'n'roll but a free-jazz background – there was a performance we did in New York, at Tonic. I was in the process of recording an album with a German free-jazz player called Peter Kowald*, and Kowald was in the Globe Unity Orchestra, which was of course the band that Jaki Liebezeit was in. He came from that world: so I've got these pictures of myself, Damo and Kowald together; Thurston Moore was at that gig as well.

So it was a funny collision of that kind of free-jazz world and Damo's improvisational aesthetic. From where I was sitting there was a whole lot of improvisation: every night we got up and played it wasn't scripted, there was nothing that we tried to reintroduce, we really tried to be in the moment. And then I had the privilege of doing all these other tours with Damo with other musicians, and that was always a completely different scenario – even with the same personnel.

DAMOSUZUKI.COM BLOG
Los Angeles, CA, USA
December 2 2007 Sunday
Damo Suzuki with Len del Rio (Percussion), Michael Esther (Guitar), Tommy Grenas (Guitar, Bass, Keyboard), Chris Guttmacher (Drums)**, Ryan Kirk (Guitar, Bass), and Kevin Lee (Theremin, Moog)
@ Safari Sams

With LA sound carriers, I released one double Metaphysical Transfer *and half of double CD* Hollyaris.

I didn't see them since 2002 (except Tommy, Len and Kevin, they performed once in between in Cologne, so I had opportunity to see them) and now, we

---

*   This was in the early days of the Network; Peter Kowald died in September 2002.
** Cul de Sac's drummer in the first decade of the millennium.

perform together... this is one of my personal highlight for this west coast tour. To meet old sound carrier friends. Perform with them is almost perform with my own band, they know each other well and there are many characters. Fortunately this time I have time to stay few days in LA.

Yesterday afternoon, I arrived, Tommy and Michael from Farflung picked me up we went Tommy's place where I will stay until fourth... In the night, I cooked foods for all LA Metaphysical Sound Carriers. Nice to see all of them since all these years... finally I got work permits and work visa after all these years.

I was almost forgetting about my gout story. Gout is horrible pain on foot bones and such a pain, sometimes you like to cut off own foot away from pain. It was sickness for rich man, people say. Then why I? It comes also from alcohol... When you are forgetting something it comes suddenly unexpected. I may stop drink alcohol... no, no I'm not such heavy drinker, just I drink a bit... I mean measurement of people thoughts is no limit and difference. This happened before performance begun. I was tired and unconscious, sitting at merchandising. Soundcheck has done without Chris who was lost in traffic jam. Now I feel slowly that I'm getting gout again... It's horrible, if this happens during tour. I have to go to San Diego... then long journey to UK for ATP* festival...

In October 2008, Damo found himself at an airport approximately forty kilometres' distance from Minsk, the capital of Belarus. "In this place you find only field after field," he describes, "sometimes reaching a village or a parking site with propaganda statues. When your car gets into the city there are apartment blocks in typical communist building style; somewhere between proud officialdom and political office building."

It was a state frozen in the materialist ideologies of the 20th century. While communism had since imploded and the Soviet Union had long since fragmented into a centrist Russia and many satellite states, the Belarussian leadership retained the authoritarian model of a dictatorship.

Its political distance from modern Europe was reflected in the lack of ease in reaching the place. Damo had to take a flight from Cologne to Prague, followed by a small chartered aeroplane to Minsk.

---

* All Tomorrow's Parties.

"I waited for a while for Sasha, a twenty-one year-old guy who was organising indie/alternative concerts in Minsk with his friend Alex," he recalls. The city, with a population of two million, accounted for almost a quarter of Belarus's citizenry. The utilitarian architecture and central planning vibe made it seem to the traveller like Glasnost had never arrived, the Berlin Wall had never come down.

"They brought me to the apartment of a Sound Carrier named Anton," the genial traveller relates. "There are many of these apartment houses, since almost all buildings were bombed in World War Two and all buildings since the war have been similar complexes. Anton's girlfriend, who was one of the organisers of this show, cooked me salmon and vegetables before I took my rest. I slept quite well and deep. When I woke up it was already dark."

Damo had been invited to the city by V.O.M. – while it may sound like a punk-rock emetic, it was actually a network of minimalist musicians founded in Minsk in 1993, which had extended its activities into Mother Russia. "Actually, these people are doing the same as what I am doing – connecting people with music," he acknowledges. "V.O.M. has different formations of anything like fifty musicians under the same name. From formation to formation they give a number – V.O.M. 4 is the Moscow band, etc."

Damo had been contacted about two years before by a Ukranian calling himself 'African'. By this time he was able to accept the invitation, obtaining work visas for Minsk, Moscow, St Petersburg and Pskov (the latter being a Russian city close to the Belarussian and Estonian borders).

"In the evening I went to a rehearsal room, in the part of the city where the V.O.M. Sound Carriers who would perform with me lived," he describes. "It was a very tiny room, fitting you in tight against the next person."

After lapsing into a night's sleep, Damo revived the next day to walk through the centre of the city with Sasha and his girlfriend, communicating in English. The travelling gourmet, curious as ever, asked them about the national cuisine, only to be told there was none – the food was the same as that of Russia.

"We went to a restaurant/bar, ordering vodka and the dish a girl beside me recommended – which was good," he recalls. "At this point we were joined by two girls, both students speaking English. One of them was a girlfriend of Sasha, a cute, friendly person.

"Sasha had to prepare things for that night's concert, so he left me alone with those three nice girls for sightseeing. Then I took a taxi to pick up all my stuff, as I had to leave at midnight: ten hours by train to Moscow, then I'd get an aeroplane to St Petersburg."

DAMOSUZUKI.COM BLOG
October 22 2008 (Wednesday) Belarus Minsk @ Goodvin

Damo Suzuki with Magical Unicellular Music (V.O.M.3 + V.O.M.5 + V.O.M.23): Batman Electricity (Guitar), Dee (Guitar), Hamlet (Bass), Lampi (Sound Devices), Mitya (Bass), Stereochuvak (Guitar) and Tubbi (Drums)

On the way to the venue, I saw thousands of people in public viewing, watching soccer at square, buildings are like dream spotlight from low... many Russian cities have this kind of illumination.

The venue is at middle of main street, clean and modern... place with restaurant/bar upstairs. During soundcheck appeared Anton from Moscow (there are many Antons), who is organising this Russian tour and also as sound carrier on guitar and another Anton (from Minsk)...

After the show we went to restaurant before take train... Drink and talk, then we went to station through middle of the city in night air. At the platform, many other young people came to say 'goodbye' to me and two Antons (one Anton, organiser/guitarist, another Anton is founder of V.O.M. lives in Minsk). Train didn't start soon we had enough time to see each face on platform and three in train through window. Very sentimental moment... when I'll see them again...? Hopefully take not long.

The long train to Moscow carry his weight forwards, very slowly, but securely. Young people are getting smaller and smaller in midnight.

OCTOBER 23 2008 (THURSDAY) RUSSIA ST PETERSBURG @ THE PLACE

Damo Suzuki with Magical Unicellular Music (V.O.M.4): Bimka (Broken Sound Devices), Grin'ko (Drums), Monochuvak (Bass), Stereochuvak (Guitar) and Zen Porno (Guitar, Noises)

After 10 hours of did-I-sleep?-or-I-couldn't-sleep situation, the night train slide into Belarus Station (Moscow has nine railway terminals), we get out from the train as last guest in that wagon, we have still enough time. Early morning at railway station has much ambience, workers going, small shops around the station have been opened waiting for customers, many things to eat already at this time, café shop, etc... nice smells and white steam smoke from the ground... I like Moscow in this period of the day. Through all this living ambience, we took metro (most beautiful tube in the world... station is like in museum or castle...) to get [to] Europe Square where we can change train to Airport. It's quite new railway and railway station.

Inside train was enough place for suitcases and stretch legs. Flight was also getting modern than last time I took exactly same line and same route a few years ago.

St Petersburg is one of most amazing city in Europe for my taste for long time. Moscow is interesting city too. But, becoming money-orientated city... as far as I heard 70 percent of Russian budget flew to Moscow. Peters (St Petersburg) is just opposite... it's cultural metropolis... It's very difficult to find one classical music composer who had never been here to study or work. Prokofiev, Rachmaninov, Shostakovich, Tchaikovski, Mussorgsky, etc... all were here... and they're sons of St Petersburg... Much power comes from deep, while Moscow is elegant and trendy. Performance at this venue is first time even [though] I perform in Peters for six times. People here are so friendly. At this stage I feel getting gout again. Concert went pretty good... After I went to Sasha's place. He told me he has difficulties with financial crisis and lost many many money. He has publishing company. Since I came to Russia people's talk number one is worldwide financial crisis.

It was kind of lucky in unlucky. This stage my gout was getting really terrible with pain. I was lucky that Sasha has also problem with gout and he had strong medicine against this painful attack. He gave me some medicine for tonight and for following days. And I tell you this helped me a lot next days.

OCTOBER 24 2008 (FRIDAY) PSKOV @ TRI CLUB

Damo Suzuki with Magical Unicellular Music (V.O.M.4): Bimka (Broken Sound Devices, Guitar), Grin'ko (Drums), Monochuvak (Bass), Stereochuvak (Guitar) and Zen Porno (Guitar, Noises)

Van ride took around four hours through grey uncomfortable ambience and smells of winter, clouds are heavy looks like they might drop from sky at next moment. This stretch is almost you can see nothing, ruin like farmer house, freezing woods, even [though] this road is head up to Minsk, quite busy road.

Pskov is a small city quite close to Belarus. People in Peter's and Moscow say Pskov is nice place to visit for sentimental reason. Buildings are standing still since long and there is no modernisation.

I mean this nostalgia is thing that only domestic people can feel and smell as they know history and situations however. So? was staying my brain whole day. 'Nostalgia?' Hmm... maybe that is feeling like if I come back to sixties. Anyway... Not many foreigner artists come here and perform – even Russian artists to perform here seems to be seldom... so, when we started full of people.

As witnessed above, on Damo's Russian sojourn his reverence was reserved for the great composers of the 19th and early 20th centuries. As much as he clearly enjoyed meeting and performing with his young hosts, he remained in ignorance of their own music up to the point where he joined them onstage.

"At home I listen only to classical records mainly," he confirms, "because I like to keep away from modern music. Classical music has many elements inside it; I don't like three- or four-minute pieces. Nowadays I make a concert of two hours with only one piece. That is enough, because I don't make any kind of arrangements and I just like to share energy with the people. That's all."

In fact, he seems to regard much external stimuli – whether from musical or other sources – as being a form of contamination. "If I was a painter maybe I'd not attend any exhibitions," he explains. "If I made movies I'd not watch so many movies by others. I like to use at least 80 per cent of my brain – that's my creative philosophy, but without taking from other people.

"Because if I hear too much music it's too much information inside my head and it's really, really difficult to create your own stuff. Maybe I do get influenced by somebody, I don't know," he concedes, "but information is a most dangerous thing for me – not only in my musical life but in my daily life too.*

* As we shall see, Damo regards information – or, perhaps more accurately, disinformation – as something that can be directly weaponised against a free individual.

"Maybe I'm an 'anti-artist' – I don't know how you'd say it. But I just like to create on the day of the performance, with the audience and Sound Carriers. This is the moment I really enjoy and the other part I like to switch off. I like to think," he says of his solitary cerebral activity, "or I like to make something else – not music.

"Years ago, I said I was making music from the Stone Age, but the Stone Age is actually very close to us. Now, when I begin playing with other Sound Carriers, we don't have any information. We are going to make the information – but it's also maybe the DNA that you get from your mother and father, or it's the state of the band or the experiences of your life.

"Because everybody is facing really different conditions; you feel maybe bad or you feel good, it's every second different. It's also a matter of the weather today, if you have trouble with your girlfriend or your tax office. All different kinds of information which are *real*.

"Maybe 80 per cent of the time, I've never tried to make any kind of specific lyrics," he says of the method that stretches back to That German Band. Because for every hauntingly remembered phrase we might lovingly recall from 'Mother Sky', or 'Paperhouse', or 'Sing Swan Song', it's just as likely our mishearing of the young Damo's broken English has informed our own personal meaning for the song.

"Because if I don't have a message, then twenty, thirty or forty years later you can still listen to it as there is actually no meaning. Sometimes there is," he concedes, "but my meaning is not connected with a specific epoch and maybe you don't understand it – so that is okay."

Indeed. Listen to some of Damo's album releases of random compositions recorded live – like *Abhayamudra*, its clanking, tenebrous, guitar-based post-rock supplied by Cul de Sac – and you may find yourself straining to hear what Damo is singing. It sounds so urgent to express itself, so tightly meshed with music created spontaneously but which sounds pre-composed, that you may find your own words in there. In this sense, he is urging the listener toward self-discovery.

Or, in Damo's terms, he is creating a new kind of energy. "The message really is energy," he evangelises, "and if I add this energy to the music then I am quite happy about this."

Energy is, in his definition, not just a byword for vitality or stamina. It is the life-force itself. "Energy is one of the most important things in music too. The foundation of life is energy.

"I had to go this way because I hadn't for so long," he recalls of the post-Can period when he was divorced from music entirely. "I needed to make music again because it's good for my body and soul. Energy is something I use mainly for creativity, but it is very important for the human species. I should not keep it just for myself, it should be shared with other people."

In this sense, music is not a career plan; not an industrial product; according to Damo Suzuki, it is just one aspect of human creativity that is galvanised by a common life-force.

"That is what I'm doing with the music and the so-called instant composing," he asserts, making a phonetic connection between the two. "Instant composing ends with 'ing', and if you say 'ING' (Ai-En-Gee) maybe twenty times then it sounds really like 'energy'.

"Energy is floating and powerful, and must be used in a positive way. Without energy nobody can live. So this is a very important thing in my musical life and also my personal life as well. Without energy I cannot conceive of myself.

"Any kind of source that makes power is energy, you can find it everywhere. Nikola Tesla was talking about free energy for everybody," he evokes the father of the electrical alternating current, "but he couldn't make it because he didn't find any sponsor to support him. All industries like to see a profit and if anybody provides free energy then they cannot make it a business.

"But I'm doing this with the music," Damo insists. "So I like to create a network of energy – everyone depends on other people, but it's not dependent on any kind of 'isms', capitalism or socialism, because it isn't a code for living but a return to the human sources of energy. Positive energy can be mathematical or physical as well. Physical and mental stuff cannot be separated – this is energy."

CHAPTER SIXTEEN

NEVER ENDING II

"I'm not thinking about 'the blues'," protests Damo, at the suggestion that his ever-deepening, non-verbal growl may be part of an indirect lineage. That something primal may run from the acoustic delta blues singers to Captain Beefheart, playing out through the other side of rhythm and blues and into another dimension – or indeed, into the improvised explorations of a Network gig.

But he demurs. "American blues singers were not original. Singers from West Africa and from the Sahara, these I think are the real originals because they went to the USA, or other countries, as slaves. If you are not black or not of a certain social class, I think you cannot sing the blues. Because it must come from somewhere deep.

"It's also the same with hip hop; there are many people doing rap music in Germany or England or somewhere else, but they're not really. They're just copying American people. It's really difficult to find originality – but if you experience many things then you can find something original by yourself."

It's a minor detour in our conversation, but it leads to the backstreets and alleyways taken by the Terpsichorean muse – dispersing it further and further from its common origins.

"So maybe it's *my* blues," Damo concedes. "If you go to Greece, or if you hear flamenco music, this is a kind of blues too, because it's spiritual. You cannot tell what is 'blues', or what is 'jazz', this is just categorising stuff. Humans made it, the music was there before.

"It's almost like krautrock – what is 'krautrock'? Before people named it there was already this kind of German music. At the point people founded the so-called blues in West Africa they just made traditional music, workers' music, women-washing-clothes-in-the-river music – music that is to do with life itself, things which come from inside the soul of the human."

The discipline of random composition, he infers, stretches all the way back to the first notes emanating from a human voice or stretched metal cords. "This has a much longer history than composed music – the modern classical note comes from the 14th or 15th century, but before that people made music too: Egyptians or Babylonians also had music, but maybe different kinds of notes to what we are using."

In random composition, notes exist but they mutate, transmogrify, evolve. They never become a frozen score to guide the next performance.

"The music of our generation allows everybody to be an artist," opines Damo, before taking it further. "Everybody *is* an artist, everybody has their own stories. That is what makes music totally different to 200 or 300 years before. Because Beethoven or Mozart had always a sponsor, paying them money beforehand to compose their pieces. But now everybody is making music for themselves and I think it's much more free. Now we have to make music for the 21st century, and it's important to find a new system."

The random aesthetics of the Network are one route to take in a new age. But suggest that it shelters under a wide umbrella called 'experimentalism' and its founder balks a little.

"If somebody tours with experimental music, I think it's not experimental *enough* because he has always planned it," argues Damo. "In totally improvised music we don't have any plan. But to me, 'experimental' is just a category. Maybe it's boring because there's no melody or musical structure – it's kind of 'art'; some experimental musicians say they're just making music for themselves and so there is no real communication."

As he points out, 90 per cent of his Sound Carriers learned how to play via mainstream rock music. When they creatively collide with Damo Suzuki, they're not going to arrive back at the same place they've come from – but, equally important to him, he's very rarely aware of their starting point.

"For me it's always 'no music' and actually has been a long time!" Damo insists. "To listen to music is quite disturbing to me; if I listen to music it stays in my head as information. At the moment that I make music, I'm not really free if I have so much information from somewhere. It's kind of a sickness.

"Sometimes I hear music," he admits, "but not in a private place. If I have a concert there is always a supporting band, so I listen to them because I like to know the atmosphere in the venue. If the band before us is making totally loud music then I make a combination of two different bands and I play very soft. If the band before us play softly then I'm able to play louder music."

ELKE MORSBACH

Damo and I are living together sixteen years [since 2002]. But we've known each other, I think, thirty years or something like that. I was born in 1956 and this was the generation after Can. I knew them because they had been really famous at the time, and there had been a crime serial on German TV [Das Messer – 'The Knife', 1971] with their music. So even my mother knew them. [laughs] And there was the theme song 'Spoon' that I loved very much.

I remember the first time I met Damo, because my former boyfriend studied painting in Düsseldorf and at that time there was a man, Ingo Kümmel, whose dream and vision was to bring all artists together – painters and musicians and so on. And so there was a concert because they were told that Damo was coming back from his recovery. He had been in hospital because of the cancer and waited a few weeks to recover. He just came straight to the stage event. His first words were: "I was dead, I was born."

The event was in Cologne with Dunkelziffer, which was at the time a cult band. A lot of people loved this music, I think still today that it was good. At the time I studied economics, so I went to a lot of concerts. I knew The Damo Suzuki Band, and the members.

Damo's Never-Ending world tour had just started when we met again, after ten years. I think his idea was genius and it fits totally with his attitude of life. He likes to travel, and he likes to meet people, and he needs freedom in his music. There were a lot of concerts that I experienced with him together. But there was one when maybe I recognised what he was doing.

It was at a wonderful pub in London. There was an English band; Damo was singing and the band was playing. I recognised that it was like running against the wall. There was repetition and everything, but I saw that Damo made a lot of effort to destroy 'the wall'. In half an hour or something, the wall was destroyed and the band was part of the universe. For me, I understood that the band was calling on Damo to discover new ways in music for themselves. Because they were all playing together every day and there was no inspiration from outside. Damo was able to destroy everything and bring it together at a new point, it was connected.

It was interesting also that a lot of the concerts were like an instant composition, instant composing, but the audience was not recognising that anything was created in the moment. Sometimes they are coming and asking me: "I would like to buy the CD of the show." I have to tell them: "The CD may come later, but these are all live concerts created in the moment." This is really special, not only for the music but the process, as the musicians have got to know him at the same time as they create an experience for this evening.

The quality of a lot of the YouTube things* are so bad that I don't like to see them, sometimes the sound is so bad. But I think that a lot of bands are really proud to play with Damo, and a lot of them have material saved and sometimes they're asking to make a CD of that. So there is a lot of material that can bring back this moment, even if it's not available now. Sometimes the band are sending Damo pieces for their CD.

I think his system is much better than going in the studio with a big, major company telling you what to do and all these commercial things. If you're not so commercial you have to go another way. I think his way is okay, but at the time Damo made a lot of concerts I didn't always feel like that because they were new experiences. But now I'm missing it! [laughs]

I think it's part of him. It's always a risk to make all these concerts – he doesn't know the people, he has no mobile phone and he's trusting them. It's funny that he can deal with all these situations but then he's not really a normal individual. I think this was part of his personality even when he was young.

I'm sure he's always been a really free person – but with a Japanese attitude. [laughs] Damo has always a structure in his life, everything needs a structure. He is concentrating even when he is cooking; on the one side he

---

* Some of the live shows later released as albums can be found online. Their quality is highly variable and rarely matches the CDs or vinyl LPs, which were recorded direct from the mixing desk.

wants everything to be perfect, on the other side he is able to work with a lack of control, like on stage.

JONATHAN LAMASTER
Ex-Cul de Sac / Damo Suzuki's Network

The last time I performed with Damo was I think 2007 at the Knitting Factory (NYC), which was probably I think the most musically rewarding, most successful performance I've ever done with him. The musicians were just amazing: the drummer from Oneida, John Colpitts; David Daniel, a Chicago-based guitar player; guitarist, Seth Olinsky, and bass player, Miles Seaton, both from Akron Family; cellist, Okkyung Lee and a couple of other people I can't remember. But it was just unbelievable musicianship, right on the money. I think Damo, from talking to him, was maybe a little bit drunk that night, or high – I don't know if he remembers so much, I think he laughs about not knowing if it was a good gig or not. But I do have a DVD of that performance and it's just exceptional. I mean, in every gig with Damo there would always be moments that were absolutely magical – but it's the nature of playing spontaneously composed music, you're going to have some hits and misses. For me that was a real highlight. I know I've played a hundred if not more shows with him – Alex Schönert has played with him quite a bit, Dominik, I guess it depends how you slice it, but I'm probably one of maybe five to ten people who played with him most.

As a Network member, I was there early on and during the times when he was beginning to move towards not bringing people on the road with him. I have to say I weaselled my way into a couple of gigs because I just love the guy! I love playing with him, I love him as a human being. I was doing another project in Taiwan when I kind of convinced him: "Hey, let me come to Japan and play with you guys!" So I jumped on those gigs, I don't think I was paid for them and I could care less. It was not about the money at all. It's just about being around Damo and having the time of your life doing what it is you love doing – with a pretty magical dude.

I mean, he's definitely channelling some ancient energies. He has interesting ideas, and his ideas change over time. But I believe 'shaman' is a very appropriate term for him, and I think his role – he's the travelling medicine man, right?

You feel it. The audience feel it, and the musicians feel the audience feeling it. I'm not trying to be intentionally touchy-feely or hippy-dippy about this at all. I remember the performance we did in St Petersburg, Russia in November of 2002, the I Was Born, I Was Dead DVD. I was so excited that was documented and came out, because at that time it was the greatest musical experience of my life. Maybe 200 people there, but the absolute incredible energy of those moments in that place! I know he pushed my playing to probably beyond my natural abilities. I was pushed to play at or beyond the best of my capabilities, and I've many experiences with him like that.

So what is it? Is that magic, is it religion, is it spirituality? [laughs] I don't know, it's pretty powerful stuff and the audience was a part of that. I mean, if you asked Damo, he would absolutely say that the audience is just as important if not more important than the musicians on the stage. He says it all the time: "We're creating time and space together," and he talks to the audience in those terms, he lets them know, he communicates with them directly that they're a part of it, that they're important and that what's happening is a kind of biofeedback loop – he wouldn't use those terms but it is kind of what happens.

And after most performances he comes down into the audience – that was the other great thing about touring with him, the amazing people we got to meet and hang out with. He's so approachable and friendly, the guy is almost egoless, you know. He's really all about the moment.

Of course, everybody has an ego – but in Damo it's certainly not obvious. He has ideas, he has strong ideas about his aesthetics, but he wants people to be free – he values freedom, I think, above anything. He wants people to be themselves, because he knows that is when people will be their best selves; when they feel welcome, they feel part of it, they feel equal contributors. Again, I think that's probably why he likes that term 'spontaneous composition' – like, okay, it's happening in the moment, but it is a composition and it's collectively arrived at. It's not 'Damo's music'. All the records I'm on, the copyright lists every member of the band, he's not copyrighting that as his song. The copyright goes to every musician – and that's very much part of his collectivist identity.

I mean, I've played great gigs in shitty places with terrible audiences with him, and not-so-great gigs in fantastic places. Some you win, some you don't, it's all subjective anyway. But I certainly have many, many fond memories of meeting amazing people and having amazing musical experiences, great parties afterwards, staying up till six in the morning and meeting the coolest people in the world – then moving on to the next city and doing it all over again. Remarkable stuff.

He'd be horrified, I think, if people perceived him as a rock star. Before our performances, he was very intentional about having no rock'n'roll played in terms of recorded music. If a band was not playing he would play Shostakovich and Prokofiev and nature recordings – I remember some recordings of running water and rivers and things like that. He felt that was important in terms of getting people prepared to experience something together.

And he doesn't like to listen to a lot of music before he's mixing a record – I had the great fortune to spend a week with he and Elke in Canada, going through every single recording that Cul de Sac had ever made with him: we're talking like for most gigs we'd play for three hours! And I'd listened to everything in advance, I'd made these spreadsheets and I'd go through and say, "Okay, this was a great gig but the recording's bad." I'd highlight certain passages, I'd go in there all organised and think, 'This is great, we're gonna bang through this in a day or two,' and Damo was like, "No, I wanna listen to everything." [laughs] So I had to listen to all this stuff again for like the ten-millionth time – which ended up being great fun. We'd spend hours and hours, like eight to ten hours a day, just listening to this stuff and documenting and taking notes, and basically arrived at what he thought and recommended that we use. He was certainly open to my suggestions, after he'd heard everything – but he wanted to hear everything for himself.

So there you go, there's some ego there, he didn't want to just trust other people in terms of their opinion of what we should use or not use. But maybe that doesn't have so much to do with ego as it does with him wanting to be a part of that process. And then there are other releases that came out, like the Finland CDs and the DVD in Russia – I wasn't involved in selection of any of that material, he handled all of that. So it was interesting to have that one experience with him selecting and doing some initial mixes for the Cul de Sac collaboration.

DAMOSUZUKI.COM BLOG
April 29 2009 (Thursday)
Germany Lüneburg @ Wunderbar
Damo Suzuki with Quichotte: Gregor (Bass), Matthias (Drums), G. Ott (Guitar) and Rea (Keyboard, Theremin)

I've appointment at destination Lüneburg around 3pm with Gunnar, arranger of this show and Francesco from Milan, who is processing Never Ending movie, documenting *My Never Ending Tour*, he wanted film me, come out of the station...

I was in West Africa few times for my sickness called adventure, whenever take bush taxi, generally after half an hour, the cab break down and have to stay there for long, sometimes for few days. If I have time I enjoy even, I take it as new experience. But, here in Germany one of most modern country, economically top-flight, known as technological, discipline, etc. you know G.E.R.M.A.N.S!!!...

When I arrived Lüneburg (twice changed train from Cologne) outside is pouring rain. Francesco came with sweet lady Valentine, a cameralady, they drove two days from Milan.

Today's accommodation is in middle of this tiny charming soft-smelling (lavender?) city with around 100,000 inhabitants, at house, eight young people in community living. The venue you can reach very comfortably and good walk through old town. Northern Germany you can see houses so different than western part of Germany. People are also different. I know Gunnar for a couple of years since he invited me for interviews at his two-hour local radio show, Wellenrausch...

Two different local electro musicians performed as supporting bands. Good atmosphere covered the venue. After the show some people came together for drink in relax.

Next day I, Francesco and Valentina took time to visit Kunsthalle in Hamburg... to see Sigmar Polke's exhibition. This is really nice museum even so close to central station. Amazing arts from the master himself. Also I found there five paintings of Caspar David Friedrich's, one of my favourite painter beside Joan Miró. Also two paintings from Edvard Munch, these I saw in Melbourne, Oslo and here in Hamburg... kind of nostalgic feeling... like seeing my friend. In the night more than dozen people came together for drink and relax... next party night keeps going.

KENICHI IWASA
Synthesizer and percussion, Xaviers/founder, Krautrock Karaoke
I was born in Osaka, as was my guitarist, Yuki Bo Ningen. *I've been in London for over twenty years; I came here in 1996. I think the first time I played with*

* See Damo's reference to Bo Ningen in Chapter Thirteen.

Damo was like 2006 or something. I played with him for a really long time with my early band, Miso Soup. I didn't really know much about Damo Suzuki but we became really good friends – he used to stay at my house in Whitechapel when he came over here to London. He stayed a few times but I moved around.

I first played with him without knowing much about him – so I didn't have any 'this guy is a legend' or anything. I knew Can but I never really listened to it. I was very 'who is this guy?' [laughs] And then we became friends and I realised he was an amazing guy – I didn't have any 'oh my God, Damo Suzuki!' Not at all. I don't normally judge people. If I find the person really interesting, afterwards we talk – he definitely has influenced me a lot because we spent a lot of time together.

I now have a band called Xaviers. When Damo played Café OTO* 2010, I'd been invited to play with him and a few of the Bo Ningen guys. I think it was Damo's sixtieth birthday. After that we formed Xaviers because of Damo: this guy Francis Xavier, I think he's originally from Spain or Portugal, he's a missionary who came to Japan to bring Christianity. But we're not religious at all.

I think the way Damo does things is quite interesting because he'll just go anywhere and there are musicians everywhere in the world. I've been doing this event called Krautrock Karaoke for three years: I invite musicians from different bands and let them play for the first time [together] on the stage; it's kind of similar to what Damo does. Even Michael Rother [of Neu!/Harmonia] came and played, and Jean-Hervé Péron from Faust, all the way from Germany.

It's quite crazy – I started it as a joke: how can you take a krautrock song for karaoke? But I thought it was the perfect platform because it's so diverse. I love jazz too but that can be too interactive, it's not easy to understand for ordinary people. I used to do events at Café OTO when it opened, a very similar concept to Krautrock Karaoke – but I invited jazz musicians. I did another five events but I thought, 'Something is not right.' The audience was a load of jazz lovers, quite serious people, and it was great but it wasn't really entertaining to people who didn't know the music. I was looking for something that everyone could enjoy but what they're doing is improvisation.

---

* An ultra-hip music venue in Dalston, north-east London – in decades past a working-class neighbourhood of the borough of Hackney, now partly gentrified and a hipster enclave.

So-called 'krautrock' is improvised but this means there's so much space on top of it; you can pile many musicians on top of it but it still sounds like the song. Krautrock has many of the same elements but very simple rhythms. It covers everything so it's perfect music. It's got so much space to it, so many different influences.

I've performed with Damo five or six times, but with Xaviers maybe three times. The other time was like all the London musicians on the stage, a festival or something. I'd never played with them before. I don't even remember who it was, who was on stage. That's what I love – I only do improvisation. Xaviers is purely improvised; Krautrock Karaoke, there's no plan; I formed the band on the spot on the night. To me what Damo's doing is very natural.

A lot of musicians are scared of doing improvisation – even with Krautrock Karaoke, I invite musicians and they're scared. Even quite famous people – the more famous, the more popular, the more scared actually. Because they feel that they might lose something, they are so aware of how the audience sees them.

When I first played with Damo I wasn't happy – I almost walked off the stage! [laughs] Because he called his thing 'instant composing' and to me, to improvise with people I think you have to listen to others. When I first played with Damo he seemed as if he wasn't listening at all. Like he was just doing his own thing and he expects people to follow him or something. So I was like attacking him! [laughs] Going off the tune. And three or four of the audience came up to the stage, shouting at me, like, "Just do it, do it!" Because people who saw him a few times, they saw him like he was doing the same thing – he's singing in the same way, it almost doesn't matter what music is in the background.

But there was one gig on Damo's sixtieth birthday, 2010 – that gig was so good, he was responding to it. So I think it depends on his mood, or if the musician is playing really well he'll respond to it.

Damo shrugs off the idea that he responds similarly to all forms of musical accompaniment, neither confirming nor denying (nor, it seems, caring if it's true). "It doesn't matter if I like it when I make music either," he underlines, "because if people have an influence on anything then it can be positive."

His main caveat is "I have to be involved only in something that is connecting with positivity – so I don't really like to make dark music, *daemon* music or something like heavy metal.

"It's just a form of egotism," he complains of melodramatic hard-rock derivatives like black metal or death metal. "I don't like egomaniacs. If I make something I want to share with other people, it's energy. It's important too, especially now when everything feels quite hard and people in Greece or Spain have hardly any jobs," he reflects on the hard times of his adopted continent.

"But in music, if you can share a little light then maybe this small candlelight will help these people. If, in a dark time, they're singing of darkness and representing dark things, to me that's nonsense. This kind of stuff I can never take."

He might have some sympathy with the poor bluesman who went down to the crossroads a century ago with his battered guitar, and found the Devil by his side. But Damo would regard some grandiose metallist boasting about his relationship with that dark deity as a fool, courting dangerous forces he doesn't really understand.

DAMOSUZUKI.COM BLOG

Late summer 2010

First of all, I apologize for cancellation of show near Brussels, end of August if you planned to visit that show. For first time I have got cancellation from promoter so short before (a week before planned concert).

A couple of days before I've got information as usual about sound carriers I perform with from the promoter, I was really surprised and shocked to see the name of the band (for me it's impossible to have such a name). Nowadays there are many band with strange names... it's freedom to call themself what they like. Wait... but, I cannot understand and never will understand if someone call themself xxxxxxx Satan. (xxxxxxx part I cut as might be better not inform complete name). I claimed the promoter I've no interest to perform with them.

1) They must be silly, they don't realize such power source exist.

2) They're into Satanism or interested in... for me there are only these reason to call themself like this.

I'm performing around the world with ever changing local sound carriers, creating time and space of the moment and energy share. For my Network I don't need that kind of name. Also they're friend of the promoter and other sound carriers, supposed to perform with me, discussed about this situation. I received mail which says they decided not perform with me. Small stone in my heart felt down. I had few days not good feeling with this, but they decided to perform to create positive energy is not possible.

You might think this is overreaction from me. I believe in Bible and I believe in positive energy. So there is no place for such a name.

Actually, there was one concert between two London performance... Strange thing is that since I saw small ugly figure in the city of London, I feel they are following me somehow.

I met Shige, the bassist of Drum Eyes, his side project is called 'Devilman'... I will perform in Graz, Austria in October, I have my performance on Saturday, on Sunday performs band called Devil Music... I know members of them they are from Boston. But, why people must make such satanic name for their band? This has no positive energy. I said to Shige he should change to another name. An advice from friend. Nowadays young people don't take it serious. They bring this sort of name as fun. They don't know what is meaning. Am I sensitive for this? Ok. Ok... time will tell.

SIMON TORSSELL LERIN
Musical partner of Bettina Hvidevold Hystad/Damo Suzuki's Network
Our CD and book project was in February 2012. It was our names it was issued under: the title was Simon Torssell Lerin/Bettina Hvidevold Hystad with Damo Suzuki.* When the book came out we also did a concert together with Damo in Stockholm, that was after a Japan tour and we were very interested in this Network – not only with Damo, but also in Japan we noticed that the Sound Carriers made other collaborations. Maybe some of Damo's shows went really well and so the collaborations within the other Sound Carriers continued – maybe forming a new band or doing other things together without Damo.

So we were interested in the whole idea of the Network and all these musicians collaborating together; we wanted to invite the Network to play at the concert in Stockholm but it wasn't possible to invite all these musicians, so instead we sampled a lot that we recorded in Japan. In our concert with Damo, we improvised on top of samples of these short pieces of music that Damo had already improvised with Japanese musicians. We played them back and improvised on top of that, and Damo sang again on top of it. My role was also

* See Chapter Two.

part of that, I was making the samples, Bettina was controlling them live but I created these little soundscapes or samples that she could control, based on these recordings. We improvised on top of that; Bettina had more of a role of putting the pieces together and designing it. But the start of it was when we travelled and wrote together.

When he talks about the 'free energy' and these things, I think it's very interesting. I'm not sure (we've been talking about that) if it comes across in the concerts, if the audience also experiences it. Maybe – I think when people meet him after the show, because he usually goes out and talks with people afterwards, and he talks about his philosophy of free energy, then I think it comes across in that way. But during the concert I'm not sure – I think some people just come because they enjoy maybe Can, or they enjoy improvised music and they just go for that, but I don't know if in the concerts the audience get that philosophy. But certainly, if they meet him afterwards and talk to him I think they will.

There's a bass player who's from London, but he lives in Oslo, his name is Leon. We first met him at an avant-garde festival in Germany; we played with him there with Damo and we became friends afterwards, played together in another project. Since we travelled together with Damo on one of his tours in Japan, we met a lot of Japanese musicians who we have also stayed in touch with afterwards. We haven't played together with them but we have helped them. Me and Bettina have been to Japan and played our own shows, and then some of the musicians we became friends with helped us to book shows and different things. So the Network has been a really good place to find new collaborations.

As a musician I learned a lot, because when I first played with Damo I had played a little bit of improvisation before, but I was more used to performing songs or more structured music. Since then it has really opened my eyes to what music can be and how I play my own concerts. When me and Bettina have projects, maybe half the show is songs we have prepared and then the rest of the show is improvised – and that's definitely something that comes from playing with Damo. It just helped us a lot in evolving as musicians I think.

CHAPTER SEVENTEEN

NEVER ENDING III

In the second decade of the 21st century, the latest complement of Sound Carriers gave a performance that was at once both historical and futuristic. Reacting to images from Germany's early expressionist era of cinema, they telescoped an antique view of the future into a contemporary idiom.

"I performed live soundtrack music at a film festival in Reykjavík in Iceland, in 2012," describes Damo, "with two Sound Carriers from Iceland and two from Germany."

The preserved work of celluloid that sparked the performance was Fritz Lang's 1927 science-fiction epic, *Metropolis*. It's an iconic vision with a theme of mechanism vs. humanism that periodically clanks and grinds its way back into popular culture.

Kraftwerk paid tribute with a namesake track on their 1978 *The Man-Machine* album, at a time when their image was hardening into that of *Maschinenmenschen* – a neat reversal of the scenario by Lang and his screenwriter wife, Thea von Harbou, whose archetypal mad scientist, Rotwang, creates a 'Robotrix' which impersonates and undermines the female lead character.

The film's original orchestral score is seldom heard*, but the writer of this book remembers being captivated as a child by a 1975 BBC2

---

* Created by composer Gottfried Huppertz as a live orchestral score for a silent film, it was rarely played after its German premiere. The score would be revived in 2010 by the Berlin Radio Symphony Orchestra to commemorate the film's restoration to its full length, in performances at the Berlin Friedrichstadt-Palast and Brandenburg Gate.

screening featuring an electronic soundtrack by William Fitzwater and Hugh Davies. Metallically industrial for its time, its clanging, Stockhausen-influenced tones seemed the perfect accompaniment to a techno-dystopia.[*]

But of course, denial of the human element is not the Damo Suzuki way. "It was a long improvisation because *Metropolis* has many versions and this was an enormous film – a 180-minute version!" he says of its historic restoration to premiere-length director's cut.[**] "We made a live soundtrack, which was much more interesting than if you composed something for a movie. If you're playing live, behind you they're showing the film and all the mixing is being done there; it's totally different to a normal concert because there's a visual thing going on."

The Network's random soundtracking of *Metropolis* is more organically human than Kraftwerk's tribute (or indeed the cyborg textures of Fitzwater and Davies' soundtrack). The extracts online show them reacting with guitar/bass/drums/voice to the pulsating action of the suppressed metropolitan masses – rather than syncing electronically with the infernal machine heart of the city.

"*Metropolis* is an amazing film and it's kind of a movie of today – it's what's happening all over the world, people are becoming enslaved by machines," accuses Damo. It's an old charge, dating back to the Industrial Revolution.[***] But you can hear its echoes in the Third World's rush to industrialise, often at the cost of its workers or the environment, while

[*]   Other soundtracked versions include the absurd 1984 re-release with an eighties rock soundtrack (complete with crashing syndrums) produced by Giorgio Moroder. Its stylistic mismatch was akin to *The Old Grey Whistle Test*'s Led Zeppelin track accompanied by dancing 1920s flapper girls – except the latter was intentionally tongue-in-cheek. Far worthier of your attention is former Cluster composer Dieter Moebius's *Musik Für Metropolis* – released in 2016, the year after his death.

[**] Shown in various edited prints over the ensuing decades, the official length of the original print is said to be 153 minutes – although this may have been lengthened by the transfer from flickering frames-per-minute to a video version.

[***] On release, *Metropolis* was lambasted by SF visionary H. G. Wells as "silly" for its mythic, almost folk-tale elements – but mainly for its lack of faith in technological progress. But then, for all his brilliant imagination, Wells's vision of progress entailed the euthanasia of 'inferior' human beings and criminals – until his realisation that the Nazis had put that principle into practice dragged him into despair.

office workers in the developed world are tied to the inter-timezone demands of the internet – the great millennial innovation which promised to set us all free.

"Although it's an old film, it fits together with the world in which we're living," underlines Damo. "This was quite a wonderful concert because I never performed a soundtrack live before and we were playing it in probably the oldest cinema in Iceland. As it was part of a film festival, many people came but they were not expecting musicians. After the concert a musical professor came to me: 'Do you have the score for the music?' I told him it was all improvised, but he was a little bit suspicious and went away."

At the same time, Damo claims not to be impressed by the art of creating soundtracks. As with any industrialised form of music, its formulaic methods don't interest him. "With the few people that perform together with me and the people that come to the concert, it's like this," he drives home: "if you're creating this kind of music then every time it is an exercise. Improvising and composing is an exercise. So if I hear some other music then it has a stake in my brain."

ALEXANDER SCHÖNERT
Guitarist, Jelly Planet/Damo Suzuki's Network

I received two, three emails a year in which he said, "Let's go to Iceland and visit Bjork." That was several years ago. One of my best gigs I ever played together with Damo – maybe you know the film Metropolis *by Fritz Lang, this black-and-white thing? There is a film festival in Reykjavík each year, and we played there on the stage. The film was running and we were standing beside the screen and playing live music to the film. It was amazing – we were just watching on a monitor.*

Even for this gig we didn't rehearse. I did my homework, I watched the film several times before and thought, 'Okay, at this point I could go on the guitar this way,' but actually in the end I did it completely different. It was a very nice gig and the next day – I never experienced it before and nor had the rest of us – we played in jail in Iceland. In the middle of this island there's a big, super, modern, hi-tech prison, but there were hip-hop gangsters who didn't like our music! But some of them were happy at the time and said: "Next time you come bring some LSD please!"

FRANCESCO DI LORETO
Director, *Neverending*

I started my documentary at the end of 2008 and I finished at the end of 2013. But then I stayed one year for the editing because it was really difficult – I changed editors and in the end I edited by myself with only Samantha [Vecchiattini], but I used five editors. It's quite difficult to use some editor that didn't like the music, you know. I tried – some of these were very able with the editing but they didn't understand the meaning of the music of Damo Suzuki. So I needed to respect the music – my editing was not really professional, but I think what's most important is the music and the ideas of Damo.

So I lost one year to the editors, to the restarting of the editing, and then I think I lost one month to the sound editing. Because some of the concerts were not very good – so I take all the sound and go into a mixing place, and they do a really professional, workable sound. It was quite important for a documentary about Damo.

I am a fan of Can, of course, but when I met Damo for the first time at the first concert, I understood that he was making something different. Because he was making a new project, working with new technologies. He calls them by email, the 'Sound Carriers', but he never met them before and he never knows the music they make. So that is a great idea – if he finds a good musical experience, but sometimes he plays with not-interesting groups, you know? So you have different concerts: sometimes the concert was very nice, other times it was not so interesting. But the music works at the same time! [laughs] Sometimes he plays with groups that make really simple music – like rock stuff, really not interesting. But sometimes he plays with really experimental musicians. In this case it's more interesting for me.

I think the philosophy was to connect people from all parts of the world. The Never-Ending Tour started, he said in my film, in JFK Airport in New York, just on the day the US decided to start bombing Iraq. So in this moment he decided to begin this project. I don't know the motivation but I think it was to make people more close, not divide people. But it's quite a difficult concept – I think his idea was to create contact with people from several countries, several cultures.

Sometimes it is more easy for him in Europe or Japan – because he lived in Europe for forty years, he knows he will be with people and it will be quite easy. In United States too, but I think he has a problem with the US – but for *what I don't know.* Sometimes it's quite difficult, he never played in China – because they didn't like Japanese people, you know.** But for example he plays in Russia, he plays in South America, he plays in Australia. I think he connected the world as a person [laughs], with his travel from place to place: in Sydney, two days after in Tokyo, a week later in England – and Germany, of course.*

I filmed him in some towns in Italy, in Milan, in Turin, in Reggio Emilia, then in Germany I filmed him in Berlin, in Lüneburg, in Würzburg, then in Switzerland in Zürich, in Ticino and Geneva. And then Samantha filmed Damo in Australia, in Sydney because she was there and I told her: "Go to the concert of Damo and shoot something." And then some other people gave me some concerts, because I asked the people who played with Damo if they had some friends who were shooting. So I used something that came from Buenos Aires, Argentina, one from Russia and only the sound of an English concert, and then the sound of Damo Suzuki on a record in New York City, in 1997 maybe.

We sent the film to some festivals, but recently (end of 2015) I've been invited to Hamburg, to a film festival there – Unerhört!, it's a festival about musical film especially. The jury decided to make a special mention of my film, so I'm very happy for that. A guy from Paris asked me to show it at a festival

---

*	DamoSuzuki.com blog, late summer 2009: *"Many US friends are asking me why I don't have any shows in US... Reason is just simple... I have work permits until 2010, but US embassy in Frankfurt avoids issuing me work visa. (Strange, or?)*
 "Wait... thing is not only reason.
 "I'm not interesting to be treated like criminals... At checkpoint, I have to give them my fingerprint and shoot eye-cell photo. No other countries in the world are treating passenger like this. Ugly Bulls are shouting 'Come here!!, Come here!!!' ...
 "Unfortunately last time I went to embassy in Frankfurt was middle of winter, it was really cold and have to stay outside for around one hour... Uncomfortable lady at the window (behind security window) said through microphone... I'm not able to have work visa. She was so cold like weather outside reaction like an old robot, don't hear anything just ignore what I said or even she made face like if she see a criminal stand in front of her. I just put x on if I had cause to leave States...
 "You know, I really don't like to have such situation anymore... there are many countries in the world which are much [more] open than USA.
 "So, sorry to friends in USA I honestly say, I perform somewhere else not in USA... what an uncomfortable system... Control, control, and have to shut mouth."
**	The legacy of the invasion of Manchuria by the Japanese Imperial Army in 1937, and the 'rape of Nanking'. The grand irony is that few could claim to be more opposed to militarism and war than Damo Suzuki.

in March 2016. And then it has been to a festival in Italy, but I think it has been quite difficult in Italy to show a film about Damo Suzuki because people didn't know the music, didn't know Can, just some friends know it.

We have a lot of Sound Carriers – I think forty musicians in several different groups. I am very close to Xabier Iriondo, a guitar player that is really interesting – he plays with a group in Italy that is really famous, they're called Afterhours. I didn't like the music of the band but sometimes when some of them play with Damo their music is really different, it's much more experimental, more interesting. But I didn't know every person that played with Damo, because I shot maybe three or four different sets with Italian musicians but I didn't use everything. For example, I shot something with a group from Reggio Emilia – it was an interesting concert, in that location was the drummer of Nick Cave* I think. But I didn't use this concert because the audio was not good – for me it was important to have good sound so I put it aside.

Damo is making something completely different from rock music. I think he is making a more spiritual thing, something shamanic, something tribal. He is discovering something that is not easy to explain – the interior energy of people that all together communicate in the form of art. I think it's something like Pollock the painter, some improvised, abstract things. Damo is making something like contemporary art, or contemporary music, more than rock music or jazz music – or improvised music too.

I think it was interesting, this approach – it was one of the real motivations for me to make this documentary. Because I am interested in musicians that make something that gives a new point of discovery now. The best part of contemporary music you can hear is not so interesting – I don't know, it's 'entertainment'. But Damo didn't make entertainment – every concert had a point to discover something about humanity.

A lot of people, a lot of my friends, play with him – for example, Tiberio Longoni** and Saturnino, the bass player of Jovanotti who is very famous in Italy, who played violin with Damo. Or Fabio Marinoni – he's in a punk band, but after the concert he said to me: "Damo makes in me something completely different. The way I hear music this night changed completely." So sometimes

---

*   Thomas Wydler, former Bad Seeds drummer.
**   Founder member of Italian neo-psychedelic band Peter Sellers & The Hollywood Party.

there is something magical in these collaborations – with the audience, but sometimes I think with the musicians too, they're restarting with a new idea of music that before they never considered.

SIMON TORSSELL LERIN
Musical partner of Bettina Hvidevold Hystad/Damo Suzuki's Network

When we first played together I think it was 2010 and the last time we played with him was in Gothenburg – that was the last show he did before he got sick, before he stopped playing for a while. So it was the summer of 2014, I think. It was at the Jazz Är Farligt festival, it's called in Swedish 'Jazz Is Dangerous'. The show was quite fun because it's at the biggest amusement park in Sweden and they have a big stage there, and in the summer they have one week which is a jazz festival. One day of this festival they book more free jazz and experimental music and improvisational music, so we were a part of that.

It was quite interesting because it was one of the few shows when it was just me and Bettina and a Swedish vocalist – so there was Damo and one more vocalist. We had played one show in Stockholm before where it was only me and Bettina and Damo, but otherwise we were used to having more musicians together with us. So it was quite special. I was only playing guitar and Bettina did some synthesizer stuff, so it was more ambient, a little bit slower and we played for quite long as well – over an hour with just guitar and synth. It was very stripped down, mostly just about Damo and this other vocalist, how they interacted together, and we made ambient soundscapes behind them.

His name is Simon Ohlsson – he was the vocalist in a Swedish band called Silverbullit, which was a rock band from Gothenburg, and he also sometimes does vocals in a Swedish band called Fire! Orchestra, which is a big band, free jazz from Sweden. Silverbullit are not really commercial but they are quite mainstream rock. It was maybe ten years ago they were active. Since Silverbullit he has done more instrumental things with his voice.

This other vocalist called me a few days earlier and asked if we had some sort of plan. I think this singer was used to having a little bit more structure – because as you know, Damo doesn't want the musicians to decide anything before we start to play. So I think at first that was a bit challenging or new; this vocalist wasn't used to it, he wanted a little bit more structure so I think maybe he went in with a few ideas at the start of the show to prepare himself. But I think a little bit more into the show he observed what Damo was doing *and was adapting to that. He let go of these ideas that he had, maybe some plan that he had, and was able to be more in the moment.*

So he probably did it more like Damo; in the beginning as well for me, when I was playing guitar in this project, if you haven't done much improvisational music before you're more used to having structure and it's easy to go into a jam session, with maybe some riff or some chord progression or some idea from that. So after more and more shows it was just easier to go with no plan and see what happens. But when you're not used to it you usually want some sort of idea when you start.

At first I think they were both doing quite a lot at the same time. But the more we played during the show, they learned to listen to each other more and gave each other more room to complement each other – it took a little bit of time for them to learn how to support each other interactively. So I think the second half of it became really nice when they were able to give each other space and help each other.

After that I think Damo had a break for about a year or something, when he didn't play.

ELIZABETH MURPHY

He looked quite strong when I saw him in Camden four or five years ago, however long ago it was; he looked muscular whereas he never used to be. I must say I was very impressed with his performance. I don't like those sorts of very loud things, but it was mesmerising in a way. He was going for over three hours non-stop – we had to leave because we had to get the last tube! It must have been about half-eleven or twelve by the time we left and he was still going, so I don't know how long it went on for after that. He is amazing really.

In early 2014, this writer first contacted Damo with the idea of writing his biography. On Saturday February 15, I went to see him when he was performing at Klub Motorik in the Windmill Pub in Brixton, a haven for anyone who enjoys krautrock and all its psychedelic minimalist descendants.

The Sound Carriers for the evening were the group Eat Lights Become Lights, the club's house band. They seemed like the perfect accompaniment: founder Neil Rudd's synth rhythms weaved snakily seductive as stark,

293

monochrome, geometrical patterns were projected onto the wall, taking the listener on a static journey.

It might have been called 'ambient' if it hadn't been bolstered by a traditional band line-up. Damo's vocals filled any empty space with viscerally ascendant tones that rose effortlessly from the guts. He didn't use so much of his trademark growl this time – unlike some of the other Network gigs witnessed over the last few years – but it was trance rock that did exactly that: mesmerised the listener into a state that fixated his or her attention, rather than acting as a soporific.

We had a dialogue now but it would be some months before our commission on the book was confirmed. Meanwhile, Damo's intermittent return to the UK continued. The writer had to miss the April 22 gig at The Macbeth in Hoxton (traditionally the rough north end of Hackney, now a hipster haven) with electro trio Astral Pattern, but it seemed to go down well. Check it out on YouTube and you can hear him start with a vocal abrasiveness he might not bring to a louder band – point and counterpoint.

As we've seen, in the summer he continued eschewing the traditional band format to play at the Jazz Is Dangerous festival in Sweden, with Simon Torssell Lerin and his partner. The Never-Ending Tour went ever on. But gradually, almost imperceptibly, our intermittent correspondence fell off. It wasn't until the beginning of the autumn that Damo was in touch again – to confirm he'd been revisited by the spectre that stalked his health in the early 1980s.

Elke, his partner, has kindly provided her personal account of how he fell into sickness over thirty years after surviving the first serious attack on his wellbeing.

ELKE MORSBACH'S DIARY*
Monday, September 7, 2014
For about three weeks Damo is already between life and death in this hospital.

He is in an absolute blood-pressure crisis. Steadily staring at the monitor, I tremble and finally instruct the nursing staff. A carer helps, because at the moment neither brain nor kidneys are perfused.

---

* Translated from its original German.

Damo's body is bloated, because the blood splits through the sepsis and flows into the tissue; his coma is unbearable for me, I fear every day for his life. I pray, reading the Book of Hiob* in The Bible and hoping that God will save him; I cannot imagine Damo dying, and yet my inner voice tells me that his life is hanging on a very thin thread. I would never have imagined that they would cut his belly and then not be able to sew him up.

11.11 H

I have only a short time with Damo again; although I am always in the clinic, I am not allowed to be with him continuously. Damo suffers from phlegm in the lungs, the coughing affects his open stomach heavily, it is almost impossible, his pulse is racing. Blood pressure goes up and down. He tries to say something, but I do not understand him; it may also be that he speaks Japanese.

Then he breathes: "Too much, too much. My heart hurts."

"Do you know who I am?" I ask

"Yes, beautiful woman," he breathes and only looks at me with half-opened eyes. I'm crying, with happiness – no, I'm touched, touched, but he's so weak, his condition is fragile, but I'm not giving up hope. His oxygen supply, which is measured via a clip on the finger, is very bad. I am not only worried about his life, but also about his reason.

Later Damo turns to me, very gently, and then he starts to sing: "Rock'n'roll never wants that," he sings again and again: "Rock'n'roll will never die," never before has he said something like that. Basically, rock'n'roll does not mean anything to him – 'or does it?' I ask myself. I find that his oxygen supply, oxygenation in the blood, which was previously questionable, has optimised. Unbelievable: even in this pitiful, threatened state, his creativity helps him to survive. I'm amazed, I'm crying.

Then he holds my hand, squeezes it firmly and breathes again and again: "Please stay, do not go away." He grips my hand and does not let go. I have to ask Sister Anna to give me my bag, so that I can use it to dry up my tears.

---

* The Book of Job, in the King James Bible. Job is the personification of the suffering of the righteous: bereaved of all his children, afflicted with open sores, left destitute and abandoned, he refuses to renounce God and continues to shun Satan. The almost parodic extent of his suffering inspired the metaphorical phrase 'the luck of Job'.

DAYS LATER

23:00 h

I'm still watching over him. He gets Propofol – the remedy Michael Jackson took, the nurse tells me, but it's really good for sleeping – and Arterenol, I think, so his kidneys will not stop working, in which case his life or death would be sealed. The carer explains "without the medication and the machine he would be dead immediately". No, no, for God's sake no, that's not true – and yet I wonder why he's in this pathetic state today, because yesterday when I had to leave him behind because of the rules here, he felt better, he recognised me directly, chattered and held my hand firmly. But today he does not even breathe. Does not smile any more, cannot hold my hand, only once he breathes: "Stay here!!!"

I think of his mother's smile. I first met her at the nursing home in Japan, near Yokohama. She looked at me and then she smiled and I had to cry and could not stop. Never before has anyone smiled at me with such intensity. A smile that immediately creates a deep closeness at a speed that makes space and time seem unreal. He had that very same smile yesterday and as in Japan, it touched my heart immediately, compensated for all the days and hours of unbearable suffering and today, today I stand alone again, without that smile that goes beyond the limits and makes everything seem possible. Today it is he, Death, that stands also here.

Remember a saying from The Bible: "Sorrow is better than laughter, for if the face is sad, the heart will be bettered."

Damo is feverish – absorption fever, explains the sister, dead tissue parts are transported away. A good sign, I conclude – but you cannot say that either, she says.

15/09/14

Foolish year; I remember that in the spring I always said to Damo: "There are no birds. I miss the birds." We live in a very large park, larger than Hyde Park in London, and since I've lived here the birds wake me up. Sometimes it sucked, especially their cheerfulness, when I myself had to struggle with the adversities of everyday life. But when they were completely silent, that was scary. I knew then that it was not a good sign, but what it really meant was that we would be in this darkness a few months later.

15/09/14

Damo is pretty angry, annoyed. "Will go somewhere else!" I could stay, but he wants to leave. Does not understand that I have to leave him behind. Fights with his nonexistent strength in his bed. Is very, very angry.

"You can stay here, I want to get away," he says, with force.

It breaks my heart. I talk to the doctor. But they find it quite normal, they call this 'hospitalism'. Always occurs when patients are in the clinic longer. "It rips my heart!" They just raise their shoulders and let them fall again. I am alone with my despair and helplessness and Damo is fighting for his life.

His monitors play crazy. I explain to the doctors that we want to stay awake because of the risk of another sepsis. I cannot let Damo down.

At home I think of Damo's request to get out of there; it's his life and he'll know where his salvation lies. For that I need his signature. "Didn't I tell you a thousand times?" he furiously cried in his despair; did he mean to get out of there, had he said that to me a thousand times in his coma?

I have to pick up Damo's CDs and LPs from customs. Maybe the last ones ever to arrive here. He will not be able to sing any more with an open stomach, but that's our least problem.*

14:15 H

Get up in the corridor in front of the intensive care unit as they bring him back from the operating room to his bed. "Eh, you are here?" he says and smiles.

16/09/14

11:58 h

Power of attorney for Damo's transfer request printed out by our neighbour Martin. When I was at the hospital around 12:20, Damo did not want to leave, but did not say why. He only had pain. And then he said that I smell bad; yesterday he scolded me about my garlic odour, although I have not eaten for days – garlic certainly not and for two days nothing at all. But before his very first surgery I had eaten garlic. Reality only comes true in the past or only scraps of memories appear; perhaps the present is unbearable without mixing them.

---

* At this stage, the LPs were most likely the collaboration with Simon and Bettina and *Damo Suzuki Møder ØSC*, by Damo with Øresund Space Collective.

'How did they suppress his will?' *I ask myself.* 'Does he not want it any more, can he just endure everything?' *It seems to me that he gave up. And me? Am I just letting that happen?*

17/09/14

My girlfriend Marita is on her birthday. I am tormented with my nervousness. Damo lies with his eyes open. I leave him.

I'm cold, feel hungry, but I probably will not eat. Damo works majestically in spite of this cruel situation; he realises that he will probably never be able to sing again and thinks about being creative otherwise, because he actually wanted to be a comic artist. And then he is suddenly very far away. I think I'm shattering, but I'll stand it and reassemble piece by piece.

Damo had two nightmares, twice the same dream:

He drove a motorcycle. He first came across cold, smooth roads to the Japanese company he used to work for. What for, he did not remember, only that he wore his hospital pyjamas. He said that it was very cold and that he was hungry, always hungry. In the Japanese company, he saw a motorcycle in one of the warehouses – although they did not build any motorcycles, but he insisted that it was a Mazda. He drove and it was so cold, no one was on the street and he was so hungry. So hungry that he stopped and ate the tyre of the motorcycle.

He had not eaten for weeks and with the parenteral nutrition they were so sparing. How bad the hunger must be, despite the description of the dream, I could hardly imagine. God save us.

Clear up a bit. The table under the perfusor is sticky, dirty, not cleaned for days. And dust everywhere. Damo's bedside table is dirty, too. I do not want Damo's silence to hold out, but I'm strong.

27/09/14

Have not taken any notes for days, because they always turn off the light and the monitors. It makes them nervous here in the ICU when I'm sitting next to Damo's bed, checking his vital signs on the monitors and writing them continuously. So I use the light of the streetlight that shines through the window and read The Bible over and over again, the words of Solomon and the Book of Hiob.

There is no end in sight. Nobody can tell me how long he has to stay here in the intensive care unit. But I see progress: he is no longer ventilated, he sometimes has clear moments.

And suddenly, one day later, he is transferred to the normal ward. Yesterday it was still not clear whether he has overcome his second sepsis.

Damo was in a bad way, very bad, he complained of nausea, choking off white mucus as far as he was able to do with his open stomach. His eyes showed his despair, I called the doctor several times, the senior physician came, the ward doctor later and always said everything's OK. Damo held my hand tight again. But what should I do? He made me promise that I would come back, even though it was already 8 p.m.

At about 10:30 p.m. I was back, but Damo was not well; the doctor, who I called again, advised him to take a sleeping pill. At midnight I left him and I still had the doorknob in my hand when I heard a strong rattle. I ran to him, holding his head, for he could not lift himself, as light as he was with his 38 kg, which he still weighed. He vomited in a rush, not knowing what they had stuffed him with, but now it was coming out of him by the litre without being able to lift his head, too weak for anything. I yanked him up, holding out his bowl, and when we got the bed changed all that tortured him the whole day was out of him; he could finally sleep, without a sleeping pill.

Damo's contact with this book's writer began again soon after, although it didn't become regular till the following year. When we spoke on Skype, he gave details of his gradual steps back toward becoming active again – although he was still fully engaged in the battle against colon cancer, as described by Elke. It was from here that we worked our way backwards, starting from his present state of sickness and foraging ever further through the fields of memory.

It would be tempting to evoke the single-mindedness of Zen, but Damo resembles more closely a Christian stoic. "There may be much change in a person's life," he reminded me, gently implying that recent problems I'd endured myself were, on the universal scale, as nothing – certainly when compared with his own battle for survival.

But if his forbearance was extraordinary, he had not rid himself of the human need for hope. No longer had he resigned himself to the idea that, due to his sickness, music was all in the past.

"I really like being an instant composer because it doesn't matter, in any situation, whoever I play with, I make something," he admitted, with a feeling that seemed to approach pure longing. "Without that my life is quite boring."

It's arguable as to whether a man who's spent so much of his life traversing the earth has any real claim to boredom. But then, in the aftermath of much physical suffering and in the midst of a difficult convalescence, he could still recognise elements of good fortune.

"I am just doing the things that my body and soul like, and to make this moment," he said of his personal ethos. "Not many people can do this, and have the opportunity to meet with many other people. But I can live life this way so I must be very thankful for this moment."

But the sickness still made its demands. There were medical stipulations and scheduled operations.

"I'm really looking forward so much to playing a concert, it will be so interesting for me," Damo said in a reverie of longing, almost touching on nostalgia for his recent past. "But what's going to happen?"

CHAPTER EIGHTEEN

INTERLUDE – THE WAR OF INFORMATION

FRANCESCO DI LORETO
Director, *Neverending*
I wrote to him in September 2014. I wrote an email and for twenty days he never answered me. So I was very worried by that, because usually he would answer me in two or three days at maximum. So then he explained to me the problem and I called Elke, his wife, and in a couple of days me and Xabier Iriondo decided to go and meet him. He was really in a bad moment – because he was in hospital, he was under surgery, he had been for one month in rehabilitation. We went to meet him for just one day, because we were working it was quite difficult. But he was quite happy for that. Because we had been in touch for all the years, I wrote to him two emails a week, or five or six for every month, so I knew his condition.

"September 2014 was really heavy duty," confirmed Damo, looking back on his health crisis one year later. "My doctor told me eighteen months later that my stomach was quite similar to if I'd been in a traffic accident with two big omnibuses colliding.

"I had many operations in September – almost every two days for one month, so I cannot remember. I was totally anaesthetised and almost not existing, it's a kind of blank in my life. But I'm happy that I survived. The heavy stuff is, I think, all gone."

His words were as courageous as they were optimistic. He was still facing operations on his stomach and colon, for which he had to recover to a state of strength before a date for surgery could be set.

"When I had the first operation for colon cancer in 1983 it was a hard time, because I didn't know if I'd survive or not," he compared the two incidences of his family's genetic burden. "But to get back to normal life, this process was six months. By now it's much longer – already one year is gone.

"I went to the clinic at the beginning of September 2014, where they found colon cancer in almost the same position as in 1983. They cut out the cancer but then found two holes in the lower intestine; this is a very sensitive part. They cannot stitch it together, so it's taking a while to get my stomach together.*

"At the moment I don't have stomach muscles – so now it is covered by skin from my thigh. That's how I'm living. It takes one year to get better under the very best conditions before the next surgery. That's what I'm now training for."

ELKE MORSBACH'S DIARY**
07/10/14

I did not hesitate for long; the visit of E-da, a Japanese musician living in Brighton, had done Damo good. E-da called only briefly and without further inquiry he had booked a flight for the next day. They talked all day, in Japanese, and yet it was way too short, E-da said when I drove him to the airport in the evening. Damo can transform joy directly into visible energy like a transformer.

Xabier came with Francesco. In the evening I picked them up at Cologne Bonn Airport, drove to the hospital and spent some time with Damo until the rules made us leave, but Francesco and Xabier had organised their return flight so that they could stay with Damo the next day in his sickroom. When I drove to the hospital after school, I expected the three of them to tell each other stories and that Damo would have made significant healing progress,

---

* Elke confirms, retrospectively, that the two holes were actually caused by sepsis – as yet unrecognised and untreated: "Because of the sepsis, Damo was not only in a coma, but also his whole body inflated so that the stomach could no longer be sewn together and thus the abdominal muscles degenerated."

** Translated from its original German.

or at least was in a very good mood. But when I entered the room it smelled of pus, Damo sat in the surgical shirt in bed and the atmosphere was tense. "What's going on?" I asked, horrified. Damo shrugged. He was down and our friends could not raise a smile.

After Damo drove into the OR, Xabier and Francesco sat in the hallway. When asked by the caretaker who they were, I told him that Xabier was a well-known Italian musician and Francesco was Damo's cine-biographer.

I could not comply with my promise to go with the two of them in the evening to the airport, because even though Damo was not in the room, I definitely wanted to be there. I took the opportunity to discuss with one of the senior physicians the further course of action.

"It cannot go on like this," the senior physician realised; maybe he was afraid that more people would arrive. My urging was finally taken seriously and we decided to relocate. I chose the Klinikum Leverkusen. The visit of Xabier and Francesco finally got the ball rolling.

24/10/14

After days of waiting everything suddenly had to go very fast. I gathered Damo's things together, in all the weeks we had accumulated a lot of stuff including a camping fridge. The ambulance drivers came, lifted him with all his strings and machines on a stretcher. Damo was now in the ambulance and I drove with my old Mercedes behind.

LEVERKUSEN

Immediately, the doctors took care to stabilise Damo's fragile state. A dietician came and calculated exactly the parenteral nutrition. No discussion, that was superfluous as I had previously heard from the doctors in Cologne – and had to watch as Damo was getting thinner and weaker. In the meantime he weighed barely 38 kg. Access to Damo's throat was life-threatening said one of the doctors, and organised for the next day a special catheter – a so-called Hickman catheter to minimise the risk of infection. Everything went very fast and for the first time people talked about restoring the 'quality of life', even though everyone knew it was a hard road and it might take years.

It was already November and winter was coming. Damo told of a new nightmare. "I participated in a magazine programme in the 'Cooking' section, live broadcast, WDR I believe; I was suddenly pushed into bed with all the *stripping, parenteral nutrition, other infusions, the perfusor, VAC* and two urine bags. Somebody comes with seafood and a cart full of fish. I stole two fish from the cart owner." He laughed and I saw the hunger in Damo's eyes. Because he was not allowed to eat anything, although he got his diet on the vein, he was always hungry.*

The first euphoria was over. I was worried. Damo needed much more than me and the work of the doctors. I wrote to his friend Tim Peach** in Melbourne, although I did not know how he could have helped so far away. I'd visited Damo around ten years ago in Australia when he avoided the German winter. In my Christmas holidays, I ventured to the other end of the world: an eternally long flight to Hong Kong; there I stayed for eight hours. I was dead tired and booked a sightseeing tour to stay awake before another hour-long flight to Melbourne, the 24.12, which was fully booked despite the high holidays. In the end, I had been travelling for more than twenty-four hours and had a heavy jetlag for around ten days. Tim's visit was impossible, but I knew he had the same free spirit as Damo. Without thinking, I clicked 'send'.

14/11/14

Meanwhile, I had a guilty conscience, because even Tim's wife Sally wanted to take this strain. Sally is a mysterious personality, beautiful, confident, but very reserved and yet not unobservant. She sees everything without it being noticeable and she is always clear without being stuffy or conceding something. Maybe that comes from reading, if you own one of the most beautiful bookstores in Melbourne. Wow, you come – and in November! A stone falls from my heart. How many times have I asked Damo why Tim and Sally are not visiting us when they are already in Europe? "It's too cold for them here. Australians hate bad weather" – and now they come and get the best November weather Cologne has to offer: dark, rainy, windy and uncomfortable.

Tim and Sally drove to the hospital every day. Damo flourished. They had fun together, fooled around, took pictures and selfies, talked about the future. He had gained weight, bladder catheters had been pulled, and

---

* Vacuum-assisted closure.
** Damo's Australian friend, promoter and photographer – see footnotes, Chapter Thirteen.

his open abdomen had undergone another skin graft to treat his various abdominal fistulas. Then I should take him home and feed him up for the next big surgery. The hospital organised a nursing service that would add to his parenteral nutrition every day and a wound manager, but I took over his abdomen.

In October 2015, Damo told the writer of this book of his progress. "I did eighty minutes walking today," he noted with quiet satisfaction. "The weather is really beautiful; it is a little cold but the sun is shining. The landscape is really good, because I am living just a short step from a huge park. It's called Stadtwald. From one end to the other it maybe takes half a day to walk. It's a really big place. There are three or four ponds, and also there is a tiny animal park. On Saturday morning there are not so many people, because maybe they are going shopping or they had a very long party that night or something."

The small details of life had become aesthetically significant – but then to him they always were. Damo has the humility and perception to realise it's the minutiae that constitute our lives, not grandiose schemes or ambitions.

As ever, though, there was no 'now' – Damo's thoughts were several short steps ahead, in the near future. The traveller's physical world may have shrunk to the size of his apartment and its surrounding environs, but its internal dimensions still offered him creative space. The body was fragile but ideas and enthusiasm were undimmed.

"Everybody only has so many braincells," he reflects. "Everybody has the same opportunity and time to study any kind of language. I'm living sixty-seven years* and I speak four or five different languages: besides German, Japanese and English, I understand quite good Swedish and a bit of Italian, but I had so much time and still I didn't use it to learn something," he laughs with self-deprecation.

"Because I was travelling all over the world I was using mainly English, but I picked up my language on the street. So actually, grammatically

---

* This later part of our conversation took part in 2017. Several months earlier, Damo had recovered enough to perform at his first Network concert since 2014.

305

I'm totally wrong – otherwise I'd be writing some short stories or fantasy romances* already!"

Indeed, in his confinement to his home and immediate neighbourhood, Damo had started to write his own imaginative fiction. But he didn't see it as a full stop to his creativity.

"Really, there are so many things I'd like to do – I'd like to make a movie or write a book or make some fantastic food. I had time but I didn't get involved in it, so I think I'm quite a lazy person."

If so, then it's a laziness that – even in its least productive moments – always offers up a possibility for new activity.

"I need to get in as a good a condition as possible," he acknowledged earlier. "Maybe at the end of this year or the beginning of next year I'll have surgery. I cannot go on the street or on the road, it's really crazy – for one year long I didn't travel to anywhere. This has happened very seldom in my life, and also I couldn't play any concerts for this one year. It's really very strange.

"Within my mind I have always travelled – not only me but everybody else too," he corrected himself, aware that everyone has an inner world. "That is quite important, because I'm handicapped now for geographical travelling, travelling in a normal way. Besides that I must find any other solution that lets me travel within myself – so that's why I'm reading books, I'm writing short stories, or maybe I'm just thinking about things.

"If somebody I know is currently in Paris then I imagine what Paris looks like. This helps me quite a lot, because I've travelled around the whole world and if he's in Paris I can imagine that it's me there now: I can go to here or there, and I can eat this or that. Many things I can think about, and this is the only possibility of travel that I have at the moment."

As ever, Damo attributed his creative spurts not so much to any personal force of will as to the energy that's a building block of his world. But this energy is not neutral: there is good energy which may be charged, for example, by the positive attitude of friends; then there is bad energy which, he conceded, may affect him if he was unable to get out of the "bad sphere" he was then trapped in.

---

* By 'fantasy romance', Damo means the H. G. Wells-era term for science fiction.

But negative energy takes many forms. "If for instance you take bad food – if you have bad political ideas it's bad for your body or brain too." As a keen chef who enjoys mixing different ethnic cuisines*, Damo stresses the importance of food "because everybody is eating at least two or three times in the Western hemisphere every day. I can see it on the faces of the people – if they eat good food they have much more communication; if you're eating bad food, bad energies come into the body.

"But if you are using local ingredients it's much more fresh and you support farmers; there is a kind of communication before the cooking starts. If you are using this energy then you will have good food."

As a lifelong omnivore, Damo devours meat and fish as enthusiastically as he does fruit and vegetables. But he feels a similar dismay at factory farming to vegetarians: "Animals like cows have horrible lives in small cages and chickens don't see any sunshine, living in a small space like a slave. They are the product.

"Think about how many McDonald's there are all over the world, maybe more than 200,000. In every restaurant each day they are making maybe more than 1,000 hamburgers. Ask yourself where these giant amounts of meat are coming from – these are industrially made animals, not happy animals who are running or walking in nature."

Bad energy will follow, he reasons, from a diet of corporate junk food, high in saturated fats, salt and sugar, which addict working people in the manner which he parodies in his cartoon painting, *Junk Food*.

But all of the worldly evils cannot be laid at the door of bad diet, as Damo concedes.

"Something like the death penalty is never good," he extrapolates, at odds with the Old Testament morality of the USA, "because if somebody has killed somebody else then this is already a negative energy; if people send him to the electric chair then all that's behind it is pain and

---

* "My own cooking is all improvisation," says Damo. "What your stomach says is from your traditions and your DNA maybe. So if I am cooking food, maybe it's not real Japanese but I am using one or two drops of soy sauce because it makes a much more interesting taste and soy sauce has amino acids, which are good for the body. But actually I just create it by myself and it's a kind of anarchy in the kitchen that has no nationality. I'm not cooking French food, or Italian food, or Japanese food, or Indian food."

judgement. It's surely difficult for the family of victims, I know, but still – let's try to forgive this person and bring positive energy to our society. Then we will win many rewards."

In this sense, 'energy' seems to be an almost supernatural force that feeds off of our own attitudes – a physical embodiment of a kind of moral karma, perhaps. But it's also redolent of persecuted American sexologist Wilhelm Reich's concept of positive orgone energy, which, first theorised in the late 1940s, became popular again during the hippie era.*

"That's a really good thing in Europe: there are no executions," Damo expounds. "The USA, the Chinese, the Japanese and many Islamic countries have them. But who can decide that this person must be killed? Who is making the judgement? People shouldn't judge any other people, this is stated in the New Testament. Because Jesus is love – He is different from Mohammed, who was always making war and attacked other people many times."

Damo speaks with confidence as both a student of history and a former traveller in Muslim West Africa.** There are many admonitions towards mercy in The Koran (albeit selective mercy) and Mohammed was initially a persecuted prophet without honour, besieged by his former hometown of Mecca. But it's an historical fact that his religion grew rapidly as Mohammed made converts at the point of a sword – progressing in his later life from an outcast with thirty-nine followers to a theologian warrior leading an army of 10,000. Islam has always been unapologetic about this, for its very name equates with 'surrender' or 'submission' (to the will of God).***

"Why Islamic countries are carrying out so many punishments in front of the people, stonings and things like this, is because they haven't changed in the 1,400 years since Mohammed," reasons Damo – a man often charmed by the qualities of individual Muslims but wary of Islam's stern, unforgiving nature.

---

* Hawkwind paid tribute on 'Orgone Accumulator', from their 1973 double live set *Space Ritual*.

** See Chapter Eleven for his curiosity about Islam and interest in visiting a West African mosque. This is in no way negated by his discomfort at the aggressive dogma of Muslim adherents.

*** This is an etymological fact undisputed by Muslim theologians. The disingenuous insistence that Islam means 'peace' can only be made by someone who equates peace with a state of submission.

"Because they believe in war as a spiritual value, and Jesus preached about love. This is why true Christianity doesn't attack – although it does if it's another religion that calls itself 'Catholicism' or something," he demurs. "Mohammed himself killed many people. Jesus killed nobody."

Damo's stance is clear: he stands with the man who would implore the mob not to stone the adulteress to death; not with he who'd insist she should die for her very human weakness.

"Maybe many people in this world are carrying negative energies because their countries send young people to the battlefield," expounds Damo, "or some rich person is making many people slaves, or some dictator is making money from poor people – all negative energies."

And all anathema to the musician traveller, in his pacifism, antimaterialism and disdain for egocentricity. The music business, too, is "capitalistic and controlling", and antithetical to Damo's ideas of freedom.

"There is nobody standing over me except God," he asserts. "You can see now the whole history of human life: there is always a battle of kings, or a battle of churches, or power. If you become powerful you step into another world."

In his worldview, Damo does at least concede the possibility of positive and negative power – but then the travelling gourmet also draws an analogy between food and political power:

"If there is one good restaurant, if the restaurateur seeks to open another one because he's getting successful, then another place, then another three or four restaurants, he changed his idea of good food to make a business. If he stayed with his positive energy he wouldn't need another place.

"There is the same thing, I think, in politics too: so when Napoleon stayed in France, he did some really good things for the French people*; but he went to Germany, Austria, Russia. Then it becomes much more personal: because he came from Corsica, probably from quite a poor family, he has this ideal for the French people – and this moment is good, but he wanted to go to other

---

* While Napoleon is sometimes wrongly characterised as a Hitler figure, the little general was, in his pronouncements at least, faithful at first to the French Revolution's ideals of 'liberty, equality, fraternity' (debased by the Terror, which he played a vital role in ending). That he became an incursive threat to much of Europe seems to follow naturally from crowning himself Emperor.

places where there were much bigger pickings. Families in other countries were destroyed. This," Damo very reasonably asserts, "is ego."

While he recognises no one can live an existence without any kind of ego at all (in the Freudian sense, the lack of personality would make you an impassive object), he stays as true as he can to his own philosophy.

"I think that everything I do is always connecting with one source – I'm making organic food; if I watch football, which I really like, I support teams that are not really based on capitalism. I support Dortmund because they have yellow and black on their team uniform, like the tiger.

"In China and Japan there are twelve different animal cycles," he elaborates. "I was born in the tiger (tora) cycle – the tiger year, month and day. In Japan every year becomes a different animal. People say it's not really good to believe in this kind of superstition, but everybody born in this tiger cycle is a strong person. My grandmother told me that when I was a child," he recalls, with perhaps a little fond nostalgia.

"In a way I am strong," Damo acknowledges, "because I survived major surgery and, in the hippie time, I lived as a young adult in a foreign country. Many times I wasn't supported by any kind of institution, but I survived. I have found the strongest way to seek truth now."

Chez Suzuki, the parameters of his physical world may have shrunk. But there were still internal journeys to be made. "There are many books that I've read, but nothing connected with my music," he reflects, "which is good.

"I'm interested in any kind of history: the history of Israel, the history of The Bible, the history of the Japanese."

In terms of his biblical studies, Damo has long since cast off the dogma of the Jehovah's Witnesses – but for all his fervent belief, this doesn't make him an orthodox Christian.

"I'm now believing in the same god but under another name, He's called Yahuah – the Jewish people say 'Yahweh'. Also we don't say 'Jesus Christ', we say 'Yahshua'.* I use much more Hebrew because it's in the Old

---

* Elke further defines the holy etymology of hers and Damo's faith: "Yahweh = YHWH pronounced 'JaHuWah', meaning 'I am the I am'. the name of the Son is related to the name of the Father: 'JAHUschuaH', meaning 'I am the one who saves', or 'I am your salvation' (see Isaiah 12:2)."

Testament, and part of the New Testament is also written in the Hebrew language, so it's better to refer to His Hebrew name.

"I still find The Bible to be the most important and compelling book in our history," he reasserts, "there are many things in it that connect with me. Normally, people who believe in the Church, or any kind of organised religion, do not really read The Bible. They believe in priests, but people should try to find *themselves* in The Bible – because there are many aspects of the Catholic or Protestant Church that are nothing to do with it."

Faith, in Damo's case, is not unquestioning. In fact he denounces organised religion, debunking the tenets of the Catholic faith* with the zeal of an iconoclast.

"When the Catholic Church says that the Sabbath falls on Sunday, it is not so: Sunday is the first day of the week, the seventh day is Saturday, but which end of the calendar are we at this point in our history? Before the solar calendar of today, the moon calendar was used; after this, Caesar founded the Julian calendar; then, by the end of the 16th century, they were using the Gregorian calendar.

"So actually, dates are counted totally differently and everyone is moving with the human-made calendar. But if I believe in The Bible, I can't say every seventh day is the Sabbath. I must check how the sun and moon are moving.

"All of Christianity is celebrating Christmas on the 25th of December," he continues his fundamental debunking. "But there's nothing in The Bible stating that Jesus was born then." Damo, who doesn't celebrate the festive season, recognises its pagan origins in the winter solstice before Scandinavia converted to Christianity. But he takes it a little further.

---

* In the tradition of Martin Luther, perhaps, he is most critical of Catholicism's iconography. He sees elements of paganism in it and believes that, on its establishment in the 4th century AD, the Catholic Church incorporated some of the symbolism of ancient cultures. Damo: "Iconography actually came from Egypt before Christianity; their god was the sun – Ra – and they also worshipped some others. These were the first icons. (In Germany, people say *Ikone*: one such icon is 'the eye of God', this bright image like a sun.) What happened with Christianity was, in the 4th century, Constantine founded today's Catholic Church. He was a Roman Caesar and he wanted power everywhere, so he put religion and politics together, many different kinds of customs and icons."

"The pagan religion had a god, Odin – like Zeus in the ancient Greek[*] – he looked like Santa Claus and his solstice was celebrated in late December. The 25th is also the birthdate of Nimrod from Babylonia. Nimrod was the first king, he went against God to make the first kingdom on this planet. You may even find further connections here with the name 'Santa Claus' – 'Claus' comes from 'Nikolaus', which comes from 'Nimrod'.

"Many things to do with so-called Christianity are nothing to do with The Bible. I'm living in Cologne, which is famous for a cathedral: if you look inside the cathedral, death is worshipped via the cross[**], and outside the cathedral you can see ugly creatures which are demons."

These hellish gargoyles – so integrated into medieval Christianity that they can still be glimpsed in the decaying exteriors of many preserved European buildings, not only churches – appeared as warnings of damnation in the afterlife. From Notre Dame cathedral to the triptychs of Hieronymus Bosch, their demonic aesthetic remains repellent to Damo's personal view of Christianity.

But still, it's difficult for a devotee of Christianity's Good Book to totally escape the taint of demonology. The infernal creeps back into its verses whenever it finds its niche, determined to scare all hell out of the believer.

Damo goes so far as to claim the state of our modern world is predicted in The Bible's final book, the Revelation of St John the Divine – the most phantasmagorical compendium of prophecies in Christendom, from which you can pick up the sulphurous stench of the pit.

"If you read it, with its imagery of women sitting on beasts, its meaning is quite important, as in the future all religion is going to be destroyed."

With this statement Damo stands revealed. Not a Gnostic. Not a heretic. Not a fanatic. But a sincere apocalyptic – in the Greek etymological sense of 'apocalypse', as much a mystical revelation as it is the end of all worldly things as predicted in The Bible.

---

[*]   Zeus ruled over the Greek mythological kingdom of Olympus, just as Odin did its Norse equivalent of Asgard.

[**] It's tempting to draw some analogy with the Cathars – the 12th/13th century French heretics who denied the sacredness of the crucifixion. But to them, Christ was said to represent pure spirit and so the idea of his physical death was a falsehood. To Damo, who sees Jesus as both Son of God/Son of Man, it's the refashioning of his execution into an icon which gives offence.

"This I believe because all religion went a totally different way to what God said, and also because many people in different societies don't believe that God exists. If you go to school you learn evolutionary theory, and evolutionary theory is totally against God – because it has no God. They are changing their morality from generation to generation.

"Because people are believing that humans once looked like a kind of ape, evolution has turned into a religion. They believe nothing is the truth – so I can say that this is a direct attack by Satan. There are many forms of attack and Satan is the creator of them all. His most important business is to part humankind from its one true God.

"What is God to do? He knows the time when He will be attacked and it will be very soon. Satan is the greatest liar; everybody knows the story of Adam and Eve. At that time he was already on this earth – for his lying we got punished, and that's why there is death. That's why people are dying. But before, in the paradise of Eden, there wasn't such a thing."

Damo is a fundamentalist Christian. He shares beliefs with End Timer sects, and with Baptists in the American South who seek to ban the teaching of Darwinism in schools. Yet he is as far away from the stereotype of the hellfire-and-brimstone preacher as it's possible to be; his endless curiosity about other human beings would never allow him to threaten damnation to anyone who deviates from doctrine. Instead, Damo sees a personal interpretation of The Bible as each believer's duty. He is his own theological pastor.

"For me it's always good," he testifies. "It's also helped me in my situation now, where I've been awaiting two operations for cancer. It's made me feel a lot stronger, because it's not the philosophy of the system. I'm an anarchist – but actually the real 'anarchists' are those who are standing over the people, controlling them. They do what they like and they don't believe in God, only in His opponent.

"Everything they do is as an outlaw – they don't pay tax, but politicians make laws only for taxpayers. I'm an anarchist but I don't hurt anybody, but these people can hurt everybody in society. Some quote from The Bible may give them power over the people, but they are pushing the people."

CHAPTER NINETEEN

INTERLUDE – THE WAR OF INFORMATION II

In common with those Westerners who eschew religion, Damo Suzuki sees it as a potential weapon of control. All the more reason, perhaps, why he feels he should reclaim The Bible as his own, as a template for living in which personal choice and individual responsibility are intertwined. Still, he will always be an Eastern man who rejected his own cultural traditions – traditions that interest him more in later life, viewed from the perspective of an outsider.

"For me, Europe was easier to live in because it is a continent," he reflects. "Germany is the middle of the European continent, everything is quite near. Also, everyone has a different kind of mentality and there is a kind of socialism. But if you think about the crime rate," he concedes, "then Japan is much safer."

All the same, he continues to look at the land of his origins with detached interest – as if studying a fascinating alien culture.

"Like everywhere else, its history is really criminal," he muses. "If you are talking about Japanese history, the tradition of Tennō, the 'Japanese Caesar'; is very important. Caesar's dynasty originated maybe at the same time as Christ – Tennō's 'Ten' applies to 'Heaven', so it's something like 'King of Heaven' if you translate it."

The emperor as a god. It seems like an ethnically quaint concept now. It's also the ethos that led an often courteous and intelligent island race into regarding obedience and duty as the highest virtues; the extreme conclusion of this was made manifest in the war years.

"This is totally arrogant and I really don't like that they are labelled 'God', who is the creator of a human being," seethes Damo with quiet disdain. "This is Shintoism which originated the Japanese Caesar's dynasty."

It's clear by now that he must have always been a little uncomfortable with his parent culture. But at this stage of his life, Damo is happy to reflect, read and speak about it without really feeling himself a part of it.

"At the moment I'm reading folklore about the beginnings of Japan, about how ancient Japan had about a million gods," he confirms. "I don't believe in all this but I read it as if I'm reading a comic book. It's fantasy, something like twopence-a-word cheap fiction."

Both Damo and this writer share an affection for the Japanese ghost stories of Greek-Irish writer Lafcadio Hearn. Less a teller of creepy tales in the Western M. R. James tradition than a folklorist who went native (the Japanese know him as Koizumi Yakumo), Hearn would have been well known to Damo's generation when he was a schoolboy.

"Japan has many mysteries," Damo acknowledges of the fables Hearn retold in his own literary idiom. But when asked about *Kwaidan*, the classic 1965 fantasy film based on four of Hearn's tales, the Japanese traveller displays more European cinematic tastes.

"Back when I was busking, I never had time to watch the movies or anything like that," he says of the late sixties/early seventies. "But recently, when I was sick, I was not mobile enough to do anything else. It was the best way to concentrate my brain.

"I have quite a lot of filmmakers that I enjoy," Damo acclaims. "There is an Italian called Tornatore who made a film called *Cinema Paradiso*. This is wonderful, his best work, but he also made good movies like *The Legend Of 1900*."

Cinema Paradiso is a bittersweet, tragicomic 1988 Italian film. A testament to the power of movies themselves, its central character, a young boy called Toto, is based on Giuseppe Tornatore as a screen-struck youngster. *The Legend Of 1900*, made a decade later, adopts a similarly melancholic/romantic attitude toward music, with Tim Roth as a liner-ship musician whose world does not extend beyond the parameters of the boat. With his own world shrunken to the size of an apartment, Damo may have felt empathy for the title character at this point.

"He is a really good director because you are just taken out of yourself, into the film," he says of Tornatore's deceptively simple human narratives. "It's really exciting because he knows how to tell stories, he's writing the script himself, and also the music is always good – composed by Ennio Morricone." The eclectic soundtrack maestro creates understatedly evocative themes and incidental music for both, ranging from neoclassicism to ersatz New Orleans jazz.

"Also I like Julie Taymor – she made *Frida* about the Mexican artist Frida Kahlo." Salma Hayek's acclaimed 2002 performance as Frida matches the intensity of her surrealist art, which informs the film's design. The scenes of her taking refuge in creativity as she convalesces from injury may also have chimed with Damo. "Taymor also made a film based on The Beatles, *Across The Universe*." This 2007 collaboration with UK TV dramatists Dick Clement and Ian La Frenais is a 1960s odyssey, where the characters' lives are described by Beatles songs. While it seems a little too forcibly contrived to this writer, "It's very interesting because it's a kind of patchwork she is making," counters Damo – by his own admission not a Beatles fan.

"I watch quite a lot of movies – for instance, yesterday* I saw a French movie from 1986, *Betty Blue*," Jean-Jacques Beineix's erotic drama with a career-defining performance by Beatrice Dalle. "I quite like French movies because they have a different way of thinking to the German or Anglo-Saxon, totally different humour – actually, everywhere has a different opinion or a different perspective," Damo corrects himself.

DAMOSUZUKI.COM BLOG
December 1 2006 (Friday) Italy Cavariago Calamatia
Luca [G] and his girlfriend... picked me up from Bologna airport... Luca and his girlfriend run bookshop, special for films and also DVDs... we spoke lots about film. I like Italian film lots... I am fan of European film... of course Italian film with my favourite Fellini... Amarcord and Roma are my favourite**...

---

*   At the time of our conversation.
**   Federico Fellini's vividly baroque semi-autobiographies of his own life and times.

316

I like most of films from Sergio Leone*, too. There is Pasolini**... Soundtrack composer Ennio Morricone is one of best accompanist of 20th century and also this new century. I love actress like Loren and Gina***... And so and so... until deep in the night we spoke about movies. If there is any ? they pick up dictionary of film and they find answer.

As is characteristic, there is also a philosophy to how Damo watches movies.

"If I have a DVD I can see it at ten o'clock; if you are watching TV your time is controlled – a football game is at nine o'clock and you must see it at this time. If I spend my time on this it means I am losing my own time for anything else, and there are advertisements for washing powder or something.

"The main point of this whole book is my philosophy and dreams. My time is becoming less and less, so I'd like to say that it's important to have your own time which you control yourself, and not to be influenced by information which has a hidden agenda telling you not to make your own choices."

In terms of his native East Asian filmmakers, Akira Kurosawa is an artistic touchstone for Damo. But he doesn't see his breakthrough work, *Rashomon*, as a movie so much as a philosophical statement. Nor does he see Kurosawa as quintessentially Japanese – despite the trappings of the *jidaigeki* (period drama), the auteur was seen as a critic of Japan's cultural mores.

"I'm thinking of it totally as movie art like Mizoguchi," says Damo, making comparison with a more classically traditionalist director, "how he's using perspective and black-and-white film. At that time many directors didn't have so much technical sophistication, unlike now, but with less technical know-how they made such good films.

---

*   Leone's operatically stylised violence may seem a little extreme for a pacific soul like Damo – but stylisation is the key. From his antiheroic westerns to a swansong gangland masterpiece, his sense of drama was matched by Morricone's soundtracks – encompassing styles from light opera to Duane Eddy-esque guitar twang.

**   An unflinching cineaste's eye marked the career of Marxist filmmaker and writer Pier Paolo Pasolini: from a humanist reading of *The Gospel According To Saint Matthew* to pagan sacrifice in *Medea* and a grotesque relocation of Sade's fantasies to Fascist Italy in *Salo*.

***   Vivacious Italian actresses Sophia and Lollobrigida respectively.

"*Rashomon* is a fantastic film, because it's showing 'truth' as four or five 'truths'." In medieval Japan, an attack by bandit Toshiro Mifune on a nobleman and his wife results in murder and rape. Each of the three characters (plus a witness woodcarver) gives their version of events; none dissent from the end result but all are radically different – whether they seem true or false depends on the viewer's perspective.

In his autobiography*, Kurosawa gives an explanation for the unreliability of human perspective that seems Damo-esque: "Egoism is a sin the human being carries with him… This film is like a strange picture scroll that is unrolled and displayed by the ego."

"So it's depending on the perspective of one person," reasons Damo, "if you're believing in lies then this may be your truth. Life is always like that: misunderstandings; for me it's normal."

It's also, it seems, something that can be painted on a universal canvas. "Like if you see any kind of news on the TV, Western countries are always giving bad news about Putin** – I think truth is always something in between. I don't believe in so-called 'news', newspapers and stuff like this. All truth is things that you can experience and you can see.

"People cannot see three-dimensionally – many people are thinking in only two dimensions, front and back. The other things that you get so much information from are not really 'yourself'. That's why I think Kurosawa's movie is quite deep; in many situations people can tell lies – including the director himself, telling the good side, and some people are believing this too.

"Listen!" he urges all of us. "One of the real crimes in life sometime seems to be harmless and without cost: but stealing someone's lifetime is criminal. As everybody is born as a freethinking, creative person, don't give them your worthy time and protect your freedom."

So far, so virtuous.

---

*   *Something Like An Autobiography*, Vintage Books, 1983.

**   It should be acknowledged that President Putin is a former director of the KGB, for whom a sleight of hand with the 'truth' (along with a disregard for basic human rights) would be a virtue. But it's also evident that, as Damo suggests, the West may utilise him as an external aggressor to unite against, just as the West provides a common enemy for him to unite his population.

But it'd be very wrong to think of Damo – who's both a child of the age of hippie libertarianism and a little sceptical of it – as buying into the whole canon of liberal piety. In our era of mutual distrust and 'fake news', he's as averse to consensus reality as any alienated blue-collar guy on the other side of the Atlantic.*

"The period of history we are living in at the moment is, for me, a war of information," Damo confirms. "You can find information in a magazine or something, or you can go to the internet to find another perspective. But eventually you don't know what you can believe. Only if you have some kind of belief in a god, for instance, or if you have some other firm foundation, can you find a way to walk."

Of particular concern to him is how the *Willkommenskultur*, as introduced by German Chancellor Angela Merkel, was disseminated by the media. "She doesn't recognise the reality of the people," insists Damo, chiming with everyman populism. "If you are a private person you can decide for yourself which people you invite to your party, but she's inviting just everybody and it's dangerous to have such a person at the top in Germany and Europe."

Before anyone smarts at the idea of Damo Suzuki, the Far Eastern world traveller, resenting later *arrivistes* to Europe, consider the background of his presence here: curious and eager to engage with Western culture; keen to work and appreciative of the families who took him in; sympathetic to a fundamental (and seemingly now dying) form of liberalism that listened to everyone's views and didn't consider anything 'unsayable'.

"The danger is that in the beginning they didn't establish any controls," he says of the refugee crisis that grew from Middle Eastern upheavals – particularly the civil war in Syria. "They don't know who these people are. If I say 'refugees', they are mainly young, male, eighteen to thirty-five years old, and don't have any luggage. But they have mobiles and they don't

---

* Damo would return to London to perform in autumn 2016, several months after the Brexit referendum. While someone in Hackney hipster pub The Shacklewell Arms had written, 'This chair stays in the European Union' on the back of a seat, the performer was in favour of Britain leaving the EU. Responding to this writer's pragmatic concerns re short-term economic damage, to Damo freedom was an idealistic principle at odds with a vast international bureaucracy: "I hope that other countries will get their freedom from the EU."

look like they are hungry – some of them look like they are bodybuilding. So I can't help thinking about the dangers of this, because it could get ugly."

Indeed, sometimes it does get ugly. But to pre-empt facile accusations of some kind of cultural 'phobia', consider the true nature of human diversity: our internal landscapes are created in part by our geocultural backgrounds; our views of reality diverge to such an extent that neurologists theorise on how the brain itself is literally shaped by our early experience.

It's therefore hard to draw too close a comparison to the open-hearted and questing Japanese boy, who left his national borders in the late sixties, with those migrants who believe Western cultural mores are unimportant; that our societies are in decay and will soon fall to the most radical forms of Islam.

But then, to those Europeans too virtuous to even consider the nature of our changing societies, 'diversity' is just a catchphrase. In believing that all human beings are really the same, they deny that any kind of diversity exists at all.

According to Damo, the dogma of tolerance that accompanied the 2015 influx of Arabic refugees was reinforced by disinformation. "Someone says that anything up to 1.5 million refugees will come to Germany this year; one newspaper says 800,000 – the information is totally different. Okay, we accept them all, but next year there comes another million, or two million, but we don't have enough capacity or the financial grounds to help them."*

In a slight twist to his worldview, he sees the problem as originating with the control of Western media by American interests, to which he's grown increasingly averse. "Germany has been censored by the USA since they won the last world war," he asserts. "They are in control; they are checking all the telephone calls of the Chancellor. All their spies are everywhere, and they're probably checking what their neighbours know

* From DamoSuzuki.com blog, 2011: *"Revolution at Islam countries. They fight for human right, Islam or non-Islam. They need minimum right to live."* Damo's sympathy for the Arab Spring, and for the oppressed Muslims and non-Muslims of Islamic countries, is plain to see. What he and the rest of us would come to realise is that sometimes, 'freedom' in Islamic countries equates with the right to identify with a radical Islamist theocracy.

too. Information has really gone crazy. Remember that AP, AFP and all those news agencies control 90 per cent of the news sources, and who do the agencies belong to?"

In this sense, he believes, Europe is sometimes forced to accommodate hostile newcomers when the US and its allies fail in their interventionist policies – when attempts to impose Western-style democracy result only in further bloodshed and the blowing open of geocultural borders.

"I believe this," he asserts with sincerity. "If you are leaving refugees together with several hundred people in a big hall for an unlimited time in this one space, and they don't even know if they can get a stamp to be in the country, then people will get mad. Because you are not living in a private atmosphere; maybe in your normal life you've never had contact with these kinds of people – so you get really mad. The place where you're living is a vitally important element in your life. From this you get a creative energy – positive or negative energy."

"It's not the US media that creates 'reality', it's the people behind it," insists Damo. "All their media is owned privately."

If the phrase 'fake news' springs to mind, bear in mind that President Trump came to power during the period of this book's research and composition. As an egocentric, materialistic braggart and bully, it's hard to conceive of anyone that Damo Suzuki might feel less sympathy with.

But there's one aspect that Damo and the most ardent 'Make America Great Again' cap-wearers have in common: their conception of current affairs and external reality has been informed for years by a mass media they have no faith in. It's true that the mainstream media mostly abides by stringent journalistic codes that purveyors of 'alternative facts' on the internet are untouched by; but then, the media always takes ascertainable facts and spins them so much that the same event becomes several totally opposing stories, as dictated by corporate editorial policies.

Damo sees this as a historical process that has taken place throughout his life. "This control has been in place for many years – always throughout the fifties, sixties, seventies... so you can read human history, but how much of history is the truth? Because the winner is always changing history and they never show the perspective of the losers. The USA has always spoken bad things about the Germans and the Japanese; it is still like this if you see US war movies, which show how angry we all are. But it's just propaganda," he insists, perhaps a little angrily.

For Damo, as for many other people, consensus reality is dead. Or maybe it never really existed. While this is a situation fuelled by internet culture, it wasn't created by it. Idiosyncratic worldviews are common to very many of us – going online just gives the opportunity to contact other believers (or sceptics).

"Many people don't know how, when Pearl Harbor was attacked by the Japanese, the US military knew that they were coming to attack Hawaii from their secret agents. But they didn't do anything because they wanted to allow an attack by the Japanese to legitimise their own counterattack," insists Damo. "There is a parallel to September 11th: they are using these types of events to brainwash the people."

This may sound like the politics of paranoia. But take a trawl back through the millennial newspaper archives: the neoconservative Bush administration hadn't been elected long when one of its members was quoted as opining that what the USA needed was an event on the scale of Pearl Harbor to unite it. This writer also spoke to a police intelligence operative, close to the time of 9/11, who confirmed Western security services were expecting a major terror attack – they were merely unsure what form it would take. Meanwhile, the neocon administration in the US had downgraded terrorism as a priority for their intelligence agencies.

When these historical synapses join up, it seems like the paranoids amongst us may actually possess a more acute awareness. As far as Damo is concerned, it's a human being's duty to doubt the official history of our times.

"It's so strange that, since 1972, nobody has gone to the moon and walked on it," he adds, expressing one of the classic contrarian beliefs of our time. "It's nearly fifty years since the USA is supposed to have landed – but still we are not able to travel to the moon. One of my cousins is a student of astronautics, I talked to him about this and he said it's still not possible to send people to another planet, because the technology we have is not advanced enough.

"The reason the USA said they did it at that time was that, in 1969, the Soviet Union was in front in many ways. The US told lies all over the world – schoolboys were able to see this on TV and they believed it. Many things in our history are really strange and, if you research deeper and deeper, much of it is actually quite wrong.

"You think I'm a conspiracy theorist?"

Well, *yes*.

But there's a problem with that term. It's too easily weaponised to ridicule or diminish the views of anyone who strays too far from the officially sanctioned, consensus worldview. But who'd dare claim that conspiracies aren't real? Take a look on the statute books of most Western countries – 'conspiracy' itself is an offence that can attract a harsh prison sentence, depending on what the conspirators are alleged to have been planning.

A further problem is that conspiracy is, by its nature, always secret – so any conjecture by an outsider as to what's really going down is necessarily theoretical. In this Damo is little different to many thousands of other theoreticians across the world. But he holds a set of beliefs that are emblematic of him – their primary virtue is that they're the product of his own sensibilities. No one can mediate his views of reality.

It'd be easy to see his beliefs as an emblem of online culture and the age of social media. But it'd also be quite wrong – to him, the electronic communications which we live by are just more weapons of misinformation.

"People are very easy to control," he laments, "it is very easy to brainwash them these days with technological media, the internet and so on. Many people are believing in what never happened."

His distaste for the consumer-tech age seems to be one of his most fervent convictions – but then it's not just theoretical, but personal.

"Several years ago, there was an article saying 'Damo Suzuki captured' on YouTube at Christmas. Many people saw it and there was some kind of video with photos – my photos and my friends' photos. With this shit, maybe 200 or 2,000 people were thinking, *'Who is Damo Suzuki? He must be dead,'* or something like that."

In another of those online disruptions all the more annoying for their pointlessness, Damo was targeted by a hacker. "There were some internet actions and some person got into my mailbox, sending emails that said only bad things about me. It was nothing to do with me but many people totally believed it.

"And these are young, intelligent, modern people?" he asks with incredulity. "They are no better than their predecessors who believed in all those war heroes; both are brainwashed."

DAMOSUZUKI.COM BLOG, JANUARY 2010

Gosh!!! ...Already three weeks of 'Tiger' year is gone...

Hi everyone, hope you're well and in good shape.

After Christmas I received some claims by mail as some saw in YouTube 'Damo Suzuki hacked YouTube... Damo will capture YouTube and name it to DamoTube.' They're saying if I'm Damo Suzuki, please don't do it (capture YouTube) and some nasty words against me.

(They were not my fans, even they don't know my music.)

With development on internet, exists not existing person... phantom. You know, there are surprisingly quite a lot of people using name Damo Suzuki as their mail address, also appears in chatrooms or blog.

When I start surfing in net around one decade back, I was chatting sometimes and found all those behind masks. Lady is not lady (behind mask is man) kind of stuff. Crazy world. It's easy to identify into phantom. Even criminal things happened like steal money from old single lady who found in net good looking and good situated gentleman... a dream man (this man not exist) and paid money, lost quite amount of money.

Criminal thing is [more] popular than ever... it's easy to do something with mask... anonymous.

That Damo who want to capture YouTube use my photo. And worse many internetgoers believing in every small thing in net.

Nowadays Facebook or MySpace sort of things I don't go.

I just don't like to sit in front of monitor all day.

I'm working with laptop average four hours a day... it's just enough or may be too much... I don't go to any kind of chatroom, blog, if somebody invites me for.

"This is a very difficult world in which to find the truth," concedes the man who still fires off sporadic blogs to Network fans, but disdains social media. "There are many, many types of information on the internet, and they have so much time to make so much bullshit – sending it from many different places. Many people, me too," he admits, "are slaves to this information.

"What a dangerous world! The internet is not really a good place because if you believe one thing then it's quite hard not to believe in another – whether it comes from a conspiracy theorist or normal TV broadcasting. Once you have got into all this, it's really hard to get out of it and find yourself."

For Damo, the War of Information is not exclusive to the cyber age but a perennial strand of human history. "This is a problem that originated in The Bible because Eve talked to the snake, Satan, which was the beginning of misinformation," he testifies. "Bad information is the most dangerous thing."

And the ultimate aim, as he sees it, is societal control – the very antithesis of his pacifist anarchism.

"It is not part of God's will to make a kingdom for somebody so that they are standing over the people. The people should be free like God – free to decide and to hold your own opinions. This is the most important thing for everybody's lives: to go our own way and to find our own selves, not influenced by anybody else.

"I found my freedom. I was like this long ago, spiritually like Lot in The Bible.*

"Internet, newspapers, magazines, radio and TV are not telling the whole truth – nowadays especially, but previously too – because they are run by governments or private persons who put their ideology into it. There is nothing you can really believe in."

In such an ongoing situation, it seems incumbent upon everyone to define their own vision, their own *Weltanschauung*. Their own reality. Their own God.

"What I'm following is really a parallel to religion," Damo dissents. "I'm following truth. I need to find my personal truth and I need to know who I am, where I come from. This is the main theme and the main mission of each person who is living on this earth," he evangelises. "Many people are believing in things which are based on tradition which they don't research – but how have these traditions begun? For what reason?"

Media disinformation in all its forms is, he believes, exploited by the infernal one himself. "This is a time, an epoch, when people cannot believe anything, so this confusion will work for Satan.

---

* The nephew of Abraham, who, with his family, fled the decadent and damned city of Sodom in the Book of Genesis. While Lot became a righteous traveller, his wife was turned into a pillar of salt by the angels when she dared to look back at Sodom.

"It's the work of the USA and the Freemasons," Damo insists, seeing American power as always the arch-manipulator. "There are only a few American Presidents who weren't Freemasons. At the beginning of US history there was a contract drawn up by their new establishment: I think there were sixteen people who signed and it was connecting them all."*

"For me there is no 'conspiracy theory' – all the things that are happening are, I think, a conspiracy. Because if you discover the truth then big power will push you or punish you."

"Tomorrow I'm going to read my short story and Jan from Mouse On Mars will come here to record it," Damo told me in the autumn of 2015. Jan St Werner of the MOM electro duo had already taken the path less trodden, teaming up with post-punk surrealist visionary Mark E. Smith of The Fall a decade previously, later recording an album together as Von Südenfed.

"He's going to make music out of it," said Damo of his spoken-word performance. "They're coming from another field as they make electro music; I made a sound installation with this person last spring." The installation, at the Museum Abteiberg in Mönchengladbach, was entitled (in English translation) *Apparatus with which one potato can circle another (Experiment of an electroacoustic composition in memory of Sigmar Polke**)*. It

---

*　From 'Introduction: A Nation Of Conspiracy Theorists' – *Conspiracy Nation*, edited by Peter Knight, New York University Press, 2002: "Just check out the dollar bill: … To the initiated, the great seal on the reverse tells the whole story: the pyramid with the eye at the top is a Masonic symbol, not surprising given that many of the Founding Fathers were Freemasons. The Masons, the story continues, were themselves under the control of the Bavarian Illuminati, a secret society that orchestrated both the French and American Revolutions, and has been ever since secretly leading us to a New World Order of Satanic misrule." This writer should perhaps declare an interest, in having edited and proofread on occasion for a Masonic publishing house. Having never been a Mason and never invited to join, it was hard to discern any kind of satanic conspiracy. Freemasonry's adherents live in a world of private ritual, but it seems entirely informed by Christian esoterica. But then, given their disdain for 'the profane world', they probably saw me as being from 'the dark side' myself.

**　One of Damo's favoured contemporary artists – see Chapter Sixteen. The late Polke's juxtapositions of expressionistic images, photography and explosions of colour was created by random processes which share something of the Network ethos.

ran from April 23–July 5, 2015, with Damo's fragile state of health allowing him a visit to the opening. St Werner recorded him for the installation.

Now he was going to do likewise for one of Damo's first pieces of original fiction. "I wrote many short stories," the debutant author said. "I don't know whether they're good or not, I didn't make anything out of them until now.

"But I have enough time and sometimes I'm able to write them down, as making music at the moment is not possible. I can use only my hand or head, so writing is not a bad way to train my brain. It's a kind of fantasy fiction.* I'm not sure if people will be interested in it, but I have to do something. I cannot just hang around here, it's impossible when I have the opportunity to do something I didn't do before.

"If you have a sickness like mine, you must work with your head to create. That's why I've found time to write some stories, to create some fantasies. I think it helps me quite a lot. I'm writing in German; writing in Japanese is quite difficult because the meanings of words are always changing and every word can take on quite a different perspective. It's really good to train my brain.

"I like to write fantasy which is quite nonsensical, and a bit of science fiction. I did it because I don't like to read a book that from beginning to end stays the same; if the beginning is sad then the end is sad as well. So my beginning may be sad but after that everything is happier."

Damo read voraciously during his period of convalescence; as we have seen, his reading was largely restricted to non-fiction and history. As with his music, his literary work took no lead from what he consumed in private.

"It makes it free, almost as if when you make an abstract painting," he underlines the links between different creative media. "It shouldn't be truth, it shouldn't be reality or historically 'fixed' stuff. But I think any kind of creativity must have some kind of message: the writer likes to show people what he's thinking and what is his opinion, what is *his* truth."

---

* Sadly, although the writer is a fan of science fiction and *le fantastique*, Dàmo has declined to read him any translations!

ELKE MORSBACH

I think creativity is always a great healer; on the other side is believing in The Bible. It is interesting because I was born a Catholic. I went to Catholic school and to mass. I find it astonishing when I now read The Holy Bible how different my belief is. It's amazing how much wisdom and genius this book contains. I can't imagine why less people are reading it, but it's a problem if you are Catholic – you think you know The Bible but they're giving you pieces and telling you that you don't have to read it because you don't understand it; instead they are showing you pictures.

I was astonished when I left their system and all this stuff was going around the world like New Age, and all these esoteric things. You can read in The Bible about how it works and what is coming. I have come from the dark side and I experienced a lot of yoga and all this stuff.* So I was really astonished by what it said in there and I can say it is a support.

Damo's strong character helps him a lot. It's amazing to see a strong personality in situations like he is in now; he is always dealing with his situation and he is never in a bad mood. He enjoys his creativity and he's grateful for that; him and Jan St Werner (of Mouse On Mars) made an art installation because he couldn't sing or make a concert. He said of this exhibition: "There is a new world on the other side, not that I'm forgetting my music – it's what is possible now."

MARTIN SUZUKI

I think it's a great thing to see how my father's Network works. Different people meet, make music and have a nice time. If everybody in this world were like this, we'd really have love, peace and harmony.

His attitudes to human creativity have influenced me. I like his way of trying to make the world a better place. In a way, what he is doing is also a part of what I am – I am also peaceful and like to live in harmony.

I think music as his setting to the illness is important. He's got a lot of love in his body, and at this moment he can't cry it out. So he will get back on stage

---

* Elke and Damo both regard Eastern disciplines such as yoga, and more millennial fads such as New Age belief systems and pagan revivals, as inherently antichristian. Damo: "There is much doubt about New Age stuff, with yoga, or Zen, or meditation. Many people believe in Christ but they are doing the yoga, they are doing the meditation. Nobody is really clear on the route to God on a godless road."

to tell everybody how he feels. With all the musicians out there he can make music to help him to recover. There are three simple things in his life to keep him happy and smiling:

Family.

Music.

Cooking.

I love him. I am proud of what he is doing and I wish him all the best for his fight against his illness.

MIRKO SUZUKI

I really like the Damo Suzuki's Network concept – and I think the other artists appreciate making music with him for a little session. There are no rules, so it's just meeting friends and doing whatever you want to do.

I think it's more a development which came later – but maybe he was thinking about it during his harder times in life? In my opinion positive thoughts are helping through the struggle with cancer. The more positive you are, the easier it gets to fight against the illness. I think there are a lot of quotes of Tupac which can really help: "Hold on be strong," "Keep your head up" and "After a dark night there will be a brighter day." Since my father's surgery in 2014 we make way more family meetings, because you never know what happens the next day.

MARCO HEIBACH

We've always been in touch, sure. There were periods when we didn't hear from each other for one or two months, but mostly we stayed in contact all the time. For him, this is the way his life turned out to be, I think this is one of the best ways he could possibly go. From my perspective he has a quite nice life. From his perspective it's a perfect personal freedom. But I don't think it's for every individual.

I'd kind of known about his illness, but it never really came to the table. It was never like a topic. I knew way before I was born he was in a hospital – but that it was getting like a problem again, that it was related, I wasn't aware. I'm quite sure my mum told me, because she heard it from Elke. I became aware of it in that moment – because he's of a generation that doesn't actually like to go and see doctors. [laughs] I feel that in the past he probably missed his check-up or something like that, but I don't really know. That's not my thing to judge.

I don't really know its effect, I don't know any medical facts that could support this, but I would say somebody who's living a life where he can actually do what he wants to do probably has a stronger spirit, or animus, a stronger will to survive than somebody who's not living the life he wants – who's not happy or something like that. I think these factors of negativity probably have an effect – but I couldn't support this by any medical texts, so…

HIROFUMI SUZUKI
After several surgeries I talked with him by email and Skype. People who are doing creative things choose ideas from next time to next time, regardless of location. I think that becoming a future-oriented and living energy, to try to embody it, is useful for treatment.

CHAPTER TWENTY

I WAS DEAD, I WAS BORN

For much of the latter part of 2014 and the early months of 2015, Damo Suzuki fell in and out of the arms of Morpheus. Drugged by emergency palliative care, much of this time was lost to bouts of unconsciousness.

At the same time, in the world outside his hospital ward, his friends and peers continued with their own struggles. Those battles with an ageing constitution and failing health that are wired into us all by the human condition. Erupting at random, with the outcome just a roll of the genetic dice.

"When I heard of the passing of Stefan Krachten, I myself was in a coma for weeks," wrote Damo with regret in early 2015. "I feel sad that I couldn't show up for his last."

The former Dunkelziffer drummer succumbed to a long illness on September 16, 2014. As with a number of his peers, he'd drawn on his own musical eclecticism in recent years to expand into electro: dance and trance. Back in the day, he'd been the one to invite Damo to join the young Cologne band – offering him a path back into music.

DAMOSUZUKI.COM BLOG, JANUARY 2015

We had many good times together.

*Before he passed he played in Blue Shell, Cologne, I had opportunity to see him with Goldman around a few months ago.**

---

* Goldman is a band with an amorphous line-up which has included old buddies from the Stollwerck chocolate factory in Cologne – like Helmut Zerlett from Phantom Band on keyboards. Their laid-back yet never-quite-ambient sound is representative of Euro jazz-rock fusion in the late 20th/early 21st century, understated but nicely suited to film and TV soundtracks. In the wake of Stefan Krachten's death, they would return to the same venue in tribute and to complete the *Live At The Blue Shell* album – augmented this time by Rosko Gee on bass and Jaki Liebezeit replacing Stefan on drums.

He was long time not healable ill and last year most of times he had to spend on his bed wasn't mobile.

Still he wasn't weak, performed sometimes and produced his own and other artist recordings.

Stefan forever.

ELKE MORSBACH'S DIARY*
Spring 2015
*Together with the neighbours, we are building a new kitchen so that Damo can move better with his IV pole. The whole apartment is in a mess, three neighbours – Martin, Roland, Alfred – are engaged in our small kitchen and then the whole of Julie's Haircut.** Luca had already called the Cologne hospital more often and was very worried. On their European tour, they decided to stop briefly to visit Damo. A total of seven people stood between all the boxes and furniture, for whom I cooked on a small stove on the floor a Cologne lentil soup.*

In the autumn of 2015, the secondary interviews for this book got properly underway. Damo offered a gradually evolving list of personal contacts and Network Sound Carriers whose detailed discussions would inform much of our content here.

Convalescing and relatively isolated, our main man was keen to offer guidance. His world had shrunk to the size of his apartment – but his inner universe retained the dimension-defying scale of his psyche.***

Before this writer could contact anyone, Damo fired off emails to a small selection of his old Sound Carriers. What, he was curious to know, were their initial impressions of playing with the Network?

EMAIL TO DAMO FROM MATHIAS HILL
Vocalist and bassist of Rockformation Diskokugel**, October 4, 2015**
It's good to hear that you are well, I wish you all the best about that!!!

---

*   Translated from its original German.
**   Luca Giovanardi's band – see Chapter Thirteen.
*** Damo may prefer the angular rhythms of early Captain Beefheart and not care too much about the lyrics – but I'm guessing he might also feel some empathy with 1972's 'My Head Is My Only House Unless It Rains'.
**** Rockformation Diskokugel is a post-punk/indie-pop band from the Rhein region. Even to a non-German speaker, there's a playful sense of humour evident in the album title *The Boy With The Zorn In His Side* (referencing both The Smiths and US experimentalist John Zorn) and the single release 'The Day With Sid Vicious'.

As for your request about the 'Sound Carrier impression', I can tell that I've twice had the pleasure and the experience to share the stage with you: First time at 603qm in Darmstadt some years ago as part of a big 'orchestra' of thirteen musicians, second time in 2013 in Finkenbach (as bass player in Rockformation Diskokugel).

603qm was a nice and unexpected gig for me: Jens Engemann from 603 and some friends had the idea and wanted to start a 'super backing group' of Darmstadt alternative musicians and they asked me to join. As it was clear that there'd be a couple of bass players, it was clear to me that I should play some other instrument. Stefan from Rockformation lent me his Stylophone and a guitar synthesizer, so I was able to throw in some strange electronic noises from time to time.

We all thought that it wouldn't work to have all thirteen musicians on stage all the time, so we decided that we'd start with a few musicians, then the others join and leave just as they think it serves the flow of the music – less is more. And as I had some kind of 'extra instrument', I wanted to stay in the background as much as possible in order not to annoy anyone...

The soundcheck (a day before the gig) was quite strange... it took ages to get everything on stage, and afterwards everyone wanted to jam which started a total noise... and some discussions about who was to blame afterwards... so we stayed with the 'less is more'-attitude.

As the gig started, I was astonished that Damo immediately joined us. I had thought that there would be some kind of 'dreamy introduction' and the maestro would join the musicians after fifteen to twenty minutes. But I got to get the point: for this kind of music, you have to be focused, and it's not easy to be focused if you've been off stage for a beer for some minutes. So I guess the concert was enjoyable for the audience and for the musicians as well, I had a lot of fun and I got to understand what the task of a sound carrier should be.

Some years later, my band Rockformation Diskokugel stayed with our friend Rainer Csallner in Switzerland. As we asked him which other musicians visited his house lately, we came to talk about Damo. It was Rainer who created the idea that Rockformation might be a good sound carrying unit for Damo. I was very astonished that the other guys thought so as well. Usually, we play rock concerts with three-minute songs, which is fun, but something totally different. But we all thought a new experience would suit the band and so we got in contact and planned to play the Finkenbach festival with Damo.

In order to do it right and to get to a new horizon with the band, we started to jam at the rehearsals. In fact, we didn't do rehearsals at all for months and months... we just met at the rehearsal room, someone started off with a lick and then we carried on for hours... that was something totally new to us.

As the gig came close, we were quite nervous... What would happen? Of course, there was a front man (to hide behind in case of emergency), but for the first time, we didn't have a set list to hold on [to]!

As in Darmstadt, we planned to start with some slow, dreamy keyboard and guitar sounds, but before we went on stage, Damo said to start off a festival, you should begin with a bang! And so he jumped on stage and we all did a storming, rocking start... we played for a while and everyone was into it, and when I glanced at our drummer Matthias for the first time, I was astonished that he was covered with sawdust – his drumsticks were already getting thin... I remember it as being like a well-oiled machine and I remember Damo singing something like 'Rave into the night' (during bright daylight, by the way) and in Rockformation we still talk about the 'Raven to the night' when we talk about this gig.

As we didn't know how to stop a song, we played for forty-five minutes until the flow silenced for the first time of the gig. It was a strange feeling for me as I didn't know how the audience would react. At first, there was silence, which is the worst reaction of all(!), but then the crowd started to cheer and to applaud – so we had another go.

For me, this gig was totally different from the Darmstadt concert, as I was a part of a solid, enduring crew of five musicians and a singer – together on a festival stage for the whole of the gig. And being the bass player is being the backbone of it, whereas the Stylophone playing was more the icing on the cake or some extra gimmick or whatever.

The backstage party was nice, Stefan nicely asked some guy from the festival crew to fill up the beer in the fridge – it turned out that it wasn't a crew member but some guy from Ton Steine Scherben. All the other musicians were nice, laid-back and highly enjoyable, especially Damo and Mani.*

---

* Mani Neumeier – drummer of Guru Guru and organiser of the annual Finkenbach 'krautrock' festival.

So all in all, both concerts changed my view on how to play and listen to music – not totally, but to a large degree. Thanks for giving me the opportunity to experience this, Damo!!!

EMAIL TO DAMO FROM KEITH MARKS
October 5, 2015

Damo, I remember the show in Seoul, South Korea where they forbade you from performing. You sat in the audience and cried. I'll never forget that moment – how passionate you are for this music.

We met, randomly, in Cologne in an art exhibit where we walked from room to room in different colours, wearing different colour vests.

I would still love to see you perform. I live in Jacksonville, Florida, USA now. One day...

My friend has a recording studio in Cologne. He does a lot of hip hop, but is a great guy. If you ever want to meet new, great people in Cologne, let me know.

EMAIL TO DAMO FROM MASON JONES
Founder and guitarist of Numinous Eye*, October 8, 2015

Hello! You asked about impression/feeling during our performance together, and it's interesting. My friend Mike** and I performed with you and Steve Eto*** in Tokyo some years ago (Pink Noise, March 8, 2007). My impression was a little strange because we flew from San Francisco and landed at Narita about three hours before our performance. So I was kind of like 'high' from jetlag! Ha-ha. But I really enjoyed the performance because we had never played with you or Steve before and I always enjoy improvising in a new situation. I knew Steve's playing, and of course I knew your past, so I was comfortable, but of course I didn't know how we would combine or what would come out. That's a great thing, I think. But at first, there is always the question of 'how to start?' and

---

*   The San Francisco-based band is a space-rock descendant too febrile in its textures to be termed 'ambient'. Founder Jones has collaborated with a number of Japanese musicians, including Makoto Kawabata. He also founded psychedelia/experimental/noise label Charnel Music.

**   Michael Shiono of Jones' previous band, SubArachnoid Space.

***   Japanese self-styled 'heavy metal percussionist' – utilising instruments from bongos to car bumpers.

'what will happen?' and a little bit of waiting. I wondered if someone would 'push or pull' the others along, and I always listen and think about whether to add something or not, and when to change. I thought that the performance went very well, and really enjoyed it.

Thank you! I hope that you're continuing to do well, and someday in San Francisco or Japan or elsewhere I look forward to performing together again.

DOMINIK VON SENGER

I finished a new record (Dominik Von Senger & Montezumas Rache EP*), which comes out in London by Emotional Response and by Golf Channel Records in New York; I did this with Christian Pannenborg, who was the founder of a record shop in Berlin which was really famous for DJs, and with Jan Schulte from the Salon Des Amateurs.** He is today in Australia, he has become famous. Both were very young people I met who got me into a project which took two years.

The last thing I did was a concert with Jaki Liebezeit last Saturday*** with two other drummers, called Drums Off Chaos. We played in Cologne – this was the kind of highly charged and fantastic concert that I didn't have for a long, long, long time. Some days before I talked with Damo on the telephone. If I speak with Damo it is always lunchtime, most of the time he is cooking. I am just getting in, so I have to break off the call; this goes on for years: it's always perfect timing with eating, it's always the same.

I've known Damo for a lot of years. What we've seen from the eighties to now are very long and strong, deep connections. I'm very grateful for the connections that have been sustained so long. Jaki told me just a week ago it was like '83, when he was having his sickness like he has now. He's so strong, stronger than other people – but I don't know many people so closely as I do Damo.

ELKE MORSBACH'S DIARY
February 2016
Damo once again had another very long operation to restore his independence. I had gone to Leverkusen early to see him before the surgery, but when I

---

* Electro-ambient music with some distinctly funky undertones.
** The Düsseldorf music collective project, known for its experimental approach to dance music.
*** January 2, 2016 – almost exactly a year before Jaki's passing.

arrived at seven thirty he was already gone. Only in the evening was I allowed to visit him in the monitoring station.

He's feeling sick, he does not want to get up. Suffers. There are complications. He needs a VAC again; in addition, his lower leg had to be cut open. After two hard months, he will be released in April so he can recover for the next big surgery. No one knows if Damo can ever sing again. The senior physician still believes that he can perhaps restore the abdominal wall.

In May 2016, Damo gave the writer of this book a progress report as to how he was recovering from his last major operation, back in February. His candour was humbling.

"I'm not good on walking as my feet had trouble during surgery," he confirmed. "That surgery took nine hours, to clear my colon and put it in its original place; during this surgery they used ten litres of water; somehow this came into my feet, which became almost three to four times larger. In another emergency operation, I needed further surgery to cut into the muscles of my feet."

In his matter-of-factness lies the will to overcome adversity. We are all frail flesh and blood – but the impetus for overcoming our frailty, Damo will argue, comes from another energy entirely.

"So my left foot is getting better now, but part of the foot is almost in electric shock all the time. Another problem is I've a new artificial stomach, which sometimes makes it not easy to sit or stand for a long period. Occasionally I have to rest myself.

"And another problem is the stoma," he said of the surgically imposed opening that allows waste to be cleared from his diseased stomach. "I've an artificial output on the small intestine, that means my colon is not functioning now but my small intestine is active. Quite often this stoma gets broken, then I have a problem as I cannot prepare it by myself. It's not in a place that I can see.

"So therefore my condition is not well when one of those things goes wrong. But it's a matter of time," he insisted, with an optimism that took him way beyond stoicism. "Later it'll get better for sure."

A visceral lesion in the gut. A crack of light that shone through anaesthetised darkness.

"My condition is only just beginning to take me outside of the life I've lived in hospital since December 2014," he said of the first of several return admissions. "After the surgery this February, I have to try to get well from the very beginning.

"But I'm okay," Damo insisted, "I have to solve this and I've only one way.

"Since the day before yesterday we've had spring weather finally, so I try to walk a bit step by step. I've done thirty minutes yesterday, so I'll do the same today as I can see the sun is shining this morning."

Acceptance. Resilience. Defiance. Energy.

ELKE MORSBACH'S DIARY
Summer 2016

At home, Damo accepts a festival offer. It will be the first time he will be back on stage. He chooses the band Jelly Planet. He knows them for a long time and knows he can count on them. They pick us up and we drive to southern Germany. On the border with Bavaria, the police (four policemen, believe me) search our car. They are looking for drugs, but they only find parenteral nutritional pouches, syringes for vitamins, medications and lots of bandages.

Finally arrived in Bavaria, the festival area shakes us. Heavy metal! I'm worried, I want to leave right away. Turn the crosses over and pray.

Damo seems lost on stage, has to sit down. Thinking that he will not make it, I would like to spare him a disappointment but cannot stop him; he wants to know if he can perform. I trust the guys in the band, who will not let him down. And then he gets up, very slowly, takes the microphone and I think I'm dreaming when I hear his voice, very gentle but moving. 'How does it work?' I ask myself, and then the people from all the other stages come and listen to him, although his music is very different and has nothing to do with heavy metal. What a riddle.

On the way back Damo's wounds break through. I put him on a blanket in an Aldi parking lot and reconnect him. People are very reserved, sensitive, realising the seriousness of the situation.

As he can sing without abdominal muscles, he himself does not know from where he takes the strength. Or maybe he does. His unwavering faith never left him, even in the worst of times. While some wardmates complained about their fate and accused God, because they were good people and others were in much better condition, such thoughts were completely foreign to Damo. On the contrary, every day our faith grew stronger, but it changed. We understood more, everything was much deeper.

"So the first concert was on the 5th of August (2016) at a festival," confirms Damo, giving his own take on the event. "I was quite worried. We travelled seven hours by car because it was in the Bavarian forest, just close to the border with the Czech Republic, so it's quite far from here. It was summer season and there was much traffic.

"When I arrived there had been an accident with my artificial output, so I had to run to the hotel and change it." As ever now, he was dogged by his own physical limitations. But his feeling of vulnerability wouldn't last.

"Then I made a soundcheck. In this moment I felt quite astonished by myself," he recollects, as if still slightly disbelieving. "I thought I was not able to raise a voice as I hadn't trained or prepared for two years. But when the live concert started I felt quite free, realising I'd been missing something. It was a really great moment and I felt quite well at that point."

At this time, Jelly Planet, the Dortmund psychedelic band, hadn't played together for eleven years either – in fact their last gig had been in London in the mid-noughties, with Damo. The Bavarian festival gig was a double resurrection. The vocalist's voice reached the most resonant depths that many metalheads will have experienced; the band managed to be psychedelically freeform while holding tightly together.

"It was a really young audience," observes the resurgent performer, "limited to 1,000 people and they sold out all 1,000 tickets. It's an exclusive club so it's a private atmosphere – people of maybe twenty to twenty-eight, far younger than my age.

"I spoke with many young people after the concert – they were really surprised, they'd never heard this kind of music," he recalls with obvious satisfaction. "It was a really good moment because I could be motivated by it in the future. If you are handicapped you need to give more than 100 per cent. It was really something."

As with much of the post-2003 history of the Network, the performance was an open-ended piece that twisted and turned, taking the audience with it on its wilder detours.

"A special energy came from somewhere else, because I didn't think that I could make it for ninety minutes. I thought that I could only do twenty minutes or half an hour," Damo marvels at his own physical and spiritual resurrection. "But from the moment that I was on the stage and began to sing, from this moment I was totally free – free from my pain and free from my illness, free from everything.

"I felt in a way spiritually free and mentally free, and free from my body. It's quite difficult to find words, but I think it was a kind of miracle. I went into a different space. I felt real joy, when you have such real happiness that you are crying. Nothing that is possible to say in words, just a really special moment."

ALEXANDER SCHÖNERT
Guitarist, Jelly Planet/Frankenstein's Ballet

I wrote an email. He said: "I make a break and I'm very sick. Please don't contact me – but I'll be back." Half a year ago he was back and wrote me an email. Now I'm in regular contact again. At the Void Fest in August 2016, we had this gig, Jelly Planet and Damo Suzuki, for the first time in eleven years we played with him. He was sick for two years and it was his first travelling and his first gig.

He looked quite cool – because of the illness he's fucking thin! Before he was a little fat and now he's thin. He's bit more grey. He was very sick and Elke, his wife, had this medical stuff to care for him.

But when he entered the stage he was like twenty years, almost thirty years ago – the same. It's always the best: his voice was clear, powerful, and his mind was clear – he makes breaks at the right time. As you know, we have no rehearsals before. He has his very own unique style, and it's Damo! Nothing changed that much in all those years. That's my opinion.

There was a big range of very quiet songs but also loud songs, and then he was singing like an animal! What I liked very much is that I'm standing behind him as a guitarist, he's the frontman. After minutes of continual singing, he stopped and was waving his hair to the rhythm, his long hair – that gives me the feeling, 'Wow, we're doing a good job! He likes it.' And this can happen for several minutes – he doesn't give any voice, just waving in the sound, like a mantra. This he did when I met him the first time as well – so he's still Damo!

Ten minutes before the gig, if you watched him he was like a sick old man. On the stage he wasn't. It's the same with a friend of mine – he has a very, very bad sickness; it's the spine, he cannot stand up properly. And he's always in pain, but when he plays the guitar he doesn't feel the pain; maybe it's the same with Damo. The audience – or we the musicians standing behind him

– couldn't recognise that he's sick or he's in any pain or that his voice was suffering from that – it wasn't at all like this.

I'm sure he needs to be on stage, he needs to sing. Because he avoids being in a recording studio, he avoids being in rehearsal studios, I think he doesn't make music at home – so he needs the stage. It's always new.

I hope for the future we are now going to release this album we recorded eleven years ago. When Jelly Planet was in the studio in Cologne we had an off day. It was so boring so I gave Damo a call and he came. It was the first time in many, many years that he entered a studio, and I could tell him, "Okay, we are not playing Jelly Planet songs – we are just improvising with you from the moment you enter the studio." And he did, he came.

It's two songs, two long tracks – it's thirty minutes and thirty-four minutes, and I love it so much, it's so cool. It's real krautrock – with beat, without beat, with psychedelic parts, with Damo at his best. The songs are called 'Wildschweinbraten' and 'Venushügel' ('Walk On Venus'). The first in the forest, the wild pig. When we were playing his lovely girl, Elke, was cooking for us these wild boar things and that's why it's called 'Wildschweinbraten'. So I'm very much looking forward to releasing this record as soon as possible.* Maybe in this connection we can have more gigs with Damo. I hope so.

In early October 2016, Damo gave a further update on the state of his health which seemed more downbeat. It came in the wake of his first concerts in two years – indeed, in the middle of a mini-world tour that was ongoing – but seemed to be the words of a man who knew how much his strength had dissipated.

"I'm okay but I'm quite handicapped," he admitted. "I cannot do anything alone really. I cannot travel alone, because I have an artificial output and a stomach without muscles. So that is not fine as I cannot carry anything and I cannot do much physical stuff.

"I have final surgery in December this year, and then early 2017. So maybe after that I could be quite normal," he reflected, rekindling his old optimism. "But I'm not sure, because I do not know how long it takes to recover.

* *Damo Suzuki & Jelly Planet* was released by Purple Pyramid Records on CD, double vinyl and digital formats in February 2018. On 'Wildschweinbraten', a burbling undertone of electronica accompanies a vocal that is typically Damo – urgently communicating thoughts and feelings hidden deep within the 'Damo-ese' language.

"It's in between stations. Not everything is good every day, because every day is quite up and down mentally and physically. The balance is not good. But for me now it's quite important to be relaxed; to do things very slowly, not to be too busy."

It sounded like a realistic assessment of where he now stood – but at the same time, it was a big contradiction. The Network was finding its way back to life; Damo had already performed again in his adopted German homeland and was due to come back to England in the next fortnight. If this was 'doing things slowly', it was only because Damo was not able to globetrot at his former prodigious rate.

"For over two years I have not been in a normal condition," he acknowledged, with very slight melancholy, "because I must carry this artificial output. I sometimes need a person near me to be of service. It's actually really difficult; you are not able to plan anything. Sometimes an accident happens and therefore I need somebody to attend to me, everywhere I go. It's not a very good moment."

Still, there was no taint of self-pity; no 'why me?' Just a recognition that a man who had formerly travelled lightly, as a 'small, mobile, intelligent unit'*, now had to carry a physical burden.

"Now I am doing quite okay by myself as well, but still I'm always handicapped. I think they are preparing in February 2017 to get my stomach muscles together.** Before, in February 2016, they put my colon back into its original place. I stayed there in hospital for almost two months, from February to April. Now I have a small intestine which has to be put into its original space in December 2016.

"I have endured many things!" Damo laughed aloud, as if at the absurdity it all. "You cannot have all this surgery at once together because you need special conditions. Everything at one time is impossible, so my doctor doesn't like to do this and I understand.

---

* To appropriate Brian Eno's aspirations for himself, early in his solo career.
** Elke: "They did not want to get the stomach muscles together because there was no chance to do it, but they hoped to gather skin about the open stomach. Until now there are no muscles. They offered to bring it together in a very long operation, but after the last one they said no chance, it would be too dangerous for Damo."

"Since then I'm not doing so many things – although I did two concerts in August and September 2016." The first of these, as we've seen, was with Jelly Planet. "At the second concert, only thirty-five kilometres away in Bonn, I performed together with musicians I don't know, I never saw them before that day. The musicians in Bonn were quite oldish persons* – the youngest one was maybe middle forties; the other people were maybe the same age as me, or a bit younger. So they have an approach to German music from within the same generation.

"I performed one piece for more than two hours – it's not a commercial product so I don't have to end it within ten minutes, or five minutes. Maybe it's possible some Sound Carriers want to stop?" he conjectured aloud. "I really don't like to end anything at all – is it my ego?" Damo jibed at his own expense.

"I was due to play a concert with Simon Torssell Lerin, but it didn't happen. It was the organiser's fault – they booked the wrong aeroplane and things like that," Damo laughed. As we will see from Simon's words below, he may have been downplaying his own vulnerability.

SIMON TORSSELL LERIN
Experimental musician/Damo Suzuki's Network
We have written some emails back to each other – checking on how he's been doing. So we've stayed in touch, and then maybe not last summer but the one before [2016], we were supposed to play a concert in Stockholm together when he was feeling better. So the show was booked and everything but just the day before he had a problem with his stomach, so he couldn't come and he had to cancel last-minute.

*I haven't met him or seen him since he became sick. The last time I saw him was in Gothenburg [2014] at that festival**, I haven't met him during his illness or the operations, but I think it's quite amazing that now he seems*

---

* At the Stadtfest in Bonn on September 4, 2016, Damo's Network included Lothar Stahl, xylophone and percussion, and Jens Pollheide, kaval, flute and bass – both veteran krautrock musicians and former members of Embryo.

** The *Jazz Är Farligt* festival – see Chapter Seventeen. "This show with Simon in Gothenburg was my last before my illness," confirms Damo. "I'll perform with Simon for the first time since 2014 on October 4, 2018, in Skien: where Simon and Bettina teach art at the moment, around two hours' train ride from Oslo."

to be dedicated to performing again. My impression from reading the emails and everything is that he seems like he's still full-focused on touring again and performing. He wrote to me about how he'd been to South America and I think he was going to the UK for a tour there, and he was playing some festival in Germany as well.

He wrote a little bit in the last email about how his girlfriend was retiring in a few years and they were thinking about buying a house in the countryside. So maybe he will retire – but I'm not sure, it still seems like he's very focused on performing. I think it's amazing after everything that he's been through, that he doesn't want to slow down.

It seems like this drive to going back to performing and meeting people again, if he had that as a vision when he was sick – 'When I am well again, I will be back performing and meeting people again' – I'm sure that must have kept him strong and kept him focused on getting better, so I think that must have helped him.

JONATHAN LAMASTER
Ex-Cul de Sac/Damo Suzuki's Network
2007 was the last gig I played with him.* But I've seen him play and anytime he's been over here I go out of my way to meet up with him, and have him stay

---

* Post-Cul de Sac and Damo's Network, Jonathan remains musically active, as he describes here: "I've been playing and recording with a band called Brian Carpenter and the Confessions, and I've got a small tour that I'm organising in Europe; we've got a date that's been offered in Ljubljana, Slovenia with The Psychedelic Cinema Orchestra – that's a band with Dana Colley, the saxophone player from Morphine, and a drummer called Ken Winokur who most notably plays with The Alloy Orchestra, who do a lot of soundtracks for silent films. I'm playing all kinds of twelve-string guitar, electric guitar, violin, electric sitar, small synthesizers. Dana can't make this tour so I've roped in some friends from Zagreb, Croatia (Hrvoje 'Niksha' Nikšić, who I actually met on tour with Damo in 2003, Hrvoje Radnić and Ivan 'Chado' Čadež from the band Šumovi Protiv Valova) who will be backing us up. We're performing to these amazing films by an artist called Ken Brown, who was the backdrop projectionist for the Boston Tea Party rock club, back between 1966 and 1969, and he had the dumb luck of buying a Fuji 8 camera instead of a Super8 – you can do all this interesting double-exposure work and in-camera editing with the Fuji8 apparently. He made these films just as kind of visual candy to accompany performers at the club – some of the people who would have performed to these films back in the sixties would have been Jimi Hendrix, the Grateful Dead, The Velvet Underground, Led Zeppelin, Frank Zappa & The Mothers."

at my place, help him in any way I can – although he hasn't been back, maybe 2007 was the last time he was here in the States. I most recently hung out with him, my wife is from Germany, so I visited him and Elke at their home when he was, you know, between surgeries. And it was great to see him, he was in good spirits, we had a really nice visit, but it was hard to see him in that way too. This guy who's just so incredibly full of life brought down, you know? So I'm just so happy that he's doing it again.

And you know, he is not crazy about Western medicine, he has significant doubts particularly about medication and chemotherapy – I don't think he did any chemo with his cancer. So I know when I visited him a couple of years ago in Köln, of course he had to have the surgeries done, there was no way around that – but I think the main issue with his illness was him getting sepsis in the hospital. He was quite keen on his diet, I think he tries to address his health needs through dietary means. It's a big part – as was a kind of re-emergence of spirituality, I think, at that time.

In the time I was working with him, we never talked about spirituality or religion beyond these ideas he had around creating time and space, collectivism – I would say 'spiritual' in the loosest of terms. I'm not a particularly religious or dogmatic person, despite the fact I'm the son of a Lutheran minister. (Maybe I was ruined because of that.) I'd say probably agnostic, so maybe it just didn't come up for us. But when I saw him again it certainly came up. I think he's become very spiritual again. And I don't know what I would even call that – it's his take on Christianity.

But of course it was a fun party and I got to drink quite a lot of the whiskies he'd collected on his travels! I think that's one of the things that really connected us, that mutual love of life and people. He's interesting: he's introverted in some ways; he kind of has an introverted style, and yet I'm sure he's got to be a hardcore extrovert just based on his love of people and meeting new people. So it's like an extroverted interest in people but an introverted way of communicating.

What I'd like to say is the universe isn't ready to let him go, and we need him more than ever. We need these ideas about free expression, collectivism, not letting your ego just pollute everything you do. I'm so heartened that he's back doing what he's doing. It's really quite incredible when you think about how lucky I was to have that time with him. As sad as I am that I'm not able to do these tours with him, because he's moved onto this idea of *playing with individuals in their town, I'm more happy about the fact that, not only did I get to have that experience, but all these other people get to have that experience with him now. So he gets to touch way more lives now by going off to do these one-off performances with people that have never met him. I mean, that's amazing!*

I would work with Damo again in a heartbeat. I'll look at his schedule from time to time and say, 'Mmmm... think I'll pull that thing I've pulled a few times in the past where I just say, "Hey, any chance you need a performer in Copenhagen?"' Whether I do or not, I just feel so lucky to do all those performances with him and put out all that material. It's life-changing.

The week after we spoke on the state of Damo's health, in October 2016, would see his return to England: "Sunday the 9th of October at a festival in southern England; then two days later in Brighton at The Hope & Ruin, it's not such a big venue, and two days later in London at The Shacklewell Arms.

"I won't be travelling to London directly as I like to stay at the seaside much more than in a big city, which makes me quite stressful," he reflected, hinting at the rest and recreation element of the Network lifestyle. "I think it will be good in Brighton to just relax."

The Shacklewell Arms gig was packed wall to wall. Whether conscious of Damo's gradual emergence from crisis or not, the north and east London crowd turned out in legion. His Sound Carriers for the night were Xaviers, the band formed by his fellow expatriate friend Kenichi.*

They opened the evening as support band; their electronic bass notes could be felt within the upper torso, a visceral descendant of motorik's undulating drive. But when Damo took the stage with Xaviers as his Sound Carriers, they softened their tone.

The primal growl that arose from the diaphragm – from deep within the pit of a now surgically assisted stomach – transcended its animal origin to float above itself. To float free.

The repetition of his opening line became mantra-like. But with each rhythmic reinvention of itself it soared higher. The prehistoric howl took flight with a spiritual elation.

* See Chapter Sixteen.

In his personal imperium of time and space, measuring just a few square feet of space on a stage, Damo Suzuki broke out of the box that hemmed in the human spirit. Its restrictions, its physical agonies and wounds, were shrugged off. For one endless moment, he stepped off the greasy sliding rail that moves us all inexorably towards our extinction. In the realm of total sonic freedom, there is no death and there is no despair.

KENICHI IWASA
Synthesizer and percussion, Xaviers/founder, Krautrock Karaoke

We played with Damo in October 2016, after his stomach operation. His energy had changed, I thought – he was so open. His energy was so positive, it really touched me. He's changed a lot lately. He's quite a cynical and sarcastic person, but I love him too – we always kind of joke, taking the piss out of each other, always. [laughs]

I play music in a very free space as I'm not a trained musician, but it's definitely about the textures; I listen to what others are doing and try to find a spot where I can fit in. It's very dynamically sonic, and Damo is singing in such a strange language. Sometimes I understand some words, because it's mixed with Japanese. But it's very made-up I think. It's like it's coming from his stomach, this feeling. I like the way he plays.

I was a bit worried that he wouldn't make it because he'd been cancelling a lot of gigs last year, or the year before. I was quite surprised that he was able to play for one hour. I was quite emotional looking at him singing, even more powerful than before, thinking, 'Oh my gosh, his sound, his voice,' his energy was so different. It made me want to cry or something, it really did.

But I didn't quite feel the togetherness at that gig, I wasn't really sure. But the audience, a lot of them came up to me afterwards – even Damo's girlfriend, she said to me that was one of the best ones she had seen, which means a lot because she has seen a lot. But strangely you don't feel it. Sometimes it feels really distant – as though I'm just watching myself doing it. It's a strange feeling – maybe it's just my state.

Damo has no gut – and afterwards we went for a meal, and he was saying, "Ah, I want to eat meat!" I was saying, "Can you eat meat? How are you going to digest it?" And he was smoking as well. I was saying, "Can you smoke?" and he was saying like, "Smoking is good for you. It will protect you from the things the government is spraying from the sky," or something. [laughs] Smoke will protect you from that!

347

He's a survivor. He almost died when he was in his thirties and he had the cancer. And then he told me that they said to him maybe six, seven years after the first time it's going to come back – but it never came back for thirty years. But he was aware that it was going to come back actually, and he also told me, before he was diagnosed again, he kept having the same dream-nightmare.

It was really quite a vivid dream: he was in the middle of the desert or something. But there was nothing for dinner so he stole a motorbike – he was driving around looking for food. He was so hungry he started eating the car tyre that was on the side of the road – then he got a crazy stomach ache. He was having the dream for months, he said, and then he got diagnosed with cancer.* It's very interesting.

He's always stayed and he's always cooked a meal – he will cook like a seven-course meal, so you start eating at seven and finish at three or four o'clock in the morning. And we drink like crazy – I threw up his food a few times! [laughs] He drinks so much and smokes like crazy. I can drink and smoke but he is like fucking extreme! And full of energy.

He seems like he doesn't really care about his past too much. Maybe he does but I don't know, it's almost like he doesn't want to talk about it, he doesn't want to look at it. But then it's like he will go along with whatever comes. He will not be taken over – it's all about his attitude towards life, I think. Just going forward and maybe even if he dies, if cancer kills him, it doesn't really matter. Maybe he will keep going – his awareness, consciousness.

ELKE MORSBACH'S DIARY
15/12/16

Damo's last surgery is due. It should be relatively easy and until New Year he should be back home. But there are complications.

Body does not seem to put away its hardships and it does not regenerate well. His healing powers diminish.

So we spend Silvester** in the hospital. I come with sushi, caviar and champagne. But even the small luxury does not win over my despair.

This is followed by several interventions and then the last surgery; more you cannot do any more – either he does it or his condition remains. He goes

---

*   For Elke's interpretation of the same recurring dream, see Chapter Seventeen.
** The feast of St Sylvester, December 31.

into the observation room. The next day I sit next to him, hold his hand; he sleeps. Then I feel him pressing my hand.

"Last night in the corner I saw a kind of devil. I watched him, he made himself very small, he crouched in the corner in the chair," Damo whispers, but he is very calm. Damo had been watching him with curiosity rather than anxiety. "And you really were not afraid?" "No, not me, but the devil himself trembled with fear."

A little later, Damo tells me another dream.

"I was rolled up by an octopus, he almost suffocated me and then I was in the stomach of the squid." Damo was gasping for air.

"Suddenly I'm back in the room," says Damo. "The room is limitless and I'm still fighting against being stifled by the squid..." Damo stops. "I was scared to death," he breathes.

"Since December 15, 2016, I've been in hospital," Damo confirmed in late January 2017 of his latest bout of institutionalisation. "It's a long time now, already one month. So I don't know how long I'm going to stay here, but if my last surgery, on January 9, stays good, then I don't have to have another operation for a while.

"I'm not really in a normal condition but I'm getting better – the doctor told me too that I'm in a good way. It's a really long journey but... it happened! I treat this as a creative break," he laughed. "So the next time I make music I'll feel much better."

He seemed in a vastly more optimistic frame of mind than the last time he'd described his medical condition. For all his pain and suffering, his attitude towards it evoked healing wounds rather than a weakened condition.

"If you are thinking about sickness you never get better," he mused, back in thrall to his positive philosophy. "It's an important thing to think in a positive way, because it happened and you cannot change things like that any more. You cannot change your past days – by that I mean music too," he extrapolated from his recent predicament to other parts of his life.

"I cannot make any kind of music that is involved with the industry. I like to find myself; I like to do anything that is provocative in this money-controlled world.

"Jaki was also moving in quite the same direction," he said of his erstwhile Can/Damo Suzuki Band mate. "I don't know what he was thinking, but he was attacking time – his life was always in time!"

For the great motorik timekeeper had died suddenly and – to fans and other interested parties, if not perhaps to those closest to him – unexpectedly. He'd expired on January 22, 2017*, within less than three weeks of the interview which informs parts of this book.

JAKI LIEBEZEIT
I fear there are no recordings. I have not heard anything.** Damo makes spontaneous happenings wherever he goes – he meets musicians at their place, without rehearsing. Chuck Berry used to do it like that! [laughs] All over the world he met people who knew all his songs, so he could find people who could play them. He'd put the band together in Seattle, or in Hawaii, with local people. It seems to work. For Damo it can make a travelling music kind of thing.

When the conversation with Jaki had concluded, he wished this writer a hearty "Happy New Year!" – though it seemed more generously aimed at the wider world, all of us together. On replaying the recording, there was a slight but noticeable bronchial crackle. But it didn't make the news of his death from pneumonia any less of a saddening jolt.

Of course, this is written from the distant perspective of a music lover. To Damo, still convalescing in the hospital, the loss of his old comrade in rhythm was almost unbearable.

"I was told about Jaki late on Sunday the 22nd," he confirmed mournfully. "He died in the morning, but four people emailed me and I didn't know. One came from my friend in Australia; one came from my friend in Italy.*** Then I got a call on the phone from a musician who is playing at his funeral. Two days before, these musicians who were working with Jaki will come to make music for him at a place in Cologne.****

---

* Jaki Liebezeit was born on May 26, 1938; at the time of his death he was 78 years old.
** Jaki made the easy mistake of thinking the Damo Suzuki's Network era has left us no recorded output. In fact, though it's mostly come live from the mixing desk rather than the recording studio, the total amount of CDs and limited-edition vinyl LPs easily outstrips Damo's total number of recordings with Can.
*** Tim Preach and Francesco di Loreto, respectively.
**** Damo would make his own 'Jaki Tribute' together with Dominik von Senger, Drums Off Chaos and Rosko Gee a year after his old compadre's death, at the tribute concert at the Kölner Philharmonie on January 22, 2018. Damo's urgently improvised vocal and Dominik's crystalline guitar beautifully complemented DOC's understated yet intricately percussive rhythm, coloured by jazz-flexed sax.

"I was really so shocked on that day that I wasn't able to do anything. Especially if you're in a condition like mine, sickness, then you're much more sensitive. I was really quite sad – maybe I cried.

"But the whole day I was listening to his drumming, maybe twenty hours or more, especially in The Damo Suzuki Band – in between '86 to '90 it was a special type of music. It was a most interesting time for me with Jaki."

For now, though, Damo was lost in memory. Lost in sound and rhythm. Requests for comment from two journalists were politely declined.

"I heard that Irmin Schmidt and Holger Czukay were also like that. I don't think they said anything about his loss in public. Maybe they didn't talk about it because they were much more with him; the passing of Jaki is practically the end of Can – okay, everybody else is important in that band, but they have had to experience the loss of the motor of their sound.

"I remember many things about me and Jaki," Damo ruminated on the personal, "it's quite sad. But his wife told my girlfriend that he died satisfied because he was free energy, he was all the time free; he was a creative person and I think he was also one of the most innovative musicians.

"I'm trying to think in this way," he said with barely restrained melancholy, "but instead I'm getting really down." Damo's sadness was increased by the fact that he couldn't attend Jaki's funeral – on February 6, before he'd be able to discharge himself from hospital.

"'Love Time' was Jaki's name," he said of the literal German translation. "He was always a really happy person because he was doing what he wanted and he found his own style. How many drummers and musicians are able to find their own way? Most of them have a uniform style and yet they are like a 'star'," Damo shook his head sceptically.

"He was quite shy, but he created so much. I'm happy that I had maybe seven or eight years together with him to make music," he reflected on the eras of Can and the Suzuki Band, almost two decades apart. "It was my good fortune."

Damo spoke with near-reverence of Jaki's continued relevance among younger musicians. Of his penchant for innovation, right up to the last. "In his last days he had another style which fits together with electro music: his drum kit was getting smaller; last time he didn't have any pedals.

"Because the drum kit is actually like an artificial musical instrument, different kinds of percussion connected together. There is really only one kind of percussion instrument, djembe drums and things like this; there are no cymbals, they are for somebody else to play.

"So in a way Jaki was going back to his roots: the drumming was becoming more simple, monotonous, and he found his way again. I think it's quite interesting because his life was like everybody else's: if you're thinking about your childhood dreams, if this dream you had as a child fits together with your life as an old man, then I think you are quite a happy person.

"Jaki had quite a huge musical field," Damo said, making his final summation. "He knew many musicians in the German jazz scene; he knew also the so-called 'krautrock' bands. He knew many people and many people knew him, not only from the city of Cologne. So he had a rehearsal room and every day he was drumming, playing minimal percussion behind a band. Even at his age, the minimum amount of time he was practising was eight hours, still exercising every day. He was all the time keeping rhythm."

After his final operation in January 2017, Damo gradually resumed his Never-Ending Tour in the spring. It began to retrace the strands of experience that had crisscrossed his life since the turn of the millennium.

"I come back to London in May 2017, to the Moth Club," he confirmed. "I don't know what Sound Carriers are on that day.* It may be possible to have a lot of people on stage, or it may not be possible, but it's okay. It'll be a really creative month." His anticipation – heading towards electrification – was tangible.

"I'm going to Dublin, Belfast, Letterkenny, and also Dundee – I never performed in Dundee before – in Scotland; Edinburgh; Glasgow; Brighton again." Indeed, before long he'd be going to the top of the world.

"I may perform in the Himalayas, I've an invitation from Ziro Festival. I'll perform with an Indian new-wave band; the place is 1,700 metres high from sea level."

He continued with a revitalised enthusiasm. Rekindled and kinetic. "Also, at the end of this year I'll perform in Santiago and Buenos Aires for

---

* It was Nervous Vibrations – a very young Cambridgeshire band with a sax player whose Coleman-ish airs made a perfect fit for Damo's voice.

the first time in ten years. I'm so happy that my life is getting slowly like my old days."

But first, he'd again have to contemplate mortality – not his own, which he'd already looked in the eye many times, but that of his old comrades and peers.

DAMOSUZUKI.COM BLOG, SEPTEMBER 21, 2017
R.I.P. Holger Czukay (March 24 1938 – September 5 2017)
I didn't see Holger for many years, we didn't have relationship, so I didn't know what he was actually doing.

Last time I heard about him was that he didn't appear at Jaki's funeral early this year, after while I heard Holger was sick that time. (Unfortunately, myself was also in hospital, not able to join Jaki's funeral.) Even I didn't know his wife U* – she died a month before him.

If you're at Network performance, creating time and space of the moment with ever changing local sound carriers and you're into it and enjoy that energy and you keep smile, I say, if I didn't meet Holger on that beautiful spring day in Munich 1970, I'm not able to bring you this experience of joy and share energy with you.

Holger is the person [who] open my door to music activity. So, you know, everything begun on that day, Holger Czukay invited me to sing. (I still don't know what moved him to stand up and come to me and ask if I can sing with Can on that day)...

Holger was workaholic.

He was first one to enter Inner Space Studio and last person to leave day after day. He was into wire, equipment and electric substance, eating sweet bread and drinking coffee, seemed to be no interest to get any other food, my picture in my brain is Holger in that form.

Sometimes he watched us (Irmin and me) during chess match looked very angry while he had problem with equipment. We're concentrating next move. He was working, if he doesn't he say some wits (near to philosophy) that often nobody's able to understand.

Very first day, I was quite surprised from him was playing bass with white glove. I thought of Mickey Mouse, has four fingers, therefore he is bassist?...

* Ursula.

He was, I guess in nineties, somewhere on the street of Cologne I met him, he was saying, "Can is the best band and there will be no band like us… also not in future…"

In fact as he was a hard worker, he was mostly with the band, take care about equipment, lay cables, even drove bus when we didn't have roadies. Then, at Inner Space, preparations, recording, editing…

He was action in person…

Holger left us at age of 79.

U – she is beside him and Jaki's grave is just few metre distance.

He was Inner Space, he chose his last moment in Inner Space.

It may [be] right place… space of creativity.

Holger, rest in peace.

ELKE MORSBACH'S DIARY
October 2017

Again it took months, but his little body made it, somehow.

Damo and I only have a short time until an offer comes from India. He is supposed to play in the Himalayas, at a place where even Indians need a visa and which is controlled by the police. But it is one of the most beautiful places the organiser has ever seen.

"Impossible," I say, but I feel Damo's wanderlust is bigger than anything else. So I try it in a rational way. "You need an accompaniment, you cannot do anything. How are they supposed to do that?"

"They give me a companion," says Damo, unmoved.

"And how will that work?"

"I fly to New Delhi and meet him. However, Indians are only allowed to enter the airport for their flight."

"So you're alone in the airport for two hours after such a long flight, you have not eaten anything, you have nothing to drink, you cannot leave?"

"Don't worry, he has rented a VIP lounge, they pick me up from the plane. There is food and drink there and I can rest."

Unbelievable, I'm running out of arguments.

The family doctor of Jaki is ready to fly with Damo, but Damo refuses because he has already promised the Indian and it feels very rude. I would prefer it, but Damo does not allow for discussion.

From New Delhi, he flew another 2.5 hours and then travelled another eight hours by train, then four hours by Jeep, which was the hardest on the whole tour. The single track serpentined to the hotel – and indeed there was a real hotel, which he shared with the Kathmandu Killers from Nepal.

In fact it was a big festival, with 3,500 visitors, all of whom had come over the dangerous switchbacks. They, too, had come a long way. As young Kolkata girls shouted, 'Vitamin C', Damo laughed and gave them the vitamin C lozenges I had given him.

It was interesting that many Christian churches were there and also one of the police – who secured this once fiercely contested area – got an autograph.

At home I shivered, phoned the organiser several times, and he assured me that Damo was fine. At last he got him on the phone and Damo laughed, he had probably expected nothing else from me. He still refuses to carry a cellphone.

Damo devoted himself to this experience which was to his liking, pure adventure. His cells had probably generated extra oxygen in order to cope with the heights. From then on there was no stopping. Damo accepted any concerts that he was offered and liked, and yet they were different now. What he has experienced is from now on also in his voice. I noticed that.

On his return from the Ziro Festival, Damo contacted this writer. His effusiveness was infectious.

"Late Wednesday night, I came back from Himalayas and I still am not able to get back to daily life," he enthused. "It was fantastic, it was adventure. I'm most happy with my body and spiritual condition that I've done this short tour after three-and-a-half years of heavy illness. It was a really new experience to perform at the end of the world."

For all his fragility, Damo's rejuvenation seemed complete. He was as electrified as a kid who'd given his first performance. But as ever, the music was only part of the story. The meaning was in the motion.

"Opposite Germany on this planet is New Zealand, the shortest flight connection is around twenty-six hours," he explained the scale of his most recent sojourn. "For this open-air festival in Ziro it took me two-and-a-half days one way! Eight hours from Frankfurt to Delhi, Delhi to Guwahati two-and-a-half hours, both by flight. Then change to night train to Naharlagun: eight hours then from there to Ziro by Jeep on mountain road, holes, narrow, partly dangerous, direct to valley four-and-a-half hours.

"All this is quite hard to do if I'm in normal body," he reflected. "But I've done it with this bodily condition. This makes me proud."

Almost as an afterthought, an electrified Damo made reference to the music itself. "All festival long I was quite often together with Kathmandu Killers, ethnic punk band from (of course) Nepal. They were one of the few highlights at the festival as it was mainly mainstream like hip hop, reggae… like everywhere else," he noted, slightly cynically. But he also wrote of staying "alongside Johnny 8 Track from Brighton, as we had the same home.

"Again there is a story, it's endless."

Indeed – it really seems to be never-ending…

DAMO SUZUKI'S NETWORK
Shared Energy@

Aalst, Aarhus, Aberdeen, Adelaide, Ahaus, Almeria, Amsterdam, Ancona, Angers, Antwerp, Aomori, Arezzo, Asahikawa, Asheville, Athens, Athens/ GA, Atlanta, Auckland, Augsburg, Azpeitia, Bad Kötzing, Baltimore, Bangor, Barcelona, Barreiro, Basel, Belfast, Beograd, Bera, Bermeo, Berlin, Bern, Biel-Bienne, Bilbao, Birmingham, Blaenau Ffestiniog, Bochum, Bognor Regis, Bologna, Bolzano, Bonn, Boston, Bourn, Bremen, Brescia, Brest, Brighton, Brisbane, Bristol, Brussels, Brooklyn, Bucharest, Budapest, Buenos Aires, Burg Herzberg, Calgary, Camber Sands, Cambridge, Cambridge/MA, Cardiff, Cardigan, Carpi, Castelbasso, Cavriago, Chapel Hill, Chester, Chicago, Cleveland, Colchester, Cologne, Colle Val D'Elsa, Copenhagen, Cork, Cordoba, Coventry, Crewe, Darmstadt, Delémont, Detroit, Dewsbury, Dnepropetrovsk, Dortmund, Dresden, Driftpile Valley, Dublin, Dubrovnik, Düdingen, Dundee, Dunedin, Düsseldorf, Edinburgh, Edmonton, Erfurt, Eugene, Exeter, Faenza, Falmouth, Finkenbach, Firenze, Florianópolis, Frankfurt, Freiberg, Fruecht, Fukui, Fukuoka, Galway, Geneva, Gerlesborg, Getaria, Gdansk, Gillingham, Glasgow, Goiânia, Göteborg, Graz, Guelph, Guspini, Haarlem, Hachinohe, Hachiōji, Halle, Hamamatsu, Hamburg, Hamilton, Hannover, Hastings, Hebden Bridge, Helsinki, Hitchin, Hobart, Hoboken, Huddersfield, Huesca, Hull, Ichinomiya, Innsbruck, Iowa City, Isle of Wight, Itri, Jena, Jyväskylä,

Kami-Suwa, Karlsruhe, Kashiwa, Kawaguchi, Kiel, Kilkenny, Kitakyushu, Kloster Cornberg, Knittlingen, Knoxville, Kokubunji, Kotor, Koumanovo, Kuala Lumpur, Kumamoto, Kunitachi, Kyoto, La Chaux-de-Fonds, La Coruña, Lake Palić, Lake Windermere, La Spezia, Latina, Lausanne, Leeds, Lehrte, Leicester, Leipzig, Letterkenny, Liège, Lima, Limerick, Linz, Lisboa, Liverpool, Ljubljana, London, London/Ont, Los Angeles, Louisville, Lucca, Lyon, Lärz, Lüneburg, Macomer, Madrid, Malaga, Malmö, Manchester, Marburg, Maribor, Marina di Massa, Marseille, Martigny, Meaford, Melbourne, Melle, Memphis, Mestre, Mexico City, Mezzago, Milan, Milton Keynes, Minehead, Minneapolis, Minsk, Modena, Montpellier, Montreal, Montreuil, Moscow, München, Müritzsee, Nagoya, Nanaimo, Nantes, Napoli, Nashville, Neuchâtel, Newcastle, Newcastle/QLD, New Haven, New York, Nice, Nottingham, Novi Sad, Oakland, Oaxaca, Oberhausen, Offenbach, Oita, Okayama, Okinawa, Oldenburg, Ōmihachiman, Orihuela, Orleans, Osaka, Oslip, Oslo, Ottawa, Oulu, Oxford, Padova, Palermo, Palma de Mallorca, Paris, Perth, Pescara, Philadelphia, Piacenza, Pisa, Pittsburgh, Poitiers, Poole, Pori, Porrentruy, Portland, Porto, Praha, Preston, Pristina, Providence, Pskov, Reggio Emilia, Ramsgate, Rennes, Reykjavik, Riga, Rio de Janeiro, Rome, Rotterdam, Roubaix, Rouen, San Diego, San Francisco, San Juan Island, Santiago, San Vito di Leguzzano, São Paulo, Sapporo, Sasebo, Saskatoon, Schiphorst, Schwerin, Seattle, Sendai, Seoul, Sevilla, Sheffield, Skopje, Sofia, Solingen, Sorrento, Southampton, Spenge, Split, Stavanger, Steyr, St Gallen, St Helens, St Norbert, Stockholm, Stockton, St Petersburg, Subotica, Sydney, Takamatsu, Tallinn, Tampere, Tanworth In Arden, Taragona, Tel Aviv, Tenerife, Thessaloniki, Tilburg, Tirana, Tokorozawa, Tokushima, Tokyo, Tolmin, Torello, Torino, Toronto, Torpåkra, Totnes, Tournai, Travnik, Trondheim, Tsurugashima, Tullamore, Tunbridge Wells, Turku, Tübingen, Valencia, Vancouver, Varaždin, Verviers, Victoria, Vigo, Vigonovo, Vöcklabruck, Walsall, Washington, Waterloo/ONT, Weinheim, Wellington, Wesel, Wetzlar, Wien, Wigan, Winchester, Windsor, Winnipeg, Winston-Salem, Worcester, Wrexham, Wörgl, Wroclaw, Würzburg, Yokohama, York, Zagreb, Zaragoza, Ziro, Zofingen, Zürich

As the Never-Ending Tour resumed – an eventuality that, a year and a half previously, would have seemed improbable, if not miraculous – it remained a moot point whether the travelling musician was, foremost, a musician or a traveller.

"It's not a geographical matter," Damo insists of his wanderings. "Maybe people are looking for truth and this is it. For me, I didn't know the things I was looking for.

"I think everybody is doing it, so it's not a matter of going to a different country. Maybe this is what drives social movements too. It depends on which age you are living in. Everybody's travelling – but I did it in the geographical sense as well."

For his part, the veteran wanderer remarked on how he now preferred travelling in the countryside more than in European cities. "I'm not so interested in historical buildings because in Europe – or maybe everywhere – the history of a building is connected mainly with religion or politics, kings or queens.

"Instead I liked to walk in nature, particularly in England. I like the Lake District, because at the time I was there I was just drifting and anything to do with nature is always good." Damo also says local town Buxton has "probably the best bookshop I've ever been to; it's really not that huge, but they have three or four floors and a workshop for fixing all the broken books." It's contributed to a bibliophile's collection of circa 10,000 books *chez* Suzuki.

"In the south I like Penzance, and in the north Scotland is very different – it has the highlands and Scotch whisky, but England has not so many natural landscapes.

"Hebden Bridge in the north is also good. I like such places; it's interesting because it's such a small town but always there are many people coming to a concert – 200 or 300. Also this village has quite a good atmosphere, because in the middle it has a river and a canal, so it has a special energy. If you go to a watery environment, like a river, lake, sea, you will get positive energy from this natural substance."

This formerly obscure part of West Yorkshire has become a little artistic enclave of northern England. Thirty-odd miles from the Lancashire city of Manchester, it's started to attract migrant city-dwellers. It's also adopted Damo Suzuki as an esteemed, semi-regular guest. "The last time I played there, the master of the village – in Germany we would call him 'the Buergermeister'* – came along. I wasn't expecting him to come," he says understatedly.

* The mayor.

So it's probably fitting that a filmmaker from the region has chosen Damo as the subject of an ambitious, crowd-funded biodoc. Michelle Heighway has taken up the baton from Francesco di Loreto, whose *Neverending* is a documentary portrait of Damo's creativity, whether at home in the kitchen or randomly composing onstage. Her film, which has pre-emptively begun shooting, concentrates on one of the most crucial stages of his life, as he and Elke face life-threatening adversity and come out the other side.

MICHELLE HEIGHWAY ON HER FILM, *ENERGY*

I have known of Damo since he first played with my partner's band – they were Damo's Sound Carriers. It was 2007 in Huddersfield Parish Pump (name of the pub).

Damo has this really unique presence on stage... he is fearless, in the moment and seems to tap into the universe and/or maybe the unconscious part of his brain that naturally for him is evoking these sounds that he carries around the room with the help of his microphone and the musicians, without any kind of preparation.

*It is very spontaneous. My partner played more and more with Damo as the years went on, as part of the band The Window Right.***

Six years later our longstanding friend/drummer of The Window Right passed away due to cancer. Damo wrote a wonderful piece about Neil Atkinson on his site. His music connected strongly with Damo and vice versa.

When I found out Damo had colon cancer in 2014 I knew I had to follow this journey. As part of my self-exploration with regards to dealing with Neil and his death and also as a filmmaker, I had a keen interest in Damo's outsider viewpoints. He has been a true inspiration. Damo has such strong willpower and his positive outlook is transferable. I leave his home with lots of energy!!!

Damo and Elke make a wonderful pair and it has been a very enriching time for me as a filmmaker capturing their journey together.

---

*   Huddersfield is approximately thirteen miles from Hebden Bridge.

**   Damo: "Around that time I was travelling with a Discman, with a selection of maybe around ten CDs – my favourites of that period. First time I met The Window Right, they were very curious to know which CDs I was carrying. I didn't know exactly what was inside the disc case as I randomly changed selection each tour – but I found there were two CDs from The Window Right."

He does touch upon some important facts in the documentary: the fact that two people [from Can] have died now and that he's survived his operations. It's very poignant.

We're going to have some animation as I don't want it to be like the standard talking-heads documentary. As it's Damo, it's more of a film about his life – we have some dream sequences and memories from the past. I have some beautiful archive that Damo's been able to give me.

I don't really know what my intent for the film is because it's so organic. It's like a beautiful, poignant tale of hope and resilience as Damo recovers from cancer, and you find out how he became this enigmatic character, I guess that's kind of the premise of it.

It's just so inspirational, I've enjoyed it so much – it's just kind of scary to do the crowd-funding project. But if I reach the target then I'm going to be able to tell this story the way it deserves to be told. He's such an influential character isn't he? I like to work with freethinkers, I'm quite a freethinker myself – not to the extent that Damo is, he's been so influential on different levels, the main one being the musical level. He's just so free on stage, I really find that inspirational.

I call my documentary Energy because of a Russian doll that a fan gave him that has 'Energy' on the back. When you talk to Damo, or when you read at the end of his blogs, he says 'Energy' – but really, what resonated the most is that you realise the amount of energy that this man creates. In recovery, he was walking around the forest, the woodland area outside his house – just getting the energy to recover was so fantastic.

I was interviewing Damo closely to the time when Jaki died, but I didn't think it was the right time to ask him something about that. I actually cried when I read what Damo had written on his blog, so I'll probably mention that at some point in conversation with the camera on or off. But it did resonate with me because my best friend died of cancer and he also played with Damo sometimes – it's hard to lose people who are that important in your life.

I've got some beautiful images Damo showed me that were done by the Red Bull Academy. This artist did this wonderful image of Damo praying to God on the street and being found, and explaining the first show that Can did. I would love to have this moment animated.

I've got to find things that haven't been talked about, because those things are all the time in every single magazine aren't they? I think it's nice and refreshing that, with my documentary at least, we're seeing a different side – but also it's important to talk about the other aspects of his life. People change and move on, don't they? It was a cool part of his life but he moved on and Damo has done lots of other great projects.

My focus for this film is him as a freethinker, his resilience and his spirit. The really human side to it. It's really important for me to be able to use all this beautiful archive and information – it's like peeling the layers of an onion and Damo's the perfect person for that, because you can just take any kind of angle. He's really good at being involved and informing me of really good, cool things that he's done and images that he's got and people he's collaborated with. He's really good at putting a little bit of direction into how things go as well. I think it's really important as a filmmaker – because it is Damo's story at the end of the day, I've got to respect that and flow where he wants to flow.

I love how humble Damo Suzuki is, actually. I'm probably too aware of some of the things I ask him, because sometimes he doesn't like to be reminded of how some people perceive him. He's such an inspiring character, I can't believe how much energy he's got. Even when he was going through the operations he'd talk; it's hard to say where he gets all this energy and motivation from. To put that out there in a film, to inspire any kind of person that's in a band or struggling with illness maybe – the resilience of it, he's kind of superhuman in that way!

Damo loves the desert. One of my favourite quotes from Damo is "'The middle of nowhere' is my favourite place to be" and that may be why he removed himself from Can, because he loves to be in uncrowded places really. The only time when he allows himself to be in a room with a large capacity is on stage, I guess that doesn't bother him. But when he's not on stage Damo prefers to be where there's lots of open spaces, where there's not a lot of people around.*

---

* Damo described to Michelle his surreal hunger dream – as recounted in this chapter by Kenichi Iwasa, and in Chapter Seventeen by Elke: "Oh that's in my film! He explains that to me so I'm animating that. It's really visual because he described to me waking up in the hospital and the little pinny robes they put on you – and he escaped and ran outside and it was snowing and freezing and he jumped on this motorbike to go and get a burger because he was starving! Because he'd been on morphine for weeks, he was really, really high on that and he was starving because he wasn't allowed to eat. So he's having these really insane dreams. He dreamt he was off to get a burger and then he just started eating his tyre – so yeah, he tells me that story on camera. I love that story, so that's cool."

In 2018, Damo's activity accelerated at an unfeasible pace. As the Never-Ending Tour resumed its circumnavigation of the globe, this writer caught him at The Jazz Café in London's Camden in January. The Sound Carriers were modern jazz/electronica musician Orphy Robinson and his compadres – with percussionist Beibei Wang blowing musical bubbles from a water pipe.

Damo's vocals were suitably merged with the near-ambient sounds – though their primal essence still erupted when least expected. At his merchandise stall, he displayed his extramusical, humanistic concerns, in supporting the campaign to free Fumiaki Hoshino.

Imprisoned in 1975 for the murder of a policeman at a protest in Shibuya he'd organised four years previously, Hoshino was for years made legally 'untouchable' by the isolating tactics of the Japanese legal system.

It's clearly arguable that he's a political prisoner: any evidence against him for the riotous behaviour that killed Officer Tsuneo Nakamura is inconclusive; the prime suspect was never caught; Hoshino's primary offence was agitating against the island of Okinawa's use by US forces as a staging post for Vietnam. Crucially, Damo points out that the island was also used as a base for America's nuclear warheads in the Pacific – a sad concession by the only nation to have endured nuclear attacks.*

And so the Never-Ending Tour continued. It was randomly creative. It was interactive. It was social. Perhaps most startlingly, its least important element, according to the man at its centre, was that it was musical. Reflecting on his return, Damo concedes that certain aspects may never be quite the same as before. "Now I have to take so much medication and

---

* Damo has long been opposed to any form of nuclear power. When a tsunami hit the coast of north-eastern Japan in 2011, damaging a reactor at the nuclear power station in Fukushima, he ran the following message in his blog: "*This is the biggest damage since WW2 in Japan. Still many people are missing, every day comes Job's Message... number of dead are increasing. Horrible scenario... [but] the world is coming closer against nuclear power station... This is the turning point to think about alternative energy source and alternative lifestyle... We're standing on historical moment!!!*" It's perhaps a sad irony that the nuclear industry continues to sell itself as the 'clean' alternative energy source. Deriving power from the splitting of the atom, the building block of life itself, it may be the epitome of Damo's idea of 'negative energy'.

I have to face this drama," he acknowledges, "so I cannot meet so many people any more." It seems to be his one abiding regret.

"For me the music is not so important," he shrugs disarmingly. "I like to meet as many other people as possible and talk together. When I meet them it's not necessary to take notes, because this kind of music is not so interesting to remember."

With one casual phrase, Damo dismisses the idea of a 'music biography'. "Remembering is not such an important thing in one's life," he says – rendering the very idea of this book totally redundant! "Memory is a kind of sentimentality, repeating your life is not so important because everyone has quite a short life. So within this life, you can enjoy as many new things as possible – a new door opens which is much, much more productive."

But, for all his rejection of nostalgia, Damo can still detect one virtue in our project: the evolution of the Network; the importance to him (and by association with him, to others) of random creation; the freedom to be found so far outside of commercial constraints.

"Sometimes, through happiness, I am almost crying on the stage," he admits. "I did cry sometimes," he corrects himself, "because I was really, really happy about the audience, happy about the sound that the Carriers on the stage were making, so it was a peak moment, a really high point."

In searching for the peak experience, Damo has explored the limits of human freedom – nothing to do with licence or lawlessness, but the freedom to stake out personal territory in which your own actions, your own creation and your own meaning cannot be sidelined or dismissed.

"This point is something concentrated in time," he says of each fleetingly unique performance, "so you cannot repeat it. If I arrive at this special moment and my body's really shaking, then afterwards tears are dropping from my eyes. It's a really good feeling, a kind of link to another sphere. It's so special that I cannot find any words – but I hope you understand!"

Whether we understand or not depends, as ever, on our openness to new experiences and new modes of communication. Whether we regard music as a product or as an expressive process.

"I can only compare it with my other experiences," he insists, seeing the resurgence of the Network not as a return to a musical career but as an integral strand of his existence. "In 1983 I survived cancer," he draws past and present together, finding liberation in a crisis. "Everything went well," he says of recent events that echo that crisis of the past. "And this moment that I came back to myself was almost the same kind of thing," he grasps for the simple words to explain something so personally monumental.

"Like being reborn," Damo reflects. "A rebirth of my life."

"Revolution is every single family dining.
Serve before main dishes."
DAMO SUZUKI

PERMISSIONS

'Mushroom'
Words & Music by Caroli, Liebezeit, Schmidt, Schuring, Suzuki
© Westminster Music Limited of Suite 2.07, Plaza 535 Kings Road,
London SW10 0SZ
International Copyright Secured.
All Rights Reserved. Used by Permission.

'Tango Whiskyman'
Words & Music by Caroli, Liebezeit, Schmidt, Schuring, Suzuki
© Westminster Music Limited of Suite 2.07, Plaza 535 Kings Road,
London SW10 0SZ
International Copyright Secured.
All Rights Reserved. Used by Permission.

'Spoon'
Words & Music by Caroli, Liebezeit, Schmidt, Schuring, Suzuki
© Onward Music Limited of Roundhouse, 212 Regents Park Entrance,
London NW1 8AW
International Copyright Secured.
All Rights Reserved. Used by Permission.

CREDITS

Script
Paul Woods

Script Assistants
Damo Suzuki
Elke Morsbach

Cast
(In Order of Appearance)
Hiroko Suzuki
Hirofumi Suzuki
Simon Torssell Lerin
Elizabeth Murphy
Deirdre Nuttall
Jaki Liebezeit
Gitta Suzuki-Mouret
Dominik von Senger
Luca Giovanardi
Kenichi Iwasa
Naoume Anzai
Jonathan LaMaster
Martin Suzuki
Mirko Suzuki
Astrid Heibach
Marco Heibach
Alexander Schönert
Keiichi Miyashita
Makoto Kawabata

Francesco di Loreto
Mathias Hill
Keith Marks
Mason Jones
Michelle Heighway

Visual Effects
The Suzuki Family of Ōiso
The Murphy Family of New Ross
Damo Suzuki
Gitta Suzuki-Mouret
Michelle Heighway
Gerald Jenkins
Elke Morsbach
Dominik von Senger
Francesco di Loreto
Tim Peach
Olva Dyer
Juan Barabani (aka Rotenapels)
Kevin McCabe
Bettina Hvidevold Hystad
Dominic Thackray

Producer
Omnibus Press

Soundtrack
Continued on accompanying CD.

DISCOGRAPHY

CAN

Holger Czukay (*Bass*)
Michael Karoli (*Guitar*)
Jaki Liebezeit (*Drums*)

Irmin Schmidt (*Keyboards*)
Damo Suzuki (*Vocals*)

Soundtracks
(LP)

Liberty (LBS 83 437 1)
Recorded at Schloss Nörvenich

Side One

1. 'Deadlock' (3:27)
   from the film *Deadlock* (Roland Klick 1970)
2. 'Tango Whiskyman' (4:04)
   from the film *Deadlock* (Roland Klick 1970) – My first recording with CAN
4. 'Don't Turn The Light On, Leave Me Alone' (3:42)
   from the film *Cream-Schwabing Report* (Leon Capetanos 1971)

Side Two

1. 'Mother Sky' (14:31)
   from the film *Deep End* (Jerzy Skolimowski 1971)

1971

Tago Mago
(2LP)

United Artists Records (UAS 29 211/12X)
Recorded at Inner Space Studio

1. 'Paper House' (7:28)
2. 'Mushroom' (4:03)
3. 'Oh Yeah' (7:23)
4. 'Halleluwah' (18:32)
5. 'Aumgn' (17:37)
6. 'Pekin O' (11:37)
7. 'Bring Me Coffee Or Tea' (6:47)

Turtles Have Short Legs (Single)
A. 'Turtles Have Short Legs' (3:30)
B. 'Halleluwah' (3:30)

Liberty (15 465)
Recorded at Godolf Studio
Recorded at Inner Space Studio

Spoon (Single)   Liberty (35304 D)
A. 'Spoon' (3:03)   Recorded at Inner Space Studio
B. 'Shikaku Maru Ten' (3:18)   Recorded at Inner Space Studio

1972
Vitamin C (Single)   United Artists Records (35472A D)
A. 'Vitamin C' (3.34)   Recorded at Inner Space Studio
B. 'I'm So Green' (3.09)   Recorded at Inner Space Studio

Ege Bamyasi   United Artist Records (AUS 29 4141)
(LP)   Recorded at Inner Space Studio

Side One
1. 'Pinch' (9:28)
2. 'Sing Swan Song' (4:49)
3. 'One More Night' (5:35)

Side Two
4. 'Vitamin C' (3:34)
5. 'Soup' (10:25)
6. 'I'm So Green' (3:03)
7. 'Spoon' (3:03)

1973
Future Days   United Artists Records (AUS 29 5051)
(LP)   Recorded at Inner Space Studio

A1. 'Future Days' (9:30)
A2. 'Spray' (8:29)
A3. 'Moonshake' (3:04)
B. 'Bel Air' (19:53)

Moonshake   United Artists Records (UA 35 596 A)
(Single)

A. 'Moonshake' (3.09)   Recorded at Inner Space Studio
B. 'Future Days' (3.18)   Recorded at Inner Space Studio

1976

Unlimited Edition (Compilation)   Harvest (1C 148-29 653/54)
(2LP)   Recorded in Inner Space Studio

1. 'Doko E' (2:26)
4. 'I'm Too Leise' (5:10)
6. 'Blue Bag (Inside Paper)' (1:16)
7. 'E.F.S.No.27' (1:47)
8. 'TV Spot' (3:02)

1995

The Peel Session (Compliation)   Strange Fruit (SFR CD 135)
(CD)   Recorded Live at John Peel Session in February 1973

1. 'Up The Bakerloo Line With Anne' (18:49)

2012

The Lost Tapes (Compliation)   Spoon Records (CDSPOON55)
(3CD, Booklet Box – Limited)

CD Two
6. 'Spoon (Live)' (16:47)

CD Three
10. 'Mushroom (Live)' (8:18)
11. 'One More Saturday Night (Live)' (6:34)

DUNKELZIFFER

Oleg Gelba (*Percussion*)   Wolfgang Schubert (*Saxophone*)
Rike Gratt (*Bass*)   Damo Suzuki (*Vocals*)
Matthias Keul (*Keyboards*)   Dominik von Senger (*Guitar*)
Stefan Krachten (*Drums*)   Helmut 'Jumpy' Zerlett (*Keyboard*)
Reiner Linke (*Percussion*)

1984

In The Night   Fünfundvirzig, Furgo (EfA 12-4502)
(CD/LP)   Recorded at Mascot Studio

A1. 'Watch On My Head' (2:50)

A2. 'Sunday Morning' (4:49)
A3. 'Retrospection' (13:25)
B1. 'Q' (4:58)
B2. '(Do Watch What You Can) Prof.' (2:23)
B3. 'I See Your Smile' (3:58)
B4. 'Oriental Café' (10:04)

I See Your Smile (Single)   Fünfundvierzig (Fünfundvierzig 03)

A.   'I See Your Smile' (3.58)   Recorded at Mascot Studio
B.   'Q' (4.44)   Recorded at Mascot Studio

1985
You Make Me Happy   Fünfundvierzig (EfA 4510)
(EP)   Recorded at Projekt X Studio, Cologne in 1985

Oleg Gelba (*Percussion*)   Reiner Linke (*Percussion*)
Rike Gratt (*Bass*)   Wolfgang Schubert (*Saxophone*)
Matthias Keul (*Keyboards*)   Damo Suzuki (*Vocals*)
Stefan Krachten (*Drums*)   Dominik von Senger (*Guitar*)

A1. 'You Make Me Happy' (3:38)
A2. '1st Future Information' (3:15)
B1. 'Trailer' (2:12)
B2. '2nd Future Information' (3:26)

Various – Off Record Number 1 – Stollwerck Sampler (Compilation)
(LP)   Fünfundvierzig (EfA 4507)

B1. 'I Pinched Myself' (5:06) – Recorded at Projekt X Studio, Cologne
     in 1985

1986
III   Fünfundvierzig (Fünfundvierzig 1986)
(CD/LP)   Recorded at Projekt X Studio, Cologne in 1985

1.   'Give Me Your Soul' (4:03)
2.   'Akino Aruhini' (6:34)
3.   'Network' (7:17)

4. 'Trailer II' (5:07)
5. 'Take Off Your Heavy Load' (12:05)
6. 'No Matter' (5:41)

1997
Live 1985   Capt. Trip (CTCD058)
(CD)   Recorded live at Maschinenhalle Stollwerck,
                               Cologne, Germany on December 28 1985

1. 'Coffeehouse' (11:20)
2. 'After Saturday Night' (5:52)
3. 'The Messenger' (6:40)
4. 'Facing The Wind' (13:01)
5. 'Distant Drums' (5:10)
6. 'These Days' (4:14)
7. 'Up Date' (5:54)
8. 'Shamrock' (4:11)
9. 'You're My Melody' (9:32)

DAMO SUZUKI BAND

Matthias Keul (*Keyboards*)   Damo Suzuki (*Vocals*)
Jaki Liebezeit (*Drums*)   Dominik von Senger (*Guitar*)

1998
V.E.R.N.I.S.S.A.G.E.   Damo's Network (DNW007)
(CD)   Recorded live in Linz on January 11 1990

1. 'Date Line Today/Yesterday' (13:20)
2. 'Ballad Of Diver' (8:30)
3. 'Don't Forget Ya Job/Halleluwah/Mushroom/Day Lily' (26:39)

P.R.O.M.I.S.E.   Damo's Network (DNW008-014)
(7CD Box)

P   Recorded live in Berlin on May 15 1987
1. 'The Land Of Promise' (22:41)
2. 'Ballad Of Diver' (22:41)

3.   'Bounty Hunters' (12:34)
4.   '3,000,000 Miles Away From Your Home' (24:13)

R   Recorded live in Dortmund 1987
1.   'Sun Is Not Shining' (10:15)
2.   'A Year Of Poor Harvest' (18:55)
3.   'Some Day' (17:49)
4.   'A House On Sand' (24:43)

O
1.   'Don't Forget Ya Job' (16:20) – Recorded live in Dortmund 1987
2.   'Today/Yesterday' (8:42) – Recorded live in Münster 1987
3.   'Sometime Chinese' (20:14)
4.   'Skin Or Tooth, She Comes Twice' (16:24) – Recorded live in Detmold 1987

M
1.   'Vanilla Pudding' (14:49) – Recorded live in Düsseldorf 1987
2.   'All I Need Is You' (6:22)
3.   'Mikado In Looping' (10:12) – Recorded live in Stuttgart 1987
4.   'It's Me You're Thinking Of/Weekend Paradise' (29:28)
5.   'Ode To Emanuell S.' (7:04) – Recorded live in Nürnberg 1988

I
1.   'Room #45 Distorted' (5:38) – Recorded live in Emden on September 4 1987
2.   'Upside Down Mountain Crossing' (13:39)
3.   'Date Line' (8:57) – Recorded live in Bocholt on November 23 1989
4.   'Bitter Lemon, Sweet Potato' (10:29)
5.   'Die Nadel' (6:39) – Recorded live in Bielstein on November 26 1989
6.   'Rice Field Of Vietnam' (14:42) – Recorded live in Linz on January 11 1990

S
1.   'So Far In Mellow' (10:36) – Recorded live in Wien on January 12 1990
2.   'Another 3,000,000 Miles Away From Your Home' (9:44)
3.   'City Park Avenue III' (7:33)
4.   'Date Line Today/Yesterday' (9:57)
5.   'Stone Hawk In Marshall Island' (10:56)

6. 'Waterfront Wizard/Mother Sky' (15:31) – Recorded live in Graz on January 13 1990

E
1. 'Yume No Nakani' (11:43) – Recorded live in Cologne on December 26 1989
2. 'Cozmic Fall' (13:10)
3. 'Han Over The Rainbow' (4:39) – Recorded live in Hanover on December 22 1989
4. 'Open Song' (14:01) – Recorded live in Saarbrücken on December 28 1989
5. 'Sadda Dome' (7:09)
6. 'It's Me You're Thinking Of' (6:38)

DAMO SUZUKI'S NETWORK

Mandjao Fati (*Bass*)
Michael Karoli (*Guitar*)
Matthias Keul (*Keyboards*)

Mani Neumeier (*Drums*)
Damo Suzuki (*Vocals*)

1997
実況まつり
(2CD – Limited)
Damo's Network (DNW001/002)
Recorded live at On Air West, Tokyo on April 30 1997

実況まつり
(2CD – Limited)
Damo's Network (DNW003/004)
Recorded live at On Air West, Tokyo on May 2 1997

実況まつり
(2CD – Limited)
Damo's Network (DNW005/006)
Recorded live in Muse Hall, Osaka on May 4 1997

1999
Seattle (2CD)
Damo's Network (DNW018/019)

Mandjao Fati (*Bass*)
Thomas Hopf (*Drums*)
Michael Karoli (*Guitar, Violin*)

Alex Schönert (*Guitar*)
Damo Suzuki (*Vocals*)

Upper Disc   Recorded live at Fenix, Seattle on October 4 1998

1. 'Half Of Haven At Half Past Eleven' (12:42)
2. 'Fall Of Fire Bird' (7:30)
3. 'She Crosses The Universe' (7:30)
4. 'Light Of Fortune' (8:09)

Lower Disc

Guest: Mark Spybey (*Toys, Fx.Processing*)
Dustin Donaldson (*Sound Effects*)

1. 'Seattle Shuffle' (8:51)
2. 'Port Of Timeless Situation' (17:46)
3. 'N.J.S.O.L.W.O.Y. Mother Sky' (16:40)
4. 'Bellevue Cocktail/Floating Bridge Mix' (29:54)
5. 'Leaving Fenix' (7:02)

2000
JPN ULTD Vol.1   Damo's Network (DNW015)
(CD)   Recorded live at On Air West, Tokyo on April 30 1997

Mandjao Fati (*Bass*)   Mani Neumeier (*Drums*)
Michael Karoli (*Guitar*)   Damo Suzuki (*Vocals*)
Matthias Keul (*Keyboards*)

1. 'Inquisition' (21:05)
2. 'Brain Watch' (9:52)
3. 'Living Planet' (24:25)
4. 'Lonely Subway' (8:56)

Odyssey (Journey Into Japanese Cosmos)
(2CD)   Damo's Network (DNW020/021)

Tommy Grenas (*Bass, Synthesizer*)   Alex Schönert (*Guitar, Bass*)
Nicolle Meryer (*Drums*)   Damo Suzuki (*Vocals*)
Carlos Robalo (*Percussion, Voice*)   Dominik von Senger (*Guitar*)

Input
1. 'Lover Behind Mirror (Sweeter Than Paradise)' (13:52) – Recorded live at Loft, Tokyo on September 22 1999

2. 'Amazing (Electric Yellow Bag)' (9:17) – Recorded live during Odyssey on September 24 1999
3. 'Walking On Fire (Don't Give Him Water)' (14:47)
4. 'Without Piano (Memories Of Early Days)' (11:22) – Recorded live at Loft, Tokyo on September 22 1999
5. 'Cyber Walk (Mobbing Occasion)' (8:43) – Recorded live during Odyssey on September 24 1999
6. 'Winner Writes History (XX XXX XXXX)' (8:28)

Output
1. 'Planet Of Heartbreaker (End Of Material)' (21:27) – Recorded live at Loft, Tokyo on September 22 1999
2. 'Dance Of Thousand Tarantulas (Party Has Long Legs)' (20:56)
3. 'Every Side Open (No Way Out)' (21:17)
4. 'Odd Essay (No Comment Left)' (11:22)

2001
Metaphysical Transfer (2CD)   Damo's Network (DNW022/023)

Len Del Rio (*Percussion*)   Brandon LaBelle (*Drums*)
Tommy Grenas (*Bass, Guitar,*   Kevin Lee (*Synthesizer, Theremin*)
Synthesizer)   Damo Suzuki (*Vocals*)
Ryan Kirk (*Bass, Guitar*)   Dominik von Senger (*Guitar*)

Open
1. 'Slave Dancer & Taxi Driver' (9:21) – Recorded live at the Crocodile Café, Seattle on October 8 2000
2. 'Manager Cinderella' (6:34)
3. 'Hotel Orchidee' (6:30) – Recorded live at Sam Bond's Garage, Eugene on October 6 2000
4. 'Source Of Third Violence' (6:44) – Recorded live at Richards On Richards, Vancouver on October 11 2000
5. 'Crossroad Gas Stop' (7:00) – Recorded live at Sam Bond's Garage, Eugene on October 6 2000
6. 'Nineteen Sixty Night' (9:39) – Recorded live at the Crocodile Café, Seattle on October 8 2000
7. 'Big Foot Skelton' (11:09)

Closed

1. 'L.A.Tibet' (18:27) – Recorded live at Spaceland, Los Angeles on October 3 2000
2. 'Terry White Meets J.B.' (5:39)
3. 'Sun, Sun, Sun' (6:36) – Recorded live at Richards On Richards, Vancouver on October 11 2000
4. 'Silver Shadows On Ruin' (6:29)
5. 'Sweet Poison' (6:44)
6. 'Give Me More Light' (13:20)

2002

JPN ULTD Vol.2   Damo's Network (DNW016)
(CD)   Recorded live at On Air West, Tokyo on May 2 and
                                Muse Hall, Osaka on May 4 1997

Mandjao Fati (*Bass*)   Mani Meumeier (*Drums*)
Michael Karoli (*Guitar*)   Damo Suzuki (*Vocals*)
Matthias Keul (*Keyboards*)

1. 'E.G.A.Y.O.V (No Return)' (18:34)
2. '13 Steps To Freedom' (13:54)
3. 'Buridan's Donkey' (20:21)
4. 'Halleluwah' (10:20)

2004

Damo Suzuki & Cul De Sac
Abhayamudra   Strange Attractors Audio House (SAAH2728)
(2CD)

Robin Amos (*EMI 101 Synthesizer,*   Jonathan LaMaster (*Bass, Violin*)
Harmonica, Autoharp)   Jon Proudman (*Drums*)
Glenn Jones (*Guitar, Bouzouki*)   Damo Suzuki (*Vocals*)

Disc One
1. 'Beograd 1' (14:58) – Recorded live at Dom Omladine, Beograd on March 29 2003
2. 'Halle 2' (20:36) – Recorded live at Objekt 5, Halle on April 1 2003
3. 'Baltimore 5' (13:34) – Recorded live at Ottobar, Baltimore on February 14 2003

4. 'Berlin 4' (8:59) – Recorded live at Magnet, Berlin on March 31 2003
5. 'Frankfurt 4' (12:59) – Recorded live at Café Nachtleben, Frankfurt on March 24 2003

Disc Two
1. 'Beograd 6' (8:10) – Recorded live at Dom Omladine, Beograd on March 29 2003
2. 'Cambridge 1' (8:06) – Recorded live at Middle East, Cambridge on February 5 2002 – Jake Trussell (*Bass on Cambridge 1*)
3. 'Berlin 6' (3:54) – Recorded live at Magnet, Berlin on March 31 2003
4. 'Kopenhagen 3' (9:10) – Recorded live at The Church In Møllegade 7, Copenhagen on April 5 2003 – Jim Siegel (*Drums on Kopenhagen 3*)
5. 'Berlin 3' (10:36) – Recorded live at Magnet, Berlin on March 31 2003
6. 'Zagreb 3' (18:14) – Recorded live at KSET, Zagreb on March 28 2003

Sixtoo-Chewing On Glass & Other Miracle Vures   Ninja Tune (ZEN CD86)
(CD)

Sixtoo (*Sampling*)   Damo Suzuki (*Vocals*)

16. 'Storm Clouds & Silver Linings' (8:52)

2005
Hollyaris   Damo's Network (DNW26/27)
(2CD)   Recorded live at Knitting Factory, Los Angeles on August 31 2003

Len Del Rio (*Percussion*)   Ryan Kirk (*Bass, Guitar*)
Tommy Grenas (*Bass, Guitar,*   Kevin Lee (*Synthesizer, Theremin*)
Synthesizer)   Damo Suzuki (*Vocals*)
Chris Guttmacher (*Drums*)   Keiichi Miyashita (*Guitar*)

Hollywood   Recorded Live at Café De La Danse on October 5 2003
1. 'Road Music Package' (13:13)
2. 'Hypnotic Orange' (7:55)
3. 'Nihilist Convention' (7:55)
4. 'Hot Tuna Express' (7:34)
5. 'Last Stage Of Being Out' (6:52)
6. 'Dino's Lunch Time' (8:51)
7. 'Breez Of New Morning' (12:24)

Damo Suzuki & Les French Doctors:
Sebastian Borgo (*Guitar, Electronics*) Nicolas Marmin (*Bass, Electronics*)
Franq De Quengo (*Electronics,* Edward Perraud (*Drums*)
Noises) Damo Suzuki (*Vocals*)
Olivier Manchion (*Bass, Acoustic
Guitar, Electronics*)

Paris
1. 'Ouverture' (14:25)
2. 'Un Pantin Sauvage' (8:07)
3. 'Parfum' (7:47)
4. 'Une Rue Sans Visage' (8:03)
5. 'Un Voyage A Travers Toi' (14:38)
6. 'Fin Du Traitement' (10:50)

2005

3 Dead People After The Performance Ektro Records (Ektro026)
(CD) Recorded live at Jyrock Festival,
Jyväskylä on April 11 2003

Jyrki Laiho (*Guitar*) Mika Rättö (*Drums*)
Jussi Lehtisalo (*Bass*) Damo Suzuki (*Vocals*)
Jorge Ledezma (*Guitar*)

1. '3 Dead People After The Performance' (52:21)

Damo Suzuki's Network Tip Top (Tiptop001)
The Swiftsure Session Re-released from Research Records
(LP) (Reserch 01) in 2017
Recorded live at Corduroy Records,
Melbourne on November 24 2004
Free energy cut direct to vinyl in real time

Oren Ambarchi (*Guitar*) Damo Suzuki (*Vocal*)
Edmondo Ammendola (*Bass*) Davey Williams (*Drums*)
Emil Sarlije (*Guitar*)

1. 'The Swiftsure Session, Pt.1' (23:57)
2. 'The Swiftsure Serssion, Pt.2' (23:54)

2006
Damo Suzuki & Now
Tri (Tri9)
The London Evening News
(CD)   Recorded live at the Bull and Gate, London on March 8 2004

Damo Suzuki (*Vocals*)

Now:

Caspar Gordon (*Percussion, Trombone, Synthesizer*)

Peter Lowis (*Bass*)

Yuhi Nakano (*Acoustic Guitar, Synthesizer, Sampler*)

Giles Narang (*Drums*)

Justin Paton (*Guitar, Percussion, Synthesizer*)

Craig Tamlin (*Percussion, Trumpet*)

1. 'Knopf Off' (25:48)
2. 'Metro Girl' (12:01)
3. 'One And One Equal One' (5:20)
4. 'Acid Test' (1:03)
5. 'The Zero Game' (15:13)

Tutti I Colori Del Silenzio
Palustre Records (PAL4)/Wallace Records
(CD)   (Wallace105)
Recorded live at Circolo Culturale Luogo Comune, Faenza on 15 July 2006

Andrea Belfi (*Electonics*)

Mattia Coletti (*Guitar*)

Xabier Iriondo (*Guitar, Mhai Metak*)

Diego Sapignoli (*Drums, Percussions*)

Damo Suzuki (*Vocals*)

1. 'Tutti Colori Del Silenzo' (46:50)

Suomi (2CD)
Damo's Network (DNW28/29)

Jens Küchenthal (*Drums*)

Jonathan LaMaster (*Bass, Violin*)

Boris Polonski (*Synthesizer*)

Alex Schönert (*Guitar*)

Damo Suzuki (*Vocals*)

Turku
Recorded live at Säätömö, Turku on October 23 2002
1. 'Finland Episode 1' (15:04)
2. 'Heat Me' (11:10)
3. 'The Night Before First Snow' (8:53)
4. 'Never Give Me Enough' (8:06)

5.   'Sparking Lady Lake' (7:24)
6.   'Emerald Tear Drop And Sun Dance' (8:12)

Helsinki   Recorded live at Gloria, Helsinki on October 26 2002

1.   'Don't Heat Me' (7:20)
2.   'The Day After First Snow' (10:40)
3.   'The Button' (6:13)
4.   '2040-The Truth At The End Of Tunnel' (11:36)
5.   'Little John Puppet' (7:20)
6.   'Mother Goose Universe' (10:17)
     Guest: Mother Goose   Anti Laakkonen (*Guitar*)
     Kare Karhu (*Drums*)   Eija Roisko (*Bass*)
7.   'Finland Episode No.4' (16:26)

2007

Omar Rodríguez-López &   Gold Standard Laboratories (GSL 131)
Damo Suzuki   Recorded live at Gebäude 9, Cologne
Please Heat This Eventually   on November 14 2005
(EP)   Recorded on The E-Clat Disaster Portable Morgue Unit

Damo Suzuki (*Vocals*)   Money Mark Ramos-Nishita
Omar Rodríguez-López Group: (*Keyboards*)
Adrian Terrazas Gonzales (*Sax, Bass,*   Omar Rodríguez-López (*Guitar*)
Clarinet, Percussion)   Marcel Rodríguez-López (*Drums*)
Juan Alderte De La Pena

A.   'Please Heat This Eventually (Parts I, II, III)'
B.   'Please Heat This Eventually (Parts IV, V & VI)'

Safety Magic   Goatica
Voices (Compilation)
(CD)

Damo Suzuki (*Vocals*)   Dan Lerman (*Tres Guitar*)
Magicians: Oleg Mariakhin (*Sax*)
Mikhail Avsharov (*Bass*)   Arkady Marto (*Electronics, Sampling,*
Kosta (*Trumpet, Flugelhorn*)   *Kalimba*)

Nazaar (*Violin*)

Sergej Nebolsin (*Percussion*)

Pavel Novikov (*Tabla, Flute*)

Oleg Pankratov (*Guitar*)

Raghu (*Didgeridoo*)

Andrey Romanika (*Drums*)

3. 'Highway Retrospection' (6:03)

The Fire Of Heaven At The End Of Universe (Live At UFO Club)

(CD)   Vivo Records (vivo2007030CD)

Recored live at UFO Club Tokyo on March 5 2006

Hoppy Kamiyama (*Keyboards*)

Yuji Katsui (*Violin*)

Kenji Sato (*Bass*)

Damo Suzuki (*Vocals*)

Tatsuya Yoshida (*Drums*)

1. 'The Crystal Desert' (12:30)
2. 'Moonlight Warrior' (17:41)
3. 'The Last Night Of The Sun' (11:02)
4. 'Dress Your Girl' (28:45)
5. 'Another Dirty Weekend' (5:41)

Sgt. With Damo Suzuki

Penguinmarket Records (PEM-005)

(CD)   Recorded live at Shimokitazawa Era on March 2 2007

Kouji Akashi (*Bass*)

Toshitaka Mukaiyama (*Guitar*)

Mikiko Narui (*Violin*)

Hitosi Oono (*Drums*)

Damo Suzuki (*Vocals*)

Guest:

Daichi Kanbayashi (*Saxophone*)

Taichi Miyagi (*Drums*)

秘められた女の生活事情/傷だらけのあかね雲/スクリーンの中の天国にいちばん近いおへそ

1. 'Session' (14:07)
2. 'Session' (12:12)
3. 'Session' (09:57)
4. 'Session' (12:09)
5. 'Session' (06:15)

2008
Damo Suzuki With Metak Network/   PhotoMetakLaboratories (01-08)
Damo Suzuki With ZU & X.Iriondo   Wallace Records (Wallace101)
PhonoMetak Series #4   Recorded live at SoundMetak,
(LP)   Milano on December 9 2006

Damo Suzuki (*Vocals*)   Xabier Iriondo (*Mahai Metak,*
Metak Network: *Objects*)
Paolo Cantu (*Guitar, Clarinet*)   Alberto Morelli (*Kalimba, Melodica,*
Mattia Coletti (*Guitar*)   *Harmonic Tube, Piano Harp, Voice*)

A1. 'Dove Siete Stati L'Ultima Estate?' (6:46)
A2. 'Un Oceano Di Due Mezzelune' (8:32)

Xabier Iriondo (*Guitar, Mahai Metak*)   Recorded live at Berako Kultur Etxea,
Damo Suzuki (*Vocals*)   Bersa on June 10 2005
Zu:
Jacopo Battaglia (*Drums*)
Luca Mai (*Baritone Sax*)
Massimo Pupillo (*Bass*)

B1. 'La Citta Nascosta' (6:51)
B2. 'Il Territorio Proibito' (6:04)

2009
Damo Suzuki Network Featuring Makoto Kawabata
And Dublin Sound Carriers   Farpoint Recordings (fp030)
One More Universe   Recorded live at Crawdaddy on
(CD-Limited Edition)   December 2 2008

Makoto Kawabata (*Guitar*)   Fergus Cullen (*Clarinet, Keyboards*)
Damo Suzuki (*Vocals*)   Barry Murphy (*Laptop, Percussion*)
Dublin Sound Carriers: Bryan O'Connell (*Drums, Percussion*)
Paul Condon (*Bass*)

1. 'Universe 1: Newborn Steel Unicorns' (14:10)
2. 'Universe 2: Pneumatic Distorted' (7:01)
3. 'Universe 3: Hullabaloowah' (6:09)
4. 'Universe 4: Delete History' (9:03)

5. 'Universe 5: Music For The Long Now' (20:09)
6. 'Universe 6: Lost Between The Space' (10:21)

2010
Damo Suzuki & The Holy Soul
Dead Man Has No 2nd Chance   Repressed Records (REP001)
(CD)   Recorded live at The Toff In Town, Melbourne on Feburary 19 2008

Damo Suzuki (*Vocals*)   Trent Marden (*Guitar*)
The Holy Souls: Peter Newman (*Electronics*)
John Hunter (*Guitar*)   Kate Wilson (*Drums*)
Dan Luscombe (*Keyboards*)   Sam Worrad (*Bass*)

1. 'Stone Of Fortune' (34:52)
2. 'Strangers In Blue' (26:41)

Live In Dublin Featuring Electronic Sensoria Band
(CD)   Last Of Our Kind (LOOK1)
                             Sleeves hand-drawn by band members
                    Recorded live at Crawdaddy, Dublin on March 21 2005

Damo Suzuki (*Vocals*)   David Carroll (*Percussion, Casio
Electronic Sensoria Band*:   *Keyboard*)
Anthony Carroll (*Percussion, Casio   Fergus Cullen (*Guitar*)
Keyboard*)   Adrienne Flynn (*Percussion*)

1. 'The Last Mohican' (7:39)
2. 'Eye To The Ear' (10:02)
3. 'Unfortunate Concubines' (10:51)
4. '20,000 Words Under The Sea (She Is A Lonely Hunter)' (7:03)
5. 'Sirens Of Titan' (10:51)

2011
Damo Suzuki & CUZO   Alone Records (AR031)
Puedo Ver Tu Mente   Recorded at Centro Cultural Matadero (Huesca),
(CD/LP)   Spain on November 4 2009

Pep Caravante (*Drums*)   Jaume Pantaleon (*Guitar, Effects*)
Alvaro Gallego (*Bass*)   Damo Suzuki (*Vocals*)

385

1. 'Puedo Ver Tu Mente' (17:41)
2. 'Tiempo Que No Tiente Ojoys En Medio' (11:07)
3. 'Billete Sencillo Para Dos' (7:15)

Killer – Damo   Black Smoker Records (BSJ-003)
(CD)   Recorded live at Chikyu-Ya, Kunitachi on November 5 2010

Killer Bong (*Electronic*)   Damo Suzuki (*Vocal*)

1. 'Live At Chikyuya' (32:32)

Damo Suzuki's Network
Sette Modi Per Salvare Roma   Goodfellas (GF2714)
(CD)   Recorded live at Circolo degli Artisti, Roma on January 20 2011

Manuel Agnelli (*Keyboards*)   Xabier Iriondo (*Guitar, Effects*)
Cristiano Calcagnile (*Drums*)   Damo Suzuki (*Vocals*)
Enrico Gabrielli (*Winds*)

1. 'Scuola D'alta Farmacia' (1:27)
2. 'Alphabet Zoo' (11:53)
3. 'Un'altra Versione Dello Stesso' (7:52)
4. 'Siamo Interessanti Come Pensiamo Di Essere?' (9:48)
5. 'Il Papa E'fuori Dal Paradiso' (4:34)

2012
Bo Ningen With Damo Suzuki
Foreign Affair Confidential   So I Buried Records (SIB002)
(CD)   Recorded live at Catch, London on April 7 2010

Damo Suzuki (*Vocals*)   Kohei Matsuda (*Guitar*)
Bo Ningen: Akihide Monna (*Drums*)
Taigen Kawabe (*Bass*)   Yuki Tsujii (*Guitar*)

1. 'Episode 4' (15:10)
2. 'Epispde 5' (18:55)
3. 'Episode 6' (16:15)

鳥獣戯画 (CD)   Donburi Disc (DON-03)
                    Recorded live at UFO Club, Tokyo on September 5 2011

Chiyo Kamekawa (*Bass*)   Damo Suzuki (*Vocals*)
Michio Kurihara (*Guitar*)   Ikuro Takahashi (*Drums*)
Shinsuke Michishita (*Guitar*)

1.   '鳥の歌' (55:00)

2013
Simon Torssell Lerin/Bettina Hvidevold Hystad
With Damo Suzuki   Clouds Hill (CH058)
(LP & Book Set – Limited)   Recorded live at Fylkingen,
                                    Stockholm on February 11 2013

Peter Falk (*Guitar*)   Damo Suzuki (*Vocals*)
Bettina Hvidevold Hystad   Simon Torssell Lerin (*Guitar,*
(*Electronics, Synthesizer, Sampler*) *Programming, Sound Manipulation*)
Tobias Noren (*Drums*)

A.   'Ripple Effects And The Impossible Loopholes Part I' (20:14)
B.   'Ripple Effects And The Impossible Loopholes Part II' (21:18)

2014
Damo Suzuki-Seven Potatoes   Lance Rock Records (LRR-44)
Live In Nanaimo   Noiseagonymayhem Records (NAM-009)
(2LP – Limited)   Recorded live at Globe Hotel in Nanaimo,
                                   British Columbia on July 6 2013

Angus Barter (*Guitar*)   Luke Nixon (*Drums*)
David Bean (*Drums*)   David Reed (*Bass*)
Michael Breen (*Guitar*)   Damo Suzuki (*Vocals*)
Willi Hills (*Synthesizer*)   Arlen Thompson (*Electronics*)
Ian James (*Drums*)

A.   'Enter The Abyss'
B.   'No Sleep 'Til Extension' (18:28)
C1. 'Terror Crabs Of Shack Island … Attack!' (12:51)
C2. 'Buried Alive In Wax At Fascinating Rhythm' (12:10)
D.   'As Heavy As Mount Benson'

Damo Suzuki Møder ØSC
(3LP – Limited)

Space Rock Productions (SRP020)
Recorded live at Dragens Hule,
Copenhagen on February 14 2013

Birk (*Drums*)
Mikael (*Guitar*)
Mogens (*Keyboards, Synthesizer*)
Nick (*Guitar*)
Niklas (*Guitar*)

Pär (*Bass*)
Rasmus (*Keyboards, Synthesizer*)
Dr. Space (*Keyboards, Synthesizer*)
Damo Suzuki (*Vocals*)

A. 'Damo's Første ØSC Flyvtur' (23:56)
B. 'Energisk Reaktion 1' (14:09)
C. 'Energisk Reaktion 2' (17:18)
D. 'Jeg Kan Ikke Vokse Op' (20:51)
E. 'Dit Glimtende Øje' (23:57)
F. 'Datid, Nutid, Og Fremtid' (23:02)

Damo Suzuki & Tree
Live At The OzenBar Tel Aviv
(CD – Limited)

Third Ear
Recorded live at The OzenBar,
Tel Aviv on February 9 2014

Damo Suzuki (*Vocals*)
Tree:
Ben Koren (*Guitar*)

Dor Koren (*Bass*)
Nave Koren (*Drums*)
Yair Vermouth (Organ, Piano)

1. 'Untitled' (5:29)
2. 'Untitled' (5:30)
3. 'Untitled' (15:04)
4. 'Untitled' (21:29)
5. 'Untitled' (5:17)
6. 'Untitled' (4:25)
7. 'Untitled' (6:33)
8. 'Untitled' (15:58)

Damo Suzuki & The Fume   Centre d'Art Neuchâtel
Superamas (Evolving Show From April 2012 To May 2013)
(2LP)   Recorded live at Centre d'Art Neuchâtel on
September 21 2012 for the opening of
the exhibition *Superamas*

Damo Suzuki (*Vocals*)   Laurent Burki (*Guitar*)
Fume: Franz Hausammann (*Bass*)
Christian Addor (*Keyboards*)   Julien Rousson (*Drums*)

A. 'Untitled'
B. 'Untitled'
C. 'Untitled'
D. 'Untitled'

Afterhours
Hai Paura Del Buio? (Compilation)   Universal (0602537769889)
(2CD)   Recorded live at Studio2, Vigonovo on October 19 2013

Afterhours: Xabier Iriondo (*Guitar*)
Manuel Agnelli (*Piano*)   *Guest:*
Roberto Dell'Era (*Bass*)   Cristiano Calcagnile (*Drums*)
Rodrigo D'Erasmo (*Violin*)   Damo Suzuki (*Vocals*)

2.1. 'Hai Paura Del Buio?'

2015
Mugstar & Damo Suzuki
Start From Zero   Important Records (IMPREC393)
(LP – Limited)   Recorded live at Kazimier, Liverpool on June 22 2012

Damo Suzuki (*Vocals*)   Neil Murphy (*Guitar*)
Mugstar: Peter Smyth (*Guitar, Keyboards*)
Steve Ashton (*Drums*)   Jason Stöll (*Bass*)

A1. 'Waken To The Night' (13:25)
A2. 'Subway Sound' (04:27)
A3. 'Innanwah' (04:25)
B. 'Zero Coda' (22:50)

2016
Damo Suzuki's Network Featuring The Elysian Quartet
Floating Element Purple Pyramid (CLO0308)
(CD, 2LP)   Recorded live at the Purcell Room, London on April 2 2007

Damo Suzuki (*Vocals*)   Jennymay Logan (*Violin*)
Elysian Quartet: Vince Sipprell
Laura Moody (*Cello*)   Emma Smith (*Violin*)

LP: A. 'Floating Element: Season 1' (23:56)
     B. 'Floating Element: Season 2' (13:43)
     C. 'Floating Element: Season 3' (25:14)
     D. 'Floating Element: Season 4' (14:10)

CD: 1. 'Floating Element' (76:09)

2017
Damo Suzuki & Sound Carriers   Play Loud! Productions (PL-63)
Live At Marie Antoinette   Recorded live at Marie Antoinette,
(2LP)   Berlin on November 24 2011

Dirk Dresselhaus (*Baritone Guitar,*   Tomoko Nakasato (*Dance*)
Effects)   Damo Suzuki (*Vocals*)
Claas Grosszeit (*Drums*)   Ilpo Väisänen (*Electronics, Effects*)

A. 'Geheimnissvolles Treffen Auf Der Anderen Seit Des Nebels' (33:45)
B. 'Stern Des Narren' (26:54)
C. 'Die Leere Füllen' (31:19)
D. 'Wirkliche Antwort Auf Unsichtbaren Spiegel' (28:27)

Damo Suzuki's Network Featuring Château Laut
Ausland The Tapeworm (TW99)
(Cassette – Limited)   Recorded live at Ausland, Berlin on April 30 2010

Damo Suzuki (*Vocals*)   Andrew Maler (*Guitar*)
Château Laut: Steno Glenolak (*Bass*)
Stefan Fähler (*Guitar*)   Max Stolzenberg (*Drums*)

Side 1. 'Part 1' (27:54)
Side 2. 'Part 2' (30:46)

2018

Damo Suzuki & Jelly Planet   Purple Pyramid (CLO0723)
(CD, 2LP)   Recorded live at Bluebok Studio, Troisdorf in 2005

Felix A. Gutierrez (*Bass*)   Alexander Schönert (*Guitar*)
Stehan Hendricks (*Keyboards*)   Damo Suzuki (*Vocals*)
Jens Küchenthal (*Drums*)

LP:
1. 'Wilschweinbraten' (14:11)
2. 'Rest von Wildschweinbraten' (13:46)
3. 'Venushügel' (19:45)
4. 'Andere Seit Des Venushügel' (15:08)

CD:
1. 'Wildschweibraten' (27:59)
2. 'Venushügel' (34:51)

Damo Suzuki Live At The Windmill   Rough Trade (BM001)
(Cassette – Limited)   Brixton With Sound Carriers: Black Midi
Recorded live at The Windmill, London on May 5 2018

Damo Suzuki (*Vocals*)   Matt Kelvin (*Guitar*)
Black Midi: Cameron Picton (*Bass*)
Geordie Greep (*Guitar*)   Morgan Simpson (*Drums*)

Side 1. 'Part 1' (19:01)
Side 2. 'Part 2' (19:05)